For Eleanor Feinberg

Large cities are hotbeds in which neuroses and low morality are bred, as is evident in the history of Babylon, Nineveh, and the mysteries of modern metropolitan life.
—Richard von Krafft-Ebing, *Psychopathia Sexualis*

My own sexual nature was a mystery to me.
—Case History 7 in Havelock Ellis, *Studies in the Psychology of Sex*, vol. 2, *Sexual Inversion*

The more we learn of a person, the less we know.
—Djuna Barnes, *Nightwood*

Queering the Underworld

Queering the Underworld

Slumming, Literature, and the Undoing of Lesbian and Gay History

SCOTT HERRING

THE UNIVERSITY OF CHICAGO PRESS CHICAGO AND LONDON

SCOTT HERRING is assistant professor of English at Indiana University.

The University of Chicago Press, Chicago 60637
The University of Chicago Press, Ltd., London

Printed in the United States of America

16 15 14 13 12 11 10 09 08 07   1 2 3 4 5

ISBN-13: 978-0-226-32790-7 (cloth)
ISBN-13: 978-0-226-32791-4 (paper)
ISBN-10: 0-226-32790-6 (cloth)
ISBN-10: 0-226-32791-4 (paper)

Library of Congress Cataloging-in-Publication Data

Herring, Scott, 1976–
Queering the underworld : slumming, literature, and the undoing of lesbian and gay history / Scott Herring.
p. cm.
Includes bibliographical references (p.) and index.
ISBN-13: 978-0-226-32790-7 (alk. paper)
ISBN-10: 0-226-32790-6 (alk. paper)
ISBN-13: 978-0-226-32791-4 (pbk. : alk. paper)
ISBN-10: 0-226-32791-4 (pbk. : alk. paper) 1. American literature—20th century—History and criticism. 2. Gay culture in literature. 3. Slums in literature. 4. City and town life in literature. 5. Homosexuality in literature. 6. Lesbianism in literature. 7. Homosexuality—United States—History. 8. Lesbianism—United States—History. I. Title.
PS288.G38H47 2007
810.9′920664–dc22   2006101403

♾ The paper used in this publication meets the minimum requirements of the American National Standard for Information Sciences—Permanence of Paper for Printed Library Materials, ANSI Z39.48-1992.

Contents

Illustrations

Acknowledgments

This book could not have been accomplished—let alone imagined—without the helping hands and watchful eyes of many people. For archival assistance ranging from the book's inception to its final production, I thank Pat Bakunas at the University of Illinois at Chicago's University Library Special Collections Department; the staff at the Jane Addams Hull-House Museum; Wendy E. Chmielewski at the Swarthmore College Peace Collection; the staff at the Beinecke Rare Book and Manuscript Library at Yale University; the Special Collections staff at the University of Wisconsin–Madison's Memorial Library; Bill Brockman at Pennsylvania State University's Pattee Library; User Services Coordinator Shawn Wilson and other curatorial staff at the Kinsey Institute for Research in Sex, Gender, and Reproduction at Indiana University, Bloomington; and Beth Alvarez, Curator of Literary Manuscripts at the University of Maryland Libraries, whose legal knowledge regarding Djuna Barnes aided me in the last stages of this project. I thank the staff at the Rare Book and Manuscript Library at the University of Illinois at Urbana-Champaign for guiding me through a thicket of artifacts in the first stages of my thinking. I also offer appreciation to a living archive in Lancaster, Bruce Kellner, who once served me a very weird lunch and confirmed a hunch about the scene called Harlem. I consider him a friend.

That said, this book also could not have been imagined—let alone accomplished—without the aid provided by the following: various fellowships from the Department of English and the Graduate College at the University of Illinois at Urbana-Champaign across the beginning, middle, and end of my graduate training; extended release time, a summer fellowship, and a welcome subvention from the College of the Liberal Arts and the Dean's Office at Penn State University; and the generous support offered by Diana Fuss, Jeff Nunokawa, Valerie Smith, Christine Stansell, and others at a critical moment in my professional career.

As an undergraduate, Bill Hutchings, Ada Long, Michael McConnell, and Andre Millard were central fixtures in the departments of English and of history at the University of Alabama, Birmingham. While moonlighting for Blockbuster Video, Subway, D.J.'s Orchid House, AmeriCorps, various ticket booths, and an on-campus catering company, I managed to learn much from each of you. I also have many debts to pay to my primary mentor at Alabama, Amy Elias, who has always been a model of contemporary self-fashioning.

Many of the ideas presented here emerged in a University of California, Berkeley, Summer Research Seminar titled "Sociability, Sexuality, and Community" with Leo Bersani. For someone so legendarily antisocial and so infamously negative, Bersani always impressed me with his conversation skills and intellectual openness. During that seminar, I also met John Paul Ricco and Michael L. Cobb. Each has helped me a great deal in professional and personal matters over the last half decade. I thank John for once driving me up to the Russian River. I thank Michael for once flying me out to Philadelphia and for his boundless curiosity over the years. I'm so glad that our friendship took.

Back to the heartland: it was a pleasure to be in the ether at the Department of English at the University of Illinois. Carol Neely helped secure funds that put me at financial ease (no small task, for those in the know). Bill Maxwell, a constant interlocutor, pretty much taught me everything I like to think I know about American modernism. And Stephanie Foote first introduced me to the mysteries and miseries of Progressive Era realism—and fiddleheads.

I also keep the *communitas* of two Illinois reading groups in high esteem: the Comparative Queer Studies Reading Group, led by Matti Bunzl, C. Cole, Stephanie Foote, Martin F. Manalansan, and Siobhan Somerville as well as the Body Studies Reading Group, maintained by Debra Hawhee and Julia Walker. Though she arrived late in the process of the writing of this book, Siobhan galvanized its focus with a few piercing questions after it was drafted. Last but never least, Tim Dean, that enfant terrible, read countless drafts of these chapters. He has seen this project through Champaign, South of Market, Chicago, Buffalo, Madison, Bellefonte, Bloomington, and Atlanta. I learned much by his counsel, and I will return the favor.

In the Department of English at Penn State University, I had the great good fortune of having great good colleagues in an environment that rarely felt like work. During an extended leave, Carla Mulford sent a package that enhanced the introduction. Janet Lyon and Michael Bérubé were so instrumental to my upkeep. Janet read and gave commentary on the final chapter. Some years ago, she taught me how to teach. This was everything. Michael was often an elemental force in my intellectual development. Besides his boundless generosity, I thank him for showing me how always to play it as it lies. Across a stream in Happy Valley, Hester Blum and Jonathan Eburne plied me with enough osso buco and intellectual ferment that I'm glad we shared the same borough. Robert Caserio offered me commentary on every word in this book. Susan Squier lent me her unruly garden, her pool, and her chicken coop for several weeks one summer. The walks we took then helped enormously. Julia Kasdorf was more like a big sister than a colleague down the hall (or, in our shared case, the street). Rachel Teukolsky provided much for me during my first year at Penn State—food, a place to do laundry, wit, drink, lodging, someone to mock mercilessly. Thanks as well to my graduate assistants, Jessica Jones and Angela Ward, whose attentions to the final draft made my professional life that much easier. Thanks also to students in my Sexologies seminar and in my American Masculinities and Introduction to Queer Studies classes for their conversations and disagreements: it made my thinking sharper. Finally, to the administrative assistants and other support staff in the Department of English—especially Amy Barone, Amy Bucha, and Kim Keller—whose diligence keeps the first floor of Burrowes in business.

Others beyond my former institutional base have offered advice, guidance, and, most important, encouragement at moments least expected and most needed. I thank Ed Comentale, Margo Crawford, John Duvall, Justin Edwards (for glancing at my fourth chapter and for offering a helping hand from Denmark), Mary Esteve (who commented on the first and second chapters), Jennifer Fleissner, Beth Freeman, Jane Gallop, Jonathan Goldberg, Susan Gubar, Sharon Holland, John Howard, George Hutchinson, E. Patrick Johnson, Richard Kaye, Eric Keenaghan, Kenneth Kidd, Christopher Lane, Heather Love, Dana Luciano, Dwight McBride, Richard Meyer, Wendy Moffatt, Michael Moon, Kevin Mumford, José Muñoz, Ann Pellegrini, Kathleen Pfeiffer, Marjorie Pryse, Guy Reynolds (who read the second chapter), David Román, Judith Roof, Shelley Streeby, Michael Trask, Joseph Urgo, and Steven Watson. Michael Davidson was also elemental to my professionalization and to the recognition of some inchoate ideas that did not make it into this book. I thank him for that.

I have much, much to say for a lengthy roster of friends: Rochelle Rives, Travis Foster, Tom Davis, Jason Rassmussen, Brian Rich, Alan Godfrey, Dori Landry, Karmie Johnson, Melissa Ojeda, Molly Hurley, Sarah Blackwood, Bill Wilson, Ed McKenna, Alice Davidson, Jenell Johnson, Keguro Macharia, Vincent Lankewish, and, especially, Melissa Girard, a queen of hearts if there ever was one. Across three states, Jake Bishop was vital to me as I began and as I concluded my graduate work. Also know that these easy identifications don't go far enough for any of those mentioned in this paragraph.

Doug Mitchell, my editor, and his assistant, Tim McGovern, supported this project from what felt like its beginnings. Doug has been a pleasure to work with and a constant object in the book's long march to present form. Yvonne Zipter did a supreme job with the book's copyediting.

I also thank the two anonymous readers of this book, whose careful suggestions for final revisions fine-tuned the overall argument and enhanced my knowledge base of nineteenth-century sensationalism.

Portions of these pages were delivered at the Modern Language Association, the Narrative conference, various Modernist Studies Associations conferences, the New Directions in African-American Literature, Theory, and Culture Conference at the University of Illinois, an American Comparative Literature Association conference, the University of Connecticut, Storrs, Penn State University, and Indiana University. Audience members offered invaluable critique that they will see recast in the following pages.

Prior segments of chapter 3 appeared in *African American Review* 35, no. 4 (2001): 584–98, as "The Negro Artist and the Racial Manor: *Infants of the Spring* and the Conundrum of Publicity" as well as in *Modern Fiction Studies* 52, no. 1 (2006): 66–91, as "Catherian Friendship; or, How Not to Do the History of Homosexuality." A condensed version of chapter 2 appeared in *Arizona Quarterly* 60, no. 2 (2004): 87–116, as "Willa Cather's Lost Boy: 'Paul's Case' and Bohemian Tramping." I thank, respectively, the Arizona Board of Regents and the Johns Hopkins University Press for permission to reprint.

To the heart of these matters: I thank my immediate family in Alabama for their unhistorical acts as well as their ceaseless hounding. Outside the deep recesses of the U.S. South, this translates as emotional and financial support. My great aunt, Mary Willis, spoke volumes with her chocolate pound cakes. My mother, Martha, sent me countless boxes of Dreamland rib sauce, Golden Eagle brand syrup, and Red Diamond iced tea bags. My dad, Terry, was always quick to infuse in me a "Git-R-Dun" mentality. And my brother Matt forced me to sit through hours upon hours of Japanese horror film whenever I headed down home. Where I come from this means love and like.

And speaking of love and like (and care and cure): Shane Vogel. When I turned to catch a glimpse of those Vancouver pines, I didn't expect to see you on that sighting. Thank you, now, for keeping your eyes on me. It is easy enough to fall in love, but trust, as everybody knows, is a horse of another color. I trust you with all of it.

Introduction: Queer Slumming

Underworld Unknowing

What you don't know would fill a book. Near the beginning of Mae West's 1927 play *The Drag: A Homosexual Comedy* ([1927] 1997), Barbara Richmond, a wealthy white New Yorker, asks her brother, the eminent sexologist Dr. James Richmond, to tell her more about a strange book that she spots in his library. The unnamed book, the audience learns in the play's opening lines, is by the even more eminent sexologist Karl Heinrich Ulrichs. Dr. Richmond's replies to his sister's inquiries are short, sweet, and, at first glance, silencing:

DOCTOR: What some people don't know, my dear, don't trouble them.

BARBARA: In other words, it's a good thing one half of the world doesn't know how the other half lives, eh?

DOCTOR: Excellent—in most cases.

BARBARA (*Crosses to the table right—picks up the Ulrich* [sic] *volume*): Now this book—

DOCTOR (*Takes book from her and places it on table center*): Yes, but you wouldn't understand.

BARBARA: I'd rather not. (100)

Though Barbara tells her knowing brother that she'd "rather not" understand the homosexual "other half," the exchange that occurs between Dr. Richmond and his sister is ironic, given that *The Drag* presents nothing less than an underworld menagerie for its audience. Over the course of three short acts, West introduces spectators to working-class trade, to middle-class inverts, to fairies, to perverts, to sissy-men, to husbands, to closeted homosexuals masquerading as heterosexual, to a literal drag performance that brings them all together (and brings the play to a screeching halt), to raunchy gay slang, and to extended closing remarks on the immorality of homosex and the mysteries of modern homosexual identity in the United States. As historian Marybeth Hamilton argues, "West brought homosexuality to center stage, treating it as a lurid local sensation from which she crafted her own kind of metropolitan 'freak act'" (67).[1] Though Barbara learns nothing when she picks up—and puts down—Ulrichs, *The Drag*'s audience learns everything when it attends the play's production.

Let's put this another way: *The Drag*'s sexology participates in an established genre of slumming literatures, and the play's throwaway allusion to Jacob Riis's *How the Other Half Lives: Studies among the Tenements of New York* ([1890] 1996) substantiates this claim. Like Riis, whose 1890 photo-text on Lower East Side immigrant and working-class bodies functioned as armchair tourism for late nineteenth-century white middle-class audiences, *The Drag*, too, goes slumming when it stages a lurid local population for mainstream consumption and strives to make freakish bodies sexually readable for audiences in the late 1920s.[2] Instead of deviant Bohemians or Jews or Italians or Chinese migrants, however, West figures deviant white male homosexuals as objects of sexual knowledge. She turns "shadowy and mysterious" figures into dramatic homosexual sights and sounds, and she exploits homosexual subcultures for personal profit (Hamilton 1997, 62). To do so, the playwright delivers fascinating sights for fascinated viewers, and she offers you the chance to eyewitness a developing urban U.S. subculture that makes the "other half" into a quick study, an easy sight, a good show, and, don't forget, an uproarious tour. Through her slumming, West—like so many others both past and present—contributes to the ever-increasing visibility of U.S. homosexual group identity as her controversial play brings enigmatic bodies into sexual comprehension.

But what, I ask, might have happened if West made good on Barbara's contention that "it's a good thing one half of the world doesn't know how the other half lives, eh"? What if West's slumming performance closed after Barbara's question, leaving her curious audience in the lurch? Or if *The Drag* declined to grant underworld knowledge? Or if it refused to stage a sexological laugh riot even though it advertised itself a *Homosexual Comedy*? This book contends that these are the strategies undertaken by the slumming writers considered in the following pages. Contrary to the generic expectations of slumming literatures such as *The Drag*, *Queering the Underworld* argues that a handful of U.S. writers and artists in the first half of the twentieth century queered the popular genre, turned the slumming narrative against itself, used it to manipulate homosexual identifications, and frustrated the compulsion to reveal underworld sexual knowledge. As I show, the logic behind Barbara's willful ignorance informs this book's productions, all of which make good on the challenge of Miss Richmond's "I'd rather not."

The cultures that I examine sweep across three cultural and aesthetic movements—Progressive Era realism, the Afro-modernisms of the Harlem Renaissance, and expatriate sapphic modernism. The writings range from settlement house sociological tracts to realist tales of bohemian tramping to sensational Harlem tour guides to exposés of the transatlantic invert underworld. Every chapter centers on writers and artists deeply invested in slumming literatures, each of whom who could be considered tour guides that thwart a reader's expectations. Philanthropic slummer Jane Addams, the focus of chapter 1, often gave tours of her Hull-House settlement in Chicago's Near West Side, but her sociological autobiography reveals nothing about her mysterious same-sex relations. Willa Cather, the spotlight of chapter 2, wrote as a muckraker at a pivotal moment in her late-blooming literary career, yet her early urban tramping tales question the value of subcultural legibility for lesbian authors and male invert adolescents alike. Carl Van Vechten, Wallace Thurman, and Richard Bruce Nugent—the centerpieces of chapter 3—each published sensational exposés about Harlem's demimonde, yet all three members of the so-called Van Vechten School cultivated an aura of sexual mystery about this community. And chapter 4 argues that Djuna Barnes, once a sensational journalist in New York City, spent nearly half a decade scripting an impenetrable guide to Parisian invert nightlife. Each of these writers was quite familiar with historical emergence of urban lesbian and gay U.S. subcultures. None of them had any desire to expose its secrets. Through their queer slumming, they bungled the project of sexual knowing promised by a production such as *The Drag*. Along the way, their subterfuge pushed their mysterious selves beyond recognition.

Like West, this book too goes slumming. But unlike her homosexual comedy, it takes Barbara's ignorant question at face value since it never stages a metropolitan freak act. Throughout these pages, it has nothing to show you—or tell you—about lesbians or gays or their subcultural fashioning in the modern United States. Unlike other works, it has nothing to reveal to you about the debut of homosexual (or, for that matter, heterosexual) group identity in major urban environments during the late nineteenth and early twentieth centuries. It does nothing to advance productions of underworld knowledge in the 1920s or today. And it complicates the intersectional knots of race, class, and gender as these identity categories dovetail with modern homosexual group identity formations. West's play advocates a politics of sexual visibility and sexual exposure. This book does not. It instead reveals how U.S. writers used the conventions of slumming literatures—conventions that continue to haunt (homo) sexual populations—to undermine slumming's intentions. It undoes underworld knowledge-productions. And, at its most disappointing, it breaks any promise of sexual legibility for readers then and, I expect, for readers now.[3] What starts off as close reading thus snowballs into a polemic against contemporary studies of subculture. But before I reveal these disruptions, I need to back up a step. Despite the intentions of my chapters, I must first clarify the mysterious contexts of slumming literature's shadowy history.

The Hermeneutics of Sexual Suspicion

The Drag relies on conventions inherent in earlier nineteenth-century slumming literatures, a well-worn genre that scholars type as city mysteries. Though "an undercurrent of ambiguity" was sometimes present, much of this genre dedicated itself to exposing the supposed secrets of "foreign" urban bodies (Reynolds and Gladman 2002, xlix). It first gained momentum in U.S. literary public spheres following the transatlantic success of Eugène Sue's *Les mystères de Paris* (translated into English in 1844), a work that "unveiled the city's mysteries by telling tales of criminal underworlds, urban squalor, and elite luxury and decadence" (Denning, [1987] 1998, 85).[4] As critics such as Justin Edwards have noted, scads of city-mystery slumming stories such as Ned Buntline's *The Mysteries and Miseries of New York: A Tale of Real Life* (1848) and George Thompson's *City Crimes; or, Life in New York and Boston—a Volume for Everybody: Being a Mirror of Fashion, a Picture of Poverty, and a Startling Revelation of the Secret Crimes of Great Cities* (1849) soon followed suit. The genre was ingrained in the U.S. cultural imaginary by the turn of the nineteenth century, so much so that it fragmented into tramping tales, detective fictions, philanthropic reform tracts, and, as I show momentarily, modern sexological studies of homosexual bodies.[5]

The formula for many of these mysteries was deceptively simple: a narrator inspires curiosity in his middle-class audience; tells it a story of startling revelation about urban classifications in cities such as Boston, New York City, Philadelphia, Baltimore, Louisville, and New Orleans; and leaves said middle-class audience with what counts for knowledge about a criminal underworld. Like so many discursive inventions of the nineteenth century, slumming literatures were often designed to comprehend and codify social contact across borders segregating social classes, including classes based on ethnicity, race, capital, gender deviance, and, in due time, sexual identity. The typical preface to a slumming literature has the narrator present the city and its sights as a lurid local sensation that both inspires curiosity and demands revelation. As James W. Buel writes in a prologue, "Why the Veil Has Been Uplifted," to his 1883 *Metropolitan Life Unveiled* (fig. 1): "The following pages, descriptive of five distinct phases in American civilization, have been prepared solely for purposes of enlightenment, which, it is my earnest hope, may be regarded in the light of wholesome revelation" (1).

For Buel, America's shadowy cities encourage revelation because "the social life of New York is so anomalous as to defy analyzation: it is antipodal in the abstract, and concretely indefinable" to middle-class audiences (30). After announcing the city to be an indecipherable spectacle, Buel then contradicts himself so that he can analyze this incomprehensible metropolis: "In describing the hidden or secret vices of city life, I have tried to remove the seductive masks which sin assumes and expose its hideous deformities" (2). He next begs for "the reader's assent" to accomplish his moral task, and he informs his captive audience that they "will now make a tour of the Metropolis, and pay a special visit to some of the more noted dives of this dreadfully wicked city" (43).

Throughout this literary tour—which all slumming mysteries of the nineteenth and twentieth centuries undertake—the narrator operates as a demystifying tour guide, one who details a plethora of sights for the curious reader.[6] In its sensational exposés of America's "Great Cities," *Metropolitan Life Unveiled* closely reads the mysteries of "painted harlots" (4), "dive bars," "assignation houses," and the "mangled bodies" of New York City's Chinese and Italian immigrant poor (5). It uncovers spectacles of polygamous Mormons in Salt Lake City. And it unveils "Negro hoe-downs" in New Orleans (18). Time and again, the narrator insists that these revelations are "valuable exposures" for the reader since immoral urban mysteries must, of course, be solved (6). In so doing, works like *Metropolitan Life Unveiled* present literary "armchairs" for stay-at-

FIGURE 1. Frontispiece to James W. Buel, *Metropolitan Life Unveiled; or, The Mysteries and Miseries of Americas* [*sic*] *Great Cities* (1883).

home slummers that make metropolitan enigmas intelligible to their gaze (Chauncey 1994, 39). Fictive urban bodies are imagined, identified, reified, categorized—and, lest we forget, hierarchized—into races, ethnicities, and nationalities, and socioeconomic distinctions are memorialized as the urban mystery exposes the "hideous deformities" of urban modernity.

Exposure is the operative word here. The end result of many of these slumming literatures was nothing less than the wholesome revelation of what Edward Winslow Martin, in his 1868 *Work Descriptive of the Virtues and the Vices, the Mysteries, Miseries, and Crimes of New York City*, calls the city's "great secret" (fig. 2). It enables readers to become participant-observers in a disciplinary genre as the slumming literature disciplines the genre of the "dreadfully wicked city" through the act of closely reading it. Better: it takes a "concretely indefinable" mystery out of the streets and puts it into a concretely definable form in the reader's hands. James Dabney McCabe, Jr., author of the 1872 *Lights and Shadows of New York Life; or, The Sights and Sensations of the Great City*, is the best theorist of such reader response: "It has been my effort to bring home to those who cannot see the city for themselves, its pleasures and its dangers, and to enable them to enjoy the former without either the fatigue or expense demanded of an active participant in them, and to appreciate the latter, without incurring the risks attending an exploration of the shadowy side of the Great City" (14–15). Such noble "effort" on McCabe's part ensures that "the curiosity of all persons concerning the darker side of city life can be fully satisfied by a perusal of the sketches presented in this volume" (15).

Framed in this manner, it's safe to say that many shadowy slumming literatures across the nineteenth-century board help normalize and realize metropolitan spaces in a sustained and satisfying act of Foucauldian discipline that, according to Edwards, "attempt[ed] to control and undermine their threatening features" (131). To build on his findings: in the city-mysteries genre, the fictive construction of spectacular urban bodies takes on the odor of abject social reality. It is, as Buntline's subtitle to *The Mysteries and Miseries of New York* notes as early as 1848, *A Tale of Real Life*. And even if armchair viewers forget this during their literary slumming, the narrator-cum-tour guide reminds them at the close of the mystery that these urban scenes are far more fact than fiction. "In closing the details of the fearful scenes and circumstances which are nightly occurring in one shape or another in this degenerate city," the narrator of Buntline's *Mysteries* confides, "I would unhesitatingly assert that there has been nothing too highly wrought up in the various incidents" (285). Paradoxically, the historical constructions of urban slumming fictions are anything but, as one half of the world learns—again and again and again—how the other half lives.

Yet it must be also said that this set formula was, from its outset, prone to undoing. As scholars such as Christopher Looby and David M. Stewart have shown, the genre's earliest practitioners frequently called into

FIGURE 2. Frontispiece to Edward Winslow Martin, *The Secrets of the Great City: A Work Descriptive of the Virtues and the Vices, the Mysteries, Miseries and Crimes of New York City* (1868).

question the knowingness that they promised.[7] In *City Crimes*—by anyone's account an exemplar of the genre—Thompson informs readers that "we shall drag forth from the dark and mysterious labyrinths of great cities, the hidden inquiries which taint the moral atmosphere" (126). But when Thompson later begins to describe a "dark" scene of interracial sex between an aristocratic white woman and her "Negro" servant, he then retracts his narration regarding this elite decadence: "But why dwell upon such a subject so degrading to humanity? We will pursue the loathsome theme no longer" (149). This is not merely a matter of authorial self-censorship decades before the 1873 Comstock Law. In the same volume, Thompson spills pages of ink to depict gory tongue removals, male-male sexual revelries, female rape, and other instances of interracial sex. Rather, Thompson here toys with his audience's established expectations for the urban mystery. He undoes their desires for sensational realism, and insists that "the particulars must be supplied by the reader's own imagination" (248).

Withholdings like Thompson's were not uncommon to the nineteenth-century mystery, and they crop up again when we turn to twentieth-century writings on interracial demimondes. Nevertheless, the tropes of spectacularization, sensationalism, and revelatory satisfaction that many earlier slumming literatures successfully achieved had a remarkable longevity in later nineteenth- and twentieth-century U.S. cultures. Even as the mysteries of the city morphed into other genres, turn-of-the-century yellow press newspapers such as Joseph Pulitzer's *World* and William Randolph Hearst's *Journal* offered readers sensational slumming exposés that inflamed fears of interracial mixing and national decline on an almost daily basis (Chauncey 1994, 39). Confronted with cosmopolitan urban publics, these mass-circulated slumming literatures represented working-class immigrant populations as degenerates that must be reformed—if not necessarily assimilated—into the national U.S. body politic. In an extended overview of the mysteries of this urban press, Alan Trachtenberg comments that the "exploration of forbidden and menacing spaces emerged in the 1890's as a leading mode of the dailies, making spectacles of 'the nether side of New York' or 'the other half'" (1982, 126).[8]

This is not to neglect that, like several of their precursors, some turn-of-the-century slumming literatures confound the engines of ethnic, racial, and sexual knowing that fuel the genre. I say more about this when I turn to Jane Addams's cosmopolitan slumming in chapter 1, itself a bridge between later nineteenth-century city mysteries and more modernist takes on the genre.[9] For now, I note that reformist exposés such as Charles Loring Brace's *The Dangerous Classes of New York; and Twenty Years Work among Them* (1872) and Riis's *How the Other Half Lives* all too often depict working-class racial and ethnic groups as criminal, lascivious, and slovenly—a "queer conglomerate mass of heterogeneous elements" according to Riis—that are sliced into neat chapters titled "Chinatown" or "Jewtown" or "The Color Line in New York" (73). Alongside the ghetto sketches, the white slavery pamphlets, and the tramping expeditions that chapter 2 details, these "spectacles of 'the netherside of New York'" function as literary gatekeepers that made mysterious populations and "untold depravities" intelligible to a curious audience (Riis [1890] 1996, 63).[10] Through these literatures of exposure, knowledge about "social life" in the U.S. metropolis was realized through sensationalism, reproduced through spectacularization, and contained through generic formula.

So too, Riis's mention of "untold depravities" alerts readers, were emergent identity categories of urban homosexual bodies realized, reproduced, reified, and contained. In the words of historian Judith Walkowitz, slumming literatures "encouraged an exploration in the dissemination of 'sexual knowledge'" (1992, 125), and the recurrence of rhetoric such as "anomalous," "degenerate," "vice," "queer," "shadowy," "depravities," "hideous deformities," and "wickedness" supports her claim. As I noted with regard to *The Drag*, modern slumming mysteries were by no means unrelated to a modern development that inspired curiosity within U.S. readers: the historical emergence of homosexual group identity. If nineteenth-century urban legends set out to define "hideous deformities," and if turn-of-the-century slumming literatures such as the sensational press deciphered the enigmatic writing of "wicked" cosmopolitan bodies, then modern slumming literatures (like so, so many others) took this project of classifying social perversions and ran with it. To be more theoretically precise: they contributed to what could be called a hermeneutics of sexual suspicion, a mode of analysis that seeks to expose and to explain away the sexual secrets of modern metropolitan U.S. life.[11] Or, as cultural critic Jennifer Terry notes in her overview of modern U.S. sexological literatures (yet another off-shoot of the nineteenth-century mystery), "the subject of *homosexuality* was approached simultaneously as a mystery to be solved and a social problem to be managed" (1999, 35).

While historians and cultural critics such as Terry, Chauncey, Lisa Duggan, Siobhan Somerville, Marlon Ross, Mason Stokes, and Jonathan Ned Katz stress that this concern with homosexual (and heterosexual) classification was at times uneven, the epistemological toolbox present in slumming literatures such as *How the Other Half Lives* and *Metropolitan Life Unveiled* nevertheless abetted individual and communal identifications of bodies that seemed to "defy analyzation" and that began to dominate middle-class cultures in the twentieth-century United States.[12] Just as earlier slumming literatures set out to demarcate the secrets of the great city, so too was the later nineteenth-century homosexual and her collective group identity represented as a "mysterious physiology"; an "immense curiosity"; and a focal point for sexual "classification and intelligibility" (Foucault 1990a, 43, 77, 44). Writes Richard von Krafft-Ebing in his monumental sexological treatise *Psychopathia Sexualis* (first translated into English by American psychiatrist Charles Gilbert Chaddock in 1892): "Large cities are hotbeds in which neuroses and low morality are bred, as is evident in the history of Babylon, Nineveh, Rome and the mysteries of modern metropolitan life" ([1893] 1998, 4).

That modern slumming literatures would establish these classifications is really nothing new. They were part and parcel of larger technologies of sexual taxonomy that occurred in complementary mediums such as film, law, anthropology, musical performance, and the visual arts. For our interests, what is striking about this historical equation between sensationalism, sexology, slumming, and literature is how the rhetorical realizations of nineteenth-century mysteries of modern metropolitan life slip into the rhetorical realizations of twentieth-century mysteries of U.S. homosexual group identity; how earlier urban secrets of the city meld into the open secrets of urban homosexual selves; and how the identification of dreadfully wicked metropolitan bodies becomes the identification of dreadfully abnormal sexual subcultures via slumming literatures. Alongside West's *The Drag*, the best instance of these continuities occurs in Ralph Werther's 1918 modernist memoir *Autobiography of an Androgyne*, where a self-professed white middle-class invert from New York City—who also self-identifies as a working-class fairy—goes slumming in "the southern end of the Bowery" ([1918] 1975, 66), discovers Irish immigrants receptive to his sexual advances, and reprints "a letter to the family physician" telling his doctor that "I desire to know the mysteries of my peculiar life. It seems to me I have a right to know.... If the science of medicine knows anything about my peculiarity, I demand of you to know it" (52–53). An exemplary male homosexual body, Werther comes out to readers and sexologists alike as he considers himself a walking "secret of the great city," one of the many mysteries of the early twentieth-century New York City

ANNOUNCEMENT OF THIRD OF TRILOGY

The Riddle of the Underworld

Sequel to *Autobiography of an Androgyne*
and *The Female-Impersonators*

By Ralph Werther—Jennie June

Edited by
Alfred W. Herzog, Ph. B., A. M., M. D.
(Editor MEDICO-LEGAL JOURNAL)

To be published, in the fall of 1922, by the MEDICO-LEGAL JOURNAL. At least 65,000 words and a dozen illustrations. Cloth. Price three dollars, including postage within United States. The three volumes of the TRILOGY, (an aggregate of over 200,000 words) ordered on the same date, eight dollars, including postage. The AUTOBIOGRAPHY OF AN ANDROGYNE, ordered on the same date with one other of the TRILOGY, six dollars. Price of AUTOBIOGRAPHY alone, four dollars including postage.

****

The author of the TRILOGY, one of the half-dozen most remarkable bisexuals known to medical science, while living in New York City as college student and subsequently professional "man," had, incidentally, a six years' variegated experience (age nineteen to twenty-five) in the Underworld of the metropolis. In

[283]

FIGURE 3. Promotional advertisement included in *The Female-Impersonators* (Werther 1922).

demimonde. As he writes at the end of his 1922 follow-up, *The Female-Impersonators*, he is a textual participant in his *Riddle of the Underworld*, an unpublished (and perhaps unwritten) hodgepodge of sociological investigation, sexological case history, slumming literature, and sensational exposé (fig. 3).

This growing obsession with underworld riddles—a growing obsession with knowing one's individual and collective sexual mysteries—becomes a guiding creed of modern U.S. slumming as it swerves through a variety of aesthetic and cultural forms. Municipal governments in New York City, for instance, commissioned anti-vice squads like the Committee of Fourteen (founded in 1905 by members of the Anti-Saloon League) to unveil the sexual "deformities" and sordid secrets thought to characterize the "queer conglomerate mass" that was the metropolitan "vice" district.

In a historical analysis of later nineteenth- and twentieth-century U.S. literary slumming that spans from Riis to the Harlem Renaissance, Kevin J. Mumford argues that these organizations—like earlier city mysteries—marked "wicked" urban spaces alongside their more sexually normative counterparts. In his recovery of a committee investigative report that mirrors the "Negro hoe-downs" of *Metropolitan Life Unveiled*, Mumford details the surveillance of a New York lesbian and gay speakeasy in which a male city inspector "was introduced to a 'Pussy Party,' located in a basement where 'various forms of sex perversion [were] committed.' Near the top of the entry, his hastily penciled note reads: 'Very bad'" (1997, 81).[13] I discuss such naughty sensationalism in chapter 3, which explores how queer artists of the New Negro Renaissance undid sociological investigations hell-bent on demarcating the "various forms of sex perversion" to be found in American underworld parties. For now, I stress that modern slumming literatures by writers as diverse as Eugene O'Neill, Edna St. Vincent Millay, Robert McAlmon, Floyd Dell, Gertrude Stein, Stephen Crane, and Claude McKay often helped facilitate the dissemination of modern (homo)sexual knowledge that was occurring in very bad basements.[14] In tandem with translated sexological tracts and in line with earlier urban mysteries, they contribute to what Dana Seitler terms "the new visibility of homosexuality" (2004, 74); what West, following Riis, euphemistically terms "how the other half lives"; and what Eve Kosofsky Sedgwick terms "the epistemology of the closet," "a chronic, now endemic crisis of hetero/homosexual definition . . . dating from the end of the nineteenth century" (1990, 1). But, as I outline below, there has always been another half to this now endemic story of homosexuality's emergence in the United States. Like *City Crimes*, some modern productions wrecked this trajectory I just overviewed—an overview that has become one of the open secrets of modern U.S. sexual history—not from outside the genre's disciplinary constraints but from inside them.

The Suspicion of Sexual Hermeneutics

Queering the Underworld, that is to say, tries to thinks outside the epistemology of something like the collective closet. It surveys the same terrain (and sometimes the same works) as Denning, Trachtenberg, Edwards, Walkowitz, Terry, Hamilton, Somerville, and Mumford as it revisits a standard set list of mysterious underworlds, urban squalor, and elite luxury and decadence. But it also augments these scenarios of sexual knowledge production. In contrast to the now-canonical accounts of slumming that I rehearsed above, I explore how some play variations on its standard formulas—its basic mystery of the city themes—in order to sidestep sexual group identifications. To be blunt, I am less invested in tracking the shifts in U.S. sex-gender systems or in outlining alterations and aberrations in modern sexual taxonomies or in detailing the numerous developmental narratives of homosexuality than in how my writers skew these macroprojects in toto. I'm interested in those who disrupt slumming's conventions to thwart classificatory knowledge about the mysteries of homosexuality as an "unveiled secret" (Bersani and Dutoit 1998, 13). While others have shown the genre's success across the decades, my readings focus on its failures, its misfires, its interruptions, and its departures from established goals in a few choice settings. Hence as slumming literatures help inaugurate U.S. sexual case histories—taxonomic technologies with which later modern subjects continue to grapple—I focus on the undoing of this project at the moment of its historical assumption.[15] Rather than wholesome revelation for eager audiences, I keep you in the dark.

I admit that this task is paradoxical. But I believe it is a paradox that has been inherent in many explorations of so-called sexual deviance, from the literary representation of nonnormative sex acts in U.S. antebellum sensation fiction to the post-bellum rise of sexology to the present-day institutionalization of queer studies in several American academies. Indeed, any literary critic or social historian will most likely tell you that later nineteenth- and early twentieth-century slumming literatures most likely facilitated insidious distinctions between bodies.[16] But though I rely heavily on previous accounts of mysteries that expose the social constructions of homosexual group identity, my aim is to move beyond demystification by embracing mystification. The book cancels out a hermeneutics of sexual suspicion by concentrating on its embedded inverse—a suspicion of sexual hermeneutics. To do so, it stitches together formal reading, cultural and subcultural studies, poststructuralist queer theory, materialist-minded queer-of-color theory, gender studies, American studies, and critical race studies to address slumming literatures that deform the genre and its relentless allegiance to sexual knowledge, sexual visibility, and sexual revelation. It thus investigates how modern writers reformat the genre's conventions to achieve what Willa Cather terms an "Art of 'Escape,'" a distancing mechanism from the compulsory identifications of modern sexual underworlds (1992a, 968).[17]

Viewed theoretically, this book shows how slumming literatures—literatures about modern (homo)sexual group identity—were reinterpreted not as reverse discourses but as minor literatures. By a reverse discourse, I refer to Michel Foucault's exemplary definition in *The History of Sexuality,* volume 1, *An Introduction*: "Homosexuality began to speak in its own behalf, to demand that its legitimacy or 'naturality' be acknowledged, often in the same vocabulary, using the same categories by which it was medically disqualified" (1990a, 101). This is a strategy of subcultural recognition with which slumming literatures such as Djuna Barnes's *Nightwood* refuse to comply. In chapter 4, I show how Barnes presents readers with an antislumming guide to the night worlds of Paris, one where—in the words of her not-so-eminent sexologist Dr. Matthew O'Connor—"the more we learn of a person, the less we know" (111). Such sexual mystification defies easy reading (and acknowledgment) as it frustrates slumming's sensational realism from within. Barnes's queer slumming refuses to speak on homosexuality's behalf, and it resists the cultural solicitation to identify homosexual bodies, including what some later critics have assumed to be the author's own.

Though a work like *Nightwood* deploys the "same vocabulary" and the "same categories" as other modern slumming literatures, it manipulates this rhetoric into a minor literature rather than a reverse discourse. By minor literature, I refer to Gilles Deleuze and Félix Guattari's succinct definition—"a minor practice of major language from within" (1986, 18).[18] As my writers face the "impossibility of not writing" themselves into modern sexual subcultures that demands the revelation of one's sexual riddles, they turn the "major language" of the slumming literature's sexual revelation into the "minor practice" of queer slumming (16). This book thus charts how some twentieth-century writers used slumming literatures as minor literatures neither to legitimate themselves or visible subcultures nor to demand minoritizing recognition within U.S. literary public spheres. Instead it argues that appropriations of slumming literatures undid sexual and communal categorizations by manipulating mechanisms that best inspired homosexual legibility, namely, sensationalism and spectacularization. It shows how these appropriations resisted sexual identifications at the moment of sexual identity's historical emergence across a variety of disciplines in the United States. And it reveals that convention-cracking early twentieth-century slumming enabled sexually suspect writers to lose themselves in the metropolis rather than to secure an identifiable and policed collective culture. In so doing, it offers welcome respite from the ongoing imperative to identify sexually, to affiliate sexually, and to band together sexually under the aegis of reverse discourse. And it maps how deformations of conventional slumming literatures allowed writers to distance themselves from the confines of that sure-fire vehicle of sexual classification, social control, sexual knowledge, and sexual visibility—the epistemology of the closet. What audiences want to see in these texts is never what they expect.

I marshal a slew of minor slumming literatures to support these last claims—unpublished poems, letters, essays, prefaces, introductions, autobiographies, short stories, sociological accounts, newspaper articles, newspaper headlines, scrapbooks, clipping books, sensational urban exposés, tramping tales, supposedly sapphic novels, critic reviews, interviews, aesthetic credos, and spectacular tour guides. That said, each chapter pivots around a primary instance or cluster of queer slumming—Addams's *Twenty Years at Hull-House* ([1910] 1990) in chapter 1; Cather's 1905 "Paul's Case" (1991) in chapter 2; Bruce Nugent's 1926 "Smoke, Lilies, and Jade" (2002c), Van Vechten's *Nigger Heaven* ([1926] 2000) and *Parties* ([1930] 1977), and Thurman's *Infants of the Spring* ([1932] 1992) in chapter 3; and Barnes's *Nightwood* ([1937] 1961) in chapter 4. As I demonstrate, these disparate writings share a deep structure. Each undermines the genre's promise of subcultural legibility to muddle what "normal" society likes to think it knows about "perverse" bodies. Each revolves around mysterious individuals who refuse to self-identity as homosexual or to self-affiliate with a homosexual milieu. And each seeks out terrain perceived as indifferent to modern constructions of sexual knowledge: abstracted cosmopolitan spaces in a settlement house for Addams; glitzy hostelries indifferent to sexual eccentricity for Cather; after-hours parties where nobody knows your name for Van Vechten, Thurman, and Nugent; and the unknowable recesses of the unconscious night world for Barnes.

In Cather's "Paul's Case," for instance, when an effete white suburban bohemian under constant surveillance flees to Manhattan, he does not seek an emergent gay community even as he samples the slumming "night side of the town" with a "Yalie" from San Francisco (1991, 233). Instead, he tramps into the elite luxury and decadence of the Waldorf Hotel where he "lost himself" (223). And in Thurman's *Infants of the Spring*, a reluctantly "New" Negro writer yearns for "slightly known territory" outside the parameters of Harlem's identifiable lesbian and gay subculture, a utopian space that he finds through slumming ventures undertaken with close friends, both black and white ([1932] 1992, 199). While some of these works (like *Twenty Years at Hull-House*) betray elitist observations concerning racial and socioeconomic classifications that continue to smart, all reconsider the value of making homosexual subculture knowable in an act of "cultural desperation regarding . . . the control of language over the social construction of identity" (Somerville 2000, 9). And though the book constricts its focus to black and white literary productions in the modern United States, I should point out that these chapters also engage with London's Jewish immigrant populations, Chinese commercial spots in New York City, working-class Sicilian communities in Chicago, German aristocrats and opera singers in Pittsburgh, anti-imperial African circus performers in Berlin, Latin bodies in Greenwich Village, Austrian Jews, Eastern European immigrants, rural French vagabonds, and transatlantic Tangiers sailors to present varieties of cross-class, cross-gender, cross-racial, cross-ethnic, cross-sex, and cross-national contact whose purpose is not to consolidate identifiable sexual group identities in U.S. sexual history but, rather, to unknow them. The works I address do little more than discourage sexual revelation because the social lives they represent are so anomalous as to defy analysis, are antipodal in the abstract, and are concretely indefinable to curious audiences.

If this is the case, the slumming literatures I introduce should best be read as scripted fantasies that think outside the ongoing calcifications of modern U.S. sexual history. Like many mysteries of the city writers, I too see these writings as fictive imaginings that spark a reader's interest. Only my archive de-realizes modern metropolitan life when it refuses to show you anything even as it solicits your curiosity. In so doing, these textual acts could together be viewed as collective fantasies that resist not only what Adrienne Rich memorably termed "compulsory heterosexuality" (1993, 229) but also what I call "compulsory homosexuality." Much as *The Mysteries and Miseries of New York* and *Metropolitan Life Unveiled* turn mysteries of the city into the mysteries of real life, the slumming literatures this study examines warp the genre's sexual formulas into fictive wish fulfillments that deflect a knowable sexual group identity that was becoming all too real. And since these minor literatures refuse to articulate a politics of sexual recognition or a politics of sexual visibility, it is best to view these works as fantastic tours that enable readers to re-mystify their cultural moments. By refusing subcultural affiliation and by offering something other than what mainstream audiences want to know or desire to see, these slumming literatures make strange—one meaning of the word "queer"—what was presented as spectacular to modern U.S. urban cultures both yesterday and, I argue in my epilogue's turn to "down low" bodies, today. At their most audacious, they long to pitch themselves outside their historical contexts through fantastic manipulations of a historically entrenched genre.

But let us return to the start of the book for an overview. In chapter 1, "Terra Incognita: Jane Addams, Philanthropic Slumming, and the Elusive Identity of Hull-House," I examine the life and writings of Progressive Era reformer Jane Addams to argue that her sociological autobiography *Twenty Years at Hull-House* renders moot any epistemologies of her sexual self. Though Addams had two extended passionate relationships with women, she never affirmed a sexual invert identity, and she chose to live in Chicago's immigrant neighborhoods rather than as a part of the city's emergent Anglo-lesbian subculture. The reformer undertook this project at a moment when nationalist and imperialist U.S. discourses cast spinsters such as herself as perverted threats to the middle-class Anglo-American family. To sidestep these discourses, Addams "disappear[ed] into the bulk of the people" by philanthropically slumming on Halsted Street ([1910] 1990, 179). Manipulating her public persona as an international Anglo-American matron of various races, she casts her slumming venture as a form of impersonal cosmopolitanism. This way of life, she presumes, privileges basic likenesses between working-class immigrants and middle-class Anglo-Americans over "the less essential differences of race, language, creed"—and, I argue, sexuality ([1910] 1990, 66). Advancing a queered form of cosmopolitanism rather than lesbian subcultures, *Hull-House* becomes a terra incognita rather than a closet, in which Addams's sexuality remains unknown—yet nonetheless indebted to—Progressive Era slumming literatures of exposure and reform.

Unlike Addams, Cather's Paul does not try to connect with an ethnic or racial underworld. Through an extended reading of the realist short story "Paul's Case," in chapter 2, "Willa Cather's Experiment in Luxury," I instead show how Cather's lost boy goes incognito tramping to make his perverse behaviors inconspicuous to the paranoid others that surround him. In so doing, my second chapter charts how Cather revises a popular turn-of-the-century slumming literature—the bohemian tramping narrative. Several realists and social commentators, such as William Dean Howells, Stephen Crane, and Jack London, wrote about their tramping excursions into underworlds in an attempt to experience underclass life. These excursions always fascinated Cather, as her early essays on tramps such as Walt Whitman and Paul Verlaine, as well as her obsession with bohemia, attest. Yet while her critics claim that Cather used male bohemians to voice her closeted lesbian desires, I argue the reverse and suggest that Paul, the protagonist of her favorite short story, tramps to flee from homosexual classification. In my reading, Cather first casts Paul as a transient bohemian dandy reviled for his effeminate attire. His teachers gossip that he is a homosexual pervert, a bad secret of the city. To escape this sexual exposure, Paul first tramps into the fantastic "portal of Romance" that is Carnegie Hall (1991, 228). When this fails, he then leisurely tramps into the elite Waldorf Hotel, where "he had no especial desire to meet or know any of these people" and where nobody cares about his sexuality (233). Like Addams, his sexuality, too, becomes unreadable, though he engages with elite luxury and white decadence to avoid dangerous classification.

Chapter 3, "'Slightly Known Territory': Renaissance Admixture and the So-Called Van Vechten School," builds on the queer accounts of philanthropic and leisurely slumming developed in chapters 1 and 2 by turning to two Harlem Renaissance writers—Wallace Thurman and Richard Bruce Nugent—who interacted loosely with bohemian patron Carl Van Vechten. Although some scholars contend that black and gay pride informed the Harlem Renaissance, my research reveals that the Van Vechten School (as it was then known) uses discourses of interracial slumming to question the value of an affirmative, knowable minority community, homosexual or no. With its calculated misinformation and confusing interracial scenes, Van Vechten's best-selling slumming narrative *Nigger Heaven* builds on an earlier queer slumming text by his friend James Weldon Johnson to obstruct sexual knowledge that slumming whites (and, I argue, blacks) might like to think they have about Harlem's underworld. His later slumming narrative, *Parties*, complements this signifying slumming, as German octogenarians, downtown American whites, and underworld bootleggers engage in a queer admixture in New York and Paris, indifferent to communal or subcultural affiliations.

Thurman's roman-à-clef, *Infants of the Spring*, and Nugent's stream-of-consciousness prose poem "Smoke, Lilies, and Jade" complement—as they critique—Van Vechten's work to champion anticommunitarian spaces predicated on earlier slumming literatures like that of James Weldon Johnson. Nugent's Alex wants a space where no one, including himself, understands his sexual desires, and this bohemian finds it by traversing the streets of Greenwich Village. Likewise, Thurman's anti–New Negro Ray also longs for a gathering indifferent to sexual (and racial) categorizations. He briefly finds this social scene in the company of a Scandinavian graduate student; yet the Prohibition Era's obsession with difference soon ruins this "slightly known territory" ([1932] 1992, 199). In so doing, Thurman validates and critiques the social agendas that Van Vechten's slumming literatures inspire.

Taking the writings of Djuna Barnes and her nemesis Radclyffe Hall as its primary focus, chapter 4, "Antisapphic Modernism," broadens the book's scope to query the possibility of a knowable gay and lesbian past. From December 1913 to August 1914, Barnes worked under Van Vechten as a journalist in New York City, and her perplexing, antihistorical slumming literatures augment the Van Vechten School's confusing textual strategies. Building on Barnes's earlier sensational accounts of bohemias found in Chinatown and Greenwich Village, my close reading of her modernist classic *Nightwood* maintains that the text is anything but an autobiographical lesbian novel about homosexual underworlds that a writer like Hall offers in her best-seller *The Well of Loneliness*. While many read Barnes's novel as a slumming literature that lifts the curtain on expatriate invert night life, I argue the opposite: Barnes undermines discourses of perversion to present an unknowable underworld removed from a sensationally real gay or lesbian historical body. For Barnes, this underworld is fantastically antimimetic, a representational wasteland. In lieu of an identifiable subculture, she asks that readers become "something not yet in history" ([1937] 1961, 44), much like her "eternal[ly] incognito" sleepwalker, Robin Vote (88). *Nightwood* thus completes the arc of my main argument as it presents a sensationalized urban exposé—a Sue-like *Mystery* of the Parisian night—that paradoxically resists sexual exposure of any sort.

Rotten Politics

Some quick remarks about my political aims: they're rotten. Slumming literatures are, of course, nasty business, and their spectacular politics are, of course, unpleasant. But there might be perverse value to them when they are recast as minor literatures. When seen in this light, this book's strategies forecast a model for subsequent dealings in interdisciplinary queer studies, American studies, and studies of modern American literary cultures. It does not contribute to a hermeneutics of sexual suspicion. It does not present a collective subterranean history that gradually emerges into the light of mainstream visibility.[19] It fails to recuperate or redeem anyone's sexual past, including your own. It has little faith in a politics of sexual recognition. It makes nothing more—and nothing less—than trouble for curious readers or investigative critics. And though it draws on close reading, archival research, and the intellectual labors of prior decades, it has no particular investment in decoding bodies or in decoding the cultures so invested in coding these bodies. The closer critics examine the following texts, the less the texts reveal and the more they annoy. This is precisely their antihermeneutical point.

These antirevelatory readings of queer slumming do, however, take inspiration from legal studies scholar Martha M. Umphrey's succinct account of one early twentieth-century Pittsburgh millionaire murderer—Harry K. Thaw—whose sensational narrative of elite luxury and decadence "makes trouble" for recent descents into the past (2003, 26). Trying to situate Thaw into modern U.S. sexual history, Umphrey finds that the more she digs, the less his archive shows: it foils her identitarian—and her communitarian—intentions. Thaw does not fit into a knowable schema or a legible sexual taxonomy, and he "stood outside the politico-historiographic laws of identity formation, which require a self-conscious association with the group subject to historical excavation" (27). In other words, Thaw is a one-man queer slumming literature. As such, he disappoints the disciplinary frames of middle-class sexual identifications in the twentieth-century United States. A privileged white mystery of Pittsburgh, he ruins Umphrey's historical expectations and the designs of one version of U.S. sexual history. His archived body spoils, makes rotten—another meaning of the word "queer"—a communal politics of homosexual recognition in the first decades of the twenty-first-century as it ruins a communal politics of sexual visibility in the first decades of the twentieth (Umphrey 2003, 25).

I stress spoilage and ruination. As Umphrey notes when she cites several etymologies of "queer" from the *Oxford English Dictionary*, the word does not have only the adjectival meaning of "strange" or "odd" (2003, 25). Nor does it only have the nominal and often recuperated meaning of "homosexual" (*OED*, 2d ed.) or only a definitional focus of "nonnormative," as in "not in a normal condition" (*OED*, 2d ed.). "Queer" also functions as a transitive verb that frustrates these popular definitions. When deployed as a universal (as it often was at the turn of the century) it can mean "to puzzle" or "to spoil, put out of order" (Umphrey 2003, 25). Delving a bit deeper into its etymology, it can mean "to spoil (a person's) undertaking" (*OED*, 2d ed.).

It is this earlier "self-conscious" usage of "queer" as an active process of spoiling or ruining or making rotten the "undertaking" of sexual communitarianism that intrigues me the most. Unhinged from its nominal role in the sexual "identity formation" of any queer "group subject" across race, nation-state, region, class, or historical time, the word may ruin the best-laid schemas of slumming cultures still dedicated to the sexual surveillance, the sexual exposure, and the sexual revelation of communal formations such as *The Drag*. It may "interfere with or spoil the business (of a tradesman or showman)" like West, or, more to the point, like a literary or cultural critic committed to queer studies (*OED*, 2d ed.). It may also spoil or deform or interfere with the "historical excavation" that enables contemporary subjects to associate themselves with the business of a showy lesbian and gay body or to reify themselves into a knowable sexual present as a queer "group subject." In so doing, "queer" may also disrupt the now-institutionalized reading regime of the "open secret" that slumming literatures often advance, a regime that is "still the mode of producing, transmitting, and receiving most discourse around homosexuality" (Miller 1992, 16). In this sense, the trade of queer studies that this book promotes is one of knowing impairment regarding the production of sexual epistemology across any period and across any media. It is a project of disabling the psychic, social, and material functioning of sexual identifications—of self, of group, and of everywhere in between. It is a puzzling acting out of queer slumming, not the lurid local sight of a queer slumming. This may, to return to another adjectival meaning of "queer" rarely cited by critics, be a productively "worthless" task (*OED*, 2d ed.).

This is also to say that sketchy bodies like a Harry Thaw—or a Carl Van Vechten or a Djuna Barnes or a Wallace Thurman or a Jane Addams or someone on the down low (DL)—grant a distinct vantage point for surveying the spectacular regimes of a modern sexual epistemophilia that continues to haunt the idea of *us*. Indeed, Umphrey contends that it is "engagement with unsavory characters" like Harry Thaw that should be a key focal point for contemporary queer studies (2003, 28). To further build on her understudied claims: none of my writers or characters is particularly pleasant. Some, like Thaw and Cather's Paul, are woefully committed to the wealth of whiteness. All have fraught relations to sexual, racial, and class politics, usually to an embarrassing degree. None take comfort in making sexual mysteries visible to larger audiences even though most engaged in same-sex activities. None promote the collective lesbian and gay worlds that sprouted in major U.S. urban centers. And none put on a good show. But if these queer slummers each have nothing much to say about the historical doing of modern sexual group identity, they have a lot tell about the spoiling of sexual modernity in America.[20] And if they have nothing much to tell with regard to redeeming communitarianism or subcultural ways of modern lesbian and gay life, their riddles of the U.S. underworld do have something to say about anticommunal unbelonging.

It is important therefore—before I turn to my chapters—that I stress the anomalous position of this literary slumming in U.S. cultural history, modern U.S. literary public spheres, and late modern queer studies. Their refusals to represent homosexual bodies, alongside their unwillingness to champion burgeoning homosexual communities, were the main reason why I was drawn to their interferences. They just don't fit into conventional narratives of modern U.S. lesbian and gay underworlds that often guide queer American studies, despite the desires of biographers, cultural critics, literary theorists, and social historians over the past half-century to make them do so. Given their antirevelatory strategies, they also do not defer to a logic of the closet, a predominant mode of reading that is still intrinsic to many understandings of U.S. sexuality. They instead give a distinctive resistance to sexual exposure since what they expose, finally, is that there was nothing to hide. Hence while these writers confront the "terrible one-directionality of the culture's spectacularizing of gay men [and women]" in the modern United States, they have no interest in "opening channels of visibility" as a reverse discourse for any spectacular body (Sedgwick 1990, 60).

Nor do I. I only trust that my attention to what these writers fail to show fosters desires to render more incognito sexual moments of anyone's historical period. If such is the case, then this book's refusal to grant any sexual insights within a supreme classificatory genre may offer unforeseen ways to put out of order the perpetual quickening of sexual visibility and sexual recognition. This is, unfortunately, the predominant politics that governs understandings of nonnormative sexual bodies of any color, class, and gender in the United States for the past three centuries. A synonym for "to put out of order," it needs to be said, is "to displace."

Underworld unknowing, the following chapters propose, is not a homophobic project. To make rotten a will-to-knowledge may sideswipe sexual politics as "we" have come to know it. When read against the grain of the sensational homosexual mystery, queer slummers overturn historically conditioned desires to legitimate sexual group identities in the distant past, the immediate present, and the near future. They thwart the generic expectations of compulsory homosexuality by inhabiting them, and their spoilage of the mysteries and miseries of sexual modernity prohibits an invasive gaze. They ask that readers wait to see—or know more about—the sights and sensations that have come before. They present a rotten politics that is, as *The Drag*'s Barbara could have had it, just another way of saying that what some people don't know about the other half may be a good thing. Barbara didn't stop pressing sexual matters. These pages do.

CHAPTER ONE

Terra Incognita: Jane Addams, Philanthropic Slumming, and the Elusive Identity of Hull-House

We must say that there is a bourgeois sexuality, and that there are class sexualities. Or rather, that sexuality is originally, historically bourgeois, and that, in its successive shifts and transpositions, it induces specific class effects. —Michel Foucault, *The History of Sexuality*, volume 1

She never thought of herself; even her autobiography is the story of Hull-House. Was there ever a more impersonal autobiography?...Miss Addams does not ask us to consider her, but only the society she served. —Henry Steele Commager, foreword to the 1961 edition of *Twenty Years at Hull-House*

Disappearing Acts

Foucault's dated claim that Western formations of (homo)sexuality historically originated from within the middle classes should have given scholars in U.S. queer studies pause, if only because the field has yet to exhaust the interclass dynamics of this most recent technology of normalization and modernity. Currently, scholars are quick to agree that the "nineteenth-century homosexual became a personage, a past, a case history, and a childhood, in addition to being a type of life, a life form, and a morphology" (1990a, 43). They then connect the homosexual body to burgeoning disciplines such as criminology, sexology, sociology, and psychology, and they confirm recent breakthroughs in understandings of the intertwined emergence of racial and sexual categorizations. Yet despite these advancements, relatively few have focused on the interconnections between developing class identities and the production of homosexual group identity in America. Predominantly social historians, these scholars—George Chauncey, Jeffrey Weeks, Lisa Duggan, and Lillian Faderman, among others—have charted the insular, in-the-know nature of early twentieth-century U.S. gay and lesbian subcultures and their complex relation to middle-class notions of sexual identity.[1] Chauncey, in particular, has documented the trickle-down effect of an urban male heterosexual and homosexual binary as it leaked from the white middle classes into the working classes throughout the 1920s, and thereafter. Following Foucault's lead, we might now ask what "class effects" emerged from the "shifts and transpositions" of urban interclass contact prior to these formative years (1990a, 127).

I have in mind the question of the philanthropic Progressive slummer. One of the more influential U.S. social movements of the late nineteenth century, Progressivism emerged as a middle-class response to the perceived mysteries and miseries of the metropolis—immigrant migrations from locales other than Northern Europe; rampant industrialization; and the development of cosmopolitan neighborhoods removed from the watchful eye of developing suburbs. The white middle classes often regarded these working-class immigrant residencies as a terra incognita akin to what Jack London, in a shrill 1903 slumming narrative, terms the "Abyss" of "Darkest Africa or Innermost Thibet" ([1903] 1982, 22, 8). In tandem with London's metaphors of primitivism and geographic isolation, others derided these ethnic regions as an underworld, a "no-man's land" (Sante 1991, 19), an "interzone" (Mumford 1997, 19), a "nether life" (Riis [1890] 1996, 187), or a "nether world" (Trachtenberg 1982a, 142); and, for many, they were dismissed as the slums. These seemingly lurid social spaces—New York City's Tenderloin and Bowery and parts of Chicago's Near West Side, to name but three—were notorious and notoriously visited for vice, shorthand for activities that did not promote standards of propriety, industry, sobriety, and sexual restraint. For much of the white middle classes then, the denizens of such quarters, precincts, and districts constituted an underclass that terrified and titillated.

Somewhat akin to populism, a working-class rural reform movement aimed at stifling emergent corporate capitalism and aiding impoverished Midwestern communities, Progressivism attempted to clean up, control, and categorize these spaces in a classic Foucauldian act of social management. Some male and female reformers even went so far as to inhabit working-class immigrant neighborhoods as self-styled philanthropic slummers and to publish detailed accounts of their interclass activities in U.S. literary public spheres.[2] Embracing a type of life far removed from the havens of privatized white middle-class identity, the Progressive slummer often championed temperance, suffrage, and corporate reform while ministering financial and emotional aid to immigrants from a new form of cohabitation—the settlement house.[3]

Scholars have charged that the social activities undertaken in these settlement houses advanced, unconsciously or not, assimilation and internal U.S. imperialism, but I have chosen to forgo a negative critique of philanthropic slumming and concentrate on its connection to novel technologies of homosexuality, a connection both historically rich and theoretically underdeveloped.[4] A philanthropic act that was less about the increasingly popular phenomenon of ethnic and sexual tourism than about altruistic urban aid, Progressive Era slumming emerged around the same time that another discourse—sexology—and one of its corollaries—the epistemology of the closet—began to achieve prominent notice in U.S. media. On American soil, both discourses originated from within white professional-managerial classes and gradually seeped into working-class immigrant populations. Both were indebted, as Siobhan Somerville has shown, to scientific racism.[5] Both investigated nether regions, whether these were the psyche or the deprecate slums. Both specialized in literatures of exposure—the closet and the pathological case history for one and the muckraking photo-essay for the other. And both, at times, found these similarities condensed into symptomatic conflicts over another novelty, the suspect body of the mannish New Woman. Historian Carroll Smith-Rosenberg, in a claim to which I return, finds that "as Progressive women reformers increased their political power in the years immediately preceding the First World War, and as the suffrage movement reached a crescendo of public visibility (parades, arrests, forced-feedings) and of political power (the passage of the Twentieth Amendment), articles complaining of lesbianism in women's colleges, clubs, prisons, and reformatories—wherever women gathered—became common" (1990, 242).

But if, as Foucault asserts, sexuality "induces specific class effects" (1990a, 127), we might ask how the heightened visibility of Progressive interclass contact enabled some lucky few to manipulate—rather than to realize—technologies that produced identity categories such as the "lesbian" reformer in the first place. According to historian Kevin P. Murphy, some philanthropic slummers in their settlement houses managed to cultivate "sexual identities and practices that conformed neither to the middle-class norms of their day, nor to current binary notions of heterosexuality and homosexuality" (2000, 290). In dialogue with Murphy, this chapter asks: How did some female participants in the Progressive settlement movement short-circuit sexual surveillance in U.S. literary public spheres to found what I call an alternative terra incognita? How did narratives about their philanthropic slumming enable some white middle-class women to slip past a burgeoning epistemology of the closet, despite the media's obsession with identifying the mannish lesbian? How, that is, did reformers manipulate representations of their interclass contacts to fracture the chronic, now endemic crisis of homo/heterosexual definition that increasingly structured U.S. sex-gender systems as they came to know them?

To answer these questions, I focus on the autobiography and unpublished writings of one philanthropic slummer and settlement house reformer—Jane Addams—whose sexual proclivities have been the cause of much debate. While I spell out this controversy as the chapter progresses, a brief synopsis of her public and private life might be useful for readers unfamiliar with the details of her life-long slumming venture. After an agonizing back surgery, a neurasthenic depression, and a painful rest cure supervised by famed clinician and novelist Silas Weir Mitchell, Addams, along with her good friend Ellen Gates Starr, cofounded the Hull-House settlement in Chicago's Near West Side during the spring of 1889. Providing emotional, intellectual, and material aid to working-class immigrant populations, her settlement house patterned itself after British models such as East London's Toynbee Hall and promoted itself as a cosmopolitan arena that gathered middle-class reformers, immigrants, and women disgruntled with the constraints of suburban (or, in Addams's instance, rural) domestic life. While some scoffed at Addams's slumming venture when she and Starr first publicized their efforts, her settlement house soon received widespread recognition, thanks in large part to the encouragements the reformer received from her second longtime companion, Mary Rozet Smith.

Save for a brief period when pundits chided Addams for her World War I pacifism and her stringent anti-imperialism, the reformer gave public lectures to welcoming crowds, wrote praiseworthy tracts on prostitution, juvenile delinquency, and immigrant life, corresponded regularly with the Chicago school of sociology, and received several honorary degrees. She also became an international icon who, on daily average, received hundreds of well wishes from anonymous citizens as well as notables such as W. E. B. DuBois, William Dean Howells, Jacob Riis, and

William Butler Yeats. This renown reached its apex in the late 1910s, her popularity so pronounced that, as biographer Allen F. Davis notes, her name recognition was used to sell tin cans of "Jane Addams Mixed Vegetables" throughout the nation's heartland. Nicknamed "Saint Jane" by the press, Addams became an icon of Progressive internationalism, a living, breathing Statue of Liberty whose "name was so well known that it was used generically" (Davis 1973, 199).

Though she was recognized for administering to Chicago's slums, nothing has been written about how and why Addams manipulated this altruistic public image for her personal benefit. Indeed, Addams courted the public image of a saintly cosmopolite but paradoxically shied away from the invasive exposure accorded by Progressive media. Included in her best-selling 1910 sociological autobiography-cum-slumming narrative *Twenty Years at Hull-House*, one of her favorite anecdotes illustrates this complicated relationship between the prying press and the philanthropic slummer:

> Years ago I was much entertained by a story told at the Chicago Women's Club by one of its ablest members in the discussion following a paper of mine on "The Outgrowths of Toynbee Hall." She said that when she was a little girl playing in her mother's garden, she one day discovered a small toad who seemed to her very forlorn and lonely, although as she did not know in the least how to comfort him, she reluctantly left him to his fate; later in the day, quite at the other end of the garden, she found a large toad, apparently without family or friends. With a heart full of tender sympathy, she took a stick and by exercising infinite patience and some skill, she finally pushed the little toad through the entire length of the garden into the company of the big toad, when, to her inexpressible horror and surprise, the big toad opened his mouth and swallowed the little one. The moral of the tale was clear applied to people who lived "where they did not naturally belong," although I protested that was exactly what we wanted—to be swallowed and digested, to disappear into the bulk of the people.
>
> Twenty years later I am willing to testify that something of the sort does take place after years of identification with an industrial community. ([1910] 1990, 178–79)

Though the club member's maudlin tale recognizes Addams's social work, she cautions that a golden rule—Love Thy Neighbor—must be broken if the white middle class is to sustain itself. Drawing on the tenets of Social

Darwinism, a popular ideology that maintained stronger races or classes would overpower the weaker, the club member's allegorical tale naturalizes class distinctions and warns against interclass contact for fear of race suicide. Attempts to aid working-class immigrants stifle the white middle class, the club member suggests. The bourgeoisie will be conned, subsumed, and destroyed by the underclass if it continues to slum philanthropically.

Seeing her self-proclaimed digestion within the Chicago slums as a blessing rather than as class kamikaze, Addams instead welcomes this incognito disappearance. Her humanitarian attempts to aid the immigrant poor cannot be written off as noblesse oblige, nor do they extinguish the middle classes. By obliterating her own individuality, her philanthropic slumming venture into an international district where she does "not naturally belong" instead makes her impersonal. Her improper public endeavors allow her to "disappear into the bulk of the people." Over twenty years, she claims, her "identification with an industrial community" benefits the benefactor as well. Though her cosmopolitan work was publicized in numerous middle-class literatures, her slumming project becomes nothing less than a vanishing act. While Addams was dependent on the Progressive public for recognition of her work in the slums and for the construction of her benevolent image as a philanthropic slummer, she uses such spectacular recognition to extinguish her self within the public spheres of her day, literary or otherwise.

To understand why Addams undertook this oddly impersonal project of disappearing into "an industrial community," and to further comprehend one relationship between class sexualities, philanthropic slumming, and white middle-class identifications, this chapter unfolds in four stages. First, it addresses both Progressive Era and contemporary accounts of Addams's relationships to the women she loved and with whom she worked. Here I argue that her public image as a selfless slummer was a calculated response to growing concerns with identifying lesbian bodies in national public spheres. Second, I show how Addams presents her settlement not as an urban home that condoned unnatural acts between women (as some conservative critics sensationally assumed) but as the embodiment of cosmopolitanism, a "cathedral of humanity" ([1910] 1990, 50) that thrusts particular persons into an abstracted world of "universal fellowship" (48). After outlining a brief history of U.S. cosmopolitanism, I next show how Addams tweaks this supposedly modernist ideal to present her public with an autobiographical slumming narrative—*Twenty Years at Hull-House*—that refuses, rather than incorporates, the genre's epistemological imperatives for sexual knowledge. In the chapter's third section, I illustrate how her commitment to such cosmopolitan slumming, combined with her self-promotion as an abstracted citizen of the world, enables Addams's autobiography to dodge any developing epistemology of the closet. Here I focus on the Progressive Era infatuation with ethnic and racial taxonomy to show how Addams, reworking popular representations of immigrants as undistinguished bodies, scripts a typological narrative that facilitates her incognito disappearance into "the bulk of the people." This elusive strategy, I argue in my final section, may have something to teach us about current desires to place queer individuals into a discernable historiography as Addams becomes one type of personage—an abstracted mass body—rather than another—a homosexual one. Or, as the reformer states in her autobiography's introductory chapter, the word "settlement" "implies migrating from one condition of life to another totally unlike it" (26).

Spinster Panic

Any attack on the spinster is inevitably an attack on the lesbian. —Sheila Jeffreys, *The Spinster and Her Enemies*

Though Addams may have attempted to skirt an epistemology of the closet, her critics have not. Much of the research surrounding her philanthropic slumming on Halsted Street centers on uncovering—or downplaying—her presumably knowable sexual identity. It assumes either that her heterosexuality was a given or that her homosexuality has been buried by decades of homophobia. Following Addams's death, early biographers dismissed the reformer's intimate relationships with two Hull-House residents—her cofounder Starr, from 1884 to 1890, and Smith, from 1890 to 1935. In the reformer's first full-length biography, her nephew James Weber Linn sidesteps any potentially erotic elements of Addams's personal life and instead characterizes Smith as "barely twenty; tall, shy, fair, and eager. From that day [when she first walked into Hull-House] until she died, forty-three years later, the interests of Hull-House remained her interests, and the friendship of Mary Smith soon became and always remained the highest and clearest note in the music of Jane Addams's personal life" ([1937] 2000, 147). Though Linn confirms Smith's centrality, he insists that the reformer's relationship with her has little to do with Addams's public endeavors. Addams and her lover are essentially nothing more than best friends.

More recent accounts of Hull-House's activities refuse to mention these relationships. Neither Mina Carson's *Settlement Folk* (1990) nor Rivka Shpak Lissak's *Pluralism and Progressives* (1989), two astute works on the settlement movement, credit Smith's or Starr's influence on Addams. Likewise, the sole biography that dares to hint at Addams's same-sex relationships, Allen F. Davis's 1973 *American Heroine: The Life and Legend of Jane Addams*, finds Addams's sexuality a moot point. "If one did not marry and preferred not to live alone, and if one rejected the role of maiden aunt," he contends, "living with another woman was often the solution. There were also, doubtlessly, sexual reasons, latent or expressed, for many women living together, but whether or not these women were actually lesbian is essentially irrelevant" (91). And in its most recent incarnation, Jean Bethke Elshtain nonchalantly asks, "What exactly would be revealed, if definitive proof were discovered of carnal activity among Hull-House women?" (2002, 24). Elshtain's rhetorical question answers itself: women did engage in intimate relations with each other, and this same-sex intimacy unnerves the conservative critic.

In their revisionist accounts of turn-of-the-century U.S. lesbian identity and community, Carroll Smith-Rosenberg and Lillian Faderman deviate from these reductive approaches that dismiss settlement movement homosexuality prima facie. The settlement house, argues Smith-Rosenberg, was doubtless a charged scene of poorly sublimated lesbian passion: "Teachers and settlement-house founders were loved as 'mothers.' Like those countless women before them, many of these women teachers and settlement-house residents formed passionate relationships with one another. Unlike earlier women, many of these New Women, eschewing men, felt they had married each other for life" (1990, 266). Though Smith-Rosenberg fails to mention Addams's relations to Smith and Starr when she refers to a certain settlement house founder, Faderman rectifies her oversight. "It is only in the last few years that we can acknowledge," she writes, "without the fact diminishing her stature, that Jane Addams—whether or not she knew to use the term about herself—was what our day would consider lesbian. She devoted her entire emotional life to women, she considered herself married to a woman, and she believed she was 'delivered' by their shared love" (1991, 28).[6]

While we would be foolish to deny that networks of female intimacy structured the settlement house movement, I want to think beyond this critical deadlock over Addams's sexual identification, since the philanthropic slummer did so herself. If we focus for a moment on her personal writings, we find an intimate same-sex relation that refuses the epistemological certainty of lesbian *or* heterosexual identity, primarily because Addams's Hull-House relations fail to conform to either a burgeoning twentieth-century sexual binary that now marks what Faderman marks as "our day" or even a nineteenth-century romantic friendship that may have marked hers. Addams, that is, situates herself outside developing sexual discourses of her day but within the sexually indefinite settlement house practices—if not the novel sexual identities spotlighted by the sensational press—that Murphy references.

In an unpublished, undated poem inscribed to fellow reformer "M.R.S.," the slummer congratulates herself and her close friend on inhabiting a settlement house relation far beyond the bounds of recognizable attachments such as an opposite-sex coupling or even a Boston marriage:

> The "mine" and "thine" of wedded folk
> Is often quite confusing
> And sometimes when they use the "ours"
> It sounds almost amusing
>
> But—You and I, may well defy
> Both married folk and single
> To do as well as we have done
> The "mine" and "thine" to mingle
> (*Jane Addams Papers*, reel 113.45.1572)

In this pithy love poem, Addams praises herself and Smith for sidestepping compulsory (homo)sexual identifications. Against all odds, she suggests in this correspondence, the two have managed to carve out an affective space enabling "mine" and "thine" to conjoin into something foreign. Traditional relational spaces, Addams informs Smith, both perplex ("often quite confusing") and please and are laughingly conventional. In contrast to such standard forms of intimacy, Addams and Smith inhabit a different form of coupling, something more akin to a relational terra incognita rather than a closeted liaison, since there is no suspicious sexual group identity to hide. Situated outside conventional Anglo-American marriage, and far removed from being "single," the two gleefully—and defiantly—"mingle" in Hull-House without any relational fusion. Eschewing men, they are adamantly not married to each other for life. Instead they "have done" well when their relationship could have been construed as perverse and pathological, given the Progressive Era's increasing intolerance for passionate same-sex relations of any kind. In brief, their settlement intimacy is beyond any discernible sexual taxonomy like the mannish lesbian: it is instead a love that does not speak any name.[7] And through such sustained, nameless coupling, the two come to exemplify what Terry Castle sees as a definitive characteristic of late nineteenth-century female relations: "a ghost effect: to ambiguity and taboo. It cannot be perceived, except apparitionally" (1993, 31).

This is also to say that this intimate relation negotiates—rather than exemplifies—an emergent binary in U.S. sexual history and the middle-class closet logic dependent on it. While Progressive Era literatures surrounding Addams's personal relationships somewhat substantiate Castle's contention that "at least until around 1900 lesbianism manifests itself... primarily as an absence, as chimera or *amor impossibilia*—a kind of love that, by definition, cannot exist" (1993, 30–31), the philanthropic slummer nevertheless lived during a cultural moment increasingly suspicious of same-sex relations between women, and one that began to define these relations in opposition to heterosexual identity.[8] Though some female relationships may have been condoned—even encouraged—in postbellum America under the rubric of romantic friendship, by the end of the nineteenth century many more were frequently identified as unnatural expressions that departed from the gendered norms of middle-class white womanhood. Following the 1892 trial of middle-class "sapphic slasher" Alice Mitchell, professional psychosexual discourses (such as the 1899 revised edition of Richard von Krafft-Ebing's *Psychopathia Sexualis* [(1893) 1998] as well as Havelock Ellis's and John Addington Symonds's *Sexual Inversion* [(1897) 1915]) and their more popular counterparts (such as the mass-circulated sensational press and other slumming literatures of exposure) freely borrowed from each other to classify passionate same-sex friendships between white women as pathological aberrations (Duggan 2003, 75).

Ellis, Symonds, and Krafft-Ebing usually focused their sexological gaze on upper-class and middle-class subjects while the sensational press often concentrated on mysterious underworld denizens or an aristocratic decadent elite, but all agreed that instances of same-sex mystery abounded in supposed vice districts like those found in Chicago. As Krafft-Ebing argues, "There are prostitutes who let themselves be known as given to tribadism [mutual genital stimulation between women]; persons who have been in prison for years; and in these hot-beds of Lesbian love, through abstinence, acquired this vice" ([1893] 1998, 623). Similarly, late nineteenth-century reformers such as Charles Loring Brace, Jacob Riis, and others dedicated themselves to uncovering the unspeakable acts that took place in the slums, to exposing and categorizing the moral "untold depravities" occurring in promiscuous houses much like the dilapidated mansion that Addams copurchased in 1889 (Riis [1890] 1996, 63). Hence Faderman's supposition that the signifier "lesbian" may not have been in widespread circulation during Addams's time could be reconsidered, given that various Progressive Era U.S. discourses coded intense same-sex female relations across class lines as fundamentally degenerate. In more theoretical terms: intimacies between women were increasingly cast as sexual pathologies ("hotbed" vices) in what now appears as a supreme instance of homosexual surveillance, a desire to render nonnormative sexual desires knowable so that they could be categorized and patrolled. Passionate same-sex intimacies between Anglo women were thus exposed as sexual pathologies disruptive to the proper functioning of the American body politic. Or, as one cultural critic has observed in a tacit nod to Smith-Rosenberg's findings, early twentieth-century media "admitted the existence of a masculine woman or her 'most aggravated' type, the female invert" only to manipulate these modern spectacles as "the catalyst for social and literary disenfranchisement" (Behling 2001, 28, 29).

As I have hinted, presses across the United States played into this growing concern with lesbian identification through panics over the role of the "single" unmarried woman within urban U.S. public spheres. Though Addams, I stress, was never singled out for the perversion of spinsterhood, regional and national newspapers published numerous editorials on the Progressive Era female slummer's lifestyle that she was well aware of, since she had them pasted into her clipping books. And while pathological same-sex activity was never explicitly named, connotations of settlement perversion abounded in newspaper reports written for the *Chicago Tribune*, the *Record Herald*, and the *New York World*, among others (fig. 4). In a December 4, 1905, *New York World* editorial ([1905] 1985, n.p.), one critic ventriloquizes that "race suicide laid to women's clubs": "Olga Louise Cadish, a young Ohio woman, has turned on her sex who belong to clubs and written dreadful things which she defies clubwomen to deny. She pictures the clubwoman as a destroyer of the home in the genuine meaning of the word. A woman who commits race suicide and encourages other women to do likewise."

FIVE "OLD MAID AUNTS," DECLARES AUTHOR HARD, ARE BOSSES OF CHICAGO

FIVE "AUNTS" RULE CITY

RACE SUICIDE LAID TO WOMEN'S CLUBS.

GENIUS OF HULL HOUSE IS "FIRST CITIZEN OF CHICAGO"

FIGURE 4. Headlines referencing public spinster. Courtesy of Swarthmore College Peace Collection.

Cadish provides her audience with no mannish images to substantiate her wild claims, yet she nevertheless "pictures" philanthropic women involved with settlement clubs as social aberrations who fail the norms of the private Anglo homestead. Her unfounded remarks—the ominous tone of "dreadful things" that no Progressive slumming reformer dare "deny"—suggest that something sordid occurs in these female clubs, clubs for which Hull-House was well known.[9] And while it might be tempting to dismiss her hysterical critique as yet another conservative attempt to contain white women within the domestic sphere (and outside the public spaces of the metropolis), Cadish's unfounded hunch that public women were "destroyer[s] of the home" was echoed in several articles denouncing the heightened prominence of the philanthropic spinster. Bold headlines such as "Five 'Old Maid Aunts,' Declares Author Hard, Are Bosses of Chicago" and "Five 'Aunts' Rule City" are but two of the numerous public attacks aimed at unmarried women in the first decades of the twentieth century; and one vitriolic editorial, written by the Reverend Elmer E. Huffner of Grand Junction, Colorado, spawned a series of intense exchanges between reformers and conservatives in cities such as

Boston, Pittsburgh, Philadelphia, and Chicago. In print and from the pulpit, Huffner lambasted Addams and her coterie by "saying that old bachelors and bachelor maids should be isolated on an island so they could not hinder the progress of civilization" (*New York World* [1905] 1985, n.p.) and charged that the unmarried woman is nothing more than "humanity wasted" (*Spokane Spokesman* [n.d.] 1985, n.p.). He further claimed that "unmarried women—'spinsters'—[appear] as even a worse class than bachelors; as almost a nuisance" (quoted in Bartley [1910] 1985, n.p.). And his hysteria continues: like unmarried men, who, if the "quality of [their] lives [with regards] to purity, honor, yes, even decency, was to be discussed I fear we would find ourselves in a very unwholesome and unsavory controversy," unmarried white females were thought to destroy the morality of the private sphere, to taint the dignity of the U.S. public sphere, and to encourage impressionable young women to lead a dreadful woman-centered life, an agenda culminating in nothing less than the downfall of heteronormative domesticity (quoted in Bartley [1910] 1985, n.p.).

To be sure, suspect settlement reformers in and around Hull-House did not ignore these insinuations: they reformatted the rigged terms of the argument. For present concerns, I note that several of Addams's close friends and acquaintances entered these vitriolic public spheres to promote themselves as domesticating icons of cosmopolitan humanitarianism, rather than as a perverse community centered on pathological spinsterhood. In so doing, they manipulated sensational press discourses in order to present themselves as selfless saints who foreclosed any knowledge about the mysterious mannish lives that they, perhaps, never lived. Sarah Elizabeth Bartley, for one, dismissed Rev. Huffner's charges, praising "the ability, the unselfishness, the sacrifice, and the usefulness that I have seen exemplified in the lives of my 'beautiful unmarried sisters' [such as Frances E. Willard, Susan B. Anthony, and Addams]." And in the *Spokane Spokesman*, a critic informed readers that, despite Rev. Huffner's call to "exile old maids to a barren island," the white unmarried woman "has shown herself to be a powerful reenforcement [*sic*] of human knowledge and the betterment of society.... No! no! It is too late in the day, if it ever were timely, to speak of the unmarried woman as humanity wasted. Without a child of her own to call her mother, she exercises a spiritual and larger motherhood" (*Spokane Spokesman* [n.d.] 1985, n.p.). Likewise, in another heated exchange that, unwittingly or not, verges on typing the Progressive female slummer as a modern-day lesbian, Helen

Gould addresses the question, "Are Bachelor Maids Useless to Humanity," sensationally "CALLS MEN TIRESOME," and presents "a list of ten world-famous" humanitarian bachelor aunts that begins with Sappho, "Grecian poetess," and ends with "Gould, philanthropist" and "Jane Addams, sociologist" (*New York World* [1916] 1985, n.p.)[10]

Linking the Isle of Lesbos to Chicago's Hull-House settlement and denouncing what Adrienne Rich would later call "compulsory heterosexuality" (1993, 229), Gould would have made a fine revisionist historian; but I am more interested in the national paranoia that incited her to such brash discourse in the first place. Through flashy headlines, spinsters were characterized by their critics as harmful to the progress of the American (read, Anglo-Saxon) race since they failed to reproduce the norms (read, bodies) of the nuclear family. And through their own sensational headlines, bachelor aunts like Addams capitalized on these paranoid claims. They created spectacular retorts that situated unmarried white women not as sexually deviant subjects, but as central to the development of "spiritual" ideals of "purity, honor, yes, even decency" even as their childless lives failed the dictates of familial heteronormativity.

New Women slumming reformers, in short, rejected the sensational libel of race suicide and social perversion to affirm instead that their supposedly unnatural interactions in international environments such as the Near West Side did more good than harm. Fostered through a worldly philanthropy wedded to immigrant populations, this well-publicized nurturing distanced them from the demands of the "mine" and "thine" of married folk while they operated under a cosmopolitan rubric. Presenting herself as an exemplary citizen who nurtured working-class immigrants, the single—though often coupled—bachelor maid tweaked an available discourse of selfless cosmopolitanism to stave off (homo)sexual identifications. This is not, I emphasize, a process of self-closeting. It is rather a deliberate cultivation of what Shannon Jackson, in an extended reading of Hull-House performativity, calls "queer domesticity," a mode of habitation that operates outside the framework of identifiable (homo)sexual bodies (2000, 164). Failing to reproduce, these wastes of humanity thus become what Licia Fiol-Matta (2002), in a discussion of another sexually unidentifiable public woman, Chilean writer Gabriela Mistral, has elsewhere termed "queer mother[s] for the nation."[11] In lieu of mannish lesbianism, Anglo-American spinsters such as Addams did well to present themselves as philanthropic slummers skirting the sexual categorizations to be found in both the domestic family and its pathological counterpart, to conform neither to the middle-class norms of their day nor to current binary notions of heterosexuality and homosexuality that often structure the late twentieth century. It is to the cosmopolitan strategies of these historically anomalous bodies—to what Jackson sees as "elusiveness of stable interiorities, sexual and otherwise, at Hull-House" (2000, 166)—that I now turn.

Queered Cosmopolitanism

As the voluminous clipping books housed at the Swarthmore College Peace Collection and the Hull-House archives in Chicago attest, Addams cultivated this image of a cosmopolitan philanthropic slummer within the same newspapers that derided single public women as unfit citizens. This public image stood in stark contrast to the common belief that "cooperative living" among settlement house women was "one of those unnatural attempts to understand life," as Addams herself notes with dismay in *Twenty Years at Hull-House* ([1910] 1990, 55). Yet despite chronic anxieties surrounding the unnaturalness of her settlement house, several popular presses did grant Addams a vaulted position within U.S. literary public spheres. In the May 2, 1912, issue of the *Kansas City Gazette*, Edwin Davies Schoonmaker ([1912] 1985) published a sentimental paean lauding her philanthropic deeds:

> MOTHER of races fusing into one
> And keeping open house with presence sweet
> In that loud city where the nations meet
> Around thy ample hearth when day is done,
> When I behold the wild tribes thou hast won
> And see thee wooing from the witching street
> By thy own saintly face the erring feet,
> I know Love still hath power beneath the sun.

With its references to a maternalized melting pot and U.S. imperialism, the poem's first line implicitly likens Addams to another famous female icon—the Statue of Liberty—who functioned as a preeminent symbol of American democracy and assimilation. With their overpowering "Love," Schoonmaker croons, these two women tame unruly impulses. In Addams's case, her cosmopolitan Hull-House settlement—an "open house" spanning across Chicago's Halsted Street—domesticates the seemingly "wild" immigrant "tribes" who inhabit the city. Like the Statue of Liberty, her "ample hearth" civilizes and acculturates the working-class immigrants entering the metropolis.

The *Gazette* was not the sole newspaper to shower the reformer with praise for these interactions, however. Depictions of Addams as a benign philanthropic slummer were quite commonplace during the early twentieth century. As thousands of newspaper cuttings in her clipping books reveal, numerous middle-class magazines such as *Ladies' Home Journal*, *American Magazine*, and *McClure's* applauded her altruistic social work and characterized her as a benevolent saint who fed, educated, and proselytized immigrants unfamiliar with American (or better, Anglo-Saxon) customs. "Reporters discovered," writes Davis, "that Jane Addams was good copy; they summarized everything she wrote, and reported everything she did.... She was an opinion leader, who not only made news, but influenced attitudes on a wide variety of subjects" (1973, 199). A veritable national treasure, a model of virtue, and perhaps the most famous woman of her era, Addams presented herself as this privatized public body—a "saintly face" as opposed to a wasted spinster—within America's regional and national public spheres. Offering her home to the homeless, the reformer was often perceived as a living institution "where the nations meet": "'The Lady Abbess of Chicago,' 'The Genius of Hull House,' 'The Only Saint America has produced,' 'Chicago's First Citizen,'...'The First Lady of the Land'" (Davis 1973, 199). In this hotbed of public "self-abstraction," to borrow a term coined by Michael Warner, Addams becomes an international body—"MOTHER of races fusing into one"—who fosters a rather queer form of "domestic cosmopolitanism" in the most unlikely of places (1992, 382).[12]

I emphasize "unlikely" because cultural critics and social historians often associate the cosmopolitan ideal not with Progressive Era literatures but with American modernism, and they often note that cosmopolitanism permitted the individual to disassociate from repressive national or sexual regimes.[13] In 1934, Malcolm Cowley suggested that one of American modernism's primary aims was to obliterate any emotional or psychic ties that might crystallize into damaging familial, regional, or national identifications. "Looking backward," he writes in *Exile's Return*, "I feel that our whole training was involuntarily directed toward destroying whatever roots we had in the soil, toward eradicating our local and regional particularities, toward making us homeless citizens of the world" (27). Much like Addams's insistence that a settlement house is a migration "from one condition of life to another totally unlike it," accounts of cosmopolitan displacements into the metropolis pivoted on the assumption that one's presumed identity must be superseded by a migration to a land and life less ordinary. For both the modernist exile and the philanthropic slummer then, the defamiliarizing interactions that U.S. metropolitan life precipitates were but one way to realize this journey. As Cowley's fellow bohemian and Addams's contemporary Randolph Bourne notes of the nation's metropolis in 1916, "America is coming to be, not a nationality but a trans-nationality, a weaving back and forth, with the other lands, of many threads of all sizes and colors" ([1920] 1969, 297).

But for Addams, this new admixture—this transnational melding into one—is not "coming to be." She argues throughout her autobiography that it is already quite manifest on Halsted. Though *Twenty Years at Hull-House* was written more than a decade prior to the height of American modernism, and though Bourne moved within New York bohemian circles somewhat removed from Addams's intimate Chicago spheres, the philanthropic slummer campaigned in the press for an internationalism on U.S. soil, one that would prove to have some interesting repercussions for eradicating local and regional sexual identifications at the turn of the century. Like the modernists who advocated this aesthetic creed (and like earlier reformers and reporters who ventured into polyglot nether worlds) the reformer, too, characterized her settlement house as a benevolent venture into the unknown, or as a trek into a "hospitable" "environment" ([1910] 1990, 75). Yet while such cosmopolitanism presages that of Cowley's, Addams's autobiography also promotes a unique version of this ideal, a queer cosmopolitanism—international and provincial—that "domesticates" urban environments while also facilitating unparalleled social and sexual interactions. To cite one example among the many given in *Hull-House*: Addams recounts a Hull-House performance of the tarantella and some "sleight-of-hand tricks so often seen on the streets of Naples" that several Italian immigrants presented before the Social Extension Committee, a group of Anglo-American women who gave "parties to people in the neighborhood who for any reason seem forlorn and without much social pleasure" (206). Following the production, one of the committee members confessed to Addams, "'Do you know I am always ashamed of the way I have talked about 'dagos,' they are quite like other people, only one must take a little more pains with them. I have been nagging my husband to move off M Street because they are moving in, but I am going to try staying awhile and see if I can make a real acquaintance with some of them'" (206).

While we cannot dismiss the Anglo-American club member's benevolent racism, it is important to note that she displays the beginnings of a cosmopolitan consciousness thanks to Hull-House practices. As Addams comments, "To my mind at that moment the speaker had passed from the region of the uncultivated person into the possibilities of the cultivated person. The former is bounded by a narrow outlook on life, unable to overcome differences of dress and habit... while the latter constantly tends to be more a citizen of the world" ([1910] 1990, 206–7). For the reformer, cosmopolitan interactions at Hull-House between Anglo middle classes and immigrant working classes—facilitated here through philanthropic slumming—are akin to entering into a new "region" where particularized persons tend to become abstracted citizens and where overcoming the habit of stifling "differences" becomes paramount.

To their surprise, Addams informs her readers, immigrants, philanthropic reformers, and Hull-House visitors often find themselves cultivating these abstract spaces of anonymous social pleasure, a brotherhood where one "judge[s] their fellows by a more universal test" (207). The settlement house's interclass transpositions, that is to say, fantastically begin to unsettle national as well as personal identifications, cherished prejudices, and particular taxonomies. Midway through her autobiography, Addams contends that her observations at Hull-House have put this idealistic theory into cosmopolitan praxis. She

> would cite the indications of an internationalism as sturdy and virile as it is unprecedented which I have seen in our cosmopolitan neighborhood: when a south Italian Catholic is forced by the very exigencies of the situation to make friends with an Austrian Jew representing another nationality and another religion, both of which cut into all his most cherished prejudices, he finds it harder to utilize them a second time and gradually loses them. He thus modifies his provincialism for if an old enemy working by his side has turned into a friend, almost anything may happen. (178)

Suspicious of such internationalism, historian Rivka Shpak Lissak finds that Addams appropriates this ideal of an international community from her acquaintances at the University of Chicago. Sociologists and philosophers such as John Dewey and Robert E. Park (whose urban investigations I detail at length in the third chapter) frequently held that "America's 'manifest destiny' was to produce a new kind of civilization, an international or cosmopolitan civilization, and thus accomplish the universal mission that Hellenism and the Roman and British Empires had failed to realize" (Lissak 1989, 141). While Dewey and his students promoted this cosmopolitan internationalism in academic journals, scholars such as Jessica Berman have also argued that U.S. cosmopolitanism was already a popularized discourse readily available to the readers of middle-class magazines in which Addams published. Berman notes that, unlike the bohemian cosmopolitanism fostered by modernists such as Cowley, turn-of-the-century cosmopolitanism was linked to and deployed by middle-class Anglo-women: "Well before she came to be coupled with Emma Lazarus's famous poem, the Statue of Liberty herself may be seen as a physical symbol of the connection of this cosmopolitan possibility to ideal images of women" (2001, 38). Given her frequent associations with the Statue of Liberty in regional and national presses, we could say the same for Addams.

Though the reformer rejected the more odious versions of this cosmopolitan ideal (she was adamantly anti-imperialist), the "MOTHER of races" did conceptualize her settlement house as a queer cosmopolitanism that melded both the academic and the popular, a universalized space where the distinctions among working-class immigrants and middle-class reformers were insignificant and where "almost anything may happen." She believed that Hull-House's imperative to love and aid thy neighbor (which both the Austrian and the Italian enact and which readers also witness in her toad allegory) elided ingrained social distinctions in an international interzone. And she was convinced that settlement house social relations transformed the particular individual into a "citizen of the world" who, like herself, becomes fantastically self-abstracted. In the closing arguments of her first chapter, Addams notes that, "at any rate, I was heartily ashamed of my meager notion of patriotism, and I came out . . . exhilarated with the consciousness that impersonal and international relations are actual facts and not mere phrases" ([1910] 1990, 13–14).

What is so striking to me about this pragmatic epiphany is that Addams comes out into the impersonal relations of Hull-House's cosmopolitan citizenry, rather than the all-too-personal relations of what sensational and sexological literatures began to construe as a modern lesbian coupling. Inhabiting—and transforming into—an "open house with presence sweet," she encourages the mingling of various peoples in her home and the surrounding neighborhoods, a gathering that becomes an alternative mingling of "mine" and "thine." Not to belabor this point, but Addams, along with her cohorts, queers burgeoning modernist ideals of cosmopolitanism and sociability that were already developing in academic circles around Hull-House, that had already achieved an imperial prominence in major middle-class Progressive Era U.S. magazines, and that we will see revamped when we turn to the slumming-based parties fictionalized by artists associated with the New Negro Renaissance in chapter 3. For now, I highlight both the obvious and the improbable: interactions in Addams's "open house" enable persons to become more alike rather than more different. And as minority cultures encourage a shared sense of universality that deemphasizes a cultural politics of ethnic recognition, this cosmopolitan climate also implicitly supports a politics of sexual nonrecognition, mainly because it refuses to engage with particular technologies of sexual identification.[14] According to Carrie Tirado Bramen, "Second-generation pluralists [such as Addams] were not exclusively concerned with making a plea for tolerance, nor were they consumed with a subcultural strategy of recognition; theirs was a much bolder strategy, which sought to lay claim to the dominant culture by transforming definitions of Americanism through the particular. The cosmopolitan and the universal, therefore, were not opposed to minority culture. Instead, identity culture was the means toward cosmopolitanism and universality; it gave cosmopolitanism a content and universality a sense of rootedness" (2000, 71). Bramen's discussion concentrates primarily on ethnic and racial distinctions as they relate to the ideological quickening of modern U.S. pluralism, but I think that an analogy to turn-of-the-century hetero- and homosexual differences may also be extrapolated from her argument. In lieu of hierarchical cultural identifications, *Hull-House* is swift to emphasize that "the things which make men alike are finer and better than the things which keep them apart, and that these basic likenesses, if they are properly accentuated, easily transcend the less essential differences of race, language, creed, and tradition" ([1910] 1990, 66). And, I would add, sexuality as Addams used settlement house intersectionality to distance her self from sexual identification.

I elaborate more on Addams's extraordinary claim when I present a closer reading of *Hull-House*'s autobiographical first chapters. I here emphasize that the idealized settlement house movement—as presented by Addams and her acquaintances in U.S. literary public spheres—impedes the charge of female perversion, since it consists of persons who have few

FIGURE 5. Norah Hamilton, "Jane Addams, Aged Seven, from a Photograph of 1867." Reprinted from first edition of *Twenty Years at Hull-House* (Addams [1910] 1990).

particularities or peculiarities about them. Whether such abstract states can now be empirically verified is outside the scope of my present concerns. What fascinates me much more is the impulse behind this desire for cosmopolitan transcendence. Since immigrants and slumming reformers together partake in this unprecedented international ideal, Addams's text anticipates that any provincialism or cherished prejudices will be fantastically erased in the social laboratory that makes up Hull-House. And through such exceptional interclass contact, these relations potentially engender what Amanda Anderson terms an "ideal universality" in its practitioners that potentially evacuates particularized identities like that of the central European immigrant or the mannish lesbian (1998, 283).[15] In brief, *Hull-House*'s queer domesticity wants bodies to mingle freely as it concentrates less on rigid racial (or sexual) classifications and more on the unprecedented delights of foreign social contact.[16]

Two idealized body images—each featured in her autobiography—substantiate this last point regarding Hull-House's cosmopolitan indifference to emergent politics of (sexual) group identity. Norah Hamilton, a fellow Hull-House reformer, did drawings of both these images and included them in the first edition of Addams's autobiography. As it appears in a chapter titled "Earliest Impressions," the first picture shows a portrait of Addams as a young white child who stares wide-eyed but purposefully at the reader (fig. 5). She wears what appears to be a white shirt, and her hair is pulled back over her brow. There is little to distinguish her from other children as she gazes at her readers; there is little that is particular to her self-carriage. As a matter of fact, a young Addams here has few distinguishing characteristics, though she does appear to have a purposeful aura to her presentation. Other than this quality, she is unspecified. Her small body flows into blank white space as the drawing tapers off around her torso, and it is uncertain where she might be best located, since readers are only presented with quick scratch marks rather than an identifiable background. The by-line underneath the drawing informs the reader that the sketch is of "Jane Addams, Aged Seven, from a Photograph of 1867," but it is also clear that "Jane Addams" is extracted from the particulars of any personal context. Given that this is one of two visual images that we see of Addams in her autobiography, it is safe to say that she is far removed from taxonomic identification with a mannish lesbian reformer. She is instead a vacant monument to ideal universality, one abstracted cosmopolite among the many at Hull-House.

So too are "An Italian Mother and Her Child," a complementary drawing that appears in a chapter entitled "Immigrants and Their Children." Just as Hamilton presents a young Addams as an abstracted type, she also sketches an Italian child in a similar manner (figs. 6 and 7). Standing next to her mother, the unnamed youth stares at the reader, her hands to her side and her hair, like Addams's tight bun, is parted down the middle and pulled back over her brow. She also appears to wear the same outfit in which a young Addams is dressed, and there are, to the best of my knowledge, no physiognomic traits that would connote a legible racial or ethnic identity that would differentiate her from an Anglo-Saxon population. A mirror to Addams, she is both nobody and anybody, a nondescript youth whose likeness parallels that of the philanthropic slummer.

Given these uncanny similarities, the two females together take on an unprecedented similarity that opposes the marked differences thought to demarcate the working-class ethnic immigrant and the middle-class Anglo-reformer. Through its commitment to such queer forms of domesticated internationalism, Addams's cosmopolitan ideal fashions an imaginary

FIGURE 6. Norah Hamilton, "An Italian Mother and Her Child." Reprinted from first edition of *Twenty Years at Hull-House* (Addams [1910] 1990).

universal space where hierarchical distinctions are rendered irrelevant, and, it follows, sexual distinctions are rendered elusive. To the "less essential differences of race, language, creed, and tradition," Addams must also include indifference to epistemological sexual exposure, since there is really nothing to expose in such fantastic terra incognita.

This is also to say that Hull-House's well-publicized attempt (at least on the printed page) to dissolve social and ethnic distinctions between white middle-class bodies and working-class immigrants longs for a breakdown in homosexual markers as well. However wistfully, Addams encourages various ethnicities, nationalities, classes, and genders to mingle impersonally within her cathedral of humanity. "Disinterested" cultural activities like lectures, salons, debates, plays, reading clubs, and painting workshops, she stresses, are "most potent agent[s] for making the universal appeal and inducing men to forget their differences" ([1910] 1990, 218). While we might now see these class effects as part and parcel of an assimilation project, Addams nevertheless uses "the practice of settling as the basis for new theorizing" against a developing sexual binary (Jackson

FIGURE 7. Norah Hamilton, detail from "An Italian Mother and Her Child." Reprinted from first edition of *Twenty Years at Hull-House* (Addams [1910] 1990).

2000, 27). She charges that the settlement house is "held together in that soundest of all social bonds—the companionship of mutual interests" (89), and in this cathedral of cosmopolitanism, social, national, ethnic, and sexual distinctions are held to be superfluous. Disparate people come together in unprecedented forms of *communitas*, rather than what the sensational press or sexological writings would describe as a recognizable hotbed of subcultural lesbian love.

Though Addams's claims for these Hull-House accomplishments have yet to be substantiated, her self-styled cosmopolitan presentations should best be read as an emphatic wish for a world beyond Progressive technologies of middle-class (homo)sexual surveillance. Her autobiographical representations of Hull-House propel the slumming bachelor maid and the working-class immigrant out of what some members of the press viewed as an unnatural nether region and into what she called "the land of the universal," a figurative space where international citizens of the world are not dependent on recognition or revelation of their differences (222). And like the reformer herself, whose utopian universality turns her into an impersonally international body rather than a sexually suspect foreign body, cultural and personal activities too tend to become abstracted in *Hull-House*. Nationalist Greek plays, she imagines when detailing the "arts at Hull-House," "have escaped from the restraining bond of one country and into the land of the universal" (222). Scandinavian weaving, despite its obvious particulars, becomes a warm gesture of intergenerational good will. Italian social clubs become "instruments of companionship" (225).

In this figurative open house where international bodies meet, individuals engage in what Anderson sees as the core component of cosmopolitanism—"impersonal cultural activities of cultivated distance"—and they begin "to enact or embody universalism, to transform it into a characterological achievement" (2001, 31). When seen in this light, the characterological achievements of the abstracted working-class immigrant and the philanthropic slummer pictured in her autobiography enable both to cultivate distance from the demands of individual interiority—what Foucault sees as a hallmark of Western sexual specification. By thrusting herself and others into this imaginative land, the philanthropic slummer is removed from the sensational achievements of homosexual typing. To fine-tune this last claim: when you scan her autobiography/slumming literature for definitive traces of a mannish lesbian body or the wasted humanity of spinsterhood, you're bound to be disappointed.

Twenty Years in Cedarville

The relationship between Jane Addams and Hull-House, between autobiography and history, is far more complicated than Addams was able to explain in her preface, as she seemed to realize herself, since she spends much of the book exploring, at least indirectly, the nature of that relationship. —James Hurt, introduction to *Twenty Years at Hull-House*

This is not to imply that Addams, as a privileged female slummer, was naive when she considered the dire realities of racial, ethnic, and economic inequality that saturated early twentieth-century Chicago, or even that she held firm to a consistent position on class relations throughout her career. "We are not willing, openly and professedly," she once argued in a college examination, "to assume that American citizens are broken up into classes, even if we make that assumption the preface to a plea that the superior class has duties to the inferior" ([1910] 1990, 26). But Hull-House's (and *Hull-House*'s) well-publicized insistence on a universality that anyone could obtain distinguishes it from other Progressive reform tracts and their realistic analyses of the slums. *Hull-House*'s cosmopolitan ideal, while connected to Chicago school sociology as well as to popular imperial accounts of taming the "wild" urban "streets," opposed how many late nineteenth- and early twentieth-century slumming narratives, particularly that of Jacob Riis, had conceived interclass contact.

As I mentioned in my introduction, yellow press publications such as Joseph Pulitzer's *World*, William Randolph Hearst's *Journal*, and the *Chicago Tribune* as well as book-length sensational urban exposés such as *How the Other Half Lives* (Riis [1890] 1996), *Metropolitan Life Unveiled* (Buel 1883), and *The Dangerous Classes of New York; and Twenty Years Work among Them* (Brace [1872] 1967) dedicated themselves to revealing—rather than surpassing—the supposed depravity of working-class immigrant neighborhoods for armchair slummers. Grounded in an "imperative of making everything, including interior states, visible, legible, and governable" (Seltzer 1996, 95), this methodology depended on a sensational realism that demarcated—rather than elided—cultural differences, that made the various mysteries of the metropolis into particular—and identifiable—types.[17] To no one's surprise, Riis discovers when he slums in *How the Other Half Lives* that "the Italian is gay, lighthearted and, if his fur is not stroked the wrong way, inoffensive as a child" ([1890] 1996, 95). Infantilized, the Italian immigrant becomes a figure of affection rather than of terror for the middle classes, and one who can be summarized in a sentence or two. For the photojournalist, such uniform racializing is applicable to all foreign elements of the metropolis. It is a "familiar fact," Riis concedes, that not only do "'all Chinamen look alike,'" but they are also prone to "acting 'alike,' in a body"—and he has a photo to prove it (127).[18] In contrast to Addams's settlement descriptions and *Hull-House*'s settlement drawings where interclass likeness leads to dynamic forms of abstract sociability, Riis's photographic essays thrust foreign bodies into categories that highlight taxonomic difference: "Unlike the German, who begins learning English the day he lands as a matter of duty, or the Polish Jew, who takes it up as soon as he is able as an investment, the Italian learns slowly, if at all" (92). Delving into the incognito populations of New York, the reformer manufactures a stereotypical idiom—a typological mania—that the middle classes could easily comprehend. Constructing what Peter Stallybrass has elsewhere termed "a spectacle of heterogeneity" (1990, 70), Riis molds immigrants into overdetermined types that crystallize developing racial, ethnic, sexual, and class differences rather than surpass them.

A fellow reformer and philanthropic slummer, Addams will also acknowledge the presence of cultural, national, and religious differences such as Austrian Jewishness and Sicilian Catholicism, but as we saw in our discussion of her impersonal cosmopolitanism, her autobiography could care less about any epistemological Progressive agenda such as that exemplified in *How the Other Half Lives*. She instead argues that the distinctions between the middle classes and working-class immigrant populations must be overcome—not elaborated—in order to produce a cosmopolitan universality that obstructs recognition of all sorts. Disappearing into the bulk of the people, she cultivates abstract mingling rather than nationalistic, sexualized, or race-based particularities. Or as she writes of a scholarly address delivered by W. E. B. DuBois at Hull-House, "color seems to accentuate [racial differences] so absurdly" ([1910] 1990, 149).[19]

This is not to neglect the familiar fact that several Hull-House reformers participated in the sociological project of making ethnic immigrants and their sexual behaviors—if not their sexual identities—legible. Several of the settlement's female inhabitants, such as Jenny Dow and Agnes Sinclair Holbrook, considered themselves to be lay sociologists who would uncover and explain the poverty and depravity thought to characterize these populations.[20] Though they were unable to participate officially in the University of Chicago's gender-segregated discipline, Hull-House female reformers produced—with men—numerous surveys, maps, and lectures on the living conditions of the city's immigrants. The most famous product of these endeavors was the 1895 *Hull-House Maps and Papers: A Presentation of Nationalities and Wages in a Congested District of Chicago, Together with Comments and Essays on Problems Growing Out of the Social Conditions* (Residents of Hull-House 1895). As we can see, *Maps and Papers* reproduced a color-coded grid of the Near West Side detailing "nationalities" from "Polk Street to Twelfth, Halsted Street to Jefferson, Chicago" (fig. 8). The publication is somewhat ironic, given that Hull-House's most conspicuous reformer would write against the absurdity of racial-ethnic differences in her slumming narrative. Nevertheless, like *How the Other Half Lives* the treatise divides mysterious metropolitan sectors into disparate ethnic types—Russian, Polish, Dutch, Swiss, German, Italian, Chinese, Irish, and "Colored"—that presents readers with a condensed grid that mirrors a sensational urban exposé. And like Riis's muckraking photojournalism (published only half a decade earlier), we find chapters such as "The Ghetto in Chicago," "The Bohemian People in Chicago," and "Remarks upon the Italian Colony in Chicago." The end product of their research is a visible representation of spectacular differences within what was thought to be an anonymous foreign horde.

Addams contributed to *Hull-House Maps and Papers* with an essay entitled "The Settlement as a Factor in the Labor Movement." Yet while several of Addams's critics have envisioned the Hull-House settlement as a continuation of the Progressive infatuation with the immigrant masses, I hope it is clear by now that *Hull-House* the autobiography refuses to delineate or categorize bodies as it stages an anti-Progressive project of "being-becoming invisible" and performs the impersonal internationalism that Hull-House the institution fantastically represents (Esteve 2003, 107). In sharp contrast to Riis's shocked rhetoric regarding the ethnic working classes, Addams moves into a tenant house that once belonged to a member of Chicago's white aristocracy—John Hull—and makes it promiscuous by mixing classes in an ideal universality indifferent to difference. Further, Addams has little interest in exposing or defining particular personalities despite the intentions of *Maps and Papers*. She is instead more than eager to muddle identifications with cultural bodies that Riis, among others, was hell-bent to demarcate. Finally, Addams revises the Progressive slumming narrative's obsession with racial and sexual typing not to distinguish herself from the working classes or to set up a sustained contrast between middle-class morality and immigrant "depravity." Rather, typology here enables Addams to render herself indistinguishable from the ethnic crowds ("forget their differences"), to become like a mass body to such an extent that her personal biography vanishes, and to thereby renegotiate middle-class Progressive technologies of sexual identification, or what scholars now refer to as the hetero- and homosexual binary.[21]

As my discussion of *Hull-House*'s impersonal cosmopolitanism illuminates, this manipulation of Progressive recognition regimes and literatures of exposure guides her autobiography from start to finish, and I now want to expand earlier claims. Combing through the initial pages of her autobiography, one notices that Addams refuses to highlight any particular aspects of what some would consider a peculiar life. This strategy is evident from the opening lines of *Twenty Years at Hull-House*, where her preface announces that "the people with whom I have so long journeyed have become so intimate a part of my lot that they cannot be written of

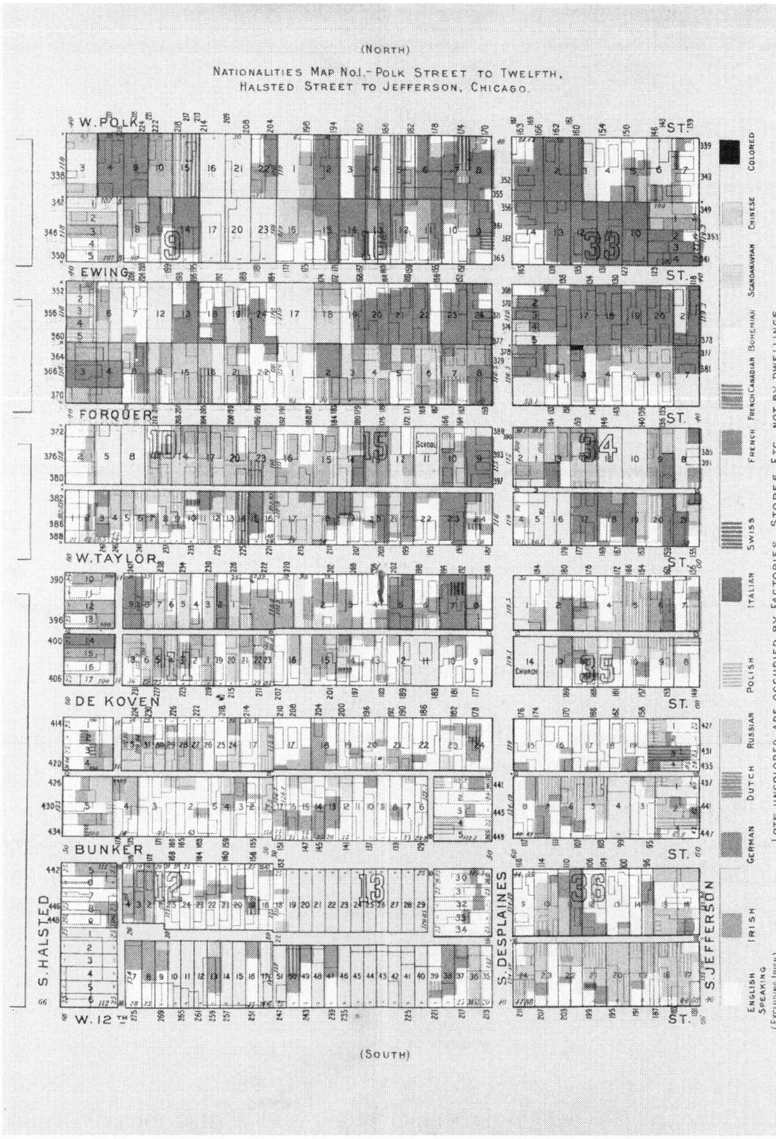

FIGURE 8. *Hull-House Maps and Papers*, Nationalities Map 1. Courtesy of Jane Addams Memorial Collection. The Special Collections Department. University Library. University of Illinois at Chicago.

either in praise or blame; the public movements and causes with which I am still identified have become so endeared, some of them through their very struggles and failures, that is it difficult to discuss them" ([1910] 1990, 1). Rather than articulating her intimate attachments to the women she loves and with whom she works, Addams informs her readers that she will tell them a story of her impersonal institution; the "people" she has "journeyed" with are simply too "intimate" to be written about. Her readers, she imagines, will be much more interested in learning how her abstract identifications, rather than her personal attachments, inform her autobiography. Thus Addams dissociates herself from any same-sex intimacies at the very moment that she announces these same-sex relations in her text.

When Addams goes on to describe her autobiography's origins in her preface, this movement away from the humanity wasted of mannish spinsterhood is made even more explicit. Her narrative was written, she confesses, in order to "start a 'backfire,' as it were, to extinguish two biographies of myself, one of which had been submitted to me in outline, that made life in a Settlement all too smooth and charming" ([1910] 1990, 2). Though she never specifies which two biographies she writes against, we can read this statement as yet another attempt on Addams's part to gain control over her public persona in the wake of pathological same-sex friendships. Like Riis, she too will recount the activities that took place over the three decades of Hull-House's operations. But it is important to note that she makes "no effort . . . to separate my own history from that of Hull-House during the years when I was 'launched deep into the stormy intercourse of human life' for, so far as a mind is pliant under the pressures of events and experiences, it becomes hard to detach it" (2). Unlike the standard autobiography or slumming literature, Addams's text will be anything but a typical retelling of her past and present ventures, since "Addams herself largely vanishes" after the text's first few chapters (Hurt 1990, xv). Her autobiographical self, as I suggested in this chapter's introduction, is both a vanishing act ("to disappear into the bulk of the people") and a failure of personal history: the reformer is spectacularly forgettable since she can hardly remember her past. Rather than discussing the sexual history of one person's life, the reader will turn the pages to find the impersonal activities of a cosmopolitan Hull-House, since Addams has conflated the abstract institution and the self who cofounded it.

Rejecting a depth model of individuated identity, Addams's personal history becomes the characterological achievement of a cosmopolitan institution, an autobiographical account of impersonal cosmopolitan slumming.

As James Hurt writes in his introduction to the 1990 edition of *Hull-House*, "There would have been no Hull-House without the personality and experiences of the person who created it, but equally, perhaps, there would have been no 'Jane Addams' if she had not created Hull-House in an extraordinary act of, among other things, self-making" (xi). This earnest identification with a working-class industrial population, however, not only makes "Jane Addams" (the public image). It also unmakes Jane Addams, the interiorized, sexually definable person. Forgetting the intimate associations that took place within this environment, she presents her audience with a detailed account of her public deeds—an abstracted life of sociology, social work, and impersonal internationalism.[22] As she states in her preface, "The public movements and causes with which I am still identified have become so endeared, some of them through their very struggles and failures, that it is difficult to discuss them" (1). When the reformer attempts to recollect any particular experiences that might serve as precedents for her contemporary actions, she "can scarcely recall the scaffolding" (2). Consequently, "it has unfortunately been necessary to abandon the chronological order in favor of the topical" (2). Structuring the majority of her autobiography, these topical essays are then reproduced from several middle-class magazines. "More than a third of the material in the book has appeared in *The American Magazine*," Addams informs her readers, "one chapter of it in *McClure's Magazine*, and earlier statements of the Settlement motive, published years ago, have been utilized in chronological order because it seemed impossible to reproduce their enthusiasm." Pitched outside individual interiority (and a temporal model of sexual development), Addams's amnesiac autobiography is nothing more than a pastiche of cosmopolitan magazine reproductions. Her life, which she cannot remember, is that of an abstracted press.

As we have seen before in her "Aged Seven" drawing, so too is her particularized spinster body an abstraction. In the November 16, 1909, edition of the *Indianapolis News*, for instance, Nellie Simmons Meier presents her readers with an image, in "Characteristics Read in the Palm of the Hand," that mirrors the abstracted self Addams affirms in *Hull-House*. The article includes an imprint of Addams's palm as well as a close reading of its lines:

> The hand of Jane Addams of the Hull-House Settlement shows a type of those rare cases where self-abnegation is combined with common practical sense, tact, and great executive ability. A mixed type of palm, in which the practical

> predominates but with such a strong love for the artistic, that the nature demands artistic surroundings in order to round out a perfect life.
>
> Fingers showing care in details, a strong love of both mental and material order, with executive ability and tact. A life line in which the strength of will and nerve force has had much to do in maintaining the vital spark, which has been threatened with extinction at times in the past. ([1909] 1985, reel 113.57.702)

Like Riis's exposé, Meier's reading transforms individuality into type, but it also traffics in mass press clichés that Addams cultivated throughout her public life. For the palmist, the slumming reformer's print reveals everything and nothing as Addams's individuality is marked by "self-abnegation," rather than unnatural identification. The distinguishing grooves illuminate a "mixed type," which could also characterize the make-up of *Hull-House*. And in the "details" of her fingers, the palmist discovers an abstracted sense of "nerve force" and vitality. A synecdoche for her moral character, Addam's handprint reveals a selfless person whose queered cosmopolitanism is inscribed into her flesh. Her abstract sainthood—an improbable state of universal and impersonal being—becomes concretized through palmistry (fig. 9).

Playing on this cultivated image of Saint Jane, Addams presents her audience with a Golden Legend in the first three chapters of her autobiography. Turning hagiographic typology ("MOTHER of races") into a typological slumming narrative, her childhood events precipitate her later activities in Chicago. These memories gravitate to the figure of her father, John Addams, a renowned miller of Cedarville, Illinois. Walking home from her father's mill one afternoon, Addams discovers her

> first sight of the poverty which implies squalor, and felt the curious distinction between the ruddy poverty of the country and that which even a small city presents in its shabbiest streets. I remember launching at my father the pertinent inquiry why people lived in such horrid little houses so close together, and that after receiving his explanation I declared with much firmness when I grew up I should, of course, have a large house, but it would not be built among the other large houses, but right in the midst of horrid little houses like these. ([1910] 1990, 4–5)

Even at the tender age of seven, Addams's slumming life has already been prescribed. This is not so much a case of foreshadowing as of rewriting a past so that it conforms to the narratives that she fed to the public press.

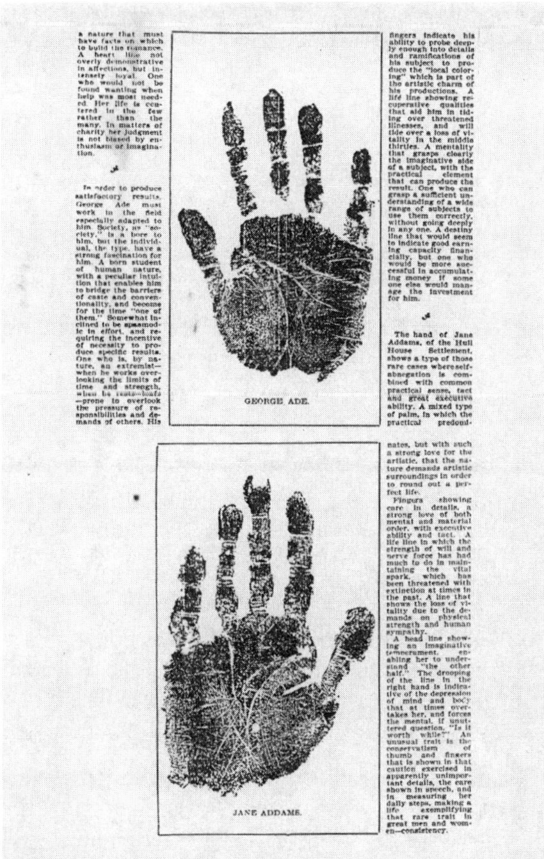

a nature that must have facts on which to build the romance. A heart line not overly demonstrative in affections, but intensely loyal. One who would not be found wanting when help was most needed. Her life is centered in the few rather than the many. In matters of charity her judgment is not biased by enthusiasm or imagination.

In order to produce satisfactory results, George Ade must work in the field especially adapted to him. Society, as "society," is a bore to him, but the individual, the type, have a strong fascination for him. A born student of human nature, with a peculiar intuition that enables him to bridge the barriers of caste and conventionality, and become for the time "one of them." Somewhat inclined to be spasmodic in effort, and requiring the incentive of necessity to produce specific results. One who is, by nature, an extremist—when he works overlooking the limits of time and strength, when he rests—loafs—prone to overlook the pressure of responsibilities and demands of others. His fingers indicate his ability to probe deeply enough into details and ramifications of his subject to produce the "local coloring" which is part of the artistic charm of his productions. A life line showing recuperative qualities that aid him in tiding over threatened illnesses, and will tide over a loss of vitality in the middle thirties. A mentality that grasps clearly the imaginative side of a subject, with the practical element that can produce the result. One who can grasp a sufficient understanding of a wide range of subjects to use them correctly, without going deeply in any one. A destiny line that would seem to indicate good earning capacity financially, but one who would be more successful in accumulating money if some one else would manage the investment for him.

The hand of Jane Addams, of the Hull House Settlement, shows a type of those rare cases where self-abnegation is combined with common practical sense, tact and great executive ability. A mixed type of palm, in which the practical predominates, but with such a strong love for the artistic, that the nature demands artistic surroundings in order to round out a perfect life.

Fingers showing care in details, a strong love of both mental and material order, with executive ability and tact. A life line in which the strength of will and nerve force has had much to do in maintaining the vital spark, which has been threatened with extinction at times in the past. A line that shows the loss of vitality due to the demands on physical strength and human sympathy.

A head line showing an imaginative temperament, enabling her to understand "the other half." The drooping of the line in the right hand is indicative of the depression of mind and body that at times overtakes her, and forces the mental, if unuttered question, "Is it worth while?" An unusual trait is the conservatism of thumb and fingers that is shown in that caution exercised in apparently unimportant details, the care shown in speech, and in measuring her daily steps, making a life exemplifying that rare trait in great men and women—consistency.

FIGURE 9. Imprint of the hand of Jane Addams, accompanying the article "Characteristics Read in the Palm of the Hand" (Meier [1909] 1985). Courtesy of the Swarthmore College Peace Collection.

Within the "horrid" nether regions of her childhood, she is always already a philanthropic slummer undertaking good deeds for the indigent, even though she previously stated that she was totally unable to "recall the scaffolding" of this enterprise.

In keeping with her universalistic principles, Addams takes this typological conflation of her self to such an extreme that she argues against any differentiation between herself and "the bulk of the people." As the child of a prominent politician and businessman, Addams claims that she was subjected to indecent public exposures. When she walked the streets of rural Illinois, the town folk would spectacularize John's daughter at her father's prodding. Addams, however, eschews this spectacular recognition in a curious scene that she reconstructs at length:

> One day I met my father coming out of his bank on the main street of the neighboring city which seemed to me a veritable whirlpool of society and commerce. With a playful touch of exaggeration, he lifted his high and shining silk hat and made me an imposing bow. This distinguished public recognition, this totally unnecessary identification among a mass of "strange people" who couldn't possibly know unless he himself made the sign, suddenly filled me with a sense of the absurdity of the entire feeling. It may not even then have seemed as absurd as it really was, but at least it seemed enough so to collapse or to pass into the limbo of forgotten specters. ([1910] 1990, 7)

Within a public space, Addams's father presents his daughter as a little bourgeois darling. The emphasis Addams gives to the "high and shining silk hat" marks both her and her parent as members of a middle class sharply opposed to the "mass of 'strange people'" that surround them. Identifying her as a lady through his "imposing bow," John Addams shines on his child a spotlight that the reformer-in-the-making abhors. For Addams Junior such public identification is "totally unnecessary." The strangers around them have little idea of who either she or her father is, save for the sartorial codes that signify bourgeois identity. As with her reply to the member of the Chicago Women's Club, Addams rejects the hyperexposure of her personal life (and her association with the middle class) that her father's cringe-worthy recognition grants her. And much as she presents settlement house life as a flattening of ethnic and sexual differences, she longs to become one with this "strange" crowd, an undistinguished type amid the masses.

Through fantastic identification with these rural bodies in Cedarville, Addams justifies why she would later desire a terra incognita where she achieves fantastic identification with urban ones in Chicago's Near West Side. Typologically speaking, the will to disappear into "the bulk of the people," though once forgotten in the "limbo" of her mind, was already in place as a young girl as she melds into a "mass" of undifferentiated social strangeness. Hence a rural Main Street presages the impersonal cosmopolitan slumming that she would later embrace in the boulevards of Chicago, much as the abstracted "Jane Addams, Aged Seven" prefigures the abstracted "Jane Addams" of Hull-House in figure 5. Disturbed by the public recognition that her father grants her, Addams modifies her childhood provincialism and opts instead for identification with the supposedly anonymous masses, rather than with the stalwart of white middle-class familial heterosexuality—her father. To do so, the reformer presents herself as a body like everybody else, one whose lack of distinction enables her to lose any particular traits and to transcend "less essential" differences. Much as she does in her descriptions of Hull-House activities, Addams again pushes her self beyond hetero- or homosexual identifications, and such an unspectacular fantasy of universalized "classlessness [becomes] a strategy for transcending being classed" (Thornton 1997, 209).[23]

I want to take these identifications a step further. Addams not only longs for merger with "the bulk of the people." She also attempts to imitate these elements that surround her in her rural environment. Though she was always mesmerized by her father, she was also interested in his occupation and longed, as a child, to mimic his milling hands: "In addition to these fascinations was the association of the mill with my father's activities, for doubtless at that time I centered upon him all that careful imitation which a little girl ordinarily gives to her mother's ways and habits. My mother had died when I was a baby and my father's second marriage did not occur until my eighth year. I had a consuming desire to possess a miller's thumb" ([1910] 1990, 7). This desire to become like her father does not necessarily imply that the reformer wants to adopt his bourgeois ideals. She is rather more interested in embracing a social position that will connect her to the masses: "I also took measures to secure on the backs of my hands the tiny purple and red spots which are always found on the hands of the miller who dresses millstones" (8).

We might recall that John Addams's status as an affluent miller was something of an anomaly during the last quarter of the nineteenth century, his wealth primarily the result of a monopoly on small town grain processing. In fact, the occupation of miller was assumed to be a working-class one. Thus when Addams writes in retrospect that she longs to possess a miller's thumb, she also argues that she longs to identify through philanthropic slumming, to be seen as, to embody, and to disappear into the subject position of "the bulk of the people." Distancing herself from the domestic imperatives of what historian Barbara Welter, in 1966, famously titled the "Cult of True [heterosexual] Womanhood" (151), the reformer presents herself as a young child who longs for what appears to be a nondescript identity, one that she will later advance on Halsted Street: "This sincere tribute of imitation, which affection offers to its adored object, had later, I hope, subtler manifestations, but certainly these first ones were altogether genuine" ([1910] 1990, 8).

Through this self-described "careful imitation"—through her capacity to become similar rather than individuated—the philanthropic slummer again short-circuits any attempts to particularize a modern middle-class sexual identity (7). Addams distances herself from familial relations at the very moment that she announces herself as one with her father. This disidentification then enables her to align herself with a rural population, one akin to the "anonymous" masses whom she will later nurture through her domesticated cosmopolitanism. Addams, that is, universalizes the regional family into an international domestic sphere that confirms queer cosmopolitanism, rather than reading the homestead as the locus of individual sexual identity, perverse or otherwise.

In her own time, her followers noted the reformer's astounding capacity for identification. A 1909 editorial in the *Record Herald* ([1909] 1985), proclaiming "Genius of Hull-House is 'First Citizen of Chicago,'" acknowledges that her "sense of identification with others... is the open secret not only of her influence with others but her capacity to interpret them to herself and to each other. She not only has this sense of being identified with others, but she also gives others the sense of being identified with her" (reel 113.57.735). Like her identification with the miller, we see how Addams's commitment to philanthropic slumming again fantastically levels social distinctions between the middle class and immigrants as each becomes more like the abstracted other. An "open secret" that well defies the production of other open secrets, Addams's multiple identifications—with Hull-House, the fantastic institution, with her father's working-class occupation, with rural Cedarville, with Chicago's immigrant populations—help fabricate her public image as a devoted follower of impersonal and international ideals; yet they also make her interior self a rather slippery subject. "The issue of Addams's sexuality vis-à-vis its impact on her reform and political work," writes historian Harriet Hyman Alonso in an overview of Addams's biographies, "still remains a mystery" (2004, 151). Though not, I stress, a *Mystery of Chicago*.

As a well-publicized international icon and an ordinary woman, the reformer pushes herself beyond any scrutiny that might lead to specification as a mystery of the sexualized city, or as a participant in an emergent white U.S. lesbian subculture. "And so," she states in a paradigmatic *Hull-House* claim, "a Settlement is led along from the concrete to the abstract, as may easily be illustrated" ([1910] 1990, 176). An extraordinarily ordinary figure that eschewed sexual revelation yet fed off inchoate technologies of sexual recognition, the reformer turns into a two-dimensional type rather than a concrete fleshed-out subject, an individual who has no sexual identity to define herself. Like the Statue of Liberty to which she was so often compared, she is a concretely abstract spectacle, a hollow woman pitched beyond sensation (in all the word's myriad meanings) and into the land of the sexually inexplicable.

The Limbo of Forgotten Spectators

Above all, her story reminds us to look beyond our sources, to read both silences and speech, and, at times, to accept the historical integrity of elusive personal identities. —Estelle B. Freedman, "'The Burning of Letters Continues'"

How do we link Addams's queer slumming to current demands on modern U.S. sexual history? I have presented several strategies for showing how Addams spoils a burgeoning sexual binary through literary and visual discourses that make Progressive Era homosexuality most legible, yet I stress again—as I have been throughout this chapter—that one will never know the truth of her sexual identity, nor am I comfortable positing one for her. Though I have examined a few instances of same-sex intimacy with her Hull-House cohorts, I have also explored several means by which she moves the settlement house beyond a hermeneutics of sexual suspicion (and a hermeneutics of the sexual self), and we might do well, as Freedman advises us, to respect the integrity of this strategic unintelligibility.

This is certainly not to foreclose further explorations of Hull-House's conflicting cultural and political aims, even as we admit to the settlement's sexual unknowing. On the one hand, given that *Hull-House* and Addams both operated as cosmopolitan mass bodies assimilating immigrants, they could be seen as disciplinary institutions par excellence. On the other hand, as Shannon Jackson points out, Hull-House's unprecedented forms of interclass contact could also be seen as a reparative example of a Progressive "'queer world,' one that is, in Lauren Berlant and Michael Warner's terms, 'a space of entrances, exits, unsystematized lines of acquaintance, projected horizons, typifying examples, alternative routes, blockages, incommensurate geographies'" (2000, 165). Though these readings may appear contradictory, neither are canceling, and we should relinquish any certainty as to whether one is sounder than the other. Either way we perceive the institution, Hull-House as it was conceived and as it developed never once offered a public world facilitating self- or other recognition for middle-class lesbian slummers, and this may be why Addams championed its ideals in the first place.

As I have been arguing throughout this chapter, *Hull-House*'s cosmopolitanism tried to imagine something—anything—other than particularized urban homosexual subcultural bodies. To repeat Murphy, the "men and women [of the settlement movement] established sexual identities and practices that conformed neither to the middle-class norms of their day, nor to current binary notions of heterosexuality and homosexuality" (2000, 290). His claim is carefully and usefully ambiguous, since it goes beyond present historical debates concerning romantic friendship's demise and modern lesbianism's spectacular emergence in the United States to suggest that there may be something about settlement movement relations on Halsted that cannot be historically recuperated. Yet I would take his argument one step further to propose that this particular settlement house and this particular act of philanthropic slumming enabled some privileged middle-class citizens such as Addams not simply to establish novel sexual practices in a calculated act of "*nonce* taxonomy" (Sedgwick 1990, 23). Hull-House residents instead avoided bourgeoning technologies of the middle-class U.S. sexual binary by cracking open the taxonomic codes embedded within conventional narratives of Progressive Era slumming—even while they may have imposed norms of sexual morality on the working-class immigrants they embraced.[24]

We will see more of such taxonomic undermining when I turn to the DL in my epilogue. For now, let's recall Foucault's sweeping claim: modern sexual identities in the West (and especially, I add, in the United States) are inextricably tied to the production and extension of class interests and class desires, so much so that the philosopher (and subsequent social historians such as Chauncey) posit that members of the working class did not adhere to a sexual binary until the bourgeoisie imposed one on them in the first third of the twentieth century:

> If it is true that sexuality is the set of effects produced in bodies, behaviors, and social relations by a certain deployment deriving from a complex political technology, one has to admit that this deployment does not operate in symmetrical fashion with respect to the social classes, and consequently, that it does not produce the same effects in them.... We must say that there is a bourgeois sexuality, and that there are class sexualities. Or rather, that sexuality is originally,

> historically bourgeois, and that, in its successive shifts and transpositions, it induces specific class effects. (1990a, 127)

Though the middle classes made discourses of sexuality a discernible mode of categorization and, hence, control, it may be safe to say that Addams constructs something else at the moment that she so desperately wants to inaugurate *Hull-House*. If this is the case, then her project might further Foucault's somewhat vague, but still relevant, hypothesis. Like Riis, Addams and her fellow female reformers dedicated their lives to aiding the masses though novel forms of social interaction. But while Foucault argues that sexuality, as a group identity formation and spectacular deployment of modernity categorization, dripped into the working classes after the bourgeoisie tested the techniques of sexuality on themselves, Addams blocks this development when she interacts with the ethnic communities that surround her. To reframe this point: Addams paradoxically uses the sensational literary and sociological tools of Progressive slumming to render herself sexually incognito, a well-publicized but forgotten specter who disappears into the bulk of the people.

By becoming this selfless personage—an abstracted institution at one with the urban poor—Addams avoids being cast as a nominal Foucauldian personage: a pervert, a wasted maid, and a mannish lesbian. Becoming somebody catering to all, she becomes both nobody and everybody, a saint who transforms into a settlement house and a personage without a past, a case history, or a remarkable childhood. In brief, she presents herself as spectacularly lackluster since such mass-mediated self-aggrandizement also functions as sexual self-effacement. Hence if conventional slumming—"traveling to 'foreign,' exotic, supposedly inferior cultures"—can also be entitled "appropriating the margins for pleasure" (Mumford 1997, 135, 133), then Addams's slumming narrative shows how the generic conventions of this Progressive Era literature blunted the prescriptive operations of middle-class sexual identity by infusing the formulaic genre with unprecedented "social pleasure" ([1910] 1990, 206). While such slumming efforts have rightly been read as confirmations of bourgeois sexuality, this reformer's slumming venture instead produces the inverse. She cultivates one type of life—the unprecedented cross-class, cross-racial, cross-national contacts in *Hull-House*—to distance herself from others more sexually legible.[25]

If one of the genre's narrative engines is a dispersal of a middle-class identity into a "foreign" lower- or working-class ethnic region and a return to the safe havens of white bourgeois culture (as exemplified in Riis and the *Mysteries* of any major U.S. metropolis), Addams's life-text reformats such promiscuous wanderings. As reformer, sociologist, matron, and impersonal celebrity, she disperses herself when she seems most grounded. In keeping with her self-characterization of *Hull-House*, the reformer becomes a flexible institution whose unprecedented boundaries are in flux though stabilized—even as she moves into a universal land of her own imagining. Her capacity to be internationally everywhere while also being located nowhere, her tendency to reveal nothing about her past while presenting herself as the exemplar of cosmopolitan values, and her strategic manipulation of mimicry transfigure her into an unknowable type that avoids the modern typology of sexuality for this middle-class citizen.

Through such self-styled cosmopolitan slumming she becomes an international citizen who cannot easily be traced or tracked, which is also to say that she ruptures now-standard shifts from romantic friendship to lesbianism by dislocating herself from inchoate regimes of U.S. sexual identity. Localized, she becomes the land of the universal. Domesticated, she leaves her home for the printed page. An enigmatic gatekeeper of middle-class conduct, she short-circuits middle-class technologies of categorization while also supplementing them with Hull-House's cultural work. Not so much appropriating the margins of the slums as fully inhabiting them, Addams's life project can be described but her privileged life narrative cannot. The author of *Twenty Years at Hull-House* hence becomes unreadable, a reversal of the Progressive epistemological agenda that she may, at times, have enforced.

Curiously, her lack of a case history continues to vex historians of U.S. sexuality. The mysteries of her private and her public life, she acknowledges on the first page of her autobiography, are "difficult to discuss" ([1910] 1990, 1). Sabotaging any attempt at historical comprehension both then and now, her recorded activities are paradoxically hidden from the Progressive record. Rather than a subject with a discernible and definable subjectivity—a person—whose interior mysteries can be pursued by sexologists or later reclaimed by revisionist queers, she becomes a generic mass body—Saint Jane, the "MOTHER of races"—hidden from historical inquiry. And the moment that she may be individually perceived by the Progressive press or by contemporary scholars, she metamorphoses into an embodied mass institution catering to the indigent. In so doing, Addams renders her public and private letters—the mounds of personal correspondence, the minutiae of Hull-House's daily bureaucratic grind, the sensational newspaper clippings, the diary notes, and the unpublished love poems preserved on microfilm and microfiche across the U.S. nation—difficult to decipher sexually. Looking for words that might hint at her sexual identity, you instead find a philanthropic slummer whose paper trail becomes everybody's autobiography.

Addams's "characterological achievement," in sum, refuses individuation by transforming into typological script, and several of her contemporaries were quick to notice this. An anonymous, undated article in the *Evening Transcript* titled "In Desert of Individualism" ([n.d.] 1985) states that "normally a settlement is a social oasis in the desert of individualism, a neutral zone where combatants who outside its doors are foes, a survival under a new urban form of the ideal that used to be summed up in the word 'neighborliness.' The settlement often is the institutional nexus between the 'ancient good' and the 'modern true'" (reel 113.58.656). Or, I might add, the ancient Isle of Lesbos and the modern "slums."

I can read this commentator's remark in Foucauldian terms to say that Hull-House's philanthropic gesture staves off discipline and the punishments of a definable sexual group identity by creating a neutral zone of internationalism that wants to see sameness as more pleasurable than sexual difference. Or I can turn to Addams's one-time good neighbor, University of Chicago philosopher, psychologist, and educator John Dewey, who also spent a great deal of time thinking through issues of universality and abstraction: "The local is the ultimate universal, and as near an absolute as exists. . . . Uniformity and standardization may provide an underlying basis for differentiation and liberation of individual potentialities" ([1927] 1954, 215). By becoming like the "mass" and by identifying with the working-class immigrants that other Progressives sought to make legible, Addams's autobiographical self does not contribute to the taxonomic rhetoric of depravity found in Riis and other turn-of-the-century slumming literatures of exposure. On numerous levels, her typological life narrative and her cosmopolitan slumming venture were instead an elusive sexual "liberation" through idealized universality. Her neighborly efforts affirmed freedom from middle-class sexual prescriptions not through their obsession with or exoticization of difference but through forced similarity beyond the mysteries of otherness, through the willful creation of unfamiliar spaces that fostered a public "ours" neglecting the reformer's "mine" and "thine" (and, I should note, sometimes ignoring the material inequalities of the city's socioeconomic conditions).

With this in mind, we must now read her earlier—and her later—receptions in a different light and return to the epigraph with which this chapter began. Oddly impersonal, Addams does not ask us to consider her voluminous archives but only the international interzones into which she served, disappeared, and forged. Directing us to look beyond psychosexual biography through her antiautobiography, Addams shows readers something other than the benefits and securities to be found in an intraclass sexual subculture and points beyond a closeted middle-class sexual identity that may have set the stage for future self-identified queers. Then as now, she presents curious readers with a contact zone surpassing sexual specification rather than a sexological case history, one entrenched in *Hull-House*'s utopian abstraction. Setting up an international house that remains terra incognita to this day, the "MOTHER of races" thus dislocates sexual identity through the cultural technologies that should—and unfortunately did—render other historical bodies less elusive. Such unintelligibility earned through foreign communications and unprecedented social interactions becomes a core creed of later queer slumming within and without the United States, as subsequent chapters demonstrate. But first, I focus my attentions on one of Addams's muckraking contemporaries and a most unlikely early twentieth-century slummer—Willa Cather—to further examine the questions of dislocation and disidentification to be found within other perverse early twentieth-century threats: the adolescent tramp and the bohemian author who scribbled him away.

CHAPTER TWO

Willa Cather's Experiment in Luxury

Put on your slumming clothes and get your car
Let's go sightseeing where the high-toned people are
Come on, there's lots of fun in store for you
See how the other half lives on Park Avenue
. . . .
Let us hide behind a pair of fancy glasses
And make faces when a member of the classes passes
. . . .
Let us go to it, they do it
Why can't we do it too?
Let's go slumming, nose thumbing, on Park Avenue
—Irving Berlin, "Slumming on Park Avenue" (1937)

Cather's Case History

As the previous chapter claimed, early twentieth-century anxieties over perversion and national decline gravitated to sensational accounts of Anglo-American bachelor maids like Jane Addams. Precisely because of their publicized disloyalty to heteronormative domestic forms, some philanthropic slummers and their settlement houses were cast as aberrant threats to the bourgeois family. The white middle-class home, however, was not immune to internal threats of moral or sexual corruption. At this point in my discussion of queer slumming and its mystery literatures we might do well to recall Foucault's generalized claim that "the deployment of sexuality which first developed on the fringes of familial institutions...gradually became focused on the family" (1990a, 110). While I do not wish to imply that Progressive Era spinster bashing transferred onto other errant U.S. bodies, it is striking to note that another sexually suspect figure—the vice-ridden male adolescent—emerged from inside the middle-class family during the first decades of the twentieth century. Like the spinster's public misdeeds, the adolescent's sexual indiscretions signaled, for some, the decline of Anglo-Saxon civilization. Novel typologies of adolescence circulated alongside typologies of homosexual vice in what Foucault sees as a primary deployment of modern bourgeois sexuality, namely, "*the specification of individuals*" (1990a, 42–43). Alongside the New Woman, there emerged a new type of boy—the delinquent adolescent.

The paramount instance of this connection between Anglo adolescence and perversion occurs in child psychologist G. Stanley Hall's *Adolescence* (1904), an encyclopedic overview of "boyology" that invents its subject matter ex nihilo.[1] Hall argues throughout his opus that "adolescence is a new birth, for the higher and more completely human traits are now born" (1:xiii). But despite the adolescent's entry into sexual modernity, various disorders—neuroses, psychoses, and abnormal morphologies—mar the individual's journey to adulthood proper. "The momentum of heredity often seems insufficient to enable the child to achieve this great revolution and come to complete maturity, so that every step of the upward way is strewn with wreckage of body, mind, and morals" (1:xiv). As a result, one cannot neglect arrested sexual developments, shrug shoulders, and invoke the folk wisdom that boys will be boys, for natural bodily changes engender unnatural tendencies. "There is not only arrest," Hall warns his readers, "but perversion, at every stage, and hoodlumism, juvenile crime, and secret vice seem not only increasing, but develop earlier in years in every civilized land" (1:xiv). In a lightning-quick logical twist, particular acts—what Hall calls hoodlumism—flower into peculiar social identities. Slipping from a perverse activity to a perverse body, juvenile delinquency is but a step removed from juvenile delinquents.

Of course the adolescent was not the only novel type of secret vice to find itself inclined to perversion, depravity, and abnormality. As we saw in the introduction and in our focus on the sensationalized lesbian, these traits also typify the late nineteenth-century middle-class homosexual male.[2] Just as *Adolescence* makes the pubescent body intelligible, so too it was the sexologist's goal to make this mysterious homosexual body discernible, to make it speak the miseries of its inverted soul. No matter how well he may hide or deny them, the homosexual's desires nevertheless voice themselves through this indiscreet body. If you are looking for an imbalanced, crime-ridden pervert, you know him when you see him. And given widespread rumors about the prevalence of homosexuality in adolescence, this pervert is oftentimes an arrested—and arresting—young lad who slums into hoodlumism.[3]

Take Willa Cather's 1905 short story "Paul's Case: A Study in Temperament," one of the first literary attempts to question turn-of-the-century discourses on perverse sexuality, middle-class white male adolescence, and vice tendencies. "Always smiling, always glancing about him," Paul lives his days in paranoia, "seeming to feel that people might be watching him and trying to detect something" ([1905] 1991, 222). His fears are not without warrant. In the story's opening, Pittsburgh High School's faculty and his father pounce on the adolescent like "a miserable street cat set at bay by a ring of tormentors." In their attempts to make sense of—to survey—Paul's particularity, the elders force the adolescent to account for his hoodlumism, "his various misdemeanors" (221). Yet throughout this grand after-school "inquisition," we hear only one direct quote from the boy: "'I don't know,' he replied. 'I didn't mean to be polite or impolite, either. I guess it's a sort of way I have of saying things regardless'" (222). Judging from his claim that he didn't intend to "be polite or impolite," it appears as if Paul is guilty of nothing more than bad manners.[4] When asked to answer for his crimes, he confesses nothing. Uncertain of what exactly he has done ("I don't know"), he can only reiterate the mystery that shrouds him and the misdeeds he may—or may not—have committed. Since he refuses to give any details about his sexual identity or communal affiliations, he relies instead on obscurities: "a sort of way"; "saying things." No specifics are given save for the insinuation that "Paul was quite accustomed to lying" (221), but his locution's indeterminacy only adds to the nagging sensation that his is a very "bad case" (229).

Yet if his teachers find it difficult "to put into words the real cause of the trouble," and if his father only admits "perplexity" when asked to explain his son's temperament ([1905] 1991, 221), the narrator has no problem outing the boy:

> Paul entered the faculty room suave and smiling. His clothes were a trifle outgrown and the tan velvet on the collar of his open overcoat was frayed and worn; but for all that there was something of the dandy about him, and he wore an opal pin in his neatly knotted black four-in-hand, and a red carnation in his

> buttonhole. This latter adornment the faculty somehow felt was not properly significant of the contrite spirit befitting a boy under the ban of suspension.
>
> Paul was tall for his age and very thin, with high, cramped shoulders and a narrow chest. His eyes were remarkable for a certain hysterical brilliancy and he continually used them in a conscious, theatrical sort of way, peculiarly offensive in a boy. The pupils were abnormally large, as though he were addicted to belladonna, but there was a glassy glitter about them which that drug does not produce. (221)

Nothing fits in this scene as all things natural are immediately inverted. Paul's winsome smile is inappropriate for the occasion. His showy attire clashes with the repentant pose his teachers expect him to adopt. And his theatrical eyes, the narrator imagines, are better suited for the stage—and the female sex—than the male body. Quick shifts between minute details and panoramic overview enhance these sharp contrasts, almost as if the narrator ventriloquizes a doctor's attempt "to detect something." On the one hand, the boy is draped in a tattered, tight-fitting overcoat, suggesting that he is little more than a dandified tramp bohemian. On the other, the narrator hones in on his dainty pin and decorated buttonhole. Likewise, in the subsequent paragraph the narrator sizes up Paul's frame and then concentrates on his dilating pupils. This odd minutia—the jittery eyes, the tan velvet, the red carnation—hold the faculty's gaze despite their revulsion, making the boy's mysterious vice both enigmatic and clear. In a descriptive panopticon, Cather's narrator turns the spectacularization of the homosexual Anglo-American adolescent into a sensational confession of his hysterical desires.[5]

These links between homosexual perversion, the dandified body, and adolescence become even more explicit once his elders dismiss Paul: "When he was told that he could go, he bowed gracefully and went out. His bow was but a repetition of the scandalous red carnation" ([1905] 1991, 222). In his teachers' minds, bodies and dress conspire to condemn Paul's very being as clothes and gestures unmake the man. And if readers need even more reason "to detect something" askew in this adolescent's development, they could emphasize the carnation's particular color. Crouched into the lapel, the "flippantly" red flower would remind readers of another "scandalous" carnation—the green one worn by the infamous slummer Oscar Wilde (222). The narrator's reference to "something of the dandy about him" reinforces this allusion, since Wilde himself was notorious for decadent sexual tastes revealed during his three 1895 trials for slander and, later, for acts of gross indecency with working-class boys at the Savoy Hotel and St. James Place in London.

As critics such as Claude J. Summers (1990) have noted, a muckraking Cather followed the Wilde trials with great interest and even greater aversion, enough so that she wrote an excoriating account of the aesthete's downfall in the *Lincoln Courier*. Such public disdain for Wilde's slumming finds its mirror in Paul's high school. "The reaction of the teachers to Paul," Summers contends, "parallels Cather's own excessive reaction to Wilde's mocking manner in the 1890s and may reflect the author's mature reconsideration of her own earlier lack of imagination in not dealing charitably with Wilde in his disgrace" (1990, 111). Together, the red carnation, the velvet garb, and the histrionic eyes thus diagnose idleness, degeneracy, and perversion, traits "peculiarly offensive" in a dandified bohemian tramp. Indicted by his teachers for "disorder," "impertinence," flippancy, and "contempt" ([1905] 1991, 221), an iconic Paul replays Wilde's slumming trials in his high school, and the faculty punish the boy for what Cather would elsewhere term, in a review of Robert Hitchen's 1894 novel *The Green Carnation*, "drivelling [*sic*] effeminacy" (1894, 135).

While Paul's tramping body speaks volumes in two brief paragraphs, however, such elaborate exposition seems strange coming from a writer whose early investments in Progressive Era realism and later commitments to a modernist aesthetic gravitated to "the inexplicable presence of the thing not named, of the overtone divined by the ear but not heard by it," as Cather explained in her 1922 essay "The Novel Démeublé" (1992c, 837). Recent critics have dissected this muted project to show how Cather infuses perverse desire into her texts. For each, the keyword for uncovering these cryptic desires is "cross-identification." Noting that Cather taught at Pittsburgh High during the 1890s, Eve Kosofsky Sedgwick reads "Paul's Case" as an ambivalent gesture on Cather's part to affiliate her mannish lesbian self with a sissy boy (1993b, 172). In a complementary psychoanalytic reading, Judith Butler sees Paul as a "site of that transference as well as the impossibility of its resolution into any of the gendered or sexual elements that it transfers 'beyond' gender and sexuality—that is, as a fictional transcendence of 'women' or 'lesbian' in order to animate a vicarious figure of the 'male homosexual'" (1993a, 163). Likewise, Jonathan Goldberg synthesizes Sedgwick and Butler to explore the multiple racial and gendered cross-identifications that permit Cather—and the critic—to voice queer desires across her oeuvre and across the decades. Goldberg's radiant introduction acknowledges: "It must precisely be the difference *in identity* that allows me (for example) to find myself solicited by Cather's texts, uncannily found by them, uncannily finding myself elsewhere thanks to them" (2001, xi). And in the most recent incarnation of this critical tradition, Christopher Nealon contends that, for Cather and her characters, "sexuality is figured as an affiliation" (2001, 79). Together, these readings affirm that Cather's closeted sexuality advances affective bonds between dissimilar individuals. Her marginalized desire culminates in a redemptive desire for community forged through artistic imagination, or what Nealon terms "the race of dreamers" (2001, 79).

These are useful readings for recuperating stigmatized desire in Cather's texts. They also equate Cather with her fictional subjects. To put the matter another way: these analyses work with the premise that if Cather could not voice her desires in public, then she will strategically express them through fictive others. According to Joseph R. Urgo, "Some critics have spent countless pages naming the unnamed thing, seemingly oblivious to the logic that would disqualify any nameable thing as being the *unnamed*" (2002, 328). If Cather cannot speak, several critics offer in their epistemologies of her closet, then her characters will. Yet through this project of claiming Cather for postmodern audiences, we perhaps repeat the Q&A that Pittsburgh High undertakes against one of its own, a pedagogical diagnosis mirroring, in turn, a sexological one. "As if [we] suspected sex of harboring a fundamental secret" (Foucault 1990a, 69), we attempt to make Cather's desires (and, with them, her sexual mysteries) intelligible by cracking the semiotic code that she herself introduces in the opening paragraphs of her favorite short story.

But if illicit sexuality is not always the focus of Cather's early fictions and later novels, then what is? While concentrating on Cather's inscriptions of sexuality, queer critics invoke—and gesture towards—the thematics that structure "Paul's Case" and many of her novels from the 1920s and 1930s: transience, mobility, and sustained *dis*affiliation. Butler notes that the story epitomizes "a certain sign of transient homosexuality" (1993a, 165); and Nealon, in an impressive attempt to revisit Catherian adolescence, also points out that "Cather wrote about vast, empty places and about young people fleeing their families" as a protest against the constraints of heteronormative environments (2001, 66). This conflict between freedom and restrictive heteronormativity structures many of Cather's best-known short stories such as "The Sculptor's Funeral" ([1905] 1928a) and "Coming, Aphrodite!" ([1920] 1928b; both included in *Youth and the Bright Medusa* [1920]) as well as novels such as *My Ántonia* (1918), *One of Ours* (1922), *The Professor's House* ([1925] 1990), and *Lucy Gayheart* ([1935]

1985). All of these works focus on the pleasure and pain of communal detachment, and each concentrates on an attempt to come to terms with disaffiliation from the familial homestead. Yet we might pause to see how wayward adolescence figures in these characters' desires and losses. For instance, in a Catherian scene that I take to be paradigmatic, Professor Godfrey St. Peter turns his back on his heteronormative house—as well as his place in U.S sexual history—in an attempt to retrieve a sexually unknowable adolescent state in *The Professor's House*. "After his adoption into the Thierault household," the narrator states, "he remembered that other boy very rarely, in moments of home-sickness. After he met Lillian Ornsley, St. Peter forgot that boy had ever lived. But now that the vivid consciousness of an earlier state had come back to him, the Professor felt that life with this Kansas boy, little as there had been of it, was the realist of his lives, and that all the years between had been accidental and ordered from the outside" (263–64). To recapture this relation to his lost boy, Godfrey goes tramping in his imagination and finds himself "lost in profound, continuous meditation" (266).

If we are to examine Cather's relationship to sexuality and mobility, then we too could mediate on this fantastic "earlier state" and concentrate more on the tramping boy, a figure who yokes these two terms together.[6] As a novel type, a model of vagrancy and vice—and, as I show, a mobile body—the pubescent male figures as a paragon of Cather's incognito writings. Throughout much of her youth, the writer adopted a hypermasculine male persona, William Cather, Jr., and her psychological investment in male adolescence has been well documented by critics and biographers. Such a facade, Sharon O'Brien argues, was both a calculated riposte to the conventions of Red Cloud, Nebraska, as well as a definitive break from the Victorian Anglo ideals that her mother embodied. "Willa Cather's reaction to such confining definitions of femininity can only be imagined from her rejection of them," O'Brien notes. "She left no written record of her response to adolescence: her William Cather masquerade is the only diary entry we have" (1987, 99). While this masquerade enabled a young Cather to distance herself from normative gender constraints, I present this persona as something more than a stabilizing cross-identification with the male sex—a commonplace sexual inversion. Truth be told, I am more interested in how Cather paradoxically uses the figure of the tramping adolescent as an artistic paradigm for social and sexual declassification. Always on the move from something and something of an outlaw, he provides readers (and Cather) with a prime instance of how transience enables perversely labeled individuals to articulate what Leo Bersani has elsewhere termed "an anticommunal mode of connectedness" (1995, 10).

If, as Bersani contends, "the category of homosexuality—even as it has been homophobically cultivated—includes within it an indeterminacy and a mobility inimical to the disciplinary designs facilitated by the assignment of stable identities" (1995, 5), then the adolescent state appears to be a supreme mode of disconnection for Cather's characters, individuals who find themselves uninterested in normative or even nonnormative sexualities. Taking "Paul's Case" as my test case, I argue that the narrative fuses indeterminacy into the perverse figure of the male adolescent through his commitment to mobility. The delinquent adolescent achieves this through a unique form of queer slumming—bohemian tramping—that facilitates a strategic mobility enabling a perverted body to flourish within a community of like individuals but not as a part of them. In fact, the story invokes a white middle-class boy's journey into an exotic community—the aristocratic enclaves of the Waldorf-Astoria Hotel on Park Avenue—to refuse sexual identifications of any kind.[7]

In so doing, "Paul's Case" goes bohemian tramping to argue against the localization and categorization of the wayward male boy in particular and queer bodies in general. In place of a legible sexuality or sexual community, Cather champions an experiment in luxury whereby degenerate individuals fail to announce themselves and instead, like Paul and St. Peter, lose their place within a growing history of U.S. sexual identity.[8] Rather than finding themselves in any material text, they disappear altogether to write themselves out of the cultural record. A precursor to the high-toned slumming that I cite in my epigraph, Cather's story presents one body's sightseeing on Park Avenue as a way of manipulating sensational forms of sexuality, of dislocating the sexual self through spectacular slumming, and of moving it beyond communal or even subcultural identifications. But before I substantiate these claims with a closer reading of "Paul's Case," I elaborate on Cather's interventions into the social and literary fields that made the tramp boy's narrative a supreme figure of social disruption for turn-of-the-century audiences and artists alike.[9]

In the Company of Tramps

I must admit that I had certain prejudices against homosexuality since I knew its more primitive aspects. I knew it was why you carried a knife and would use it when you were in the company of tramps when you were a boy.... —Ernest Hemingway, *A Moveable Feast*

Paul's tramping body is strikingly mobile. The moment his teachers release him from their gaze, he "ran down the hill whistling the Soldiers' Chorus from *Faust* looking wildly behind him now and then to see whether some of his teachers were not there to writhe under this light-heartedness" ([1905] 1991, 222). This transient tendency recurs throughout the story, almost as if the boy cannot sit still. Paul "dashed out to the front of the house" (223). "He sat down before a blue Rico and lost himself." He "lost himself as he had done before." "He was even more than usually restless" (224). He "scrambled down" (225). He "wanted to be . . . carried out blue league after blue league" (228). Always on the run from his elders, Cather's adolescent is a body in perpetual motion, one struggling to escape from the constraints of the Anglo-American bourgeois home and his teachers' stifling judgments.[10]

Yet "Paul's Case" is not the first time Cather wove together male adolescence, mobility, and escape from middle-class Anglo imperatives. As Bernice Slote has suggested, "Willa Cather's kingdom of art lay in the context of the 1890's, a time as distractingly, glitteringly 'modern' as any time is when its years are new and change is more noticeable than permanence. But this 'modernity,' in particular, had that end-of-the-century, hectic flush that seemed part promise and part disease. It eloped in terms of 'the Decadence,' 'Bohemianism,' [and] 'Philistinism'" (32). These latter three keywords were powerful weapons in Cather's critical arsenal. Throughout her apprenticeship as a theater critic and budding regionalist writer during the 1890s, her Pulitzer Prize–winning heydays of the 1920s and the 1930s, and even her fall from critical grace in the early 1940s, she attacked the provincial mentality that, she felt, typified middle-class life. In journalistic diatribes, Cather railed against "Presbyteria," her coinage for what a contemporary, Max Weber, would define as *The Protestant Ethic and the Spirit of Capitalism* (first published as a series of articles in 1904–5 [2001]). In opposition to this ascetic bourgeois mentality, she affirmed "bohemianism," a deceptively immature aesthetic that promoted creative "unproductivity."[11] For the young artist, this bohemian mentality was a necessary retreat from the stifling conventions of middle-class living, an adolescent tramping recorded on the page rather than through the youthful male body Cather embraced as a girl. Her bohemian ideal, that is, was imagined as a life-long slumming tour into the world of art. The artist's creative mobility—based on the mind's capacity to wander into foreign locales—replaced the bourgeois citizen's social mobility in a strategic combination of decadent modernity and low lifestyle, a fusion, I show, that informs "Paul's Case."[12]

This dichotomy between "bohemianism" and "philistinism" was also indebted to several circulating narratives on male mobility that Cather recast into a guiding aesthetic ethos, two of the most prominent being the genre of tramp slumming and the knee-jerk diatribe against the wayward adolescent boy. By the publication date of "Paul's Case," several Progressive Era writers had contributed to a growing body of sensational literatures on tramp expeditions that surveyed the mysteries of modern urbanism. The anonymously published *Young Sleuth and the Millionaire Tramp; or, Diamonds under Rags* (1895), Stephen Crane's "An Experiment in Misery" ([1894] 1966a), Jack London's *The People of the Abyss* (1903), Walter A. Wyckoff's *The Workers: An Experiment in Reality* (1897), William Dean Howells's "An East-Side Ramble" (1896), Josiah Flynt's *Tramping with Tramps* ([1899] 1972), and Hutchins Hapgood's *Types from City Streets* (1910) are but a few of the many dime novels, short stories, fictional reports, urban sketches, picturesques, yellow journal articles, and personal biographies that relied on themes of tramping to launch muckraking critiques over industrialization, urbanization, and widening gaps between the working, middle, and upper classes.[13] Drawing on earlier spectacular slumming exposés of New York's Fourth Ward, such as Reverend Thomas de Witt Talmage's *The Night Sides of City Life* (1878) and London's homeless workhouses such as James Greenwood's "A Night in a Workhouse" (1866), these authors strove to highlight the miseries and to unveil the mysteries of the nation's working poor by donning, like Paul, "frayed and worn" attire to disappear, like Addams, into the bulk of the people. They became, in effect, bohemian tramps that distanced themselves from middle-class ideals of proper social and sexual behaviors only, at times, to reaffirm these ideals in print.[14]

In Crane's "An Experiment in Misery," for one, a young, presumably bourgeois adolescent wonders to himself "how [the tramp] feels" ([1894] 1966a, 33). To discover the secret vices of this mysterious body, the youth imagines a "veracious narrative of an experiment in misery" where his days and nights would consist of "rags and tatters, you know, a couple of dimes, and hungry, too, if possible. Perhaps I could discover his point of view or something near it" (34). True to the conventions of this tramping genre, Crane then presents his readers with the "veracious" horrors of the supposedly perverse slums: lost boys, claustrophobic hostels, cramped living quarters filled with naked male bodies and "smells," and, to top off these atrocities, lurid criminals and an "assassin" (37–38).[15] Judging from the sordid details of these same-sex intimacies, it's clear to the nameless tramp narrator that he has witnessed a rather queer scene filled with rather degenerate males, but it is also clear that this cross-identifying youth does not abjure this "wonderfully vivid picture" even as he critiques the social conditions that gave rise to it (33).

Unlike his realist counterparts, however, Crane also supplements this formulaic account of tramp slumming with his own version of "Slumming on Park Avenue"—"An Experiment in Luxury." Building on tropes of the mysteries of high decadent society that I briefly discussed in the introduction, Crane again has the same youth from "An Experiment in Misery" go tramping to "make another social study" and unveil the life of an American millionaire ([1894] 1966b, 43). Just as he wants to know more about the supposed perversions of the working class, the youth here treks to the photographic negative of this perverse space, an isolated mansion. Wary at first of undertaking this venture, he soon decides to give his tramping another go, and he tramps to the mansion only to pause again with trepidation. "He was a wanderer in a fairy land," he tells himself, "who felt that his presence marred certain effects. He was an invader with a shamed face, a man who had come to steal certain colors, forms, impressions that were not his. He had a dim thought that some one [*sic*] might come to tell him to begone [*sic*]" (45). Despite these apprehensions, the youth does not leave, and instead stays to observe the odd activities of the Anglo millionaire and his family, whose decadent preoccupations with a kitten mirrors the sights that he had previously witnessed in the slums.[16]

I discuss Cather's manipulations of this tramp-slumming literature when I turn to a closer reading of "Paul's Case," where Paul's experiments in a luxurious hoodlumism rethink the spectacle of adolescent perversion. For now, I note that standard literatures of the tramp-slummer like that of Crane's were complemented by bitter denunciations of this novel social type. In tandem with Pittsburgh High, many commentators shared a hunch that bohemian tramp bodies such as Paul's and Crane's youth were defiant, even deviant, forms of escape and illegibility. Cultural historian Kevin White, for one, argues that, over the first quarter of the twentieth-century, "the popular literature of the youth culture introduced two new styles of masculinity, the male flapper and the tramp Bohemian" (1993, 36). Though White concentrates primarily on 1920s modernist American authors like F. Scott Fitzgerald and Floyd Dell, earlier commentators—most notably Hall and the degeneration theorist Max Nordau—were quick to see the youthful tramp bohemian as a symptom of sexual modernity. While they operated in disparate intellectual and geographic climates, these social critics agreed that male adolescent activity like tramping was oftentimes detrimental to middle-class society and its narratives of progress. Yet like the realist trampers, they too found the tramp boy's narrative to be a fascinating subject, much as Paul's teachers find his behavior to be "remarkable" ([1905] 1991, 222).

Like the elders in "Paul's Case," these writers tried to diagnose the bohemian tramp in order to make him more intelligible—and more controllable. And like the realist trampers, the catchphrases for their respective attempts at categorization are degeneration and "the Decadence," terms encompassing fears of moral and economic perversion and terms that Cather would rewrite. Nordau, for example, describes degenerate decadence as "a contempt for traditional views of custom and morality" (1895, 5). And in a similar vein, Paul's teachers define his degenerate temperament as "impertinence" (221). For each of these critics, then, the bohemian male tramp was part promise and part disease.

Acknowledging that "adolescence is the normal time of emancipation from the parental roof, when youth seeks to set up a home of its own," Hall, however, sees the adolescent quest for new experiences and stimulating adventures as a "normal" inclination in young boys (1904, 1:349). Proverbially speaking, they sow wild oats. But Hall also warns against purposeless wandering, since such mobility may culminate in deviance as promising males slum into social dissolution: "As these troubles have far more mild than grave forms, we probably see the effect of their taint in hoodlums, rowdies, hoboes, vagrants, vagabonds, dudes, spendthrifts with no money sense, ne'er-do-wells, egoists, cases of moral insanity, juvenile criminals, and hosts of people whose early life promised well" (1:319). For Hall, then, these vice-ridden men are antisocial creatures whose slumming bodies threaten domestic and national ideologies precisely because they are dissociated from these institutions, and philanthropic reformers such as Jacob Riis have proven this all too well. "The vagrant, itinerant, vagabond, gadabout, hobo, and tramp, that Riis has made so interesting, is an arrested, degenerate, or perverted being who abhors work; feels that the world owes him a living; and generally has his first real nomad experience in the teens or earlier" (Hall 1904, 1:349). Here the conflation of degeneracy, perversion, trampdom, and adolescence is made explicit: unproductive male vagabonds are forever trapped in a state of peripatetic arrested development. The liminality of their tramp bodies—the transitional status of the pervert—is only enhanced by their transitory natures. Wandering adolescent males fit in nowhere yet manage to be everywhere, and such a transient state leads to a mobile indeterminacy. Tramp boys like Paul wander themselves out of a social existence and, to an extent, out of a social identity, which is why they need to be specified and controlled.

To take a cue from Hemingway: tramp boys form company rather than community, and the distinction between the two is important. As Nels Anderson, a graduate student at the University of Chicago, a sociological expert on hoboes and homelessness, and himself an experienced tramp, writes in "The Juvenile and the Tramp" (1923): "Regarded ever as a working group, the tramp class is an exceedingly unwieldy and undisciplined body. The members of the group are always living anonymous lives, and generally they are shifting and moving to avoid responsibility. They are a group of men with no home attachments and few interests that would identify them with any community" (1998a, 100). His restless nature, it follows, surrounds the tramp "with the cloak of anonymity. Not even arrest reveals his identity.... The tramp is not identified with any community or any social group" (115). Careless of private property, morally depraved and immorally perverse, the tramping bohemian male becomes, like the wasted bachelor maid, a supreme figure of social disorder.[17] Sexually immature and socially unproductive, he inaugurates the arrested development of heteronormative society as a whole.[18] This, Anderson warns, "is the life that tempts the boy" who, like Paul, so desires the "wanderlust type" (101, 103).

Decadent Movements

Which is also to say that the transient bohemian male has the makings of either a decadent European aesthete or a slumming American dandy in the Pittsburgh suburbs. Recall that Paul's clothes are "a trifle outgrown" and the linings of his overcoat are "frayed and worn." As I suggested earlier, such lackluster attire paints the boy as a tramping Bohemian. Yet we must not forget "for all that there was something of the dandy about him" ([1905] 1991, 221). These interconnections between the bohemian tramp, the dandy, and "the Decadence" are complex ones for Cather and her glittery sexual modernity. For brevity's sake, I point out that Hall's emphasis on moral insanity and egoism should also bring to mind another turn-of-the-century text that Cather read and disagreed with—the French theorist Max Nordau's *Degeneration* (1895). A bitter diatribe against literary movements such as the decadents, the aesthetes, and the symbolists,

Nordau's book posits egomania as the central pathology of dandified artists who, like Paul, wander the subterranean city streets. "They are weaklings in will," he snarls in his case histories, "unfitted for any activity requiring regular uniform efforts, or else victims to vanity, wishing to be more famous than is possible to a stone-breaker or a tailor" (337).[19] Self-obsessed, these slumming aesthetes "have completely gathered under their banner this refuse of civilized peoples, and march at its head" (337). Like the transient American bohemian, these dandified European flaneurs are both everywhere and nowhere, princes "who everywhere rejoice in [their] incognito" (Baudelaire [1863] 1997, 133).

While it may be tempting to read Nordau's characterization of these conversant literary movements as a Tramp Boy Pride Parade run amok, we should not lose sight of the onus that he places on the wandering, decadent boy-artist. With Wilde, Baudelaire, and Whitman written up in effigy, Nordau singles out vagrant tramp symbolist Paul Verlaine: "In normally constituted society there is no place for them. Verlaine has been a vagabond the whole of his life. He has loafed about all the highways of France, and roamed as well through Belgium and England.... He has no residence, but resorts [to living] as a tramp" (1895, 123). For Nordau, Verlaine's vagabondage appears as immature and adolescent. Since he is beyond the pale of normal civilization, he brings down the European race. After all, this transient artist is a contagious degenerate; and, as Nordau's title implies, degeneration in art is also degeneration in society, a closing moment of the nineteenth century whereby an epoch declines and "moral sea-sickness abounds" (7). "Thus," he laments, "it appears as if the whole of civilized humanity were converted to the aesthetics of the Dusk of the Nations," as if civilization has become little more than a vice district (7).

Given Nordau's imperialist and millenarian tone, it is clear that *Degeneration* is a close relative of *Adolescence*'s phyletic fears. Like Hall's wayward hooligans, these limited cases of human behavior engage in perversions of the mind (their decadent art) and perversions of the body (promiscuity; same-sex passion). "As one vagabond feels himself attracted by other vagabonds," Nordau writes, "so too does one deranged mind feel drawn to others" (1895, 124). In a logical Gordian knot that Addams and Hall would have admired, vagrancy connects to artistic tendencies that connect to perversion that connects to the rise of "antisocial beings" (261). And underpinning these analyses of male transience is the inescapable fact that the tramp boy—a not-so-distant relative of the decadent artist—escapes from the confining institutions of society only to find pleasure in his international wanderlust, whether it be in the streets, the fields, or on the printed page.

In her long apprenticeship as a writer, Cather built on these crisscrossing theories of degenerate adolescence and boy tramping while simultaneously rewriting them. Though literary critics associate the decadent movement with continental or British literatures, it is important to recall, as Slote and Larzer Ziff remind us, that "the sense of decadence was very much in the consciousness of many American writers and readers in [the 1890s]" (Ziff 1966, 133). Cather was no exception. Early formations of her kingdom of art championed bohemian tramps such as Whitman, the Canadian duo Bliss Carman and Richard Hovey and their *Songs from Vagabondia* (1894), and, especially, Paul Verlaine. And her hatred of *Degeneration* attests to the book's popularity on American soil and her familiarity with egomaniacal artists: "The whole of Nordau's ponderous and on the whole rather stupid volume on degeneration is not enough to explain Paul Verlaine, though it fits him exactly," she argues in her review essay "Verlaine" (1966, 394).

We can extend Cather's interest in Verlaine's transient aestheticism to the structuring concerns in "Paul's Case." As several critics have noted, Cather admired and eulogized Verlaine, and the story's nominal allusion to the poet should be obvious, though no critic has ever emphasized it.[20] Furthermore, in a tribute to Verlaine, Cather was quick to point out the poet's uncontrollable vagrant tendencies, tendencies that mirror Paul's uncontrollable mobile body. "He spent his life like Villon, vagabonding about the highways and byways of France," Cather writes. "He had but three homes, the street, the hospital and the prison" (1966, 395). Describing the disparities between his religious sensibilities and his perverse tendencies, she then surmises that "this double life was the existence of Paul Verlaine. Both moods were exaggerated, violent, insane even, but both were perfectly sincere.... He was imprisoned again and again for unmentionable and almost unheard of crimes, but he wrote some of the most beautiful and devout religious poetry in any tongue. He was a practicer [*sic*] of every excess known to man" (394). For Cather, Verlaine is the penultimate tramp-slummer, a vagabond who moves from the suburban middle classes to the urban streets to the fields with a grace that the American artist cannot help but admire. Fundamentally, his is a double life. Like Paul, he is a wandering loner, both "indefinite" and vague, trying to escape the regulations of the social ([1905] 1991, 395).[21] Or, as Summers maintains, "Unlike many turn-of-the-century critics who saw Wilde and

Verlaine as equally dangerous figures and who linked them in a common enterprise of decadence, Cather scorns the artificiality of the aesthetes but celebrates the blessed degeneracy of Verlaine" (1990, 107).

Given her admiration for French decadence, it should come as no surprise that Cather viewed her art like a good vagabond aesthete should. Though she adopted a hypermasculine persona during her adolescence, discounted Wilde in her editorials, and imitated the regional aesthetics of her chosen mentor, Sarah Orne Jewett, she embraced—even championed—the creeds of the aesthetic symbolists in newspaper reviews and editorials. Even in her 1925 preface to Jewett's *The Country of the Pointed Firs and Other Stories*, Cather cites Pater as an unlikely literary companion to the regional writer: "Walter Pater said that every truly great drama must, in the end, linger in the reader's mind as a sort of ballad. One might say that every fine story must leave in the mind of the sensitive reader an intangible residuum of pleasure" (1992b, 850). In a twist on Wilde's classic epigram that "all art is quite useless," Cather too affirmed that art has no sociopolitical function but must nevertheless bring useless "pleasure" to its audience. Here Cather Americanizes the decadent aesthetic by turning it into a perverse manifesto for anticommunal connectedness.

For Cather, then, creative acts of tramping bohemianism contribute little to making the world a more philistine place. In a 1936 manifesto prompted by claims that she was not writing realistic (read, proletarian) literature, Cather rages, "You were asking me what I thought about a new term in criticism: the Art of 'Escape.' Isn't the phrase tautological? What has art ever been but escape?" (1992a, 968). She then goes on to suggest that her aesthetic viewpoint may be outmoded (a claim supported by the arch title of the collection, *Not under Forty*), but she also insists that the artist's position in society should be antisocial, that art should enhance one's imagination rather than one's pocketbook: "At the moment, we hear the same cry that went up during the French Revolution: the one really important thing for every individual is his citizenship, his loyalty to a cause—which, of course, always means his loyalty to a party. The composer should be Citizen Beethoven, the painter Citizen Rembrandt, the poet Citizen Shelley, and they should step into line and speed their pen or brush in helping to solve the economic problems which confront society" (1992a, 968). Holding onto a revised decadent aesthetic in the face of social realism, a conservative Cather maintains that art should bohemian tramp, that it is a disloyal slumming flight from the social prescriptions and economic imperatives that dictate the individual's philistine life.[22] Using "citizenship" as her catchall term for socioeconomic mandates, Cather embraces the tramp boy aesthetic (not, I emphasize, a tramp boy identity) that so infuriated early twentieth-century child psychologists, philanthropic reformers, and degeneration theorists. Championing an intellectual and aesthetic vagabondage, she dissociates herself from communal imperatives and opts to become, in Nordau's phrase, an "antisocial being"—or, better, a middle-class artist who turns her back on her own kind to slum into an imaginary bohemian world, the escapist fantasies that make up the kingdom of art.

She permits her characters to do likewise. Exemplified by "Paul's Case," this tramp-slumming advances an incognito realism that allows Cather and her protagonists to stand together in good company without forming a community. Eschewing civic duties, neither Cather nor Paul identifies with any community or social group, even though both circulate within the social. And neither Cather nor Paul identifies completely with each other. Though others imagine the Catherian corpus to be an extended engagement with the writer's "fervent" adolescent "desire . . . to be a boy" (Nealon 2001, 91), I offer a different take on her fascination with the wandering adolescent. Cather found this "early state" to be something more than a stable, though stigmatized, sexual identity. She transformed the category of adolescence into an operative mode of queer relations far removed from the imperatives of sexual citizenship. Her transient artists (Paul included) lose themselves by fantastically slumming into an adolescent state of artistic peregrination. Such self-dissolution is accomplished through restless mobility, a mobility that replaces the entrenched sexual and gender identifications that constitute the philistine Pittsburgh suburbs.

The Miseries of Pittsburgh

Showcasing the figure of the well-dressed vagabond, "Paul's Case" reenacts Cather's dichotomy between bohemia and philistinia that also appear in Hall, Nordau, and Crane's tramping experiments in misery and luxury. The boy's transient bohemian aesthetic ("something of the dandy about him") is a knee-jerk reaction to suburbia's philistine asceticism, an austerity rooted in the middle-class home that Paul flees in the final third of the story. But before I detail this slumming flight, I want to concentrate on Cather's descriptions, denunciations, and appropriations of middle-class fantasies in order to show how her protagonist turns bourgeois desires for social mobility and world renown into an escapist aesthetic.

Paul's domestic life initially thwarts what will become, by the story's conclusion, a rather indeterminate mobility. After a day spent wandering through museums, theaters, and the Pittsburgh streets, Paul returns to Cordelia Street, the locus of suburban banality, anomie, and normalization, "with the nerveless sense of defeat": "He turned and walked reluctantly toward the car tracks. The end had to come sometime; his father in his night-clothes at the top of the stairs, explanations that did not explain, hastily improvised fictions that were forever tripping him up, his upstairs room and its horrible yellow wallpaper, the creaking bureau with the greasy plush collar-box, and over his painted wooden bed the pictures of George Washington and John Calvin, and the framed motto, 'Feed my Lambs,' which had been worked in red worsted by his mother" ([1905] 1991, 225). In this garbled paragraph, Cather piles clause on top of clause to suggest the claustrophobia that haunts Paul. The "light-heartedness" that the boy experienced once he flees from Pittsburgh High screeches to a halt the moment he remembers his suburban life (222). Sluggish sentences (in both senses of the word) weigh the boy down, a premonition of his father's night watch and Paul's inevitable punishment. Prose conspires with paternal conscription, blocking his escape from sexual surveillance and "forever tripping him up."

But Paul fears more than his father's reproaches. Perhaps the only domestic space permitting psychic relief from his parents, his bedroom is saturated with smothering posters and even more stifling allusions. Unlike the liberating "orgies of living" he engages in once he leaves Cordelia Street, Paul detests the "creaking" furniture and the "horrible yellow wallpaper." In opposition to his aesthetic quests for adventure, these loud furnishings offend his sensual nature. His personal dislike for this garish, utilitarian bedroom in particular complements his repulsion for "respectable beds," "common food," and a "house penetrated by kitchen odors" in general ([1905] 1991, 225). This is to say that Paul's disdain for the creature comforts of family life is also nothing less than a hatred for American heteronormativity, a life centered on familialism and deadening intimacy (Berlant and Warner 1998). Like his father, the house and the bedroom—a sustained experiment in misery—are eyesores rather than sights for sore eyes.

And as with the lad's red carnation, a flower that signifies effeminacy and perversion, Cather again uses color to allude to the homestead's disturbing atmosphere. The tacky yellow wallpaper should bring to mind a controversial literary text—Charlotte Perkins Gilman's 1899 short story of the same title. Denounced at the time of its publication for inaccuracy and sensationalism, Gilman's story describes the plight of a nameless woman writer—a would-be artist like Paul—trapped in discourses of patriarchy and sexology. Confined in an attic to undergo a rest cure for nervous prostration, the narrator slowly goes insane, to the horror of her husband and sister. Though the room drives her mad, her insanity enables her to find herself in the wallpaper and releases her from the realities of domesticity. A bad case like Paul, she too must invent hastily improvised fictions and explanations that did not explain in order to survive (at high cost) suffocating sex-gender imperatives.

Three other historical references complement this allusion in "Paul's Case"—Washington, Calvin, and the motto, "Feed my Lambs." Hanging over the boy's bed, the pictures and the epigram function as fixed reminders of what Paul must become: in a word, a man. Together, these archetypal signifiers present the lad with an intelligible mode of social and sexual being, one structured around Progressive Era ideals of middle-class asceticism, Protestant masculinity, and racial and sexual normalization.[23] The picture of the Founding Father should provide Paul with a model of restraint, dedication, and national allegiance. Washington's patriotism, in turn, colludes with the picture of doctrinaire Puritan John Calvin to invoke protestant ethics and their spiritual ties to philistinism. With the addition of Christ's selflessly sacrificial motto, "Feed My Lambs," a motto sharply opposed to Paul's bohemianism, this troika of modern American family values becomes a poster board for repression. And while these not-so-hastily improvised fictions of national affiliation, moral righteousness, and rationalization may be heavy-handed, they clue the reader into the ideological noose that the home and white middle-class desire signify for the adolescent. Tacked to yellow wallpaper, these archetypes would together make a model Citizen Paul, and what should be a luxurious room of one's own becomes instead a suburban iron cage.[24]

But the boy's bedroom is not the only stifling Presbyterian world as Cordelia Street's residents commit themselves to national ideals of racially normative sexual citizenship. Cordelia is "a highly respectable street, where all the houses were exactly alike, and where businessmen of moderate means begot and reared large families of children, all of whom went to Sabbath-school and learned the shorter catechism, and were interested in arithmetic; all of whom were as exactly alike as their homes, and of a piece of the monotony in which they lived" ([1905] 1991, 225). Just as his bedroom decorations speak, in harmony, the language of productivity and repression, so too does Cordelia Street. Here Cather's use of parallelism ("where all," "all," "all of whom") suggests the push toward regulation, uniformity, and normalization, or what is elsewhere defined as "grey monotony" (234). In a middle-class world where every house, every breadwinner, and every child is "alike," this static environment implies concord, moderation, and, for Paul, madness. Given the adolescent's showy attire at the beginning of the story, it comes as no surprise that his response to this monotonous Presbyterian world is complete dread: "Paul never went up Cordelia Street without a shudder of loathing. . . . He approached it tonight with the nerveless sense of defeat, the hopeless feeling of sinking back forever into ugliness and commonness that he always had when he came home" (225). As with his namesake, in this normally constituted society there is no place for him.

What irritates Paul so much about Cordelia Street is the predictability—the sameness—of this suburban environment that clashes with his garish attire and insolent attitude. Every Sunday, the clone-like "burghers of Cordelia Street" gather to discuss business transactions and hobnob about their children's financial prowess:

> The men on the steps—all in their shirt sleeves, their vests unbuttoned—sat with their legs well apart, their stomachs comfortably protruding, and talked of the prices of things, or told anecdotes of the sagacity of their various chiefs and overlords. They occasionally looked over the multitude of squabbling children, listened affectionately to their high-pitched, nasal voices, smiling to see their own proclivities reproduced in their offspring, and interspersed their legends of the iron kings with remarks about their sons' progress at school, their grades in arithmetic, and the amounts they had saved in their toy banks. ([1905] 1991, 226)

It is interesting to note that women are absent in this social gathering. They have little place in this weekly ritual, and Cordelia Street's burghers engage in typical twentieth-century homosocial activities—braggadocio, hero-worship, and half-ass parenting. Within this male domain, fathers supervise their sons' piggy banks, and, perhaps more important, their leisure activities.[25] For the burghers, their children's leisure is also work. Toys double here as banks. Cather's none-too-subtle swipe at "iron kings" such as Andrew Carnegie and Andrew Mellon (both based in Pittsburgh) only reinforces this critique of middle-class productivity and further suggests the slavish nature of these suburban businessmen who drone on about "the sagacity" of their bosses: what should be a relaxing evening for all instead becomes yet another fetishization of "their sons' progress." Yet, for the caustic narrator, these denizens suggest suburban Protestant work ethics gone wild. Since the elders admire their own "proclivities reproduced in their offspring," these white middle-class males leisurely reproduce themselves. Within this "flavorless, colorless mass of every-day existence" (225), everyone desires—and everyone even starts to look—the same.

Take an adult who "happened to be the young man who was daily held up to Paul as a model, and after whom it was his father's dearest hope that he would pattern" (226). A successful entrepreneur, this young man renounced his life of wandering and "sowing of wild oats" so that he could "curb his appetites" and begin his professional life as a respectable businessman ([1905] 1991, 227). The pride of the community and the apple of Paul's father's eye, the nameless individual is also a hollow man. Cather signifies this physiologically. Though he has a "ruddy complexion," he also has a "compressed, red mouth," suggesting just how far he went to repress the urges that once propelled him to leave home. In lieu of adolescent exploration, he becomes a node in Cordelia Street's community. He is, according to the narrator, "near-sighted" like his mousy wife, "an angular school-mistress" who "also wore thick glasses." For the narrator, and for Paul, such visions of economic grandeur are myopic and "deadening." Essentially straight, middle-class male upward mobility is also essentially immobile.

Fairy Worlds

I like the idea of queerness as a sort of magic carpet ride to get away.—B. Ruby Rich, "The Gay Escape"

Paul's queer mobility is anything but. Paul replaces the middle-class ethic of social mobility that Cather so disdains with a bohemian ethic of transience, one that initially takes on a fantastic form. The adolescent, that is, substitutes a queer form of upward slumming on Park Avenue in place of traditional bourgeois desires for upward mobility, the cornerstone of the middle-class American Dream that structures the Sunday afternoons on Cordelia Street. In sharp contrast to the death-in-life that is Cordelia Street and his bedroom, the adolescent longs for something—anything—different and desires nothing more than to distance himself from the enforced experiment in misery that is the suburbs. Unproductive, he fails to develop himself like "the young man . . . held up to Paul as a model," though he does develop a Verlaine-esque double life. "Paul bounded upstairs, scrubbed the greasy odor of the dish-water from his hands with the ill-smelling soap he hated," the narrator notes, "and then shook over his fingers a few drops of violet water from the bottle he kept hidden in his drawer" ([1905] 1991, 227). Anointing his hands with this sweet-smelling perfume, Paul develops a tactic for coping with the suburban doldrums, one that takes on the odor of the abject.

This double life announces itself through commodities—the flashy carnation, the outmoded attire, effeminate fragrances—which permit the boy a modicum of fantasy (and the fantastic) in a privileged world of sameness, and one that retroactively makes him a repulsive object of scrutiny and surveillance. After Paul sprinkles himself with the perfume, "he left the house with his geometry conspicuously under his arm, and the moment he got out of Cordelia Street and boarded a downtown car, he shook off the lethargy of two deadening days, and began to live again" ([1905] 1991, 227). This minor scene has major implications for my larger argument. Paul complies with middle-class hygienic imperatives as he washes himself with the "ill-smelling soap." But he writes over the scent of this Protestant toilet with his violet water, much as he walks in public with his geometry book yet heads for downtown. One could dismiss these moments as adolescent duplicity, but I find it interesting to watch how the adolescent builds on middle-class protocols only to twist them to his own ends, much like Cather does with circulating discourses of youthful tramping.

With this in mind, it is important to note how Cather inverts middle-class fantasies of opulence and mobility (wandering is natural but vagrancy is abnormal), how she enables her protagonist to challenge prescriptive sexual ideals. One of Cordelia Street's favorite pastimes, the narrator informs us, is telling "improvised fictions." These tales only repeat the burghers' Sunday desires to conflate work with leisure. "The young man was relating how his chief, now cruising in the Mediterranean, kept in touch with all the details of the business, arranging his office hours on his yacht just as though he were at home, and 'knocking off work enough to keep two stenographers busy'" ([1905] 1991, 227). While these stories transpire in "exotic" locales like Cairo, the Mediterranean, and Monte Carlo, the men are more impressed with the volume of work that their ideal—the nameless, omnipotent chief—manages to produce.

Glittery "cruising," however, wows Paul more than the chief's financial prowess. The adolescent is more attuned to the fanciful transience of this tourist life than the profits that so interest the other clones. He "rather liked to hear these legends of the iron kings, that were told and retold on Sundays and holidays; these stories of palaces in Venice, yachts on the Mediterranean, and high play at Monte Carlo appealed to his fancy, and he was interested in the triumphs of these cash boys who had become famous, though he had no mind for the cash-boy stage" ([1905] 1991, 227). Though devoid of ambition, Paul desires the exaggerated results of these daring tales of vagabondage, tales that gesture to the high society chapters of many mysteries narratives. In effect, he embraces—as he appropriates—these public fantasies of the burghers, yet he also refuses to become a part of the community that surrounds him. Like the hand washing and the geometry book, middle-class heteronormative imperatives and the slumming literatures that support them here give rise to inscrutably queer desires.

When he is at school, for example, Paul captures his fellow students' imaginations with stories from his peripatetic life, stories stolen from the burghers. Oftentimes, these fantasies gravitate around tropical locales much like the ones mentioned on Cordelia Street. And when these stories grow stale, "and his audience grew listless, he became desperate and would bid all the boys good-bye, announcing that he was going to travel for a while; going to Naples, to Venice, to Egypt" ([1905] 1991, 229). Participating in what Shelley Streeby has termed a "culture of sensation," he uses these mobile experiments in luxury not to cement his heightened relation to an Anglo-American middle class but to announce his eminent departure from it (2002, 27). Sensational stories from popular culture thus enable him to momentarily escape rather than enhance his position in middle-class cultures.[26] Plagiarizing an "improvised fiction," he uses sensation to distance his self from the heterosexual spectacles of the petit-bourgeois.

While these marvelous voyages are forever deferred, however, his escapist fantasies are fulfilled in another destination—the theater. This locale, which permits the adolescent to live these fantasies and become an indeterminately mobile body, is also his "vocation" ([1905] 1991, 228), his "secret love," "his fairy tale," and his "fairy world" (225). Like Cather and

Verlaine, the young aesthete's creative slumming replaces the middle-class citizen's social mobility. Or, as Bersani notes of another "radical" slummer, André Gide, such "leisure prefigures a new society... in which vice might be reinvented *as* art" (1995, 127–28). Turning asceticism into aestheticism, Paul also turns his supreme vice—his tramplike, dandified vagrancy—into an artistic appreciation that disrupts his spectacular self.

In Paul's opinion, Carnegie Hall counters Cordelia Street with its lavish indifference to the banalities of everyday suburban life. "Perhaps it was because his experience of life elsewhere was so full of Sabbath-school picnics, petty economies, wholesome advice as how to succeed in life, and the unescapable [*sic*] odors of cooking," the narrator wonders about Paul, "that he found this existence so alluring, these smartly-clad men and women so attractive, that he was so moved by these starry apple orchards that bloomed perennially under the lime-light" ([1905] 1991, 228). Rejecting all that is good for him, that might enable him to improve himself, and that might make him an acceptable part of Cordelia Street's middle-class community, Paul instead prefers the artificiality—the *fabula*—of the theater to the social prescriptions of his philistine father and his neighbors. While the life that he lives (symbolized by the geometry book) is both petty and uninspired, this life of art permits the boy to escape what is "unescapable," namely, the toxic odors of suburban life. "In the midst of that smoke-palled city, enamored of figures and grimy toil," the narrator acknowledges, "Paul had his secret temple, his wishing carpet, his bit of blue-and-white Mediterranean shore bathed in perpetual sunshine" (228). This is one form of slumming on Park Avenue, whereby Paul queers middle-class mobility and fashions a wishing carpet ride to get away and get lost. Or, as Anderson remarks when discussing the adolescent desire for wanderlust: "The boy who lives in a dream world where he is constantly building aircastles, only to see them toppled by the stern realities of the daily routine, is strangely attracted by the tramp's life" (1998a, 101).

Inside the vast, empty spaces of this theater, Paul is indeed a different boy from the one his teachers admonish. And despite his frustrations with Cordelia Street, here he is not averse to work. After the inquisition and a few hours spent at the local museum, he returns to his current occupation—ushering at the opera house. Though a poor student and, one can only guess, a disappointing son, the adolescent is a "model usher" ([1905] 1991, 223). When he greets patrons, he is always "gracious and smiling." In sharp contrast to Cordelia Street's unspoken assumption that leisure equals work, work equals leisure at the theater. "Nothing was too much trouble for him," the narrator notes. "He carried messages and brought programmes as though it were his greatest pleasure in life, and all the people in his section thought him a charming boy."

Further, though Paul detests suburban regulations, in this pleasure palace he takes deep pride in his tramping uniform and, concomitantly, in uniformity: "When Paul reached the ushers' dressing-room half-a-dozen boys were there already, and he began excitedly to tumble into his uniform." Donning this garb, he ushers himself into sexual unknowability. The sartorial change alters his temperament and he loses the case history-like qualities that made him an object of epistemological inquiry. Now inconspicuous, Paul has an entirely different relationship to his body, its affects, and its effects: "He was always considerably excited while he dressed, twanging all over to the tuning of the strings and the preliminary flourishes of the horns in the music-room; but to-night he seemed quite beside himself." Reading this concluding clause literally, I imagine that Paul finds sheer delight (and escape) in what this occupation permits: capacities to step outside himself, to distance himself from his signifying sexual body, and to don an anonymous uniform. Within this fantastic fairy tale, there is no need to detect something because Paul is incognito. Catering to white middle-class audiences looking for spectacle and leisure, he also removes himself from white middle-class imperatives. He sees the world, yet remains hidden from the world.[27]

Within the theater, Paul erases his signifying body and puts on a brand new face, one that is "charming" and endearing rather than impertinent and hysterical: "It was very much as though this were a great reception and Paul were the host." In direct opposition to the feudal community ruled by the "iron kings" and the panopticon that is Pittsburgh High, here Paul becomes a citizen of the kingdom of art rather than the American nation. Surrounded by "fine people" and "gay colors," the boy is able to merge into the crowd: "When the symphony began Paul sank into one of the rear seats with a long sigh of relief, and lost himself as he had done before the Rico." Through this festive, theatrical lifestyle, Paul loses himself in both senses of the word and, goes slumming like Cather, into the world of fabulation.

This adolescent capacity to lose his sexual identity in work and dress is further enhanced by one aspect of his wandering tendencies: sightseeing. Pushing Cather's revision of white middle-class desires and mobility a bit further, we note that, midway through "Paul's Case," the narrator informs us that the adolescent does have a Weberian calling: the desire for looking. One minor actor on the Pittsburgh stage, Charley Edwards, recognizes this immediately. "[Paul] had won a place among Edwards's following not only because the young actor, who could not afford to employ a dresser, often found him useful, but because he recognized in Paul something akin to what churchmen term 'vocation'" ([1905] 1991, 228). Though he detests the fact that his teachers spectacularize him, Paul is constantly overwhelmed by spectacle and dedicates each and every free moment to soaking up art and culture with a capital *C*. After his teachers release him from their grasp, the adolescent rushes down to the museum and marvels at "Raffelli's gay studies of Paris streets" (223). Though he does not comprehend Jean-Françoise Raffaelli's works of urban art (most of which attempt to realistically portray the French working classes), he still basks in its colors, which "always exhilarated him." Ignorant of class portraiture, he does not view the paintings to get a stronger sense of how the other half lives in these slumming scenes. Nor does he cast the working classes as an aesthetic collective body to be marveled at and objectified. He instead loses himself in the ecstasy of a noninvasive gaze.

This sense of visual joy—the delight found in tramping into the face of crowded scenes that one indifferently views—permits the adolescent to wander around while remaining seated. "After a while," the narrator writes, "he sat down before a blue Rico and lost himself" ([1905] 1991, 223). For the young boy, the forms of these artworks and the imaginative flights of fancy that they prompt are much more intriguing than their content or their purported aesthetic value. Like Wilde's Dorian Gray ([1891] 1962), for Paul "all art is at once both surface and symbol" (18), yet the symbols in the painting have remained unread and grant the adolescent a modicum of mobility. In other words, his transient state occurs while he is sitting down and, again, looking at working-class French bohemians through the elitist lens of high museum art.

The theater functions similarly. After all, "it was not that symphonies, as such, meant anything in particular to Paul, but the first sigh of the instruments seemed to free some hilarious and potent spirit within him" ([1905] 1991, 223–24). Like the museum's objects, the stage is, for Paul, "the actual portal of Romance," a superficial scene, or a double life enabling him "to be carried out, blue league after blue league, away from everything" (228). The stage, then, represents another form of slumming into bohemia, and Paul's fantasies are fulfilled in this artificially productive orchard that blooms under the limelight. For the adolescent, the theater "was very like the old stories that used to float about London of fabulously rich Jews, who had subterranean halls there, with palms, and fountains, and soft lamps and richly appareled women who never saw the disenchanting light of London day. So, in the midst of that smoke-palled city, enamored of figures and grimy toil, Paul had his secret temple, his wishing carpet, his bit of blue-and-white Mediterranean shore bathed in perpetual sunshine" (228). In this lush paragraph, Cather inverts the standard tramp-slumming "stories" that I earlier mentioned. Much like Cordelia Street's "legends of the iron kings," Paul's exotic fantasy relies on the conventions of the tramp-slumming narrative: an "unknown" underworld, a "mysterious" population, a trek into the "subterranean."[28] Yet the boy does not dive down into the London underworld to calculate the "veracious" facts of working-class life, or to affiliate with those who are segregated from the Anglo suburbs. Pulpy narratives instead become deeply depersonalized by the young lad; and they permit Paul a fantasy opposed to the middle-class mandates that constrain him. Rather than venturing into the sensational realism of the slums, the boy paradoxically goes down into the "subterranean" underworld by entering into the hallowed halls of the middle-class theater, and decadent high art again mixes with low life.

The end product of such tramping enables Paul to vanish into the "portal of Romance," a direct cross-reference to the "portals of luxury" that mark Crane's luxurious millionaire sketch ([1894] 1966b, 45). Such queer slumming, I also note, is canned sensationalism, an urban underworld dream based largely on previous tramping literatures. As the adolescent imagines Jewish men delighting in their "subterranean" brothels filled with "richly appareled women," this setting is, safe to say, far removed from London commerce and the domestic niceties of white suburbs such as Cordelia Street. And this experiment in luxury is also far removed from hard-working realities of the actresses of the theater, who admit to an economic realism that Paul finds unviable: "They were hard-working women, most of them supporting indigent husbands or brothers, and they laughed rather bitterly at having stirred the boy to such fervid and florid inventions" ([1905] 1991, 229).

Though some might criticize Paul's low-life "inventions" as classist, orientalist, and anti-Semitic, and while Cather's portrayals of Jews across her oeuvre have rightly been called into question, I want to stress that it is unclear to me with whom Paul identifies in this fantastic scenario.[29] I cannot state whether Paul wants to be the stereotypically wealthy Jew or the appareled woman, and such uncertainty complicates any forms of damning cross-identification or insidious cultural appropriation. Paul, that is to say, identifies more with the slumming scene's setting than with those who inhabit it. He manipulates the frame of the slumming narrative ("very like the old stories") rather than identifying wholly with its characters. He replaces the spectacularization of his perverse, adolescent body with a spectacle of theatrical fantasy. In psychoanalytic terms,

> Fantasy . . . is not the object of desire, but its setting. In fantasy the subject does not pursue the object or its sign: he appears caught up in the sequence of images. He forms no representation of the desired object, but is himself represented as participating in the scene although, in the earliest forms of fantasy, he cannot be assigned any fixed place in it. . . . As a result, the subject, although always present in the fantasy, may be so in a desubjectivized form, that is to say, in the very syntax of the sequence in question. (Laplanche and Pontalis 1886, 26)

As I have argued elsewhere, fantasies depersonalize the subject to such an extent that one is able to occupy multiple positions in one's framework.[30] To his credit, Paul pushes his phantasmal mobility into indeterminacy. His subterranean slumming enables him to merge into the scripted scene, and this may have something to teach us about the political negotiations of the desire for collective cross-identification. Theoretically speaking, Paul's escapist fantasies show us that wanting to identify *as* does not mean having to identify *with*.

Here the text amplifies an orthodoxy of queer theory that maintains that disparate desiring selves can—and should—join together to form counter publics connected under the rubric of queer. Sedgwick's *Epistemology of the Closet* best expresses this utopian wish: "After all, to identify *as* must always include multiple processes of identification *with*. It also involves identification *as against*" (1990, 61). I concur with Sedgwick that any process of identification, disidentification, and nonidentification needs a narrative to jumpstart itself, but I also feel that sexual narratives (like tramp slumming) produce antinarratives that enable subjects to distance themselves from others and from norms of the social, as Paul does when he marvels at the operatic diva. Unexpected identifications with, that is, can dissolve queer or normal subjectivities at the very moment that they seem to be most stable. Thus for Cather (as for her contemporary Addams), identifying *as* someone or something you *are not* scrambles identification processes all together.

Two moments in the first half of "Paul's Case" substantiate these points. The first occurs after the theater closes, and the actors return to their homes. An avid fan, Paul waits at the backstage door to gush over his idols. On sighting the night's soloist, the adolescent follows her carriage over to the hotel and imagines what it might be like to live the life of a diva: "In the moment that the door was ajar it seemed to Paul that he, too, entered. He seemed to feel himself go after her up the steps, into the warm, lighted building, into an exotic, a tropical world of shiny, glistening surfaces and basking ease. He reflected on the mysterious dishes that were brought into the dining-room, the green bottles in buckets of ice, as he had seen them in the supper party pictures of the *Sunday World* supplement" ([1905] 1991, 224). Much like the richly detailed "subterranean hall" that Paul enters, this ritzy hotel takes on the appearance of an "exotic" world, another "mysterious" experiment in luxury. Again, Paul slums in a world akin to Park Avenue, but, I stress, this scopophilic moment does not reflect any tangible reality. Pure fantasy derived from the sensational press and the diva's room, not the diva herself, is the boy's primary love object as he inserts himself into what appears to him as the *Mysteries* of Pittsburgh's stock company. What he desires in this scenario is its sensational emptiness, its "shiny, glistening surfaces." And splendid surfaces—the sensual, decadent pleasures that Nordau detests and that Crane's youthful experimenter in luxury observes in shock and awe—are what Paul so desperately wants. Entering into a fantastic scene, the boy does not cross-identify with the regal female soloist even though "he seemed to feel himself go after her up the steps." He instead loses himself within the generic "supper party pictures." He loses himself in the rapture of white middle-class sensationalism, a sensationalism that propels the bourgeois desire to slum, uptown or downtown, in the first place.

A second encounter with a diva produces a similar sensation in the boy. This time, the obfuscation occurs the moment that Paul seems to experience acute diva identification during one of Carnegie Hall's nightly shows: "When the soprano soloist came on, Paul forgot even the nastiness of his teacher's being there and gave himself up to the peculiar stimulus such personages always had for him. The soloist chanced to be a German woman, by no means in her first youth, and the mother of many children; but she wore an elaborate gown and a tiara, and above all she had that *indefinable* air of achievement, that world-shine on her, which, in Paul's eyes, made her a veritable queen of Romance" ([1905] 1991, 224, emphasis added). In Paul's mobile fantasy, this moment should make him a "queen of Romance" as well. What's striking about this paragraph, however, is how Paul's yearning to be somebody enables him to become nobody. Again losing himself, he also retreats from his surveyed self as he marvels at the diva: he "forgot" pressing realities and "gave himself up." Enraptured by her "stimulus," the boy does not identify with her even though the narrator details the diva's body. From a few brief clauses, we learn the singer's defining traits—her nationality, her age, and her rather reproductive body—traits that differentiate her from the lanky adolescent. Yet while the narrator corporealizes the diva, what holds Paul's gaze is her aura, her "world-shine." His male gaze neither objectifies nor commodifies this female body. It provides a transient look—a sightseeing—that fixates on one body to move beyond sexual identifications. Within this theatrical world, Paul desires ambiance instead of persons. More content looking on than being looked at, "what he wanted was to see, to be in the atmosphere" (228).

While it might be tempting to read this starstruck moment as a supreme instance of gay cross-identification, it is important to realize that the stage queen, like the stage entrance, is a "portal of Romance" for the adolescent.[31] Tramping through another's body, Paul does not desire to be the diva. He instead desires the "indefinable" aura that surrounds her. "He was not stage struck—not, at any rate, in the usual acceptation of that expression. He had no desire to become an actor, any more than he had to become a musician." Contrary to most historical accounts, Carnegie Hall's symphonic harmonies do not merely enhance one's class identity or elevate one's cultural capital.[32] Inspiring fantasies and "fairy land[s]," they instead promote a deindividuating experience, an incognito slumming outside the boy's present history. A German woman becomes a queen. An adolescent loses himself in the moment. A body whose clothes once spoke volumes now becomes a body that is nothing but splendid surface. And when his teachers and his father and Cather's readers look for this "indefinable" lost boy later in the story, they will quickly find that there is no there there.

Slumming on Park Avenue

Then there were—and are—those citizens of New York City for whom invisibility was a way of life. —Luc Sante, *Low Life*

But what happens when Paul is denied access to this theatrical world? Once again, the adolescent scoffs at his teachers, and "the upshot of the matter was that the Principal went to Paul's father, and Paul was taken out of school and put to work" ([1905] 1991, 229). Paul is also barred from entering Carnegie Hall; and his pal Charley Edwards agrees never again to communicate with his most dedicated fan. Denied the fantastic bohemian life in which he achieved, for a few moments, an unproductive mobility, the boy does what Hall and Nordau imagine all adolescent boys to do. He follows his wandering tendencies and tramps forever from the home. But the trick to Cather's revisions is that the lad's queer mobility does not take him into the streets or the tramping fields, like his namesake Verlaine, but into one of the nation's most elite locales—the Waldorf-Astoria.

By the turn-of-the-century, residential hotels such as the Waldorf-Astoria pockmarked the nation's major cities and had become major talking points in the daily press. As Paul notes when he thinks about "his scrap book at home," "there were pages of description about New York hotels, cut from the Sunday papers" ([1905] 1991, 230). Combinations of permanent living and temporary respite, such residential hotels were fixtures in most major metropoles. *Sister Carrie* aside, hostelries such as New York City's Ritz-Carlton, the Tampa Bay Hotel, and San Francisco's Fairmont oftentimes packaged comfort with fantasy. As Catherine Donzel, Alexis Gregory, and Marc Walter note, "Another element characterizing the American Hotel was a sense of fantasy that went far beyond anything conceived in Europe" (1989, 15). Within these "fantasyland[s]," well-off Americans found the creature comforts of the white bourgeois homestead—running water, bath towels, single beds—alongside vicarious adventures. Indeed, hotel residents could experience the novel sensation of being both homebound and homeless as hostelries offered their residents simulated exotic worlds such as Glacier Park's canopied lobby, the Ponce de Leon's Moorish palace, and, of course, the Caesar's Grand Palace in Las Vegas (Donzel et al. 1989, 15).

A novel relational form opposed to life in the middle-class suburbs complemented these escapist fantasies that hostelries provided. As sociologist Norman S. Hayner (a student of Robert E. Park at the University of Chicago) writes in one of the first full-length studies of hotel life: "The personal hospitable contact between landlord and guest in the inns and taverns of the past has been replaced by impersonality and standardized correctness. The huge hostelries of our great cities have all the comforts and luxuries that science can devise, but they have lost . . . the friendly individuality of an earlier day" (1936, 1). Unlike intimate early nineteenth-century hostelries, early twentieth-century hotel living depersonalizes. Nobody knows your name in the hostelry, and the personal interaction that characterized the tavern or the homes on Cordelia Street is absent. Individuals instead come and go as they like with minimal knowledge of each other. Leading transient lives, each inhabitant of a room is also a modern-day tramp, an incognito vagabond outside the social but embedded within it.

In "Paul's Case," the Waldorf-Astoria functions similarly, but with a twist. Renowned for housing and serving the best of the best, the Waldorf permits deindividuating experiences amid a group of like white elites. As historian Lloyd Morris remarks, "It was the mission of the Waldorf-Astoria to bring exclusiveness to the masses" (1951, 235). Paul intuits this when he flees, moneybags in hand, for the Waldorf Hotel after stealing over a thousand dollars from his theater manager. Arriving in New York City in the middle of the night, he checks into the hotel, sleeps, and spends the remainder of the next day shopping at Tiffany's and "buying with endless reconsidering and great care" ([1905] 1991, 230). Dressed to the nines, "hot for pleasure," and astounded at the spectacle before him, the boy realizes that he has achieved the burgher's dreams (232). He has entered into "the plot of all dramas, the text of all romances, the nerve-stuff of all sensations" (232) to become a literal mystery of New York.

On entering into this fantastic Romance, Paul does not become its main protagonist, even though he goes "slowly about the corridors, through the writing-rooms, smoking-rooms, reception-rooms, as though he were exploring the chambers of an enchanted palace, built and peopled for him alone" ([1905] 1991, 232). The "nerve stuff" of slumming fiction, that is, impedes this adolescent male's degeneration into a crime-ridden pervert. Slumming on Park Avenue, he instead hides, as Irving Berlin suggests some do, behind a pair of fancy clothes to render himself a tramping spectator of modern hotel life. To play on Thorstein Veblen's *The Theory of the Leisure Class* (1899), here clothes unmake the perverse adolescent in a supreme instance of inconspicuous consumption:

> He was not in the least abashed or lonely. He had no especial desire to meet or know any of these people; all he demanded was the right to look on and conjecture, to watch the pageant. The mere stage properties were all he contended for. Nor was he lonely later in the evening, in his loge at the Metropolitan. He was now entirely rid of his nervous misgivings, of his forced aggressiveness, of the imperative desire to show himself different from his surroundings. He felt now that his surroundings explained him. Nobody questioned the purple; he had

> only to wear it passively. He had only to glance down at his attire to reassure himself that here it would be impossible for anyone to humiliate him. (233)

Paul's heart-breaking pleasure in sightseeing—his desperate hotel gaze—rids him of his perversity, his particular sexual identity. At the Walfdorf-Astoria, there is no need for the "double life" that characterized his Pittsburgh days; there is no need to hide because the adolescent is unrecognizable. The boy is no longer spectacularized: "Nobody questioned the purple." And he is no longer a neurotic, epistemological threat to the symbolic codes that structure turn-of-the-century middle-class sexual life. He loses his nerves, his insolence, and his temperament, which is also to say that he loses his self and his sexual identity on merging into this fantastic scene. Within this tramp-slumming space, questions, inquiries, detection, and surveillance vanish. Whether Paul is or is not—the central question posed at the beginning of the story and the central question of closet logic—simply does not matter. There is no need for dissimulation, forgery, or impertinence because the boy transfigures himself into a tableau vivant. He is so melded into this scene that, like the tramp, he fades into the people and the cityscape, and in this mobile indeterminacy, "the person as an object of cultural surveillance almost disappears" (Bersani 1995, 145).

No longer a case history, Paul's situation now functions as a prime instance of a short story *démeublé*, whereby the central character transfigures himself into the thing not named and becomes a social experiment in luxury. The boy's obsession with spectacle and sensation again thrusts him into a slumming venture that again moves him beyond the sensational narratives of homosexual identity and what cultural critic Dick Hebdige has elsewhere termed "spectacular subcultures" ([1979] 2002, 97). "He needed only the spark, the indescribable thrill that made his imagination master of his senses," readers are told, "and he could make plots and pictures enough of his own" ([1905] 1991, 228). Like Crane's tramp, he too is a "wanderer in a fairy land," yet his experiment in luxury distances him from—rather than enables him to present—any trace of social commentary. No longer an open secret of the great city, he instead becomes one of its lost children.

And throughout this dangerous tramp crossing, Paul continues his investment in anticommunal contact. He has no desire to "meet or know any of these people" and his is not an invasive gesture. Even though he "fell in" with a young San Francisco Yalie to embrace a "champagne friendship," he does not forge a cross-identification with any of the Waldorf's residents ([1905] 1991, 233). Nor does he desire intimacy with any of their elite circles. Rather, the boy wants "to sightsee where the high-toned people are," to observe without participating. Sedgwick reads this climactic moment as a conciliatory gesture on Cather's behalf. "By identifying with what seems to be Paul's sexuality not in spite of but *through* its saving reabsorption in a gender-liminal (and very specifically classed) artifice that represents at once a particular subculture and culture itself," Cather forges a bond with the boy and expels Wildean perversion from her mannishly lesbian body (1993b, 171). This now-standard reading can be augmented by several key factors. First, though the scene is specifically class-based, the Waldorf-Astoria's elitist decor and clientele are desired by much of the white middle class. While racially segregated, the hotel was often exclusive without excluding white customers. Second, Paul's access to the Waldorf-Astoria permits him to move beyond the bounds of both a particularly queer subculture and a heteronormative mainstream culture. As I have been arguing, the boy uses middle-class prescriptions to push him past communal and subcultural forms all together. Tramping into this elite enclave, Paul becomes an antisocial body, one who "was not in the least abashed or lonely." And third, the moment he merges into the hotel scene, Paul undoes his sexual case history; his body no longer connotes or denotes. Nobody questions the purple, and nobody questions him. Conspicuously inconspicuous, the adolescent is far more interested in depersonalizing aesthetics than in categorizing his body sexually as he stages what Lauren Berlant and Elizabeth Freeman have elsewhere termed a "queer counterspectacle" (1997, 170). "There was this to be said for him, that he wore his spoils with dignity and in no way made himself conspicuous" (233).

Capitalism and the Erasure of Gay Identity

> Who can best represent life as a chaos, and win the wreaths we have to offer? . . . We may finally find it in the honest homosexual view of life—that sincerely tragic point of view from which all those institutions and efforts and romantic hopes and ideals which center about heterosexual love are utterly meaningless. Our Tramp's Progress leads ultimately to this.
> —Floyd Dell, *Intellectual Vagabondage*

Like Addams and her Hull-House cohorts, Paul momentarily escapes early twentieth-century disciplinary regimes of homosexual affiliation when he wines and dines at the New York hostelry, even as he unfortunately supports regimes of racial and socioeconomic segregation. And like the philanthropic slummer, Paul, too, gravitates toward spectacle as a means of avoiding spectacularization. Within the Waldorf-Astoria's glittery showcase of furnished rooms, the self-eviscerating lad finds "a mobile, anonymous, individual world, a world of thwarted wishes, of unsatisfied longings, of constant restlessness"; here, "behavior is impulsive rather than social. It is a world of atomized individuals, of spiritual nomads" (Zorbaugh 1929, 86). Though Paul finds a locale where he fits in, he is also, like Anderson's juvenile tramp, far removed from communal or subculture identifications (and far removed from Wilde's hotel excursions though he signifies on them). Indeed, the nomadic adolescent discovers on his slumming venture that queerness is not an individualized stylization of life that grounds subversive counter publics. Surveying his surroundings, the wandering adolescent perceives instead that queerness can move one beyond identifications, that queerness might be defined as company rather than affiliation, that queerness functions as a situated dislocation that is also a sexual dissolution. Or, as Hayner puts it when he connects the life of the tramping hobo to the transient life of the hostelry resident: "In the metropolitan hotel the guest is only a number" (1936, 1).

But perhaps the central irony of a story abounding in ironies is that it takes economic capital—and a heap of unspoken white male privilege—to become this digit. Wayne Koestenbaum finds that "because opera in 'Paul's Case' is expensive, he needs money to be gay. Without an income, he can't participate in the aristocratic milieu of opera queendom, and must kill himself" (1993, 29). While I find that Paul's trek to the Waldorf-Astoria does not stem from his desire to join a nascent subculture of aristocratic queers, Koestenbaum's claim that economic capital structures nascent gay U.S. subcultures repeats now-standard historiographies of homosexuality that Cather's story disrupts. In his classic account of homosexuality's urban emergence, historian John D'Emilio (1993) posits that Anglo-American homosexual subcultures in the urban United States did not materialize until certain socioeconomic conditions arose during the first quarter of the twentieth century. Specifically, D'Emilio refers to rampant industrialization, urbanization, the rise of a leisure class, and the advent of free labor facilitating the breakdown of the family structure. "Only when *individuals* began to make their living through wage labor," D'Emilio argues, "instead of as parts of an interdependent family unit, was it possible for homosexual desire to coalesce into a personal identity—an identity based on the ability to remain outside the heterosexual family and to construct a personal life based on one's attraction to one's own sex" (1993, 470). The irony of Paul's case, however, is that Paul uses capital to render himself a mobile incognito at the dawn of the homosexual's historical emergence into U.S. public spheres. When the bohemian tramp takes the money and runs to the Waldorf-Astoria, stolen suburban wage labor releases him from the imperatives of having a discernible—hence, controllable—middle-class sexual identity. Hyper-consumer capitalism distances the boy from technologies of turn-of-the-century sexuality organizing both adolescent perversion within the family and nascent homosexual subcultures outside of it. A smart shopper, Paul refuses a now-standard gay migration into developing urban subcultures, and he may be one of the first fictions in American literatures to use cultural materials to push himself past the designs of U.S. sexual history. In this case, white middle-class consumption leads to the erasure of a discernible white middle-class gay male identity, the "nerve-stuff" of a sensational fiction.

Through this bohemian slumming narrative, Paul becomes faceless and unidentifiable. He moves past regimes of sexual surveillance and finds himself beyond queer visibility. While he "wore his spoils with dignity," he presents an identity that he spoils, not a spoiled identity.[33] As a matter of fact, when the money runs out Paul takes his disappearing act to such an extreme that he kills himself, merging, once and for all, into the "immense design of things" ([1905] 1991, 236). While this culminating melodrama can be mourned, it is also clear that Paul has again reworked spectacular sensation. He does anything and everything that he can to avoid becoming the sensational case history that he was in the tale's beginning: "He wanted . . . to be carried out, blue league after blue league," we are told, "away from everything" (228). And when the tramp boy throws himself in front of a fast-moving train, he continues this habit of self-divestiture, a public erasure also located in paintings, operatic divas, exotic middle-class underworld fantasies, and hostelries. You might then best read this "losing game" not only as a riposte to the repressive heteronormative climate that was Cordelia Street but also as a liberating moment in his successful attempt to push himself past middle-class classificatory regimes as he again shirks becoming "local news of a sensational nature" (234). Just as one form of vice—theft—distances him from the nameless vice that marks his tramp body in the story's beginning, so too does another novel form of mobility—the commuter train—render him indeterminate in the story's end.[34]

In so doing, a lost boy becomes as lost to U.S. lesbian and gay history as Addams and, it follows, to an archive where we might find him again. Like Cather's tacit disavowal of William, Jr., Paul's adolescent "early state" is erased from any cultural record. Transfiguring his escapist tramp tale into that of a vanishing American, he becomes, to quote bohemian Floyd Dell, "utterly meaningless," a subject outside of critical inquiry, and a prototype for later Catherian characters that lose themselves by tramping into so-called empty landscapes and so-called primitive locales. The dandified adolescent tramp's progress in this warped slumming literature thus leads to this: a company of queer transients who fit in nowhere and everywhere and whose slumming selves are placed yet dislocated elsewhere. It is this Verlainesque art of escapism—an escapism through art—that a muckraking Cather refined throughout her writings until the 1940s. It is an aesthetic creed that other bohemians of the 1920s and the 1930s, like her acquaintance Carl Van Vechten and his acquaintances Richard Bruce Nugent and Wallace Thurman, would later probe in New York City. It is these partygoers—and some of the most explosive queer slumming of their time—to which I now turn.

CHAPTER THREE

"Slightly Known Territory": Renaissance Admixture and the So-Called Van Vechten School

One of the most conceited things I can say is that I have never shaken that rascal's hand. . . . He corrupted the Harlem Renaissance and was a terrible influence on them. He was a voyeur. He was looking at these Negroes and they were acting the fools for him. And the foolisher they acted, the more he recorded them. —Sterling Brown

A Caucasian Storms Harlem

It is hard to take seriously Carl Van Vechten's queer slumming, but I ask you to do just this. Prior to his controversial participation in the Harlem (New Negro) Renaissance, the transatlantic bohemian's "weird six-foot presence seemed to be everywhere" (Lewis [1979] 1997, 182). Throughout the 1890s he affiliated with the Chicago regionalists. In prewar Greenwich Village he frequented bohemian salons. At the dawn of the Jazz Age he visited with Parisian expatriates. An extremely mobile modern, Van Vechten was also lauded as a New York dilettante whose wide-ranging literary connections were matched by substantial literary achievements. In the first half of the 1920s he forged intimate and professional ties with Willa Cather, Charles Demuth, Alfred A. Knopf, F. Scott Fitzgerald, Langston Hughes, Rudolph Fisher, Nella Larsen, Max Ewing, James Weldon Johnson, Mabel Dodge Luhan, and Gertrude Stein, among others.[1] Touted for his wit, his jazz and blues criticism, his decadent novels, and his encyclopedic history of cats, he was also praised for his rediscovery of Herman Melville's South Pacific tales and his successful attempts to secure an American publisher for British aesthete Ronald Firbank.

This generous public image shattered following the appearance of his 1926 slumming narrative *Nigger Heaven*, a novel whose title was intended as a biting satire of "white participation in Harlem" (Mumford 1997, 144). In the months preceding *Nigger Heaven*'s publication, Van Vechten had become something of a Harlem fixture. He and his second wife, actress Fania Marinoff, hosted open-invitation interracial parties. Van Vechten frequented Harlem cabarets on an almost nightly basis. He judged the annual Hamilton Ball Lodge drag shows. He urged Knopf and his wife Blanche to publish Langston Hughes's first collection of poems, *The Weary Blues* (1926b). Given the de facto segregation laws that structured many urban race relations during the 1920s, this racial intermingling was mentioned—yet by no means admired—in major black and white papers. In a 1925 society page brief, for instance, *Time* found that "sullen-mouthed, silky-haired Author Van Vechten has been playing with Negroes lately, writing prefaces for their poems, having them around the house, going to Harlem" (quoted in Watson 1995, 99). And in the winter of 1926, *Vanity Fair* artist Miguel Covarrubias published a caricature of Van Vechten as a black male entitled, not surprisingly, "A Prediction."

Immediately after Knopf released *Nigger Heaven*, magazines and journals such as *Crisis* and *Opportunity* denounced Van Vechten as a slumming profiteer, a sleazy Nordic who appropriated a stigmatized minority culture for his own profit. According to Hughes, "Mr. Van Vechten became the goat of the New Negro Renaissance, the he-who-gets-slapped. The critics of the left, like the Negroes of the right, proceeded to light on Mr. Van Vechten, and he was accused of ruining, distorting, polluting, and corrupting every Negro writer from then on" (1940, 271). Though the bulk of *Nigger Heaven*'s narrative focused on the failed romance between two middle-class blacks, these critics—most notably W. E. B. DuBois, Countee Cullen, Jessie Fauset, and Sterling Brown—were infuriated by the novel's "exotic" opening and closing nightlife scenes as well as its titular slur.[2] In their caustic diatribes, they objected that Van Vechten's literary slumming wrecked their endeavors to foster positive images of the black community and only enhanced the cult of primitivism that drew numerous white middle-class slummers to Harlem's cabarets during what Bruce Kellner sees as "the white craze for slumming in black speakeasies during what was then called the 'negro renaissance'" (2000, 119).[3]

Yet faulty race representation, as Hughes notes in his retrospect, was not Van Vechten's sole vice. He was also too friendly. Adding insult to perceived injury, critics such as Brown denounced the author as a "terrible influence" that queered New Negroes such as Langston Hughes, Wallace Thurman, and Richard Bruce Nugent, young writers who, like Van Vechten, enhanced their careers (and the New Negro Renaissance) with artistic forays into Harlem's underworld. As one Pittsburgh critic lamented, "With Van Vechten's 'Nigger Heaven' as their cue . . . , the younger writers flock to a Parnassus, which proved not to be the abode of muses but merely the bizarre den of the sensational and the salacious" (Jacobs 1928, n.p.). Charged with spoiling young men and overseeing a "bizarre den," the author is also accused of homosexual perversion. In my epigraph, Brown refuses to touch Van Vechten for fear of sexual contamination, and his rhetoric casts the white slummer as a gay pederast whose scandalous friendships fed off and fed into the wayward Negro writings that helped to constitute the latter half of the Harlem Renaissance.

In fact, Brown's claim that Van Vechten was a "terrible influence" on the male New Negro not only expresses sexual disgust for the author but also for the literary output that his writings inspired and accompanied. Unlike, say, the bourgeois realism of Fauset's *There Is Confusion* (1924), the closeted psychological melodramas of Nella Larsen (herself an avid Van Vechten enthusiast), or the masculinist folk paeans of Brown's *Southern Road* (1932), the artists of what Brown tried to dismiss as "Van Vechten's school" published sensational materials that failed to conform to a squeaky-clean image of the Negro community ([1937] 1978, 146).[4] Hughes, for one, not only contributed jazz poems to *Nigger Heaven*. He would go on to depict scenes of racially mixed Harlem nightlife with experimental works such as "Café: 3 A.M." ([1951] 1995), a poem that records the confusing identifications to be found in a dive bar:

> Detectives from the vice squad
> with weary sadistic eyes
> spotting fairies.
>   Degenerates,
>   some folks say
> . . .
> Police lady or Lesbian
> over there?
>   "*Where?*"
> (406)

To the shock of Harlem's older literati, in the winter of 1926 Hughes's friend Nugent published "Smoke, Lilies, and Jade: A Novel, Part I" (2002c), a stream-of-consciousness ode to interracial same-sex cruising that DuBois publicly vowed to throw in the trash. And Thurman became the Harlem Renaissance's gadfly with his interracial roman-à-clef, *Infants of the Spring* ([1932] 1992), a novel that infuriated New Negro mentor Alain Locke.

Given these inflammatory writings, one cannot—and should not—deny that Van Vechten delved into the sensationally primitive and that no doubt he profited from what Lewis Erenberg, in a memorable phrase, terms "the apotheosis of slumming" (1981, 256). *Nigger Heaven* went through fourteen printings in five years, sold over one hundred thousand copies, and became a popular tourist guidebook for whites and blacks interested in imbibing Harlem's underworld nightlife. That an appropriating Van Vechten and his *Nigger Heaven* supplemented an ongoing strain of New Negro writing beyond exploitation is a far riskier, though by no means outlandish, claim to consider. Discussing Van Vechten near the end of his life, Nugent once stated that, "in his usual fey way . . . he was remarkable. He was one of the few people I know who could have his mind go in two directions at the same time—the manipulative part and the feeling part" (2002b, 228). A recently published anthology of their letters (Bernard 2001) suggests that Hughes maintained an intimate friendship with Van Vechten throughout the *Nigger Heaven* controversy and well into the fifties.[5] Likewise, though he questioned the novel's artistic merits, in a *Fire!!* editorial Thurman also cited *Nigger Heaven* for how it troubled the norms of "group criticism," a strategy that Thurman, too, would consider in *Infants of the Spring* ([1926] 2003b, 194). And in 1950, George S. Schuyler proclaimed that "a great revolution has taken place in American race relations in the past quarter century, and while this phenomenon is ascribed to many causes by various authorities on the subject, perhaps the most prepotent has been the individual effort of Carl Van Vechten" (1950, 362). Yet despite this praise, recent scholars of twentieth-century African-American literary history have neglected to note that Van Vechten's friendly intermingling informed new conceptions of racial and sexual relations far removed from the communal imperatives that grounded certain strains of the Harlem Renaissance.[6] Like Brown, they hate touching him. As Emily Bernard contends, Van Vechten's detractors "ignore the fact that many black authors used Van Vechten and his work to further their own ends, and they thus obscure his most important contribution to the movement, which was not material but symbolic" (1997, 533).

Let's begin to uncover these various "symbolic" contributions by examining Van Vechten's response to an ongoing symposium by DuBois, "The Negro in Art: How Shall He Be Portrayed?" in the periodical *Crisis: A Record of the Darker Races*, a response written several months prior to *Nigger Heaven*'s publication (1926). Though the symposium's title suggests that the question of racial representation was open-ended (and it certainly was throughout the twenties and the thirties), several leading Harlem Renaissance thinkers did dictate how artists should depict the Negro race. Despite their intense ideological differences, Harlem Renaissance elders such as DuBois and Locke both sought to cultivate affirmative communal ideals in their upstanding talented tenth, ideals that they hoped would direct the aesthetic productions of younger artists. Throughout his community studies and his aesthetic proclamations, DuBois insisted that Negro art promote public, socially acceptable images of a black race, and his manifesto "Criteria for Negro Art" was no exception (Lewis [1979] 1997, 178). "All art is propaganda and ever must be," he contends, "despite the wailing of the purists. I stand in utter shamelessness and say that whatever art I have for writing has been used always for propaganda for gaining the right of black folk to love and enjoy" ([1926] 1994a, 103). Yet if Negro art is to gain the black folk joyous freedom, DuBois insists that it must have a prescriptive recipe. The racial artist, that is, must renounce pure aesthetic freedom in order to gain sociopolitical or cultural freedom. For DuBois, the New Negro artist must create exemplary works that portray the race kindly, and, it follows, the artist must stand in for the community as a whole.[7]

Similarly, Locke's New Negroes were also to become paragons of an imagined black community. Through aesthetics, Locke assumes, the New Negro will overturn the Uncle Tom stereotype once and for all. And "with this renewed self-respect and self-dependence, the life of the Negro community is bound to enter a new dynamic phase.... From this comes the promise and warrant of a new leadership" (1925, 631). Drawing on the theories of John Dewey, colleague of Josiah Royce and Jane Addams, both of whom advocated ideals of a great provincial community, Locke focuses primarily on "the life of the Negro community" and the "warrant of new leadership" as a sufficient means to political activism.[8] Presenting Harlem not as a sensational ghetto but as a phantasmatic communal ideal and a diasporic hub, he argues that New Negro writing will give "a person a sense of belonging, paradoxically allowing him to develop his own unique personality within the protective shade of a common ethos" (Scruggs 1987, 166).

Yet despite his focus on individualistic aesthetics, Locke, like DuBois, nevertheless assumes that Negro artists and "Negro group psychology" will be subsumed under the umbrella of a transnational communitarian project. "The program of the Negro Renaissance," Locke would go on to assert, "was a wholesome, vigorous, assertive racialism.... Negro writers must become truer sons of the people, more loyal providers of spiritual bread and less aesthetic wastrels and truants of the streets" (1937, 85). Centered in Harlem where individuals "discover one another," Locke's program becomes a group project for the benefit of "black people," one that utilizes "the sub-soil of native materials" (1928, 12) and one that, many felt, those linked together as the Van Vechten school were quick to disparage.[9]

They were right to think so. Van Vechten had informed Locke that he was suspicious about "group thinking" (quoted in Scruggs 1987, 165), and his response to DuBois's "How Shall He Be Portrayed" continues to probe the "protective shade" of communal ethos—racial, sexual, or otherwise.[10] The inquiry presented the author with a series of questions that centered on a desire for realistic and redemptive (read, middle class) versions of black community. I present a few pertinent to my larger argument:

1. When the artist, black or white, portrays Negro characters is he under any obligations or limitations as to the sort of character he will portray?
2. Can any author be criticized for painting the worst or the best characters of a group?...
6. Is not the continual portrayal of the sordid, foolish and criminal among Negroes convincing the world that this and this alone is really and essentially Negroid, and preventing white artists from knowing any other types and preventing black artists from daring to paint them?
7. Is there not a real danger that young colored writers will be tempted to follow the popular trend in portraying Negro character in the underworld rather than seeking to paint the truth about themselves and their own social class? (DuBois 1926, 219)

Van Vechten's reply to these inquiries regarding literary slumming reveal much about his desire to disturb the group thinking that initially guided Harlem Renaissance output: "I am fully aware of the reasons why Negroes are sensitive in regard to fiction which attempts to picture the lower strata of the race. The point is that this is an attitude completely inimical to art" (219). Van Vechten then reinterprets the questions at hand. "The question is," he asks, "Are Negro writers going to write about this exotic material while it is still fresh or will they continue to make a free gift of it to white authors who will exploit it until not a drop of vitality remains?" (219).

What's most interesting about his remarks is neither the undeniable fact that a slumming Van Vechten went on to exploit this vitally "fresh" material nor his assumption that exoticism is also a form of realism but, rather, the lack of moral censure that surrounds his reference to primitive representation and "the underworld." He refuses to view any aspect of black culture as a form of cultural property that will benefit either genteel Negroes or the working-class folk.[11] Instead, he thinks through similar communal quandaries that gnawed at Hughes in "The Negro Artist and the Racial Mountain" (1926a), and he invites New Negro "artists of the world" to join him in a cosmopolitan avant-garde that demolishes genteel modes of racial representation at the expense of the Harlem Renaissance's communal project (1926, 219). To do so, the artist—not only the Negro artist—uses racial material to shun racial group imperatives. Or, as another iconoclastic respondent to the symposium, H. L. Mencken, writes in a follow-up to Van Vechten's reply, "The artist is under no obligations or limitations whatsoever" (1926, 219). Here "exotic material" such as underworld scenes functions as a paradox. It is a departure from—rather than the epitome of—either the fetishization of racial groups or the prescriptive demand to "paint the truth about" the Negro type. Van Vechten's slumming intervention, that is, disrupts the Harlem Renaissance's central project of making the Negro community legibly redemptive. In its place, he argues for an artistic movement free from communal imperatives, a decadent movement neither black, nor white, nor both.

If this is the case, we can begin to ask how Van Vechten's so-called corruption of racial and sexual boundaries offers an alternative version of the underworld and produces an alternative version of mainstream gay slumming. Though literary critics and historians of U.S. sexuality have explored the visible gay and lesbian subcultures that emerged within and alongside the Harlem Renaissance, Van Vechten and his supposed "bizarre den" did not affirm "a sense of queerness [or race] as a *communal affiliation*" (Boone 1998, 210). Nor did these writers necessarily foster counter public modes of belonging, "where," according to Michael Warner, "a dominated group aspires to re-create itself as a public" and attempts to overturn the dominant culture's norms (2002, 112).[12] Using their "exotic material" to disrupt the Harlem Renaissance's earlier tenets, and refusing to shy away from "the sensational and the salacious," they questioned

Harlem Renaissance imperatives for a distinct minoritarian communality and advanced an alternate model of sociality removed from uplifting racial and sexual propaganda. I term this model queer admixture to emphasize how it refuses—even under the guise of realism—the epistemological imperative to paint the truth of racial or sexual group formations. Such a model, I show, rests on seemingly exotic transnational and interracial scenes advanced through slumming as well as integrated parties and involves, like Cather's tramping, an ideal of anticommunitarian contact beyond the boundaries of sexual—and here racial—gatekeeping of any sort.

To support these claims, I focus on the tight interconnections between Van Vechten's slumming narratives *Nigger Heaven* and *Parties* ([1930] 1977), and the contributions that Newer Negroes such as Wallace Thurman and Nugent made alongside these disruptive texts. Rather than upholding a Harlem Renaissance–inspired will-to-community, these writers, I suggest, affirmed a loose model of friendship promoted through queer admixture, one that renders communities incognito. I elaborate more on these threatening relations when I turn to the Van Vechten school's fictitious queer mixers as well as the integrated slumming parties that Van Vechten hosted and that Nugent discusses in interviews and "Smoke, Lilies, and Jade" (2002c). But first, I examine further Van Vechten's disdain for group formations to show how his slumming scenes, in tandem with other Newer Negro writings, short-circuits the sociological concept of affirmative minority community, as well as disrupts the celebrated artistic concept of Negro group psychology.

The Signifying Slummer

Bardacious: marvellous. —Van Vechten, "Glossary of Negro Words and Phrases"

In one of *Nigger Heaven*'s many laudatory reviews, George S. Schuyler finds that "physicians, bootleggers, lawyers, pimps, gamblers, dentists, prostitutes, hairdressers, school teachers, and vendors of stolen goods, all rub shoulders. It is often difficult to tell which is which" (1926, 14). A meld of Harlem's stratified social classes, this confusing occupational admixture also includes the fusion of middle-class blacks slumming in working-class dives, professional blacks passing as professional whites slumming in cabarets, and slumming heterosexuals mistaken for slumming homosexuals. At one point in the book an unidentified "voice" remarks, "Look at duh spagingy-spagade [a Nordic] talkin' wid duh fagingy-fagade [a Negro]." Another anonymous voice replies, "Out fo' a little hootchie-pap, Ah *pre*-sume" (208). Both visual observations are then proven incorrect in their attempts to properly identify between black and white as well as heterosexual and homosexual bodies. The novel, in short, is something of an epistemological wreck. It is also something of a complete joke when it comes to identifying disparate populations.

Such glaring racial and sexual misrecognitions could be considered one version of what Siobhan Somerville terms "queering the color line" (2000), and they stand in stark contrast to the rigid border crossings that jumpstart any standard leisurely slumming venture. For Schuyler, at least, these improbable relations are anything but standard as they occur throughout the urban geographies of Van Vechten's slumming literature: in the streets, in cabarets, in apartments, at parties, and even in the professional offices of Manhattan's literary elite. While no character or reader leaves the narrative's parody unscathed, the novel aims its satirical darts at those who refuse to mingle with others and uphold a segregated communal ideal. As Helen, one of the novel's lampooned genteel Negroes, states during a mixed race, interclass gathering, "Why there, she exclaimed, is that awful Randolph Pettijohn. In Washington we never had mixed parties like this!" ([1926] 2000, 154). Helen detests the "awful" Pettijohn because he is a pimp and a sheik, and he has the audacity to circulate with the black upper middle class. Strongly opposed to the racial, sexual, and socioeconomic mixture that surrounds her, the socialite charges, "People like that would never be received in Washington. Society is so mixed here" (155). Unlike Helen's blue-veined Washington or, implicitly, Locke's Mecca of the New Negro, Van Vechten's Harlem tells a different story about contact, one where knowing or forming a minoritarian community or subculture is less important than the unforeseeable encounters that might transpire within—or outside—any of its collective parties.

The controversial reception that met the novel's representations of these mixed Harlem parties exemplifies part of the Van Vechten school's "foolish" central project, which was to mock discourses that made racial and sexual group identities fathomable. In this regard, these artists ignored DuBois's and Locke's sociological desires to make subcultural group formations visible, comprehensible, discreet—hence, knowable. Though the term "subculture" was not coined until the 1940s, early twentieth-century white American sociologists and Renaissance Race Men like DuBois and

Locke had endeavored to delineate the marginal groups that constituted a good portion of the modern U.S. metropolis. Robert E. Park, a founder of the Chicago school of sociology and a profound influence on Locke, termed these ethnic and sexualized zones "moral regions" in his seminal work *The City* ([1915] 1997): "Fifty years ago every village had one or two eccentric characters who were treated ordinarily with a benevolent toleration, but who were regarded meanwhile as impracticable and queer. These exceptional individuals lived an isolated existence, cut off by their very eccentricities, whether of genius or of defect, from genuinely intimate intercourse with their fellows.... In the city many of these divergent types now find a milieu [or 'moral region'] in which, for good or for ill, their dispositions and talents parturiate and bear fruit" (26). Though Park makes no mention of sexual perversion in his analysis of these "moral regions," his references to impracticality, queerness, eccentricity, "defect," normative divergence, and "dispositions" repeat dominant stereotypes of the homosexual (and the Negro body) circulating within turn-of-the-century sexological discourses. Park's perverse inferences become even more explicit when he elaborates where, exactly, these sites can be found. Following his cryptic account of queer migrations into the city, he asks his fellow sociologists, "What are the external facts in regard to the life in Bohemia, the half-world, the red-light district, and other 'moral regions' less pronounced in character?" ([1915] 1997, 26). As I noted in my first chapter, the urban red-light district, like bohemian enclaves such as Harlem and Greenwich Village, was thought to be saturated with deviant prostitution and sexual perversion, a perversion exacerbated by middle-class fears of sustained cross-race, cross-class interaction. By making such urban sites into facts of serious analytical investigation, Park presents the city's mysterious—"less pronounced"—zones as communities that can be categorized, interpreted, surveyed, policed, and, fundamentally, known. In so doing, he recasts Progressive Era literatures of exposure into a new scientific discipline that "justifies the view that would make of the city a laboratory or a clinic in which human nature and social processes may be conveniently and profitably studied" (27). The sociologist, that is, becomes an objective slummer into the "eccentric" subcultures that, by sighting them, makes them so. Or, as Marlon Ross has suggested, "One could go so far as to say that [Park's] professionalization as a sociologist depended on his ability to transform [his] erotic curiosity and fleshly attraction to the mysterious other into an abstract problem of sociological method" (2004, 241).

As I claimed earlier, certain voices within the Harlem Renaissance, too, proselytized the Negro in similar subcultural terms. Before, during, and after the institutionalization of the Chicago school, Harlem intelligentsia such as DuBois and Locke complemented "the Park School model" to present the public with kinder, gentler versions of the black race (Mumford 1997, 138). For DuBois (once an assistant instructor in sociology at the University of Pennsylvania and later chairman of Atlanta University's sociology department), such racial re-presentations were offered under the now-familiar catchphrase "talented tenth." For Locke, they appeared as "the New Negro." In his introduction to a March 1925 *Survey Graphic* issue (revised and reproduced that same year in the anthology *The New Negro: An Interpretation*), Locke states that "The Sociologist, The Philanthropist, the Race-Leader are not unaware of the New Negro, but they are at a loss to account for him. He simply cannot be swathed in their formulae" (1925, 631). Yet despite the Negro's apparent mysteries, Locke, like DuBois, proceeds to meld these unknown racial bodies into his own sociological formula of aestheticized racial uplift, "race cooperation," and moral-region building. "[The New Negro] must know himself and be known for precisely what he is," Locke passionately argues. "And for that reason he welcomes the new scientific rather than the old sentimental interest" (632). Like the eccentric types that so fascinate the sociologist (or the sexologist), Negro bodies appear as mysteries that can be known with the proper analytical and epistemological tools. The Negro community, that is, is understood as a marginal group body—a subculture, so to speak—whose "less pronounced" character traits are revealed to dominant culture as wholesome and redemptive.[13]

As my introduction noted, Van Vechten is often thought to traffic in this sociocultural economy of racial and sexual legibility.[14] Critics paint *Nigger Heaven* as a misguided continuation of the New Negro/sociological project, and interpret the slumming literature as an embarrassing hybrid of Progressive Era literature of exposure, sociological/sexological treatise, and subterranean tour guide. David Levering Lewis finds that "from the point of view of racial uplift, *Nigger Heaven* was a colossal fraud in which the depiction of the Talented Tenth in high baroque barely muffled the throb of the tom-tom" ([1979] 1997, 188). In a similar vein, Mumford writes, "Like a standard guidebook, *Nigger Heaven* positions the reader as an outsider in need of guidance; it carefully describes Harlem's institutions and spatial dimensions, employing a kind of sociological realism by layering concrete details of streets, buildings, interiors" (1997,

145). As will become clearer, I do not disagree with these interpretations. Yet given the slumming narrative's supposed emphasis on revelation and cultural intelligibility, I pause when such analyses culminate in the injurious qualities of Van Vechten's sensational material. Echoing Brown and Mumford, for example, Justin Edwards surmises, "Van Vechten is unable to avoid the discursive strategies of eroticisation, voyeurism and taxonomy—all of which contradict his claims of authenticity in favor of contemporary stereotypes" (1999, 182).

Might these discursive misfires be of value? While Edwards persuasively notes that Van Vechten's text contradicts itself at every turn, I would like to add that the book's "colossal fraud" does more than confirm voyeurism, sociological realism, and salacious Negro themes. It strategizes them too. In her introduction to the novel's 2000 edition, Kathleen Pfeiffer argues that *Nigger Heaven* "effectively disguises itself as tawdry sensationalism" (ix). If so, critics might ask how Van Vechten's sloppy text deploys decadent primitivism not to reveal, like the Park school model, what sociologist Charles S. Johnson termed "family secrets" but to shatter the project of authenticity, legibility, and legitimization that was part and parcel of the New Negro Renaissance's communal ideals (quoted in Coleman 1998, 129). Throughout his life and work, some have suggested, the author's textual strategies operate "simultaneously as both critique and exploitation of the economies of surveillance and visuality governing identity aesthetics and politics" (McCoy 1998, par. 2). I supplement this analysis by arguing that Van Vechten exploits "exploitation" in the service of a critique of surveillance, of becoming unintelligible to prying popular or academic audiences.

Such a confusing technique, I note, borrows from wily textual strategies used by Van Vechten's good friend, mentor, and longtime proponent James Weldon Johnson. In his 1927 introduction to the reissue of Johnson's 1912 slumming narrative *The Autobiography of an Ex-Colored Man* (a reissue that Van Vechten convinced Knopf to undertake after he read the work in 1925), Van Vechten remarks, "When I was writing Nigger Heaven I discovered the Autobiography to be an invaluable source-book for the study of Negro psychology" ([1927] 1966, vii). The spectacular joke, however, is that *Autobiography*—with its insider-outsider narration making it an influential prototype for *Nigger Heaven*—offers anything but an insightful account of Negro group psychology. Its sensationalism appears mocking as the Ex-Colored Man informs the curious that "the colored people of this country, in reality, [are] a mystery to the whites"

([1912] 1966, 21). And though the preface to its first edition advertises the text as a *Mystery* into the recesses of a "sphinx"-like Negro life (xii), the incognito narrator transforms "the little tragedies of my life" into a "practical joke on society" (3). While the publishers of *Autobiography*'s first edition (Sherman, French, & Co., with Johnson as ghostwriter) promise that "in these pages it is as though a veil has been drawn aside: the reader is given a view of the inner life of the Negro in America, is initiated into the freemasonry, as it were, of the race," and while the ostensibly white reader is granted "an elevation where he can catch a bird's-eye view of the conflict which is being waged" (xii), the Ex-Colored Man thwarts any desire for more knowledge regarding "gas-light" Negro life (114), given that the tale told is of a successful Nordic professional—a "privileged spectator of [the Negro's] inner life"—passing and slumming into a variety of black cultural spaces with which he no longer affiliates (210). Or, as Brent Hayes Edwards concludes, "The sensationalism has been inverted, in other words—the book offers not the thrill of access to a 'veiled' world, but the threat of incomprehension" (2003, 41). Which is also to say that one shouldn't trust a word that the Ex-Colored Man, or Johnson, or, by proxy, Van Vechten has to say about what "a study of Negro psychology" really amounts to or what this sensational realism really authenticates.

Rather than presenting a close reading of *Nigger Heaven* that would confirm how useless this book is as a realistic study guide, I concentrate on the novel's confusing paratextual strategies that confound knowledge regarding minority subculture. To do so, I focus on the slang and the promotional hype that partially accounted for the book's popularity, and contributed to the sensational voyeurism that marks this literary slumming venture. For example: Van Vechten's core strategy—of delving into what counted for primitivism to thwart communal knowledge—was illustrated quite clearly in Knopf's the *Borzoi Broadside* advertisement for *Nigger Heaven*'s first printing, which promised that the sociological slumming narrative would disclose the secrets of an exceptional African-American moral region (fig. 10). In rhetoric that uncannily mirrored *Autobiography*'s 1912 introduction, the promotional blurb on the advertisement claimed that "Carl Van Vechten's novels have assured him of a leading position as a social satirist. He has abandoned that field, completely if perhaps temporarily, to write a novel whose materials are realistic and whose approach is direct and serious. In NIGGER HEAVEN, he analyses the fascinating and inscrutable drama that takes place in the gallery of the vast theatre of New York—from which the white world below can be seen, but which it cannot see." The title of the novel, the ad notes,

FIGURE 10. Knopf's advertisement for Van Vechten's *Nigger Heaven* (August 1926).

alludes to the segregated balcony where Negroes watch theatrical spectacles at safe—and segregated—remove from the whites that sit in the lower tiers. Implicitly, *Nigger Heaven* also refers to the entrenched color line that divides modern Negro and Nordic cultures. Setting up a binary between racial communities that is traversed only with difficulty, the controversial *Nigger Heaven* thus comments on the rampant voyeurism that structures interracial relationships and entices its (white) readership into an acquiescence with salacious material that they have never seen before.

Yet the blurb also works against this epistemological sociology, since the drama that the narrative reveals is "inscrutable." No matter the book's subject matter, the community remains incognito. White (and petit bourgeois black) readers may look inside the book to find the supposed primitive underworld, but in the end, they "cannot see" anything real as they descend—as the advertisement dramatically illustrates—a literary ladder into what appears to be a botched representation of Harlem.[15]

This strategic incomprehension not only marks *Nigger Heaven*'s supposedly "realistic" publication and promotion. It is part and parcel of the novel as a whole. For the first time in American literary history, Van Vechten's slumming narrative purports to shed light on the "exotic material" that is Harlem's marginalized underworld subculture. The novel opens with the spectacle of a strolling Randolph Pettijohn, a Negro sheik "to all who gazed upon him, and all gazed" ([1926] 2000, 3). Intensifying the narrator's seemingly omniscient look, the novel then follows its gaze into sensationalized Negro culture with scenes of catfights, hook-ups, numbers, rampant gambling, obscene parties, drug use, same-sex nightclub shows, and black-and-tan shenanigans. Most critics read these scenes as a corruption—an appropriation—of a minority community, the pollution of the New Negro at the hands of an infamous white slummer. According to Mumford, "Van Vechten seems determined to shock us with black/white sexual situations; he himself indulges in the kind of bohemian exoticism he critiques" (1997, 150).

Yet others, notably Beth McCoy, have suggested that the novel's attention to sociological observation thwarts the sociological gaze into a knowable minoritarian community. "Under questioning, then, the various manifestations of the Van Vechten scene," McCoy writes, "shifted . . . from being 'readable' texts that allegedly produce knowledge (i.e., providing answers to what Van Vechten was doing, what *Nigger Heaven* meant) to ones that are essentially 'unreadable,' ones that perhaps produce only the knowledge or awareness that the reader is looking at Van Vechten looking" (1998, par. 42).[16] Like the theatrical sightseeing mentioned in my second chapter, and like Addams' amnesic autobiography, Van Vechten's literary slumming narrative may prohibit an invasive gaze, one that questions the possibility of ever knowing community. Just as the novel skips from exploitative scenes of Harlem in its introduction to the prim life of librarian Mary Love in part 1, the reader is left uncertain about which social scenes best represent an accurate portrayal of the drama of contemporary Negro urban life.

In fact, the companion guide that purports to explicate Negro life thwarts the careful attention that Van Vechten apparently paid to so-called primitive Negro psychology. At *Nigger Heaven*'s close, Van Vechten presents his readers with a two-page insider's account of Harlemese, a "Glossary of Negro Words and Phrases" that aids the reader in interracial hermeneutics. Most of the terms are given brief definitions and refer to the "exotic material" that constitutes the novel's black subculture. I present five glossary terms to illustrate my point:

> *arnchy*: a person who puts on airs.
> *August ham*: watermelon.
> *bottle it*: equivalent to the colloquial English *shut up*.
> *buckra*: a white person.
> *brick-presser*: an idler; literally one who walks the pavement. ([1926] 2000, 285)

Functioning as a guidebook, these explanations seem to clue the ignorant white (or possibly middle-class black) reader into the psychology of the underworld Negro and introduce her to the supposedly foreign customs that characterize the community's "unusual" life (3). Translating Negro dialect into colloquial English, the glossary purports to make these primitive customs and persons comprehensible to a slumming audience dedicated to Standard English and standardization, and to clarify any cultural confusion that they might experience as they slum through the text.

Yet if we are to read this glossary as a definitive account of an authentic Negro community, Van Vechten soon disrupts our readiness to know more about this subculture. Three examples illustrate my point. First, Van Vechten skews authenticity even as he casts his glossary and, by extension, his slumming narrative, as a realistic guide into Negro idioms. For example, he defines "bardacious" as "marvellous" ([1926] 2000, 285). "Bardacious," however, is a malapropism for "bodacious," a term that does signify "marvelous" (not "marvellous") in Harlemese. While some may read these inaccuracies as yet another instance of Van Vechten's inept attempt to capture Negro culture, readers could also see it as a strategic ploy that scrambles a will to know and see more about Harlem's community. The phrase before the colon appears to present an unknown Negro term, and the second term a knowable Nordic explanation. Yet Van Vechten's linguistic confusion of the former confuses—mixes—easy access into black idiom. Far from "direct and serious" as the *Borzoi Broadside* ad promised, the glossary continues this strategy as Van Vechten defines words such as "*kopasetee*: an approbatory epithet somewhat stronger than *all right*" (286). The actual word is "copacetic," which my Webster's dictionary defines as slang for "good, satisfactory excellent." Under the guise of realism then, terms such as "kopasetee" and "bardacious"—words that presumably constitute a subcultural vernacular—refuse the will-to-epistemological truth that grounded the New Negro/sociological movement. Or, as Van Vechten argues in an earlier novel, *Peter Whiffle*, "my intention is not to define or describe" (1923, 48).

In line with this argument, Pfeiffer suggests that these misnomers serve "to obscure and thereby protect the integrity of that culture's meaning" (2000, xxviii). One could also expand her view to show how Van Vechten's obscurant translations undermine racial—and sexual—epistemologies. Like Van Vechten, the inspecting voyeur-reader turns the pages of the glossary and the slumming narrative to find high times in Harlem, yet she discovers an unimagined community from an author notorious for his guided tours into Harlem. Such signifying slumming, I stress, is not a case of crossing the linguistic color line in order to return with a treasure trove of African-American family secrets. Through this botched slumming venture, Van Vechten calls into question the possibility of interpreting a racial community.[17] The idiom that makes up *Nigger Heaven* becomes an inaccurate replication of Harlem life whereby minority cultures are rendered unintelligible, and this failed attempt to capture black idiom and customs produces an unexpected hybridization of both cultures that defies communal origins and racial boundaries.

Finally, the references that Van Vechten presents in the glossary operate within a closed semiotic system that refuses to answer a desire to know more about the Negro. Hence you find glib terminological dead-ends like "*boody*: see hootchie pap" and then "*hootchie pap*: see boody" ([1926] 2000, 285–86). For Pfeiffer, "The promised rhetorical explanations are inside jokes which prove more enigmatic than intelligible" (2000, xxvii). Likewise, you find a reference highlighting the absurdity of definitional practices that segregate raced bodies: "*dogs*: feet. Not to be confused with hot-dogs, frankfurters inserted with mustard between two halves of a roll" (285). An extended inside joke that closes off access to Harlem(ese) at the moment that it offers intelligibility, *Nigger Heaven* gives the reader a confusing guidebook into his or her own projected desires and racial fantasies that denies full entry into the presumably authentic subculture, or better, that mocks the idea of a knowable, legible subculture in the first place.[18] As a result, these definitional strategies transform Van Vechten into a white trickster (or what Knopf claims he no longer is: a "social satirist") since he makes any attempt to enter into the sociological and sensational realism of the Negro underworld a laugh riot (Pfeiffer 2000, xxviii). The very language that Van Vechten uses is partially illegible, and a Harlem community, which was, at times, sociologically presented as an immoral region, becomes unmapped, "a mystery," like *Autobiography*, "to the whites" (Johnson [1912] 1966, 21).

As the *Broadside* advertisement stated, *Nigger Heaven* originally hoped to present an "inscrutable" exposé of Harlem verisimilitude. Refusing to give away family secrets, yet also refusing the desire for secrecy as well, the drama remains impenetrable as those on the top see but are not seen at the precise moment that the color line is crossed. The novel "bardaciously" thwarts the celebrated concept of group psychology and the subcultural moral region as it uses the idea of an "incomprehensible" race to make race incomprehensible. Hence the exotic material of Van Vechten's supposed gay slumming renders racial community incognito, while blurring the boundaries between Nordic and Negro cultural lexicons. The discovery—or recovery—of new Negro bodies is beside the point, even though Van Vechten was noted for his avid promotion of fledging artists and their locales. Take the novel's premier detractor, DuBois, in a scathing *Crisis* review: "Probably sometime and somewhere in Harlem every incident of the book has happened; and yet the resultant picture built out of these parts is ludicrously out of focus and undeniably misleading" ([1926] 1994b, 106). Disoriented by the slumming narrative's crude techniques, readers see into Negro life, but it always remains "out of focus." Dismissing the text as a dirty glimpse into the queer underworld, DuBois is a perceptive slummer and still the book's keenest reader to date. He sees all too well that the novel's sensationalized realism is beyond visual comprehension as it thwarts the racial and sexual spectacles it invokes. The slumming literature thus produces an underworld unknowing regarding communal classification that Van Vechten himself acknowledged in a 1925 letter to Hughes at the height of his queer slumming: "It would have been comparatively easy for me to write it before I knew as much as I know now, enough to know that I am thoroughly ignorant!" (1925b).

Parties and Mixers

What a crowd! All classes and colors met face to face . . . The social revolution was on.
—Geraldyn Dismond, quoted in Langston Hughes, *The Big Sea*

When we recall that Van Vechten's erotic desires were, at times, informed by his racial exploits (Somerville 2000, 127), the author's undeniably misleading textual strategies may tell us something about how he also undermines representations of discernible homosexual subcultures.[19] Though he lived with Fania Marinoff until his death, literary critics and social historians inveterately claim Van Vechten as a "gay married man" who promoted "gay and high-society circles" (Chauncey 1994, 232, 188). Like Locke's attempts to establish the New Negro in a knowable subcultural community, such a characterization situates Van Vechten inside a stable hetero- and homosexual group identity, one that he himself attempted to disrupt through his slumming and his interracial parties.

But unlike many homosexuals when Harlem was in vogue, Van Vechten had little interest in advancing a visible subculture that affirmed victimized group thinking. Like the New Negro's sociologies, this urban middle-class U.S. subculture somewhat successfully revised and reformatted sexology's scientific analyses to forge fantastic communities that both overturned and confirmed stereotypes of the male homosexual as an underdeveloped, socially maladapted woman trapped in a man's body. In so doing, they used Foucauldian reverse discourses to create what Chauncey (1994), White (1993), and other historians have described as the "gay world," or what cultural critics in queer studies have termed counter publics (Chauncey 1994, 7). "The full panoply of tactics gay men devised for communicating, claiming space, and affirming themselves—the kind of resistant social practices . . . called the tactics of the weak—proved to be remarkably successful in the generations before a more formal gay political movement developed," Chauncey notes in his detailed exploration of emergent U.S. urban gay life (5). Like a good portion of the Harlem Renaissance, these strategies enabled minority bodies to secure an affirmative community for themselves, one that, conversely, made their visible subcultures objects of constant surveillance and control under the prying eyes of vice regulators like the Committee of Fourteen mentioned in my introduction.

By contrast, Van Vechten's 1930 slumming literature, *Parties: Scenes from Contemporary New York Life* ([1930] 1977), questions the value of a visible collective for outsiders of all kinds. *Nigger Heaven*'s confusing racial and class mingling thus finds its parallel in *Parties*, a novel in which sexual admixtures across races, across classes, and across nation-states work against knowable communal, subcultural, or sexual affiliations. Contemporary reviewers panned the book as a death knell to the high times of a gin-soaked Jazz Age (it was), but one can also interpret the novel as a threnody to a popular Afro-modernist idea—that of a protective racial and sexual community—and as a continuation of *Nigger Heaven*'s inscrutable strategy of mixing disparate cultures so that they become unreadable. The text's modernist slumming narrative, in fact, has little plot and consists primarily of impressionistic scenes in which disparate, poorly drawn characters join together only to break apart. In so doing, the novel affirms the destruction of group thinking that Van Vechten had mentioned in his letter to Locke and had also announced in *Firecrackers* (1925), a novel published the year before *Nigger Heaven*: "You must think of a group of people in terms of a packet of firecrackers. . . . The flash fires the fuse to the second, and so on, until, after a series of crackling detonations, the whole bunch has exploded, and nothing survives but a few torn and scattered bits of paper, blackened with powder" (1925, 168). Or, as the novel's transient white protagonist David informs his long-suffering wife, "Rilda, my pretty, there's no such thing as a set any more and you know it. Everybody goes everywhere" (84).

Scattering into oblivion—rather than congealing into community—is the key trope here. Rather than advancing subcultural tactics of the weak, *Parties*'s transatlantic characters embrace a cosmopolitan version of social admixture that defies cultural boundaries and categorization, and none more so than the promiscuous Gräfin Adele von Pulmernl und Stilzernl, a character whose tongue-twisting name alone makes her an impossible person. A white octogenarian aristocrat bored with the "formal affair" of a lavishly upscale Hanover life ([1930] 1977, 19), the Gräfin flees to New York with her petrified maid Fräulein Stupforsch and finds that "she might be happier in mixed company" (20). On arrival, her first urge is to go slumming and partying with the locals, rather than socializing with other German expatriates: "She was longing to drink gin in the festive surroundings described to her by the two young Americans she had met in Karlsbad" (24). "Unfortunately, she had not even learned the names of these Americans" (25), yet she soon runs into a young bootlegger, Roy Fern, who had "remarkably graceful hands, with the abnormally long fingers tipped with pointed nails. He did not appear any longer to be in the least perturbed or surprised or pleased or astonished or annoyed or even curious" (27–28). While the reference to Roy's abnormal fingers immediately signifies a certain homosexual tendency, the narrator's or Roy's refusal to dwell on difference is notable. Like the boy, the narrator is indifferent to the eccentric traits that would define Roy as a homosexual type and is, instead, far more interested in outlining the unspectacular relationship that the bootlegger fosters with the Gräfin.

Rather than highlighting the obvious dissimilarities between the two, and focusing on the sensational secrets that knowing the other might produce, *Parties*'s narrator presents them as a queer admixture, an unexceptional couple who disregard class, gender, and sexual categories. In this regard, their interactions parallel the impersonal internationalism discussed in chapter 1. No one, it turns out, comments on what might draw this "cosmopolitan" couple together ([1930] 1977, 31). "Careless of appearances" (49), they are not, as one would suppose, an astonishing or curious or perturbing or surprising item: "To the Gräfin he was an infinite source of comfort and satisfaction. . . . She demanded no more than companionship" (148–49). Part of the social fluidity that constitutes *Parties*'s narrative stream, the two could care less about the social or communal distinctions between them and are instead far more interested in a mode of queer friendship that privileges communal ignorance. Roy, the Gräfin, and the other characters in the novel thus commit themselves to meeting strangers rather than becoming a part of any knowable social set. To this end, they engage in a rampant party-going where whom you know is not nearly as important as whom you meet. Just as the liquor is poured at these parties "fairly indiscriminately," the social interactions are spontaneous rather than insular (47). "It is likely," the Gräfin thinks to herself while pondering her first cocktail party, "that Fräulein Stupforsch would have perished from a heart attack had she understood the significance of that phrase so often repeated: Bring anybody you like" (46). Like the interracial response to the call for papers mentioned in this chapter's introduction, here the partygoer is under no obligations or limitations whatsoever.

Such admixture, the Gräfin notes, has "all the essential ingredients for an orgy of the first class" ([1930] 1977, 46). Perversely, it could also be considered an alternate form of modernist cults of primitivism since it forgoes Westernized ideals of individuation and self-possession in its commitment to improper merging.[20] In lieu of propriety or social hierarchy, the partygoer instead conforms to what a contemporary, Georg Simmel, found most valuable in sociability. "In sociability," he suggests, "whatever the personality has of objective importance, of features which have their orientation toward something outside the circle, must not interfere. Riches and social position, learning and fame, exceptional capacities and merits of the individual have no role in sociability" (1971, 130).[21] At these regular Manhattan orgies, varieties of people—princes, Hollywood starlets, journalists, bootleggers, pansies, dandies, German countesses, Negroes, white slummers—experience the pleasures of sociability in an alcohol-induced merger that produces friendships like that of Roy and the Gräfin rather than an intelligible underworld community. They are the inverse of the basement "Pussy Party" mentioned in my introduction. These exotically queer "live sex acts," to borrow a term recoined by Lauren Berlant, also utterly fail to cohere into a minoritarian counter public (1997, 55). Anyone and everyone attends these gatherings, and unlike the Washington social scene affirmed by the aristocratic Helen in *Nigger Heaven*, the novel's mixed parties are relatively free from the hierarchical imperatives of class and caste.

Such infidelity to social and sexual categorizations is further illustrated in the case of rabid partygoer David, who is, according to one character, "everybody's friend" ([1930] 1977, 152). Refusing marital commitments, embracing a peripatetic lifestyle, and merging social scene with social scene, David's social and communal infidelities form the heart of the novel, and transform him into an indeterminate incognito, "the most elusive of men" (208). Like the Gräfin, who interacts with anyone and everyone, David also finds close companionship with strangers through his slumming ventures with Parisian men, with Harlem "dope addicts" (73), and with Prohibition bootleggers. Curiously, David's slumming, too, revolves around Roy, who, the reader must infer, has sexual liaisons with David. We are clued into the nature of their relationship by David's wife Rilda, who tells her acquaintance Hamish in the beginning of the novel that "David's sailed for Paris with that Fern boy" (11). Though he, like Van Vechten, is married, David also engages in frequent trysts with men at Manhattan parties and in Harlem cabarets, and not one of his partners can make sense of his indiscriminate self. "Hamish was certain that David knew everything about himself," the narrator notes, "understood even the strange necessity, the queer perversity, which made him drink, which made him sadistic, but Hamish did not understand David, anymore than he understood himself, did not understand his actions, or their motives, or even that pervasive charm which made him so frightfully attractive to all who came within the range of his personality" (204). According to Hamish, who considers himself a dear friend, David can best be defined by his lack of definition, even as he, like Van Vechten, appears to be a gay married man. Like the parties and nightclubs he enters, he is socially and personally fluid and prefers "drinking and drifting" to any stable communal relation. Through this constant state of flux, David and the other characters champion rootless mingling instead of any definable or discernible social set (203). According to Corrine E. Blackmer, Van Vechten "rejects oppositionality [of all sorts] on the grounds that defiance plays by the rules devised by the bourgeois majority" (1996, 226). Or, as Hamish notes near the novel's close, "David and Rilda . . . Rilda and David: enigmas. I understand them less than I understand myself, thought Hamish, for the hundredth time, and I don't understand myself at all. They are incomprehensible. Stranger and stranger. Paradoxes. Contradictions" (208).

These strange contacts—or unknowing underworlds—do not disconcert Hamish. Like the other characters in *Parties*, he views social relations—and the social scene these relations are based on—as part and parcel of urban disorganization. "The city of New York is difficult to describe or understand save in terms of paradox," Hamish muses, "and so, perhaps, it is more satisfactory, for those who may, to instinctively feel the metropolis rather than to attempt to comprehend her" ([1930] 1977, 119). For *Parties*'s denizens then, and for Van Vechten himself, the transnational urban scene is not a protective shade that advances minoritarian community. Like *Nigger Heaven*, it is an unrecognizable scene whose participants fail to solidify into legible sexual group identities. In their anti-Parkian and anti-Lockean refusals to territorialize this urban space, *Parties*'s characters instead feel the pleasures of incomprehension. And like the partygoers in one of Van Vechten's earlier novels, *Peter Whiffle*, "the groups separated, came together, separated, came together, separated, came together" (1923, 145).

Given this disdain for urban spaces that might materialize into a (homo) sexual safezone or a redemptive underworld, it's clear that the novel's communities are not divided according to a demarcated grid where immoral and moral regions can be distinguished. "New York," the narrator notes, "is in a constant state of mutation. If a city may conceivably be compared to a liquid, it may reasonably be said that New York is fluid: it flows" ([1930] 1977, 120). Mixing to the point of inscrutability rather than relegating themselves in a definable group, the Gräfin, Roy, David, and Hamish merge together in transatlantic scenes, yet they form neither a coherent subculture nor a locatable counter public. As the Gräfin points out when she discusses her party-going and her slumming with Hamish, "Fräulein Stupforsch has no idea where I am and I doubt if she ever discovers now" (131). Like Cather's bohemian tramping, which I discussed in my second chapter, *Parties*'s recommended strategy, too, is an art of escapism that permits anticommunitarian forms of indeterminate contact.

This form of relationality, I also note, parallels the mixed parties that Van Vechten himself hosted at his Manhattan flat during the heyday of the Harlem Renaissance. According to George S. Schuyler, these parties constituted an unknown form of cross-race and cross-class contact that became an infamous form of queer admixture: "The literary lights, the stars of the ballet, the kings and queens of the theater, the painters, sculptors and editors who had attained envious preeminence frequented his salons on West 55th Street and later on Central Park West; and to this company Van Vechten introduced their darker opposite numbers. Here they rubbed shoulders, sipped cocktails, nibbled hors d'oeuvres, conversed, sang and danced without self-consciousness. What was at first an innovation and a novelty soon became commonplace, an institution. . . . Those who came as mere faddists left as fellow travelers of interracialism" (1950, 363–64). Such indifference to social distinctions, while fostering racial intermingling, builds on a cultivated ignorance of prescriptive group forms, one that opposed the communal ideals that guided the Harlem Renaissance.[22] Van Vechten, that is, advocated relationality rather than community; and exotic material, whether in the form of an interracial party or a bankrupt slumming narrative, was a social means to this anticommunitarian end. At these mixed parties, unknown forms of contact were the only norm, which is not to say that this queer admixture did not aid Negro artists in literary networking. During these free-for-alls, Nordics mixed with Newer Negroes who mixed with white literary agents who mixed with Bessie Smith, and a friendly company, to use the terminology I introduced in my last chapter, formed only to scatter—or explode like a firecracker—by the segregated dawn. As one apocryphal story goes: a black Grand Central Station attendant told a surprised white matron that he helped the next day, "You don't remember me, but we met at Carl Van Vechten's" (quoted in Coleman 1998, 100).

Friendship beyond Understanding

Three years in Harlem have seen me become a New Negro (for no reason at all and without my consent). —Wallace Thurman, "Autobiographical Statement"

Several New Negroes matched the "exotic" materials that Van Vechten presented through his controversial slumming narratives. Each "acted the fools," as Brown (1974) claimed, to distance themselves from genteel communal representations advocated by Locke and DuBois. Indeed, Van Vechten's flat was not the only cosmopolitan interracial scene forged during the late 1920s. The author also partied hard at another rather queer locale,a rooming house located on 137th Street in Harlem (Garber 1989, 329). An apartment colony of bohemian artists notorious for its racial intermingling and decadent interior design, the building housed some of the Harlem Renaissance's most promising artists—Hughes, Nugent, and Thurman—and was satirically dubbed Niggerati Manor by its inhabitants.

Like Van Vechten, Thurman, too, presented sensational accounts of the Mecca of the New Negro in papers and journals such as *American Monthly*, the *Haldeman-Julius Quarterly*, and the *New York World*. In one article, he offered a "glossary of Harlemisms" with the playbill for his musical *Harlem* (coauthored with William Jourdan Rapp, [1929] 2003). He also presented a detailed account titled "Negro Life in New York's Harlem: A Lively Picture of a Popular and Interesting Section," where readers are told that the city has been "surveyed and interpreted, explored and exploited" ([1927] 2003e, 39). And he and Rapp complemented the paratextual rhetorical strategies of slumming narratives such as *Autobiography* and *Nigger Heaven* with headlines such as "Few Know Real Harlem, the City of Surprises: Quarter Million Negroes Form a Moving, Colorful Pageant of Life" [1929] 2003).

Throughout most of these articles, Thurman is more than willing to guide his audience through a knowing sociological tour of Negro subculture, compartmentalizing urban space into digestible moral scenes such as "Social Life" and immoral regions like "Night Life" and "Amusement Life." Such careful attention to the underworld cultures of Negro life, however, at times adopts mocking overtones that enhance what Amritjit Singh and Daniel M. Scott III have described as Thurman's "skeptical, ironic view" (2003, 29). The sensational realism of his tours takes on an atmosphere of punning racial stereotype, nowhere more apparent than in Thurman's introductory claim for an *American Monthly* "vivid word picture" that "I'm goin' to heaben when I die. Cabaret in the cellar, church on the second floor" ([1927] 2003c, 32).

While these writings, note Singh and Scott, "appear to stop short of the rejection of Harlem" (2003, 31), they do point to Thurman's increasing frustration with communal ideals and sensationalized subcultures. Though he contributed spectacular accounts of Harlem life for black and white audiences, Thurman could also be said to share Van Vechten's frustration with the group thinking advocated by DuBois and Locke. In a

September 1926 edition of the *Messenger* that was later reprinted in the November 1926 *Fire!!* he published a rather laudatory review of *Nigger Heaven*. At the end of the review, Thurman concludes that Van Vechten "has also laid himself liable to being referred to, in the provinces, as another Negro writer" ([1926] 2003f, 193). Thurman's irritation with Van Vechten's racial compartmentalization makes more sense in light of his subsequent refusals to join any racial or sexual minority body. In a published letter to Harold Jackman, he charges: "Three years in Harlem have seen me become a New Negro (for no reason at all and without my consent)" (1928, 92).

I could say the same for his supposed homosexual identity. In 1925, he was arrested for soliciting homosex in a New York subway washroom. While legal discourse typed him as a homosexual pervert, Thurman refused to self-identity as gay and derided the tabloid quality of his arrest. As he told William Jourdan Rapp in a letter: "And you can also imagine with what relish a certain group of Negroes in Harlem received and relayed the news that I was a homo. No evidence is needed of course beyond the initial rumor. Such is life" ([1929] 2003d, 139). This complaint, I believe, should not be read as another instance of homosexual panic or gay self-loathing. A closer glance at Thurman's 1932 roman-à-clef, *Infants of the Spring* reveals that the author affirmed queer—not necessarily homosexual—relations between men to advance what he called "slightly known territory" beyond the calculated stereotypes of a "City of Surprises" ([1932] 1992, 199).

After the residents of *Infants*' Niggerati Manor throw a scandalous rent party culminating in what can only be called an interracial "orgy of the first class," Dr. Parkes, a veiled caricature of Locke, comes knocking at the manor's door. Dismayed by the manor's decadence, Dr. Parkes informs Ray, a thinly veiled portrait of Thurman, that the community will no longer turn a blind eye to the house's prurient behavior. Sensational editorials in newspapers such as the *New York Call* (a lampoon of Harlem's *New York Age*) have proclaimed that:

> These young people should be brought to their senses. They should be made to realize the futility and danger of the path they had chosen, the rosy path to hell. They should be taken aside and reasoned with, then if this failed the white light of publicity should be shed on their activities and their innate viciousness and duplicity exposed to the world.
>
> Raymond laughed as he finished reading.

> "Surely you don't take this tripe seriously?"
>
> "It's not a matter of taking it seriously," Dr. Parkes answered solemnly. "It's a matter of protecting yourself from unnecessary attacks on your reputation. This is a new day in the history of our race. Talented Negroes are being watched by countless people, white and black, to produce something new, something tremendous. They are waiting for you to prove yourselves worthy so that they can help you. Scandal stories in the newspapers certainly won't influence the public favorably."
>
> "My habits and life are my own business. I intend to live just as I please, regardless of yellow journalism, or a public which might offer me material aid should I, in their opinion, prove myself worthy." Raymond's words were crisp and angry. ([1932] 1992, 197–98)

Though the subject of their fiery debate is ostensibly the manor's wild reputation, Ray and Dr. Parkes's conversation also reveals the irritation that many Newer Negroes experienced when their desires conflicted with Harlem Renaissance imperatives for redemptive community. "Watched by countless people," the residents of Niggerati Manor are forced into spectacular racial identities whose deeds are under constant surveillance. For Thurman, they are primitive folk whose "habits" and lives do not mix well with Locke's call for a "warrant of new leadership."

Infants of the Spring addresses this conflict by concentrating on a select group of artists who reside at Niggerati Manor. Critics almost uniformly panned the book when it was first published and linked its salacious themes to those of *Nigger Heaven*. In a review for the *New York Herald Tribune*, Rudolph Fisher stated that "there is too much expositional and argumentative prattle on race prejudice and communism.... The theme is the early demise of the so-called New Negro" (1932, 16). Likewise, an anonymous critic of the *New York Times Book Review* (1932) felt that *Infants of the Spring*, like *Nigger Heaven*, was a "pretty inept work. It is clumsily written. Its dialogue...is often incredibly bad. Its characters...are ciphers" (22). One critic in *Opportunity*—Louis Taylor—even went so far as to say that "there are monotonous speeches, an unclear thesis, and a lack of unity" (1932, 89). More recent evaluations of Thurman's work have suggested that "the novel is so poorly done it hardly seems possible that the best-read, most brilliant, and most uncompromising of the Harlem artists could have written it" (Lewis [1979] 1997, 277). But, like *Parties* and *Nigger Heaven*, the lack of unity and thematic incoherence that continue to trouble the novel's critics are its central point. Mimicking the style of one of Thurman's favorite writers, Thomas Mann, and building on the frustrating textual strategies of Van Vechten, *Infants of the Spring* is a misleading novel of and about "communism"—*The Magic Mountain* transformed into the Racial Manor—that wills, even desires, the New Negro's demise.

Like other better-known celebrities of their day, the artists of the manor are quite literally what film studies scholar Richard deCordova terms "picture personalities," stars whose identities are dependent on their association with an idealized institution like a movie studio (1990, 51–53). As the novel's protagonist Ray tells Stephen, a Nordic fresh off the boat from Copenhagen, "it just happens that my present landlady is a visionary as well as a business woman.... She knew the difficulties experienced by Harlem artists and intellectuals in finding congenial living quarters, and reasoned that by turning this house over to Negroes engaged in creative work, she would make money, achieve prestige as a patron, and at the same time profit artistically from the resultant contacts" ([1932] 1992, 19). More concretely: Euphoria Blake took a private home, partitioned it into apartment units, and turned the house into a public spectacle for the benefit of the Negro artist, the Negro community, and, lest readers forget, herself. For the most part, this plan has been a success, since the residents of Niggerati Manor have become well known in both the black and white press. Pelham Gaylord (George Jones), a subservient resident lacking any true artistic talent but full of artistic ambition, originally came to the manor to meet these famous celebrities: "He was overjoyed when Raymond moved into the house. For it had been bruited about that he was soon to emerge as one of the black hopes of Negro literature. George also knew that most of Raymond's friends were in some measure known to the public for their poems, stories or drawings. Their names were often mentioned in magazine and newspaper articles" (123–24).

Indeed, the residents of Niggerati Manor are sensationalized artist-celebrities who bear the burden of black communal representation and, as such, become voyeuristic objects of critique and surveillance. "You are," Dr. Parkes tells a gathering of these young literati, "outstanding personalities in a new generation. On you depends the future of your race. You are not, as were your predecessors, concerned with donning armor, and clashing swords with the enemy in the public square. You are finding both an escape and a weapon in beauty" ([1932] 1992, 233–34). Similarly, in order to emphasize their artistic scene, the narrator uses metaphors of publicity to describe the residents: under "the public gaze" (21); "forced themselves into the spotlight" (22); "the wide public highway" (220); "public legends" (200); "prate publicly" (136); "the white light of publicity" (198); "outstanding personalities" (31). This constant public exposure, in turn, becomes for Thurman a synecdoche for the larger project that is the Harlem Renaissance: "Word had been flashed through the nation about this new phenomenon. Novels, plays, and poems by and about Negroes were being deliriously acclaimed and patronized. Blues shouters, tap dancers, high yaller chorus girls, and singers of Negro spirituals were reaping much publicity and no little money from the unexpected harvest" (62).

Despite these accolades, *Infants of the Spring* suggests that this community and its infatuation with prescriptive group thinking and racial difference wrecks any attempt at lasting art and cosmopolitan contact. In sharp contrast to the Harlem Renaissance's guiding ideals, Ray tries to invert his sensationalized racial body. He attempts to distance himself from any discernible identity and any knowable communal project: "None of my likes are based on color" ([1932] 1992, 52). "Negroes won't like me because they'll swear I have no race pride," Ray later tells Steve, "and white people won't like me because I won't recognize their stereotypes.... I'm sick of discussing the Negro problem, of having it thrust at me from every conversational nook and cranny" (214–15). Unlike other residents in Niggerati Manor, who insist on becoming "most unusual Negroes," Ray refuses to "[expose his] own particular complex" and tries to discard the marker of race altogether (58). As he tells Dr. Parkes, "Can't you see that my generation, or at least the more forward of my generation, is tired of being patronized and patted on the head by philanthropists and social service workers? We don't always want to have to beg and do tricks. We want to lose our racial identity as such and be acclaimed for our achievements, if any" (200). What Ray wants is to acknowledge the force of compulsory racial communitarianism—and then forget about it: "Could not Negroes and whites ever get together and act like normal individuals or must there always be this awareness of color and this striving to gain favor?" (95).[23] Refusing the category of the public representative, he insists that the Negro artist has to be "an individualist. And that is the only type of Negro who will ever escape from the shroud of color, those who go about their own business, and do what they can in the best way they can, whether it be in business or in art" (217).

In *Wallace Thurman's Harlem Renaissance*, Eleonore van Notten reads Ray's "lack of race-loyalty" as a symptom of "[Thurman's] own sense of victimization, alienation and injustice. He had been unable to develop any satisfactory race identity in a black environment in which his dark complexion marked him as inferior" (1994, 283). This analysis, however, neglects to note that, first, Ray longs for a bohemian avant-garde scene that devalues racial consciousness. Second, like Van Vechten, Ray refuses to reside in a collective racial environment: he refuses to be an isolationist. Like the other Negro artists of Niggerati Manor, he cultivates his associations with many whites and he chastises Dr. Parkes for his hypocritical behavior, since the race leader himself "always spend[s] fifty per cent of [his] time in New York with white people" ([1932] 1992, 199). Ray's lack of race loyalty instead seems to stem from his tenuous relationship to the Harlem Renaissance. Because the movement fetishizes racial group thinking, he rightly argues that the Negro artist has become "a curiosity ... even to ourselves. It will be some years before the more forward will be accepted as human beings and allowed to associate with giants" (221). Ray instead wants the Negro artist to win acclaim for his intellectual property—his artwork—not for his spectacular communal identity. Only when Negro artists reject the role of the representative, he believes, will they be able to "go about their own business" and live just as they please regardless of yellow journalism or a public that might offer them "material aid" (198).

But when Ray struggles to "free himself from race consciousness" ([1932] 1992, 147), he is soon thwarted by Race Men. Following Pelham's scandal, Samuel Carter, a white proponent of racial uplift and an officious philanthropic slummer, arrives with Dr. Parkes at Niggerati Manor. Ray detests Sam, having noted in a damning critique of New Negro sociology that "he can't forget that he's a Nordic and that I'm a Negro, and according to all the sociology books, my taste is naturally crass and vulgar" (11). Following a brief introduction, the two corner Ray and advise him to move out of the house. "'Now don't misunderstand,' Samuel spoke hurriedly. 'We may seem to be taking liberties with your personal affairs, but you'll understand, won't you, that we are your friends?'" (196). Samuel and Dr. Parkes justify their claim by appealing to editorials in the black press that have accused these New Negroes of queer admixture, of slumming with the wrong folk, and "libeling their own people, injuring them, insulting them by being concerned only with Jezebels, pimps and other underworld fauna. Thus they aided and abetted those whites who would have the world believe that the Negro was an inferior, worthless creature, not capable of appreciating or indulging in the better things in life" (197). Ray, however, responds to this critique of his own leisurely slumming with a harsh critique of Sam's philanthropic slumming. "You're a bunch of puking hypocrites," he yells at Sam. "And that goes for reformers of your type and the lily-livered bastards that come up here seeking thrills and pleasures" (202).

As spokespersons for the Harlem community, both Sam and Dr. Parkes deride the residents of Niggerati Manor for their party-going and anticommunal slumming scenes precisely because these scenes mix too much and too improperly: "Whites and Negroes mingling so indiscriminately and drunkenly together.... It's a matter of the type of white person with whom you associate" ([1932] 1992, 199). Fearful that these artists will become disreputable "public legends," Parkes tells Ray that if the residents refuse to forgo their interactions with "underworld fauna," "the white light of publicity should be shed on their activities and their innate viciousness and duplicity exposed to the world" (198). Ray then scoffs at Parkes's remarks, telling him that "I agree with you perfectly. But I insist it is my own business" (200–201). Consistent with his individualist creed, Ray insists on his inherent right to be let alone. He affirms his independence from communal creeds despite threats that the press will ruin his reputation.

He is, however, unsuccessful in his attempts to "escape from the shroud of color" ([1932] 1992, 217) and has a panic attack after visiting one of the manor's residents in jail. Walking the streets of New York, "he wanted to be in the open, to be away from constricting walls, jabbering people, and ear deafening noises. But the street afforded a poor sanctuary.... He grew dizzy, distraught, and unexpectedly found himself leaning against a building.... He pressed harder and harder against the surface of the building. After what seemed like hours of effort, it gave way, and his body began to penetrate into its stone.... He was safe in its cranny. The protective stone had entombed him" (206–7). Since his private home has become a public spectacle, and since his private life has become a public display, Ray strives to find some public niche where he is incognito, where he can be private in public, and where he can be free from the prying eyes of the Harlem Renaissance press that patrols his sexual activities and censures his writing. Like Ralph Ellison's Invisible Man, Ray, too, desires a hole where he is free from the pressures of (racial) identity and subcultural group formations.[24] But he is called back from this "Nirvana" when two white police officers discover a "coon" lying in the city streets (207–8). Soon after he finds privacy within a public space, Ray is once again interpellated as a stereotype, a stereotyped representative of the Negro community.

But Ray once had an "inviolate" private space that corroborates the ideals of admixture that Van Vechten promoted in *Parties* and the tactics of unknowing that *Nigger Heaven* infused into its antisociological narrative frame. When Stephen enters his life, the two forge a deep friendship beyond racial or sexual understanding, one that mirrors the "strange" relationships *Parties*'s denizens create:

> Stephen had been in New York for a month now, and most of that month had been spent in company with Raymond. Their friendship had become something precious, inviolate and genuine. They had become as intimate in that short period as if they had known one another since childhood. In fact, there was something delightfully naïve and childlike about their frankly acknowledged affection for one other. Like children, they seemed to be totally unconscious of their racial difference. It did not matter that Stephen's ancestors were blond Norsemen, steeped in the tradition of the sagas, and that Raymond's ancestors were a motley ensemble without cultural bonds. It made no difference between them that one was black and the other white. There was something deeper than mere surface color which drew them together, something more vital and lasting than the shallow attraction of racial opposites.
>
> Their greatest joy came when they could be alone together and talk . . . talk about any and everything. They seemed to have so much to say to one another, so much that had remained unsaid all of their respective lives because they had never met anyone else with whom they could converse unreservedly. . . . It was only when their talk veered to Harlem that they found themselves sitting at opposite poles. ([1932] 1992, 34–36)

For all of Thurman's talk about surface and shallowness, what's most striking is this relation's lack of depth. In Stephen, Ray finds someone who could care less about the other's psychology or sexual propensities. Radical individualists, these infants experience a "precious, inviolate, and genuine" friendship momentarily free from the burdens of racial representation. "It made no difference between them," the narrator states, "that one was black and the other white." Further, unlike the affirmative communal salon that Dr. Parkes later tries to establish, Stephen and Ray want something a bit more cosmopolitan. They do not feel the need to make art socially useful, and together they talk for hours about Continental writers: "To Raymond, Thomas Mann and Andre Gide were the only living literary giants. Andre Gide was not on Stephen's list, but Sigrid Undset was. Neither liked Shaw. They agreed that Dostoievsky was the greatest novelist of all time, but Stephen had only contempt for Marcel Proust whom Raymond swore by, but didn't read" (35–36).

More important, Stephen, unlike Dr. Parkes or Samuel, does not take liberties with Ray's personal life. Like the Gräfin's cocktail party, the two inhabit what Simmel dubs a zone of "free interaction and equivalence of the elements which is the fundamental condition of sociability" (1971, 135). And since their relationship has not yet dived into identity, Ray and Stephen find "the purest, most transparent, and most engaging kind of interaction—that among *equals*" ([1932] 1992, 133). Only when "their talk veered to Harlem" do the two find themselves "sitting at opposite poles." In sum, Ray believes that this private-public space presents the optimum conditions for artistic creativity. Blacks and whites are not forced to speak from constricting racial subject positions, and singular individuals gather to discuss and debate topics. A cosmopolitan scene, or better, queer admixture, is forged. Through this ideal, which Ray and Thurman both embrace, the artist's personal life is not policed, and, through pleasurable, equable conversation, new ideas emerge that may lead to "slightly known" relational territories (199).

I could further characterize Thurman's longing for this "slightly known" territory as a fantastic leap from what historian Chad Heap, following historian Elizabeth Clement, calls leisurely slumming's "interracial spectacle" (the voyeuristic exploitation of "foreign" bodies) to "interracial sociability" (nonexploitative contact between "foreign" bodies) (2000, 119). On first arriving in Harlem Stephen confesses, "it was ghastly. The strange dark faces, the suspicious eyes, the undercurrent of racial antagonism which I felt sweeping around me, the squalid streets, barricaded by grim tenement houses, and then that depressing public dining room in which Samuel and I were the only white persons" ([1932] 1992, 15). Such racist disdain for Harlem and its geography soon wanes, and Stephen embraces the abstract sociability that Ray advances in the manor. With this focus on pleasurable contact, Thurman significantly reformats Van Vechten's inscrutable textual strategies. While Van Vechten builds on the spectacularization of the "foreign" body to confuse understanding of racial communities and sexual cultures, Thurman imagines a social space where spectacularly racialized and sexualized bodies are nonexistent. Stephen and Ray, unlike *Nigger Heaven*'s "Glossary of Negro Words and Phrases," engage with a version of queer slumming independent of—rather than predicated on—racial and sexual curiosity.

Contemporary scholars of the Harlem Renaissance have neglected to note the unspectacular nature of their relationship. Following Amritjit Singh, these critics agree that the Ray-Stephen relationship "underscores the tension between the cagey surface text and the subtext that seeks to explore the full expression of friendship and love through [homo]sexuality" (1992, xxiii).[25] In this reading, Ray and Stephen's relationship takes on a closeted form whereby friendship functions as thinly veiled homosexual desire. Such interpretations conform to conventional historical accounts of male homosexuality's emergence in early twentieth-century U.S. culture, which suggest that passionately platonic same-sex relations provided the sounding board for modern gay identities. According to David M. Halperin, "The tradition of male friendship maintains a certain distance from the world of sexual difference and sexual relations. . . . [Yet it also] provided socially empowered men with an established discursive venue in which to express, without social reproach, sentiments of passionate and mutual love . . . [that would become] an important component of what we now call homosexuality" (2002, 121).

Yet, unlike, say, Countee Cullen's closeted poems, where homosexuality is lyrically, longingly expressed as a "friendship beyond understanding" that is based on the writings of sexologists such as Edward Carpenter (Reimonenq 1993, 148), Thurman advocates a literal version of this phenomenon, a friendship truly beyond any understanding of the racialized or sexualized other. Advanced through slumming, Ray's relationship with Stephen is not an interracialized instance of the love that dare not speak its name, or a surreptitious cross-racial desire, or a prime example of the intimate counter publics that privileged white gay sex tourists forged with gullible blacks through mainstream slumming. Rather, their friendship, a model of same-sex relationality that cultural historians like Halperin have cast as a precursor to modern formations of Western homosexual identity, actually thwarts modern U.S. technologies of sexual and racial categorization.[26] Like David in *Parties*, Ray and Steve foster a queer admixture instead of a coupled gay community in microcosm. *Infants* thus queers a history of modern U.S. sexuality, disrupting that history's apparent inevitability by childishly desiring something ineffable.

Infants's novelty, then, inheres neither in its representation of the spectacular Newer Negro and his redemptive subcultural community nor in its presumably closeted filtering of homosexual desire through the lens of transatlantic interracial friendship. The slumming narrative's importance instead lies, like Addams's "limbo of forgotten specters," in its refusal to represent, in its depiction of an idealized queer admixture that enables bodies to function as incognitos to each other, persons to whom racial and sexual categorizations "made no difference," but who nevertheless find sheer delight in their inscrutable intermingling. Recording late 1920s bohemian life, *Infants* writes against any attempt to document the history of (black and white) homosexual minority identity even though Raymond is well aware that "this is a new day in the history of our race" ([1932] 1992, 198). As Thurman himself stated in a 1928 letter to Harold Jackman at the height of the New Negro Renaissance, "I like mysteries to crop up about myself" (1928, n.p.).

Unlike Van Vechten's characters, however, Thurman's are also quite suspicious about how to sustain these intimate scenes, despite the utopian impulse that guides the Stephen-Ray relationship. Stephen departs Niggerati Manor because he cannot look past the "excrescences on the essential you [Ray] that dovetail into the essential me" ([1932] 1992, 192). Though Ray is at first baffled by Stephen's departure, he later tells his friend that he empathizes with Stephen's "phobia": "This environment is enough to provoke almost any type of mental or physical malady" (193). This "emotional hangover," which Ray and Stephen both experience by the novel's conclusion, refers to a donation party held the night before. As the party escalates and inhibitions break down, "Whites and blacks clung passionately together as if trying to effect a permanent merger. Liquor, jazz music, and close physical contact had achieved what decades of propaganda had advocated with little success. Here, Raymond thought, as he continued his search for Stephen, is social equality. Tomorrow all of them will have an emotional hangover. They will fear for their sanity, for at last they have had a chance to do openly what they only dared to do clandestinely before" (186–87). Unlike Ray and Stephen's intimate talks, slumming bodies connect at the donation party solely because of racial or sexual curiosity. Though Ray does argue the morning after that this scene consists of "people who take the lead in instituting new points of view, in exploring slightly known territory" (199), this fascination with underworld differences—in public print or in live sex acts—is nevertheless "symptomatic of my generation" and constitutes the core of the Harlem Renaissance for this Newer Negro (221). "This," he kept reminding himself, "is the Negro Renaissance, and this is about all the whole damn thing is going to amount to" (187).

Nugent's Shtick

Is it wrong to love bodies? Just bodies? —Nugent, "Geisha Man"

But what—to ask a historically ignorant question—if one wanted just to enjoy a body? When Ray's friend Paul Arabian, a stand-in for Richard Bruce Nugent, is asked his sexual "preference," the bohemian replies with queer theory in a nutshell: "I really don't know. After all there are no sexes, only sex majorities, and the primary function of the sex act is enjoyment. Therefore I enjoyed one experience as much as the other" ([1932] 1992, 47). Thurman's desire for pleasurable social contact between disparate bodies was also expressed by his good friend Richard Bruce Nugent in the latter's 1926 stream-of-consciousness prose poem "Smoke, Lilies, and Jade" (2002c). Like Van Vechten and Thurman, Nugent, too, rebelled against communal prescriptions that crystallized into "group thinking" during the 1920s and early 1930s: "Almost everybody listened to [Locke's] dictates except Wally and me" (quoted in Smith 1986, 216). And in a bittersweet 1983 interview that poked fun at white sexual tourism, Nugent also recollected forms of anticommunal contact that Harlem slumming and interracial Manhattan parties advanced and that he himself helped to forge: "There was great admixture—the mixture of blacks and whites during that particular two or three years. Whites making p-i-l-g-r-i-m-a-g-e-s to black Harlem, *doing* the cabarets or Clinton Moore's private parties. Whites being able to mingle freely in every way, including sexual, with blacks. Blacks suddenly having the freedom to have white sex partners. . . . And my particular shtick was that I liked men" (2002d, 268–70). This "great admixture," Thomas H. Wirth notes in the introduction to his selection of Nugent's writing, *Gay Rebel of the Harlem Renaissance*, was "not a '*gay community*' as we currently understand the term." It was, rather, a "social matrix" that included "*networks of friendships* among men who were sexually drawn to other men" (2002, 21, emphasis added). Refusing the hetero/homosexual binary that propels desire into discernible categories and knowable communities, a bohemian Nugent, like the other Van Vechtenites, avoided identification with a minority sexual subculture and instead affirmed a controversial model of sexual and social intermingling that, fortunately, did not congeal into an institution. Or, as he once asserted, "I have never been in what they call 'the closet'" (2002d, 268). Rejecting the communal mandates that incorporate sexual and racial calls for an identifiable group body, he was much more interested in being misunderstood and cultivating a willful ignorance of communal ideals.

As is Alex, the protagonist of "Smoke, Lilies, and Jade" (2002c). Published in *Fire!!* the story charts a few days in the life of a once middle-class

Negro bohemian whose same-sex contacts refuse to congeal into a sexual awakening.[27] While Nugent gives the reader access to Alex's psyche by presenting us with a first-person point of view pockmarked by elliptical gaps in Alex's thinking, the narrative's free indirect discourse denies the knowledge that such modernist technique might illicit. Indeed, Alex spends his days in slumber, pondering his unproductive life, thinking decadent thoughts, and delighting in the fact that "he would be misunderstood . . . a fine feeling that . . . to be misunderstood . . . it would make him feel tragic and great" (79). This refusal to understand one's self—to know more about one's (group) identity—during a moment of private introspection could be considered the core of the Van Vechtenite aesthetic. As Joseph Allen Boone argues, "[The story's] wordless gaps, regularly puncturing the narrative . . . signal the possibility that some things are best left unsaid" (1998, 224).

Yet with their emphases on the unspeakable, Boone and other literary critics also go to great lengths to uncover the "unsaid" homosexual interracial desire that they assume saturates this text. "These ellipses," Boone suggests, "participate in a strategic queering of narrative that transforms modernist techniques for registering the flux of consciousness into a palimpsest of gay urban subjectivity in the making" (1998, 225). I want to extend Boone's politicized formal analyses to read the elliptical gaps in Nugent's story as an attempt to refuse any knowledge about the self—individual or communal—and as an attempt on Nugent's part to disrupt the increasingly entrenched binary logic of modern sexual identity.[28] This desire, I argue, is best illustrated through Alex's drifting thoughts and cruising body. Like David of *Parties*, Alex, too, becomes "most elusive" in his commitment to cruising, or what Leo Bersani has elsewhere called "that nameless, identity-free contact" where "we leave our selves behind" (2002, 21). In so doing, Nugent extends Van Vechten's (and Thurman's) strategy of underworld unknowing ("I really don't know") through another version of admixture.

A sophisticated bohemian, Alex opposes the genteel black community—and his black family—which nurtured him as a young boy. Refusing roots in Locke's "sub-soil of native materials," Alex also refuses the middle-class mandates that would ground him in any stable familial or national community. To do so, he embraces, like Cather's bohemian tramp Paul, a decadent and unproductive body, one that is more content lounging and smoking than affirming Protestant ethics and the spirit of capitalism: "*He wanted to do something* . . . to write or draw . . . or something . . . but it was so comfortable just to lie there on the bed" (Nugent 2002c, 75). This lazy ideal, he imagines, infuriates his mother, whom Alex ventriloquizes in his mind: "How do you feel Alex with nothing in your pockets ... I don't see how you can be satisfied ... Really you're a mystery to me ... and who you take after ... I'm sure I don't know ... none of my brothers were lazy and shiftless ... I can never remember the time when they weren't sending money home and when your father was your age he was supporting a family" (77). Yet Alex insists to himself that he "*wasn't* like his father" or any other member of the black community that raised him (76). Like Ray, he prefers to free himself from his (racial) identity and bask in the smoky haze of his thoughts, which are "nice and pleasant and comfortable" (77). This young male, that is, prefers to revel in a Van Vechten–inspired decadent bohemianism that makes his racial and sexual allegiances a "mystery" to the genteel black folk who once surrounded him.[29] He would rather be "misunderstood" than a vital part of any knowable group identity.

The mysterious aura that Alex cultivates only increases when he decides to wander the cruisy streets of New York. Like the denizens of *Parties*, the bohemian cultivates the orgiastic contact that urban nightlife offers. Following his "idle" afternoon, he attends a party where he meets other Newer Negroes and Manhattan socialites, such as Zora Neale Hurston and Fania Marinoff. Walking the "narrow" "blue" streets, he imagines "mother would be scandalized that he could think of going to a party" (Nugent 2002c, 81). These admonitory thoughts cease when he hears "someone was approaching" and "their echoes mingled" (81). The "click" of the stranger's heels sparks Alex's interest, and he begins to cruise their sound (81). Approaching Alex, the strange male asks him for a light in Spanish: "Perdone me señor tiene usted fósforo?" (81), and the two then proceed, after the exchange of a match, back to Alex's apartment for a late-night hook-up.

During this almost wordless encounter, "Alex felt like singing ... the stranger knew the magic of blue smoke also ... they continued in silence ... the castanets of their heels clicking rhythmically ... Alex turned in his doorway ... up the stairs and the stranger waited for him to light the room" (Nugent 2002c, 81–82). What's striking about their encounter in this "underworld fauna" is that, unlike the donation party scene in *Infants of the Spring*, two bodies connect irrespective of racial or sexual categories. In this "fantasy mire," they connect in a silent love that does not speak any name though not because it "dare not" (80). While Alex claims that he and the stranger "had always known each other," he also notes that there was "no need for words" (82). The contact between the two remains anonymous: he names the stranger "Beauty" rather than delving into the secrets of the sleeping person lying next to him. Since Alex refuses to personalize or even particularize this male body, his Latin lover becomes nothing more than an abstracted erotic ideal—beauty personified. Or, as Nugent stated in his unpublished novella "Geisha Man," to love "bodies? Just bodies?" as opposed to loving persons, the souls these bodies house, or the social categories that they represent, might be the central force of any cruisy queer admixture in the streets or at a Manhattan party (91).

This spontaneous queer mixing causes Alex acute psychic distress the morning after. Following his same-sex encounter with Beauty we discover that Alex also has a female lover, Melva. "He was never confused before [Beauty]," the narrator finds, "yes he would like Beauty to know Melva because he loved them both . . . there . . . he had thought it . . . actually dared to think it . . . but Beauty must never know . . . Beauty couldn't understand . . . indeed Alex couldn't understand . . . and it pained him . . . almost physically . . . and tired his mind" (Nugent 2002c, 82). While it might be tempting to read Alex's vexed thoughts into a traditional coming out narrative whereby a young male realizes his true sexual identity as he tramps through the city, or as a fine instance of "gay urban subjectivity" in the making, Nugent obstructs this attempt at sexual legibility. Alex has a female lover, and he now has a male lover; yet he adamantly refuses to categorize himself sexually, despite the egoistic and social pressure to do so. The strained attempt to negotiate between his desire for these two bodies does not signify the advent of a hetero-, homo-, or even bisexual orientation. Rather, Alex refuses to "understand" sexual categories and instead embraces the painful pleasure that loving two different bodies produces. Like Nugent, he ignores closet logic and disavows any self-inquiries into his sexual identity as he "seek[s] . . . a world less defined by identity and community than by the negation of identity through anonymous contact" (Warner 1999, 166).

Thus, at the end of "Smoke, Lilies, and Jade," we find Alex again at a party, where he introduces both Melva and Beauty to Fania, Lucricia Borl, and, curiously enough, Carl Van Vechten: "Alex lit a cigarette . . . and that florid man with white hair . . . that's Carl . . . Beauty smiled . . . The Blind Bow-Boy . . . he asked . . . Alex wondered . . . everything seemed so . . . so just the same . . . there was Melva . . . Alex loved Melva . . . in Forno's . . . everyone came there sooner or later . . . maybe only once . . . but. . . . ."

(Nugent 2002c, 86). At Forno's, Alex can embrace the queer admixture that he found on the streets and experienced in his apartment with Beauty. Much like the intimate talks that Ray had with Stephen or that David had with Roy, Alex socializes with a variety of disparate people who do not question his love for a man and a woman, nor do they inquire into the sensationally interracial nature of his relationship with Beauty. "He felt so unembarrassed" at Forno's (86), which is also to say that Alex, like Van Vechten's partygoers, experiences little self-consciousness of or compulsion to announce a stable group identity. At the party, "everything" is the "same"; and any exoticization of difference is absent. Loving both, Alex becomes unspectacular and unexceptional, a node in a party circuit who happens to fuck both men and women. Or, as he tells himself on an amusement ride with Melva the next day, "one *can* love two at the same time ... one *can* ... one *can* love ...." (87).

Though this love, he is "*accepted*, period," but not by a definably insular community (Nugent 2002d, 271). These welcome words were spoken by Nugent almost sixty years after he wrote "Smoke, Lilies, and Jade" in reference to his own sexual relations with several male members of New York's Latin community during the late 1920s. Discussing his love for Italian immigrants, Nugent writes, "in many ways I was made to know that I wasn't accepted *just* because of my sex but *despite* it, and *despite* my color. In other words, I was *accepted*, period" (271). Like the parties Alex attended, Nugent's sexual and social interactions with a disparate ethnic community enabled the bohemian to meld into a scene in which sexual and racial difference barely mattered, where his inability to belong was, paradoxically, the very condition of belonging. Despite "the American prejudice against blacks" (Nugent 2002d, 271), these immigrants enabled Nugent—and perhaps Alex—to experience queer desires outside the framework of a knowable sexual identity or community. He loved himself in this particular shtick.

For Nugent, "Italians, it seems to me, and other Latins to a lesser degree, consider and regard and accept sex as an appetite, and if their appetite is—to carry the analogy further—if the appetite is meat and potatoes, they pick ... meat and potatoes. If their appetite is a dessert, they pick a dessert" (2002d, 271). Like Alex, Nugent discovers in his "foreign" contacts that one can love "bodies. Just bodies" in bed, in the streets, or at parties without being encapsulated. Nugent refuses to acknowledge sexual identities (even though he recognizes them in the historical ether) and the emergent communities they fostered. Like his Italian-American lovers, he prefers to misunderstand bodies as pleasurable if unsexed pieces of meat. He prefers, that is, to occupy a space of "despite" and unknowing as he writes sexualized bodies that are not yet organized around a coherent, collective homosexual identity, and as he cultivates a model of desire that was being outmoded in the 1920s and 1930s. Hence Wirth's titular, revisionist charge that Nugent was a *Gay Rebel of the Harlem Renaissance* who proclaimed in more pride-filled times that "You see, I am a homosexual," could be reconsidered (2002, 268). With a little help from his friends, Nugent rebelled against the crystallizing category of "gay" to engage in "sexual activity defined not by the gender of [his] partner but by the kind of bodily pleasures that partner could provide" (Chauncey 1994, 96).[30] In brief, he operated as an indeterminate type as he went queer slumming among Italian folk.[31]

"Just a Case of Mixed Signs"

To make a truly unavoidable challenge of the question: What can be played? —Michel Foucault, "Friendship as a Way of Life"

If my analysis of their dissatisfaction with sexual and racial group thinking is accurate, then it raises a final question about the school's legacy: what to make of the pornographic clipping books Van Vechten compiled after he turned away from fiction writing and to photography and collecting as his primary aesthetic mediums? Held at Yale University's Beinecke Rare Book and Manuscript Library, the scrapbooks total twenty-three in number. Until recently, the books were sealed at Van Vechten's insistence. Now available to scholars and curious readers, an "Ex Libris Van Vechten" stamp marks each scrapbook, and each presumably contains a wealth of information about homosexual communities from the 1920s until Van Vechten's death in 1964. A hodgepodge of photographs, scandal sheets, erotic postcards, soft porn drawings, sensational newspaper clippings, advertisements, invitations, drag ball announcements, boys *en plein air*, reproductions of Renaissance paintings, objets d'art, and obituaries, the scrapbooks appear to record the emergence—and the subsequent erasure—of a U.S. gay underworld in the first half of the twentieth century. If viewed chronologically, the books chart the rise of a gay subculture during the Roaring Twenties and its downfall during the paranoid crackdowns and police raids that marked the Cold War era. They seem to exhibit the communal "gay male world" that George Chauncey details in his groundbreaking work (1994, 129).

If this is the case, then you could read these sexy scrapbooks as a campy attempt to record a teleology of homosexual subcultures. As art historian Jonathan Weinberg has suggested, Van Vechten "wants to establish the existence of homosexuality beneath the surface of the ordinary and the 'normal.' In so doing, he also expresses his own homosexuality, which at the time he made the scrapbooks was a not-so-secret secret, poorly hidden by his marriage to Fania" (1994, 47). It is this emphasis on the evidence of homosexual expression and gay experience that I would like to reframe. On closer examination, the underworld scrapbooks, like Van Vechten's queer slumming during the twenties and the thirties, reveal that entrenched boundaries between homosexuality and heterosexuality in any urban social scene are purely imaginary, that queer admixture might be more important than the stable identification of a stigmatized minority group.

Weinberg finds that "by not making a distinction in kind between photos of athletes, nude art shots, and pornography, such constricting designations as straight and queer seem to fall apart in the scrapbooks: it all becomes a matter of being, as one page declares, 'BOY CRAZY'" (1994, 42). This is also to say that any attempt to locate a "homosexual community" in this queer art proves to be a most difficult project. While it is all too easy to pinpoint same-sex desire in the scrapbooks, communal categorizations along sexual lines fall apart. Take one collage found in Van Vechten's third scrapbook. The page is symmetrically divided into two halves. On the left, we find a newspaper article that announces the advent of a politicized homosexual community on the verge of public visibility. A group of young white homosexuals, identified by an unnamed journalist as members of the Los Angeles One Inc. Society (a pre-Stonewall assimilationist homophile organization) gather around a fireplace to discuss strategy. Even though the caption underneath this photo proclaims "we are in no way ashamed of ourselves," their faces are blocked from the reader's view.

Van Vechten juxtaposes this evident fact of a politicized "homosexual community" and sociability with two cutouts of athletes, one black and one white, and the caption "OK Boys. Wipe It" sandwiched between them. Given that the two buff males, one identified as Dick Duckett and the other as Meredith Gourdine, are pasted next to the One meeting, it is tempting to insert these hard bodies into an interracial coming-out narrative, to view these images as a desire for gay urban subjectivity in the making. Such a reading misses the critical point. The athletes' sexual identities are unknown to the reader, yet the fact that they are pasted into the scrapbook makes them objects of desire. Which is also to say that anyone—or anything, since Van Vechten also includes postcards and pamphlets in his sex books—can be queered beyond communal identitarianism. As the pasted blurb underneath the photo of the homophile organization cheekily announces, "Everybody's in the Act Now." Spoiling the binary between homosexual and heterosexual sociality as well as a traditional politics of lesbian and gay visibility, Van Vechten presents his readership with another instance of the pleasures of queer admixture whereby any epistemological truth of sexual or racial group thinking is rendered indeterminate. You cannot know for certain, despite the evidence one might sift with your hands, what cross-racial desires these men, or Van Vechten, might have. Like Nugent then, Van Vechten and his pasted boys (and girls) were really "never in a closet," even at a historical moment in which this sexual regime of invisibility gained a pernicious ideological hold on a large portion of U.S. sexual culture. These scrapbooks are thus not necessarily a prime instance of Van Vechten trying "to smuggle queer representation in where it must be smuggled," to quote from Eve Kosofsky Sedgwick (1993a, 3), but of a horny adult male exploding the definitional parameters of a gay underworld again and again and again. They are, as one page advertises, "just a case of mixed signs" as they marbleize a den of sensational homophile politics with interracial mug shots of boy athletes (fig. 11).

We take this analysis one step further to argue that the scrapbooks present a historical record of the ruination of U.S. sexual history. In his essay's closing, Weinberg fantasizes that "we can imagine Van Vechten and his friends at private parties laughing over the jokes of the book, but what is perhaps most extraordinary about them is that they were intended to survive" (1994, 47). My experience at the Beinecke Library suggested something different. For several weeks in March 2003, I researched the mounds of material that Van Vechten had compiled over the decades, and I was struck by the fleeting nature of these documents. Since most of the scrapbooks were pasted together on poor quality acidic paper, some fell apart in my hands (much to the chagrin of the library staff). The large gray boxes that hold the materials are filled with bits of paper that have fallen off the scrapbooks over the years, and one can only assume that with further fondling they will crumble into a heap of scraps. Pulp—sleazy

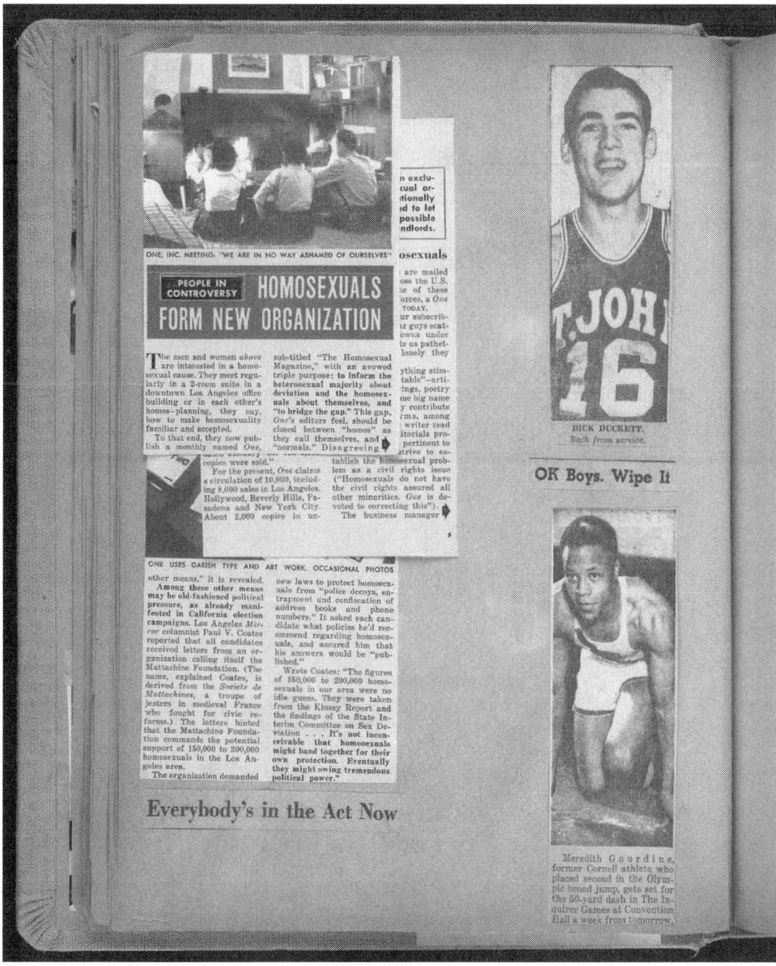

FIGURE 11. A page from one of Carl Van Vechten's scrapbooks. Courtesy of the Beinecke Rare Book and Manuscript Library, Yale University and the Van Vechten Trust.

writings and sordid photographs—turns back into pulp. Once again, the joke's on us.

If so, imagine this decay as another instance of the disintegration of group thinking that should be celebrated as a loss of constrictive group identities rather than lamented as a loss of the historical record. As with *Nigger Heaven*, you will turn the pages of the scrapbooks, but you will find no there there, whether at the bottom of the box or on one of the manuscript's cut-and-pasted pages. Any teleological attempt at discovering or uncovering a visible gay community or grounding a stable sexual identity is, once again, wrecked by the archive that Van Vechten cultivated and tossed away in one of the United States' more impressive archives for lesbian and gay letters. "Just a case of mixed signs," the scrapbooks are a decades-long act of foolish voyeurism where there remains nothing—yet everything—to see. They are a photographic extension of Nugent's gaping ellipses as they disappear before your eyes.

This is finally to say that the writers addressed in this chapter botched sociological projects that both confirmed and constrained sexual and racial minority-making in the first third of the twentieth-century United States. Rather than announcing their communal arrival into sexual modernity, they affirmed in parties and in print fleeting moments of ignorant connection in lieu of any entrenched group bond. However paradoxical, queer slumming did this for these men during the 1920s. A campy collection of queer memorabilia does likewise for Van Vechten in the mid-1950s, and, if critics allow it, for so-called investigators of sexuality today. Knowing everyone, that "weird six-foot presence everywhere" (Lewis [1979] 1997, 182), Van Vechten—and Thurman and Nugent—teach twenty-first-century queers how to turn highly public cognoscenti into highly visible incognitos. Despite their shared disdain for moralism of any sort, there *is* a lesson to be learned here: in their various scenes, everyone knows everyone else ("Bring anybody you like"; "Everybody's in the Act Now"), but nobody knows anybody. To rephrase, Van Vechten and other New Negroes exploited the Roaring Twenties fascination with sensational racial and sexual subcultures to transform it into what Michel Foucault, whose theories of same-sex friendship complement the Van Vechten school's, sees as "something desirable," namely, the cultivation of pleasurable contacts "outside of institutional relations" and the epistemological imperative to reveal one's membership in any racial or sexual group (1994, 136).

It would be best to read this Jazz Age slumming, as well as the later scrapbooks, as documents of the "death of the twenties," which is precisely how my 1977 Bard edition describes *Parties* on the novel's front cover. While the Van Vechten school records contemporary scenes in detail, they leave little evidence of an affirmative response to respectable racial or sexual communities. Readers are instead presented with the pleasures of ephemera: *Infants*' interracial book chats that don't last, *Parties*' drunken sprees that have to come to an end, Nugent's mute late-night hook-up that transforms into extended ellipses, *Nigger Heaven*'s Harlem that never was, and scrapbooks fast becoming scraps.[32] To this end, they rendered their sexual histories unreadable and fashioned themselves as cognizant incognitos whose archives and tell-alls make them dislocated and, like Cather's Paul or Addams's *Hull-House*, lost to the subcultural record.

Along the way, they introduce narratives where there is nothing but relentless sexual unknowing as the materiality of these archives fails to reveal sexual insight. Such antihistorical disclosures stand in stark contrast to the reconstructed worlds culled from detailed paper trails boxed away by undercover investigators and vice committee reformers in New York's Public Library and elsewhere. Looking for Wally and Carl and Bruce and their kind, you're going to play the fool when you envision their papers as sustained instances of gay New York subculture in the making. Or, as Van Vechten himself noted in a forgotten novel written at the dawn of his literary career, "To that extent I triumphed, and the picture still exists to confuse people as to my real personality" (1923, 33). Slumming out of their sexual histories, these misleading "fools" foreshadow the writings of another decadent modernist whose underworlds are anything but—Van Vechten's "favorite genius" and one-time employee, the antisapphic expatriate Djuna Barnes (quoted in Herring 1995, 76).

CHAPTER FOUR

Antisapphic Modernism

Les mystères de Djuna Barnes

Would you fault Djuna Barnes for hating homosexuals? Since Barnes admitted her disdain in a late interview made with photographer Hank O'Neal, I phrase this question to provoke, not to be facetious. From 1941, the year she returned to New York following a lengthy expatriation in Paris, to her death in 1982, Barnes occupied a cramped flat in Greenwich Village. Impoverished and misanthropic, she made infrequent contact with the artistic and social worlds she once helped redefine. Curious admirers sought her out instead. O'Neal, a Barnes enthusiast, recorded a series of visits he made with the curmudgeon during the early 1970s. Over several months, Barnes allowed him into her impenetrable intimacy, and she told numerous anecdotes about her bohemian life in the 1910s and 1920s, many of which ran the gamut of international Anglophone modernism. These talks revolved around her close affiliations with some of the movement's more vaunted male practitioners, and she recalled chatty walks with James Joyce as well as T. S. Eliot's dapper attire and demure persona.

Absent from these discussions was her intimate association with the expatriate lesbian communities that dotted the Parisian Left Bank from the mid-twenties to the early forties. Following her employment as a journalist and illustrator in New York City, Barnes had migrated to Paris in 1920, when she met and fell in love with Saint Louis artist Thelma Wood at the Hôtel Jacob. The two became a fixture at Parisian cafés, and a noteworthy addition to Natalie Barney's self-proclaimed Sapphic salons at 20 rue Jacob. As a stronghold for British and U.S. writers, artists, photographers, and publishers, Barney's supportive social network enabled many upper- and middle-class white women the freedom to cultivate same-sex identities and relationships in what they affectionately renamed Paris-Lesbos. Barnes, however, was unwilling to celebrate this bridge between the modern lesbian and the ancient Greek Isle. In bitter retrospect, she recalled the entrapment that this liberating moment produced. "Then back to *Nightwood*," O'Neal ventriloquizes. "After she wrote it everyone thought that she was a lesbian, that she is not, and if she had known what would have happened she would have never written it.... It was clear she cared for Thelma Wood very much and lesbians in general very little" (1991, 350–51).

What had happened was that Barnes, to her initial surprise and persistent dismay, found herself caught in a communitarian intentional fallacy. Everyone interpreted her 1937 modernist classic as a paean to lesbian night worlds, a personal tell-all that, like its infamous precursor *The Well of Loneliness* (1928), sympathetically depicted burgeoning homosexual subcultures. As Gay Liberation Front movements later intensified on U.S. soil and elsewhere, this homosexual hagiography gathered force, and, by the mid-1970s, Barnes figured as a pre-Stonewall cult sapphist much like Virginia Woolf's androgynous Orlando and Radclyffe Hall's Stephen Gordon. Avid fans sent flowers and fond wishes to her Patchin Place apartment, which became a final destination point for "amazon expeditions" that traced the byzantine paths of transatlantic lesbian literary histories (Harris 1973, 78). *Nightwood*, that is, had become *The Well of Loneliness* for the more sophisticated set, and, not surprisingly, Barnes's reply to such accolades was brutal in its disdain for postmodern sexual group identity politics. O'Neal recounts her disgust: "Then all the lesbian nonsense bubbled out. She said she hates lesbians and is rather unfeeling towards women in general, but she loved Thelma Wood in a very strong and passionate fashion, primarily because Thelma reminded her of her grandmother" (1991, 351).

Nightwood's "lesbian nonsense" not only has been integral to mainstream post-Stonewall community formation in the United States and beyond. The book has also been read as a prototype of what Shari Benstock has deemed an expatriate sapphic modernism, an experimental *écriture féminine* set predominantly on the Left Bank (1986, 189). Though this writing emerged from disparate class and national backgrounds and presented competing versions of female homosexuality, Benstock finds that writers such as Virginia Woolf, Hall, Colette, Barney, Hilda Doolittle (H. D.), and Gertrude Stein participated in a migratory woman-identified collective whose traditional and experimental writing styles disguised and voiced their lesbian desires. Despite Barnes's adamant disclaimers, Benstock positions the author as a vital member of this sapphic community, a writer whose Elizabethan-inspired parody *Ladies Almanack* ([1928] 1992) lampooned the collective's erotic entanglements, and whose *Nightwood* tracks the tortuous, failed romance between a hopelessly devoted Nora Flood (Barnes) and her promiscuous partner Robin Vote (Wood). Given trailblazing makeovers such as this, the once incognito "Garbo of letters" (quoted in Herring 1995, xvii) now appears to be a rather conspicuous writer of modernist lesbian prose, one whose convoluted *Nightwood* explores questions of silence, secrecy, and homosexual invisibility.

Central to this characterization is the claim that Barnes's oeuvre performs a closeted "ritual of self-silencing" (Broe 1991, 8), one that shrouds her deviant sexual identity in a difficult modernism that echoes her mentors Joyce, Eliot, and Marcel Proust.[1] Much like Cather's crystal-clear realism, Barnes's baroque style, too, is thought to "perform tricks while she hid behind a curtain of obscurity" (Herring 1995, xxi). Raising this curtain, scholars have fashioned her most notable achievement—*Nightwood*—into a legible cultural record of the marginally oppressed, a lesbian novel about an expressive homosexual underworld that reveals the damaging effects of Western society's intolerance and affirms minority community. Jane Marcus, for one, writes that "*Nightwood* reveals that gays and outcasts *have* a culture, a linguistically and philosophically rich culture, encompassing high and low art, opera and circus, psychoanalysis and religion, and that this culture is a vital political force" (1991, 247). In a similar vein, Julie Abraham contends that "those lesbian writers [such as Barnes] who pursued modernist experiment were . . . undoing narrative and history to change the terms of representation for lesbians, gay men, and everyone else" (1996, 35). Benstock, claiming that Barnes's sapphic modernism is a process of "entering literary history," states that "the repressed returns with a vengeance" throughout the novel (1990, 189). And in a reading informed by queer theory, Joseph Allen Boone likewise finds that "in [Barnes's] universe, the abject can begin to stand upright, the marginal to move to center stage, and the underdogs of society join together to attest to the queer communion that exists on the other side of day's 'torment'" (1998, 251).

This is a tall order for Barnes's writing to fill and, considering her misanthropy and vocal disdain for sexual minority subject positions, one that her works never entertain. Yet others maintain that *Nightwood* "takes the shape of an underworld portrait gallery populated with subliminal versions of the selves we don't wish to recognize," even as they acknowledge that "the novel presents a world in which people refuse identification and transference" (Meese 1992, 54, 55). Though "we" have failed to incorporate these debased "selves" into our normative imaginary, the argument goes, Barnes forces her reader to confront this illegitimate underworld with a legitimized politics of historical recognition. Or, as Jaime Hovey usefully proposes, Barnes, like other Anglo lesbian modernists, uses "sapphic primitivism" to "suggest a history for the queer, polymorphously perverse female subject" (1996, 548). For each of these critics, *Nightwood* reveals and champions the perverse night worlds of "the transvestite, the somnambule, the mother, the liar, the prognosticator, the wandering Jew" and the homosexual in an underworld that owes more than a small debt to Eugène Sue's archetypal slumming literature *Les mystères de Paris* (Meese 1992, 54). In current political parlance, I would say that the text operates as an underworld queer coalition.

If it does, then I could interpret *Nightwood* as a mystery of the city that addresses the social miseries of forgotten others or read the novel as a benevolent slumming narrative that articulates the unspoken, since it offers a "cult guide to the homosexual underground nightworld of Paris that Barnes shared with her lover" (Benstock 1986, 235). To substantiate such a reading, I would show that the text's perverse menagerie of characters references the Rabelaisian carnivalesque and its more contemporary counterpart, the queer shows that played nightly in international metropoles like Berlin, Paris, London, and New York City during the twenties and early thirties.[2] Barnes was always fascinated by those socially constructed as spectacularly odd, and the work certainly alludes to what historian Chad Heap has called a "pansy and lesbian craze" that took urbanites in the United States and Western Europe by storm in the early thirties, the years that she composed and revised *Nightwood* (2000, 205).[3] In Chicago and Village nightclubs, Heap finds, male and female impersonators became easy drawing cards for curious "normal" clienteles searching for novel forms of entertainment, and queers were oftentimes more than willing to oblige this audience (216). Like the sometimes stilted Negro displays staged in Harlem cabarets, speakeasies, and Renaissance writings, these "freak shows" were well attended by so-called normal slummers who, Heap contends, increasingly identified themselves as so-called heterosexual spectators gawking at so-called homosexual displays (8), and I would imagine that they proved to be a more cosmopolitan counterpart to annual country fair odditoriums.[4]

Like a master of ceremonies, Barnes, too, fashions her own freakish pansy show in the dead of a Paris night where one memorable character—Dr. Matthew O'Connor—appears as "the bearded lady" ([1937] 1961, 100). Like earlier sensational U.S. mysteries intent on "displaying the repulsive and the bizarre" (Reynolds and Gladman 2002, xxxii), her text opens with a slumming venture into this subterranean urban environment that summons readers to "bow down," a declarative that is also the title of the first chapter. During this set-up (which, I argue later, is anything but informative exposition), a stereotypically wandering Jew journeys into continental Europe's underbelly, where he encounters "the people of the underworld" (31), "the odd" (10), "the pageantry of the circus and the theatre" (11), and "the immense disqualification of the public" (12). In her more sincere depictions of these characters and through the lens of her narrator-cum-"sightseer" (43), a slumming Barnes appears to validate the perverse over the normative, to recognize and represent the silenced history of the outcast and the oppressed.

But before I uphold this now-canonical reading, I might also recall that Barnes endorsed Eliot's introduction to *Nightwood*'s first edition, where he offers some advice that contradicts the book's current reception. "To regard this group of people as a horrid sideshow of freaks [read, perverts] is not only to miss the point," Eliot warns, "but to confirm our wills and harden our hearts in an inveterate sin of pride" (1961, xvi). Barnes always admired Eliot's literary criticism ("better than anyone's"), and one might do well to take a cue from his remarks (quoted in O'Neal 1991, 353). While some may interpret Eliot's recommendation as reactionary—yet another instance of his professed disdain for popular cultural forms—I would prefer to view it as a caveat against communitarianism. At first glance, *Nightwood* has all the makings of a redemptive slumming venture that salvages history's forgotten others. It offers voyeuristic sideshows made normative, freakish underworlds made familiar, sensational personages made sympathetic. But, to build on Eliot, such a reading may focus too intensively on collective identitarianism. "The book is not," he states without a tinge of irony, "a psychopathic study" (1961, xv).

Nor, like the Harlem Renaissance writings previously discussed, is it a tried-and-true sociological investigation into the status of a stigmatized sexual subculture. To be as blunt as possible: if Barnes was "unfeeling" about the plight of modern homosexuals in general and the lesbians once around her in particular, she was also quite unconcerned about Western forms of modern homosexuality. This is not to gloss over the undeniable fact that, later in life, she disliked discussing her interactions with Barney's sapphic circle. Acknowledging her reticence, however, does not reveal that Barnes was an ex-gay *avant la lettre* or support the thesis that she succumbed to a homosexual panic that might explain her misanthropy. It would instead be more accurate to say that she was suspicious of prescriptive identity categories and the communal compulsions that structure them.

Several readers have noted this and argued that the Barnesian text "relentlessly undermines grounds for categorization" (Gerstenberger 1989, 130).[5] Or, as Frances M. Doughty perceives, "The issue is not whether Barnes was a lesbian or a heterosexual, but that she was neither.... Her refusal to take on a lesbian social identity comes not from fear of stigma but from fear of suffocation" (1991, 149–50). Following Doughty, one could say that *Nightwood* does indeed undo grand themes of history and narrative, but it does so not to alter or invert the terms of representation for minority sexual communities. It instead attempts to forgo what Barnes perceived to be the suffocation of communal representation all together. In its myriad forms, her antisapphic modernism fails to exhibit the history of a pathologized queer underworld. It obliquely illuminates how fantastic underworlds help nonnormative subjects escape the imperative to embrace a collective sexual history by putting a stranglehold on this pervasive ideal.

I use an intertextual literary history to substantiate this antihistoricist claim. Taking a cue from earlier critics of her urban writings, I first contend that Barnes's disruption of spectacular underworlds did not originate in *Nightwood* but began with earlier slumming that she undertook as a bohemian journalist. I then illustrate how the modern sapphic imagination fused the concept of the underworld to homosexual subcultures, thanks in no small part to Hall's quasi-slumming narrative, *The Well of Loneliness*. Barnes was not fond of Hall, and a close reading of *Nightwood* shows that she railed against Hall's subcultural sapphic modernism. This being the case, I next show how Barnes's intractable text undoes Hall's visible homosexual underworlds through its commitment to antirepresentation. Finally, I suggest that *Nightwood*'s battle against—not over—homosexual legibility and recognition presents an unapologetic account of an ahistorical underworld. Within this representational wasteland, narratives of sapphism fail to apply, and attempts to locate Barnes inside a modern gay or lesbian literary history miss the point. In so doing, *Nightwood* provides a fitting end to this study of queer slumming in modern American literary culture. Like the other texts, I have examined thus far, it also attempts to write the aesthetic and cultural form—the literature of slumming—out of modern U.S. sexual history rather than dwell comfortably in the genre's fantastic promise of cultural and communal unintelligibility for the non-normative middle-class citizen.

Looking for Bohemia

A door slammed in the face of the curious was the typical Barnesean response to inquiry.
—Phillip Herring, *Djuna*

While most critics focus on Barnes's dark short stories (many of which were written abroad) as a prequel to *Nightwood*'s themes, I want to follow the lead of a few others and return to Barnes's journalistic writings to explore how she confounded—rather than confirmed—knowledge about turn-of-the-century underworlds.[6] Prior to her Paris migration, Barnes was quite productive. She embraced a bohemian life in Greenwich Village; helped found the Provincetown Players; penned several experimental short plays such as *Three from the Earth* and *Kurzy of the Sea* (both produced 1919–20); and wrote a misogynistic collection of poems entitled *The Book of Repulsive Women* (1915). Guido Bruno, a notorious garret dweller who specialized in bohemian slumming tours, published the collection, and the professional relationship between the two tells us much about Barnes's ongoing interest in perverse metropolitan spectacles. Besides these accomplishments, she also worked as a theater critic at the *New York Press* under Carl Van Vechten's tutelage, whom Phillip Herring, rightly or not, speculates may have had a brief affair with Barnes (1995, 66).

As a journalist and illustrator in a male-dominated occupation, she wrote numerous pieces on the city's protean local color under a variety of male and female pseudonyms. In newspapers and magazines such as the *Press*, the *New York World*, *Bruno's Weekly*, the *New York Morning Telegraph Sunday Magazine*, and the *Brooklyn Daily Eagle*, she interviewed magnates and indigents, covered Coney Island's tango fanatics, fancied what it felt like to be force-fed as a recalcitrant suffragette, and visited numerous dance halls and glitzy hostelries. Unlike her later highbrow fictions and dramatic plays, several of these articles functioned as armchair slumming ventures for middle-class populations concerned about ongoing alterations in urban social organization. Never one to shy away from the sensational in her writings, Barnes played into these fears with first-hand accounts of ethnic locales such as Chinatown as well as gossipy chronicles of the bohemians' modern sexual revolution.

She would claim later that most, if not all, of these writings were juvenilia, scribbling for cash. When asked about possible re-publication near the end of her life, she insisted that "it [is] a great disservice to letters to reissue merely because one may have a name for later work . . . or for purpose of nostalgia or 'history' which might more happily be left interred" (quoted in Broe 1991, 251). But despite such disparaging remarks about burying her literary history, these toss-off exposés of "foreign" populations are important for my larger argument. Together, they show that Barnes initiated a minor crisis in the slumming narrative's sensationally realistic representation, one that would later enable her to by-pass Hall's realistic representation of homosexual underworlds and that would mature into *Nightwood*'s indeterminate narrative strategies. Before I turn to a close analysis of the relationship between these texts, then, I want to compare and contrast Barnes's early writings—a few on the Village, one on Chinatown, and all on bohemia—to show how *Nightwood* benefited from Barnes's engagements with these supposedly perverse ethnic and sexual underworlds.

In what could be considered an epistemology of the bohemian slum, Barnes was keenly aware of what her bourgeois audiences did and did not know. In the popular imagination, urban bohemians (some of whom were slummers among working-class Italian populations and some of whom, such as Floyd Dell and Mabel Dodge, were summer suburbanites with homes outside Manhattan) were a fascinating population that found itself the focal point of a curious white middle-class gaze, so much so that Villagers began to profit from media exposure by "decking themselves out in the costumes visitors expected of bohemians, selling their verse and etchings to the unsophisticated, and offering tours of a fabricated 'Bohemia' to the gullible" (Chauncey 1994, 233). To a conservative audience more attuned to future-president Calvin Coolidge's maxim that "the business of America is business," the bohemians were often vilified and sensationalized as antipatriotic socialist radicals (which some proudly were) in newspaper articles that "gave the raciest details . . . often inventing them, but never failing to stage a show of moral indignation" (Parry 1933, 315).

In tandem with such political radicalism and in a carryover of antebellum radical sex movements, bohemians also promoted antimonogamous sex in a conservative national climate that continued to affirm—even if it failed to practice—the ideals of Victorian prudishness; and their Village enclaves accommodated long-haired men and short-haired women at a time when the hetero- and homosexual binary was beginning to crystallize across class differences.[7] In brief, these "American moderns," to borrow Christine Stansell's (2000) memorable phrase, constituted one of the nation's most publicized cultural avant-gardes during the first quarter of the twentieth century, and more than a few of Barnes's articles aimed to satisfy her tabloid audience's curiosity about these politically suspicious and sexually renegade groups.[8]

From the outset, Barnes's professed goal is to replicate the life and times of the Village like a good urban mystery (or ethnographic account) should. In a 1916 series of linked essays on bohemianism, she guides her readers into the particularities of what, for many, was an underground subculture. Catchy headlines such as "Becoming Intimate with the Bohemians" ([1916] 1989a), "Greenwich Village as It Is" ([1916] 1989c), and "How the Villagers Amuse Themselves" ([1916] 1989d) ostensibly present her audience with a knowledgeable tourist's guide into this night world, and Barnes strives to convince her readers that the secrets of these urban legends—the freakish curiosities of this populace—will be revealed. She claims in one article that the press has never properly described or represented the Village (as if to suggest that her readers are finally getting the inside edition), and then blabs about where bohemian perverts can be found. "I, personally, have never seen one really good article on Washington Square," she opines. "The commonest spot is not recognizable. The most daring designs in the shops have all been wrongly colored. As for the long hair of the men and the short hair of the women, that type is to be found on Broadway" ([1916] 1989c, 226). She then provides readers with a behind-the-scenes account of the lurid local sensation that is the Village, one that name-drops in nearly every sentence and even pinpoints the hangouts of infamous bohemians such as Floyd Dell, Max Eastman, Charles Demuth, and Jack Reed. Following this gossip, Barnes announces: "This is real—this is the unknown. Even a basement has its basement, and this is one of the basements below Bohemia" ([1916] 1989a, 241). When they slum with Barnes, readers not only get the intimacies of bohemia. They are invited to peek below into the underworld's underworld.

FIGURE 12. Drawing of Marsden Hartley by Djuna Barnes, accompanying the article "Becoming Intimate with the Bohemians" ([1916] 1989a) in the *New York Morning Telegraph Sunday Magazine*, November 19, 1916.

Much as she makes the most unrecognizable spot visible for her mass audience, Barnes also does not object to stereotypical depictions of the homosexual type. One visual representation appears quite legibly alongside an article entitled, appropriately enough, "Becoming Intimate with the Bohemians" (fig. 12). Sketched by Barnes, the drawing shows a well-known bohemian and landscape painter, the flamboyant Marsden Hartley, perched on an invisible stool, smoking a cigarette, and staring wide-eyed at the reader. Hartley is attired in a tight-fitting suit with a polka-dot bow tie, and there is little about his effects that would connote a homosexual or an invert identity. He appears to exhibit nothing more than modern chic.

But on closer examination, Hartley's posture and his limp wrists give the game away. Like the coy fairy in Paul Cadmus's painting *The Fleet's In!* (1934), his legs are crisscrossed over each other in a traditionally feminine manner; his hand sits idly in his lap; and his pointed toes look stereotypically womanish. When we combine these features with his disproportionately large hand (itself a key signifier of Anglo homosexuality in modern U.S. literary history and visual cultures), the supple frame and the mincing composure override any sexual ambiguities. In a moment of almost Proustian recognition, readers see that Hartley is a male invert.[9] And, like other bohemian sideshows where "lesbian harems were open to the knowing," Hartley is queerly trapped in a sensationally realistic representation that Barnes deploys for all to see (Parry 1933, 327).

Having shown the conventional will-to-realism that these articles promise and that others have noted, however, I stress how devilish Barnes's tour guide/narrator is. It is never clear how to interpret Barnes's sincerity, and I cannot tell for certain whether she simulates what she thinks her slumming audience wants to see, or whether she gives it, to borrow Henry James's phrase, "the real thing." In the three articles I have been discussing, Barnes scoffs at the intimate confidence she has inspired in her curious readers and chides them for their desire to know more about these citizens: "What then? We have our artists, but we also have our vendors. We have our poets, but we also have our undertakers. We have our idlers, but have we not also our scrubwomen?" ([1916] 1989c, 227). For no apparent reason, Barnes rips the sensational out from under their feet. She deflates their expectations for insight by giving them a realism that they did not ask for nor, I would think, desire. Which is also to say that she jerks her readers around bohemia in these articles, a spasmodic technique that defers the gratification of knowledge about lesbian and gay subcultures, and one that *Nightwood*'s calculated narrative failures will build on.[10]

In one article, Barnes goes so far as to parody the sensational legibility that she first offers with a mocking account of a botched slumming venture. In the midst of a condensed overview of Village life that peeks into the boozy splendor of a ball, a "drunken Swede" whisks Barnes away from her observations and forces her to dance as he "pulled me out on the floor" ([1916] 1989d, 250). She then cuts this inebriated narrative short to highlight the presence of an avid uptown slummer, a boy playing the part of the pansy who sounds suspiciously like the Paul that Cather introduces in the opening lines of her short story:

> A boy in white flannels, white face, and rouged lips skipped lightly by, holding one perfect lily. Someone tore me from the arms of the Swedish man, and looking up, I found the tear-stained face of Alexis above me. I said:
>
> "Wherefore do you weep?"
>
> "Ah," he cried, "life has become so pure that it is no longer a pleasure to go slumming. What's the use of thrusting your hands into mud only to have them emerge cleaner and brighter, like a kitchen knife.
>
> "Why," he continued, "one can sit in the gutters of Manhattan and arise covered with nothing worse than the shadow of a star. Jean Valjean could have passed beneath our city, gone through its most corrupt sewers and have found—what?" he demanded tragically, letting go of my shoulder blade in a moment of reckless forgetfulness. "Nothing but a lot of castoff ethics and two or three discarded points of view."
>
> I took him, weeping, once around the hall.
>
> "And what did you expect?" I asked.
>
> "Do you suppose," he answered, "I left the lure of my student's lamps and my shelves of Rabelais and Moore for this? Do you think I came from upper Park Avenue, where every grocer knows delightful French jokes and wraps up the prunes with subtleties, to come here and listen to the baker's daughter talk about the possibilities of reform in New York?" ([1916] 1989d, 250)

Historians across the decades have shown that slummers in bohemia were nothing new by 1916, but that Barnes is ripped from the arms of a loving Swede to offer counsel to a disappointed lad does more than play up the stereotype of the free-loving bohemian. The scene's details—the one "perfect lily," the arch language, the boy's tragic state—also ape journalistic slumming's will-to-minoritarian knowledge in general. For the young dandy, the pleasures of fictitious slumming are more genuine than the squalor of everyday bohemian life. Yet as he goes looking, like the curious reader, for bohemia, he is sorely disappointed. He wants an Americanized version of *Les misèrables* or *La bohème*, but Barnes forces him to discard his romanticized point of view: "And what did you expect?" Such narrative disdain appears to fall in line with Village contempt for "gullible" slummers that Chauncey (1994) discusses, but here self-professed intimacy also transfigures into cutting indifference, a general unfeeling about underworld perversions that fails to satisfy readerly expectations. To reframe this point: Barnes moves beyond role reversals in content whereby a spectator becomes a spectacle as she disrupts standard forms of the journalist slumming narrative by mocking the narrative's promise of sensational realism. She refuses to deliver the goods for the slumming boy within the story and for slumming readers without it. Both, it turns out, are left tragically dissatisfied.

A similar strategy of deflated expectations and questionable realism applies to Barnes's documentary primitivism, amply evident in a 1913 slumming article on bohemia entitled "Chinatown's Old Glories Crumbled to Dust" ([1913] 1989b). Recent critics of urban travel writing have commented on Barnes's use of primitive tropes and mysterious bodies in these articles, and "Chinatown" is no exception to her chronic stereotyping.[11] Like Van Vechten's voyeurism, Barnes, too, exploits the sensational ethnic body to sustain reader curiosity and narrative tension. Here she plays on the figure of the "Heathen Chinee," a figure familiar in late nineteenth-century regionalism such as Bret Harte's and in Progressive Era literatures of exposure such as Riis's that I featured in the first chapter, to present her readers with an "exotic" ethnic night world, an abstracted China that looms over the wary adventurers.[12]

Her assignment is simple: visit this locale and report back to the front about the supposed primitivism that she and her company will encounter. Like the bohemian series and like the many ethnic tours into Chinatown undertaken by middle-class whites over the first quarter of the twentieth century, the essay offers the initial promise of sensational verisimilitude and opens with lines that invite the timid reader on a slumming excursion marked by darkness, danger, and high moralism. In an almost verbatim retread of *How the Other Half Lives* (Riis [1890] 1996), she informs her readers:

> We are just about prepared to give up looking for Bohemia.
>
> Three of us set out the other night to discover Chinatown. We were brave and faltered not; we were courageous and questioned not the other. But fear tagged behind and goaded us on with a sense of danger and of pitifully wicked things, which we must see and might not enter into: a crooked street lit with blood-red lanterns; balconies where China lolled; high, slim boards lettered in tea-packet alphabets; a shot fired into the night; narrow alleys that led into darkest China; getaways, and heavy-curtained rooms where half-dead little bundles of yellow bone and skin sucked the pipe.... We expected, the three

> of us, to eat chop suey as the mildest thing we could do, and we expected to taper it off with a tong war. ([1913] 1989b, 123–24)

These two introductory paragraphs are textbook cases of an Anglo-American orientalism that masquerade as an almost spiritual quest. Three terrified but determined Anglo outsiders venture into the enigmatic ethnic imaginary ("pitifully wicked things") to find what is most familiar: metonymic "bundles" of generic Chinese representation condensed and dehumanized into "yellow bone and skin." Barnes amplifies this primitivist strategy by emphasizing bohemia/Chinatown's threatening geography and the supposed squalor of its opium dens. The lanterns are "blood-red." The "crooked" streets (no more sinuous in its geography than those of the Village) are rife with a "sense of danger." Ominous balconies anthropomorphize into a gazing superstructure that watches over the visitors. And last, but certainly not least, we hear a shot in the dark, one that comes from nowhere but could be anywhere, given white bourgeois fears of the Chinese mafia and the stereotypical figure of the Fu Manchu that the tabloids fanned.[13] Given the swell of stereotypes that Barnes pitches at her readers, it is hard not to imagine that she has imbibed a sensational image of Chinatown whereby residents are represented as "strange," dangerous, wicked, and vile (Takaki 1989, 249). And given the article's emphasis on surveillance, spectacle, and primitivism, it is hard not to believe that she has reproduced a stereotype that matches the sensational expectations of the Anglo-American middle classes, one that ties too easily to fears of sexually suspicious Chinese-American bachelor communities.[14]

Yet, like the embedded slumming narrative in her Village bohemia series, for all of Barnes's attention to the details of Chinatown, this authentic representation seems canned. In a tortuous sentence connected only by semicolons, she piles bourgeois fears on top of cultural anxieties on top of sensational murder tropes. Such thick description is completely over the top, and a tongue-in-cheek Barnes lets readers in on the joke with her repeated use of the verb "expected" at the paragraph's conclusion. Readers *expect* the fantasy of the tiny, opium-induced Chinaman. They *expect* the simulated thrill of a foreign "chop suey" dinner pockmarked by gunshot and tong wars. But, again, her implicit reply: "And what did you expect?"

Following these introductory paragraphs, Barnes turns the tables on her audience and stages what Barbara Green (1997), in her readings of Barnes's "spectacular modernism" and sensational journalism (169), terms a "mocking critique" (173). Rather than Asiatic fantasy, readers get banalized turn-of-the-century realism: "'I want,' murmured the sporting editor loyally, 'I want to see a lantern. Above all, I want to hear the war whoop of a Chinaman, and after that I want a rice cake.' There is no Chinatown" ([1913] 1989b, 124). The narrator continues: "There are a few stacks of tea at a quarter a packet; there are a few grocery stores wherein no human can move, with odd edibles piled high. There are a few weather-beaten signs banging in the wind. There are a few Chinamen—but no one carried a dangerous weapon; hardly no one wore the Oriental costume.... And from the hundred dark windows not one face peered" (124). Though the narrator does reference the "odd" commodities, this is nevertheless an abrupt shift in tone. Barnes wrecks the formulaic narrative she had cultivated and, in lieu of exoticism, offers readers the humdrum activities of an insular community. What white middle-class readers soon discover on this particular slumming expedition is not the sensationally primitive but the all too familiar. With its bustling grocery stores and deeply privatized domestic residences under neighborhood watch, Barnes's Chinatown appears more like a stereotypical Anglo-American suburb than like inassimilable local color. Or, as the narrator later notes, "China is walking the straight and narrow path of necessity.... China has given up serving the devil and is serving America" (125).

Easy distinctions between foreign and familiar, exotic and mundane, dark and light, normal and perverse continue to break down as the article progresses, and the reader is dislocated at the precise moment that she finds herself on familiar ground. The geographic space of the Barnesian slumming scene becomes indeterminate rather than sensationally overdetermined, and the article's predicted use value becomes questionable as well, since it fails to uphold definitional boundaries between the Anglo-American middle-class self and the Chinese immigrant other. To borrow from Louise Tythacott's readings of the exotic, Barnes's "engagement with otherness engenders a reflexive attitude and a critical relativization or defamiliarization of the ethnographer's [or the sensational journalist's] classificatory premises" (2003, 3). Though she appears to present Chinatown "as it is" near the close of her article, one is never quite certain, given the article's refusal to classify, to what this "it" may refer. When they look for bohemian perversity of any sort, readers are thus thrust into defamiliarization. In "Chinatown," they find a useless tour guide to underworld knowledge, a strategy that was also shared by her mentor, Van Vechten. As Barnes again reminds disappointed readers in the essay's closing line, "There is no Chinatown" ([1913] 1989b, 130), and "we" are left uncertain as to where the other half now lives.[15]

It is this capacity to toy with readerly expectations—to tantalize with the sexual or ethnic type but to refuse to deliver—that prompts a minor crisis in sensational underworld representation, a crisis in her reader's ability to discern and categorize these populations. Tattling on unfamiliar others, Barnes shows that there may be nothing spectacular to see when she invites her readers to look into bohemia and then discredits her authority as both an ethnographic insider and as a participant-observer. Such inability to reveal extraordinary sights gets you a step closer to *Nightwood*'s indeterminate strategies and disdain for historical or sociological or sexological accuracy.[16] The refusal to represent properly what the audience expects, that is, will develop into a commitment to antirepresentation, a commitment that also owes a great deal to her impersonal modernist counterparts, Joyce, Eliot, and Eugene Jolas, editor of the influential periodical *transition*. To summarize: though Barnes dedicated herself to a journalistic sensational realism in her early career, she also sabotaged the project of capturing and recording metropolitan underworlds for an insatiable middle-class American audience. Promising insight, she undoes her slumming narratives even as these stories seem to grant geographic and cultural specificity. Within this epistemological uncertainty, ethnic and sexual freaks are lost the moment they are found. This is only to say that within the Barnesian night world, there is no perverse bohemia.

Stephen Gordon's Slumming Tour

Acknowledge us, oh God, before the whole world. —Radclyffe Hall, *The Well of Loneliness*

But there was such a bohemia after Radclyffe Hall published her lesbian novel *The Well of Loneliness*. While Barnes's early slumming narratives defy generic conventions and thwart subcultural knowledge, Hall presents a sensationally realistic narrative that makes bohemian perverts recognizable and, as a subsequent 1929 obscenity trial proved all too well, vulnerable to juridical surveillance. As Lisa Walker writes, "It was Hall's choice to write within the conventions of narrative realism and within the discourses of sexology that made the book's depiction of lesbianism blatant enough to come under broad public scrutiny" (2001, 22).

Many have interpreted this newfound visibility as a representational breakthrough for Anglo sapphics of the Left Bank. Barnes thought otherwise. Though *Nightwood* was published nine years after *The Well of*

Loneliness, she had already revealed her disdain for Hall in *Ladies Almanack* ([1928] 1992). In *Almanack*'s March chapter, Barnes, who was frequently strapped for cash and often dependent on Peggy Guggenheim's philanthropy, mercilessly satirized Hall's aristocratic pretensions and class privilege by deeming her and her lover Lady Una Troubridge "Tilly Tweed-in-Blood" and "Lady Buck-and-Balk" (18). In a caricature that now seems quite prescient, Barnes chastises the two for their commitment to gay marriage and desire for a normalizing, state-sanctioned existence. "Among such Dames of which we write," notes the cheeky narrator, "they came to the Temple of the Good Dame Musset [Natalie Barney], and they sat to Tea, and this is what they said: 'Just because woman falls, in this Age, to Woman, does that mean that we are not to recognize Morals? What has England done to legalize these Passions? Nothing!'" (18–19).

Yet despite Barnes's disdain for Hall's persona and for her pleas for homosexual recognition, critics continue to imagine *Nightwood* as a high-modern *Well of Loneliness*. Their rationale lies in the assumption that both authors, striving for lesbian visibility, presumably wrote novels that present "guided tour[s] of gay bars in Paris in the 1920s" (Marcus 1991, 398). As I have shown, Barnes dismisses the frisson of the guided ethnic and sexual tour in her early slumming; and, as this chapter progresses, it will become clear that *Nightwood* does not complement *The Well of Loneliness*. It is instead best read as a lengthy reply that builds on the defamiliarizing strategies she cultivated as a bohemian reporter.[17] It is therefore important to detour into Hall's reified underworlds to establish the social and literary fields that Barnes tried to undermine when she turned away from nonfiction prose and committed herself to fiction.

As my first chapter argued, turn-of-the-century fears over sexual perversion often gravitated around the apparitional spinster, a masculinized New Woman whose failure to advance the white middle-class family or the U.S. nation-state made her politically suspect. By the late 1920s, however, the modern Anglo lesbian had taken on a cultural form more recognizable to twenty-first-century audiences. Though sexological writings such as Krafft-Ebing's *Psychopathia Sexualis* ([1893] 1998) and Ellis and Symonds's *Sexual Inversion* ([1897] 1915), Carpenter's homogenic ruminations on the intermediate sex, sensational female-female murder trials in the U.S. south, French sapphism, and the popular sensational press all had prominent roles in this emergent homographesis, Hall's *The Well of Loneliness* efficiently cast these discourses into one icon—Stephen Gordon—

for audiences in Britain and the United States. An account of Stephen's failed search for a homo-friendly environment and a sustainable third-sex love, *Loneliness* provided readers with a sensational depiction of sapphic Parisian salons like Barney's (here coded as Valérie Seymour's), as well as underworld invert nightclubs such as the pseudonymous Ideal Bar. Through this will-to-sensational-realism, the reader really gets intimate with the bohemian pervert. Jonathan Brockett, a fey "perfect guide" of an invert who takes Stephen on a slumming tour through these subcultures, first introduces her (and readers) to this night world, and Hall's spectacularly realistic depictions easily make the homosexual a visible urban typology ([1928] 1990, 238). So successful was her account that the novel's publication and subsequent obscenity trial were "generally recognized as *the* crystallizing moment in the construction of a visible modern English lesbian subculture," notes Laura Doan. It "marks a great divide between . . . New Woman and Modern Lesbian" (2001, xii–xiii).[18]

Critics such as Doan have demonstrated how Hall's watershed book contributed to the rise of a transatlantic lesbian identity, and I do not take issue with its heightened status as an explicit depiction of the female invert that had an awesome influence on Western lesbian group identity formation throughout the 1920s and beyond. What concerns me much more, however, is how *The Well of Loneliness* idealizes compulsory homosexual community, since it offers unknowing readers a cult guide to the sexological Parisian underworlds—"the garish and tragic night life"—that *Nightwood* will attempt to undo ([1928] 1990, 378). Though Doan has rightly argued that Hall made few visits to the city's homosexual demimondes (2001, 98), Hall nevertheless presents her readers with Stephen's detailed accounts of a subterranean invert community that would assume fictive reality. Since her book was one of the first of its kind in Britain, her realistic depictions are often thought to reveal what they create and to create what they reveal for Anglophone audiences. But it is the spirit of compassionate comprehension—as opposed to Barnes's anticommunal unfeeling toward lesbian-identified women—that Hall inspires in those unfamiliar with the homosexual night world that intrigues me most, since these affections facilitate communitarian bonds between dissimilar deviants and enable invert populations to achieve a politics of visibility.

Though several critics have questioned at whose expense *Well*'s protagonist achieves this visibility, Hall shows how Anglo British homosexual (specifically, lesbian) identity becomes legible through the metropolitan underworld of Paris and how, once situated in sexological discourse, an individual invert merges into an underground urban community that demands legibility.[19] This being the case, I examine how Hall represents Stephen's communal—rather than her individual—awakening, since Barnes will erase this recognition through *Nightwood*'s incognito somnambulist, Robin Vote. In an oft-cited metaphoric passage near the novel's close, Stephen recounts her journey into the perverse Parisian underworlds where she finds herself among her own kind:

> As long as she lived Stephen never forgot her first impression of the bar known as Alec's—that meeting-place of the most miserable of all those who comprised the miserable army. That merciless, drug-dealing, death-dealing haunt to which flocked the battered remnants of men whom their fellow men had at last stamped under; who, despised of the world, must despise themselves beyond all hope, it seemed, of salvation. There they sat, closely herded together at the tables, creatures shabby yet tawdry, timid yet defiant—and their eyes, Stephen never forgot their eyes, those haunted, tormented eyes of the invert. ([1928] 1990, 387)

This "drug-dealing, death-dealing haunt" sounds strikingly similar to the opium dens figured in Barnes's Chinatown. Yet while Barnes defers knowledge about bohemian communities, Hall depicts this "merciless" locale with insider authority and lets her protagonist (and her readers) walk away with self-knowledge. And while Barnes's journalistic style questions what "you" know about the underworld ("And what did you expect?"), Hall's slumming eagerly represents "shabby" invert subculture to fulfill sensational expectations. Basically, she aims to give audiences a definitive, sociological account of a homosexual underworld.

To achieve this reality effect, Hall merges two interconnected genres in this brief paragraph—the slumming narrative of the city mystery and the coming out narrative. By "coming out," I do not mean the post-Stonewall U.S. closet. Rather, I take "coming out" in its early twentieth-century sense: "*coming out into* . . . 'homosexual society' or the 'gay world,' a world neither so small, nor so isolated, nor, often, so hidden as 'closet' implies" (Chauncey 1994, 7). For an aristocratic and pastoralized Stephen, a slumming expedition into the urban underclass "dregs" of French society is tantamount to this "coming out," an expedition into a transatlantic underworld that is also an expedition into communal self-discovery. Prior to this moment, her communal affiliation lay more with the landed British gentry than with this homosexual underclass even as she feels "the lure of the dim and mysterious bystreets"; the shock that overtakes her when she enters Alec's is entirely class based ([1928] 1990, 326). Nevertheless, though she throws herself outside her habitus, Stephen forces herself to witness the lumpen of the invert low life, even though they repulse her.

What begins as international cross-class contact, however, quickly becomes internalized cross-identification, a chance for Stephen to make her sexual mysteries legible to her self and to those around her. Venturing down into the depths of this "haunt," Stephen recognizes herself as like them, though she does not like them since she is unaccustomed to "strange places" ([1928] 1990, 168). Hall's sensational realism propels this compulsory homosexuality, since there are no particular individuals at Alec's, only a "miserable" community. In language patterned on the burgeoning discourse of group psychology, Stephen observes a "miserable army." She watches the inverts who "flocked" to this dive. She marvels in repulsion at the "remnants" of this underworld. She gapes at those "closely herded together." And she cannot avert her gaze from "their tormented eyes," which function in tandem. The slumming scene is both banal and extraordinary in its implications: homosexuals have gathered to form a subculture, an identifiable underworld that can easily be seen and, curiously, incorporated into the watchful self.

For Stephen, this sensational sight is at first magnetic, both attractive and repulsive. But despite her visceral ambivalence, she identifies with the underworld and it eventually subsumes her:

> A youth passed with a friend and the couple were blocked by the press of dancers in front of her table. He bent forward, this youth, until his face was almost on a level with Stephen's—a grey, drug-marred face with a mouth that trembled incessantly.
>
> "Ma soeur," he whispered.
>
> For a moment she wanted to strike that face with her naked fist, to obliterate it. . . .
>
> Stephen shivered and stared at her tightly clenched hands; the nails whitened her flesh. "Mon frère," she muttered. ([1928] 1990, 388–89)

As most of us know, in the wee after hours of nightlife, anything can happen, and Hall proves this as well. Her compact scene illuminates how an aristocratic British lesbian and an underclass French gay man embrace a transnational group identity in the criminal underbelly of Paris.[20] When the coked-out gay youth meets Stephen face to face and woozily acknowledges their sisterhood, Stephen, too, admits that the boy is her brother. She hates this so much, since the unwanted recognition of their communal deviance ("Stephen shivered") ejects her out of traditional kinship structures centered around class and nation-state and pitches her into bonds of an entirely different habitus—a Western European gay family. Or, as Heather K. Love explains, "[Stephen] cannot finally renounce her identity group; in the end her repulsion turns to shame, and she reluctantly avows her bond with [the French youth]" (2001, 490).[21]

I want to advance Love's strong reading here. Alongside her queer shame, Stephen also has an ingrained class bias that she hates losing, and her disgust with identifying with an underworld body is as much socioeconomic as it is sexual. The two intersect throughout *The Well of Loneliness*. Though she longs to "obliterate" the difference between her aristocratic invert self and a working-class fairy, and though she longs to forestall any compulsory communitarianism with an "identity group" that she knows will thrust her into downward mobility, Stephen does not. When she shifts from her socioeconomic class gaze to an interiorized model of sexological classification, what was once foreign to Stephen's aristocratic body has now become all too familiar. Heightened by Hall's attention to underworld details, this queer call-and-response ("Ma soeur." "Mon frère.") thus becomes a supreme moment of subcultural identification that sets the stage for the politics of sexual recognition invoked in the novel's closing paragraphs.

Unlike Barnes's parodic slumming exposés, the social scene known as Alec's betrays no crisis of historical or cultural representation. "Bereft of all social dignity," it does, however, teem with the anxiety of cultural acknowledgment, one that *Nightwood* dismisses in content and form ([1937] 1961, 388). A mirror of Stephen's self-awareness at Alec's, this politics of "demanding recognition" is convincingly the primary legacy of *The Well of Loneliness*, and an appeal to its necessity closes the novel (Love 2001, 514). After Stephen has left her lover Mary, the force of the break-up wracks her body, and she hallucinates that the familial "herds" at Alec's have invaded her house: "Who were they, these strangers with the miserable eyes? And yet, were they all strangers? . . . The quick, the dead, and the yet unborn—all calling her, softly at first and then louder. Aye, and those lost and terrible brothers from Alec's, they were here, and they also were calling" (436). The brothers' domestic invasion then becomes a corporeal one. Having located her homosexual community on her underworld slumming venture, Stephen gathers this literal body into its figurative home, her body's frame. The seedy bar's homosexual army infiltrates her corpus and forces her to recognize "her pain, their pain . . . all the misery at Alec's," to announce herself as a member of this godforsaken family (437). Though she is already a successful writer and a recognized star in her literary circles, Stephen discovers her true calling through this annunciation. "And the press and the clamour of those countless others—they fought, they trampled, they were getting her under," the narrator notes. "In their madness to become articulate through her, they were tearing her to pieces, getting her under. . . . 'Our name is legion—you dare not disown us'" (437).

In what Hall figures as an act of self-imposed martyrdom, Stephen again interiorizes this transatlantic invert underworld. Reaching into the depths of her slumming self, so to speak, she discovers the dive bars of her inverted soul. Her journey into Parisian nether regions becomes, by the novel's close, a journey into the nether regions of the self, and Stephen's voice becomes a representative for the politics of a certain vision of modern homosexual representation. "God," she cries in the novel's closing apostrophe, "we believe; we have told You we believe . . . We have not denied You, then rise up and defend us. Acknowledge us, oh God, before the whole world. Give us also the right to our existence!" ([1928] 1990, 437). In this moment of despair and homosexual infestation, Stephen loses her individuality and speaks as (and for) a subterranean "we" that demands a politics of visibility. "She must stagger and all but fall," readers are told as Stephen speaks in tongues, "beneath this appalling burden of sound that strangled her in its will to be uttered," which is also a compulsion to sensational realism (437).

To spin this reading a bit more: Hall here presents the quickening of invert interiority that then becomes a walking typology. As Stephen's particular body becomes a self-contained underworld, Hall offers something unprecedented in modern lesbian and gay Western history—a reverse discourse that (de)pathologizes how the literatures of slumming first inform and then meld into the narrative of the awakening of homosexual group subjectivity. Going down for *The Well of Loneliness* is not only the same as coming out into an international homosexual society. It is also the same as coming out into normal society. In so doing, Hall presents her fascinated audience with a highly publicized homosexual subculture that appeals to a sanctified mass public sphere for legitimization: "Acknowledge us, oh God, before the whole world." Though these decrepit creatures "seem beyond all hope . . . of salvation," one could say that Hall's religious rhetoric

FIGURE 13. Cosmo Clark, *The Well of Loneliness*, featured alongside a review of the book *The American Sketch* (March 1929). Courtesy of the Kinsey Institute for Research in Sex, Gender, and Reproduction.

propels gays and lesbians into a "salvation" history of sexual group identity politics decades prior to the rise of homophile societies like One, Inc., and the development of gay civil rights on U.S. soil.[22]

For Stephen Gordon, like Van Vechten, everybody's in the act now, but for rather different purposes. Her slumming venture, that is, turns singular bodies into spectacular communal reads that could not help but solicit the reader's curiosity on initial and subsequent publications—as well as that of the sensational field of sexology that she enabled (fig. 13). By minoritizing herself into a universal body and by obliterating her earlier class biases, Stephen Gordon's slumming tour manages to normalize via homosexual pathology an elite Anglo-invert identity via underworld possession. Or, as Havelock Ellis announces in his introductory commentary to Hall's sapphic modernism, "I have read *The Well of Loneliness* with *great interest* because . . . it possesses a notable psychological and sociological significance. So far as I know, it . . . presents, in a completely faithful and uncompromising form, one particular aspect of sexual life as it exists among us to-day" ([1928] 1990, n.p., emphasis added).[23]

Lost in *transition*

It is an entirely unique style. One sentence and you know it's Djuna. —William S. Burroughs, Letter to Mary Lynn Broe

Nightwood, by contrast, renegotiates the sensational realism of Hall's slumming narrative: it is not, to return to Eliot, a psychopathic study. The lengthy detour I have taken through Barnes's slumming articles and *The Well of Loneliness* provides an intertextual context in which to better understand how *Nightwood* obstructs the production of (homo)sexual communal knowledge and defamiliarizes Hall's subcultural and sexological work. To recap: critics maintain that Barnes's text shares many surface elements with Hall's sapphic modernism. In the general consensus mentioned in this chapter's introduction, both writers are thought to "incorporate [their] lesbianism . . . mimetically . . . into [their] writing" (Nealon 2001, 63). Both are thought to offer guided slumming tours into the queer underworld. And both are seen to legitimize the social outcast. To reinforce these parallels, I might add that each novel gravitates around failed same-sex romance. Each presents an impassioned prefatory plea to a medical or literary expert for understanding. And each occupies the same geographic turf, the invert subcultures of Paris. Adding up the various equations that readers strike between the two, you could say that *Nightwood* is a more difficult *Well of Loneliness*.

But here the correspondence ends, since the controlling themes that govern Hall's narrative are absent from Barnes's experimental text. The sensational realism that enables subcultural recognition and public visibility at the close of *The Well of Loneliness* is nowhere to be found in *Nightwood*. While Hall mimetically scripts an easily identifiable—and all too easily policed—homosexual underworld, Barnes dares disown this progress. Her text is self-consciously antimimetic and "desires," according to Donna Gerstenberger, "freedom from the prison of meaning" (1989, 138).[24] The book thus attempts to distance itself from (homo)sexual categorization by cultivating *dis*articulation on levels both formal and thematic. Or, as *Nightwood*'s quack gynecologist-cum-therapist Dr. Matthew O'Connor states in what may be considered something of a rejoinder to Hall, "There is no truth, and you have set it between you; you have been unwise enough to make a formula; you have dressed the unknowable in the garments of the known" ([1937] 1961, 136).

The doctor is replying to Nora, who has asked her fellow expatriate about the nature of invert love. His pithy commentary reveals nothing significant about homosexuality and chastises Nora for her desire to know more about this sexual type. Given this reluctance to discuss the nature of perversion, his frustrating remarks could be seen as a microcosm for *Nightwood*'s larger project. If you bear in mind Richard Poirier's claim that "it is not the substance [of difficult modernist writing] but rather the act of allusiveness or of schematization which should occupy the reader" (1987, 107), then *Nightwood*'s innovative response to Hall's realistic slumming is, like the New Negro writings previously examined, to say nothing substantial about the homosexual underworld. Even as chunks of the book seem to expound at great length on the night, Barnes refuses to offer readers any intelligible contribution to the sociological or psychological understanding of the modern homosexual.

Like her earlier slumming narratives, then, *Nightwood* is a taxing, at times exhausting, at times infuriating experience, since it aims to obfuscate what, by the mid-thirties, had become all too familiar—the subcultural underworld. According to Judith Roof, the novel is "a narrative about narrative dissolution, a narrative that continually short-circuits" (1996, xxiv). There is much formal evidence to support Roof's claim. Structurally, the text has no ending in an Aristotelian sense since it fails to conclude with a dénouement ("Acknowledge us") or an epiphany. It terminates in narrative limbo, as Nora finds her long-lost lover Robin intimately engaged with a wild dog in an abandoned chapel. This frustrating ending finds its complement in the novel's opening chapter, as I mentioned in my introduction. While the chapter showcases the sightseer Felix Volkbein, a stereotypically wandering Jew with forged aristocratic credentials, the remainder of the book fails to follow up this narrative lead. His character is soon forgotten and reappears only later, near the novel's close. Further, in the realm of character analysis, deeply psychological personages—the hallmark of many a realist novel—are oftentimes absent as distinctions between animals and humans break down. Finally, events (if they can be called that) fail to progress in an orderly fashion. A decades-long history of a Viennese family or an afternoon conversation between friends may encompass an entire chapter. Since a forged aristocratic genealogy has as much weight as casual banter, it's hard to tell what holds relevance in *Nightwood*: "No one ever knew what was truth and what was not" ([1937] 1961, 158). Meaning attaches to everything and nothing, and it is difficult to ascertain what, if anything, has "psychological or sociological significance" or symbolic weight.

Such unexpected narrative techniques are supplemented by the book's singular style, one that refuses to represent properly anything despite *Nightwood*'s recognizable syntax. "It is an entirely unique style," wrote William S. Burroughs, "one sentence, and you know it is Djuna" ([1985] 1991, 206). Yet this identifiable style paradoxically strives to queer—to make strange and unknown—the objects and events it presents on its night haunts. Joseph Allen Boone notes that the book's "strategic queering of words, imagery, and style occurs in tandem with Barnes's deliberate perversion of narrative temporality through various experimental techniques" (1998, 240). Like other high-modernist works, these temporal dislocations tend to refuse their cultural moment.[25] While *Nightwood*'s influences include modernist icons such as Proust, Eliot, and Joyce as well as the French symbolists and surrealists, its language is anything but sleekly modern. Similar to the rhetoric of her early slumming narratives, it is thick, almost turgid with mixed metaphors, endless semicolons, and archaic allusions. When Robin gives birth, for instance, the narrator tells us that "she was delivered." While suggestive of Elizabethan prose, such obsolete phrasing enables the text, like *The Waste Land* and *Ulysses*, to achieve "a manner and style of no particular era, and thus of any era" (Kannenstine 1977, xvii). Style, that is to say, fights historical substance. Or, as Boone notes with perplexity, "One is hard put, however, to imagine . . . making much progress in discovering the precise location of Paris's gay 'underground' with this largely nonrealistic novel as their guide!" (1998, 467).

Though this inscrutable style may strive for the ahistorical or the transhistorical, readers can nevertheless trace some of its experimentation back to one of transatlantic modernism's major production managers, *transition* editor Eugene Jolas. During the twenties, Jolas published numerous surrealist tracts as well as Joyce's *Work in Progress* (later known as *Finnegans Wake*), and Barnes wrote several short stories for his journal. Her professional association with *transition* was matched by an unabashed admiration for Jolas's theories on artistic creativity, the unconscious, primitivism, and their relationship to the night. Like many modernists he championed, Jolas was quick to propagandize these ideas with a manifesto—*The Language of Night* (1932)—that Barnes used to supplement *Nightwood*'s more canonically modernist influences. One of the few critics to note the book's heavy debt to Jolas, Louis F. Kannenstine suggests that, alongside its more conspicuous allusions to Joyce and Eliot, "*Nightwood* evokes even more directly the involvement with . . . the poetics of the night mind in the pages of *transition* . . . and its influence on her may have been significant" (1977, 107).[26]

For Jolas and Barnes (both subscribers to Karl Jung's psychology), the indeterminate language of the night was antisociological, a "revolt against realism" (Parry 1933, 340). "We are not concerned," Jolas writes, "with the propagation of sociological ideas, except to emancipate the creative elements from the present ideology" (1932, 34). Rather than commit to historical or sociological accuracy—the hallmarks of the realist technique—Jolas proposed that artists in general and poets in particular strive for a ritualistic search for "the underworld" (56). To do so, the artist, or "the highly sensitized individual sinks into himself, he tries to penetrate to the unutterable" (50–51). After taking this plunge, the artist (here typed as male) enters into a mystical realm far removed from cultural or geographic specificity, a space antithetical to Stephen's personal dive bar. In this realm the writer does not uncover a subcultural materialism or a treasure trove of psychological insight. She or he instead slums into the underworld of the self to return with a novel language that fails to voice (sexual) group identity politics. "His vocabulary," Jolas proposes, "runs the gamut from the lowest depths of the acherontic to the planetary reality of a sublimation" (58). This depersonalization of the night—as opposed to the personalization of Hall's dive into her underworld—then enables the artist to achieve a state of general unfeeling that propels the individual outside of temporal or historical constraints. "We must needs dissolve the personality before first constructing the new ethos," Jolas writes (42). And later: "In his night-world he feels a new sense of time" (57). And then: "The new grammar forges an elemental and a fabulous world" (60). This modernist language of night, it should be obvious, is the language of *Nightwood*, a text that offers unrealistic spaces structured through a novel and historically indeterminate grammar.[27] Or, as one historian suggests, "*transition* was for a complete experiment of freedom in expression, even to the point of absolute unintelligibility. It was for the testing of new explosives in the language, not only English but French as well" (Parry 1933, 339).

Inflected by anti-identitarian modernist ideals, *Nightwood*'s commitment to this "new" antihistorical style fights against the cultural novelty and the "present ideology" of the realistic homosexual text like *The Well of Loneliness* to create a fantastic, illegible night world. The queer narrative techniques of the book should be seen as an attempt on Barnes's behalf to escape from the invert history of modern life that Hall (among many others) had produced and that British and Anglo-American audiences came to understand as legitimate fact. It is for this reason, I suppose, that *Nightwood*'s reception as a cult novel about lesbianism infuriated Barnes. Like the poet who writes the language of night, she strove instead to achieve, "by the dislocation of old sentence-schemes" "a delusional logic that is identical with that of the nocturnal" (Jolas 1932, 60). *Nightwood*'s narrative delusions may be a revolutionary (and reactionary) fake-out, one that Barnes tested with her mocking slumming narratives and then honed when she encountered Jolasian theory. As the book dismantles the old sentence schemes of *The Well of Loneliness*, Barnes undermines the popularizing work that spectacularized the homosexual underworld. A slumming journalist turned Jolasian artist, she makes homosexuality unutterable in an effort to thwart any sociological knowledge about any minority self or the minority community. Or, as Matthew tells Nora with questionable certainty, "An image is a stop the mind makes between uncertainties" (111). Through this antirepresentational technique, a slumming Barnes offers her audience a deceptive literary art—an incognito modernism—where there is no need for disguise.

Watchman, What of the Night?

Life is not to be told, call it as loud as you like, it will not tell itself. —Barnes, *Nightwood*

If so, then one way of entering *Nightwood* (if not fully understanding it) is by viewing it as a Jolasian slumming narrative that dislocates realistic underworlds and replaces them with something unutterable, something that cannot be articulated. Such a project distresses Nora Flood. Though *Nightwood* is unfeeling about the homosexual underworld, the night and its capacity to produce insight both fascinate and frustrate Nora, primarily because it has absorbed all of her critical and emotional energies. An Anglo-American expatriate in Paris, she has lost her lover Robin Vote, who left her for the "squatter" Jenny Petherbridge ([1937] 1961, 68) and then began to wander nightly into disparate lands. In desperation, Nora tries to comprehend this promiscuity: "I sought Robin in Marseilles, in Tangiers, in Naples, to understand her . . . " (156). She seeks an explanation for her lost lover's erratic behavior and, like a standard journalistic slummer or like Thurman's revel-rousing partygoers, she probes into the night.

For Nora, this sexual curiosity has been old hat. Whenever she speaks, she typically asks penetrating questions:

> "Are you both really saying what you mean, or are you just talking?" (18).
> "Is not the gown the natural raiment of extremity?" (80).
> "What will become of her? That's what I want to know" (96).
> "What will happen now, to me and to her?" (129).
> "What is love?" (135).
> "Will Robin *only* regret?" (135).
> "Why have I always gone seeking [love] at the liar's door?" (135).
> "I never thought of the night as a life at all—I've never lived it—why did she?" (82).

These inquiries are just a sampling of her inquisitiveness, a curiosity also illustrated in her commitment to "the strangest 'salon' in America," which she nightly hosted. At this bohemian salon, the narrator informs us, "poets, radicals, beggars, artists, and people in love" gather to "rant" and "roar" "about her oak table before the huge fire" (50). That Nora should cultivate the bohemian production of political and personal knowledges makes perfect sense. While she relishes these contemporary quasi-Village gatherings, she is also "by temperament . . . an early Christian; she believed the word" (51). Nora, that is to say, puts her faith in a signifying Logos. She commits herself to representations that facilitate her understanding of social, political, and individual events.

Because her allegiance to this knowledge both discerns and edifies, "at these incredible meetings one felt that early American history was being re-enacted" ([1937] 1961, 51). Read symbolically, Nora and her fellow bohemians cultivate rationality and reason, the founding principles of the American republic. They long for enlightenment in both its eighteenth-century sense and its more modern sense—a spectacular freedom from ignorance and misinformation. Like Stephen, Nora, too, nurtures her own micropublic sphere that basks in the roar of its articulate rants, and at these publicized gatherings, she is "known instantly as a Westerner" dedicated to imperialist explorations and epistemological conquests (50). In other words, she is situated in her historical moment and summed up in a word.

Nora's interest in such conventional enlightenment parallels her insatiable curiosity about the lesbian politics of her relationship with Robin. The book's interrogative third chapter is entitled "Watchman, What of the Night?"—an echo of a line in George Thompson's 1849 urban mystery *City Crimes* where a drunken doctor wanders the streets and sings, "Watchman—hic—tell us of the—hic—night" ([1849] 2002, 215). Nora extends this searching tradition and continues her epistemological explorations by going bohemian slumming to uncover a knowledge that will shed light on the mysteries and miseries of modern invert life. To accomplish this task, she searches out her "friend" Matthew, whom she had met in the city's underground demimonde doing "advance publicity for the circus" (18). Given that Barnes links "the pageantry of the circus and the theatre" to what another character calls "the odd" (10), the fact that Nora's primary occupation revolves around making visible the spectacularly odd seems appropriate. It is her abiding career and her primary goal throughout *Nightwood*.

When Nora locates the doctor, Barnes frames the scene as a sensational venture into the exotic night world, much as she did in "Chinatown's Old Glories Crumbled to Dust" ([1913] 1989b) and her Village bohemia articles. She heads to Matthew's flat in the middle of the night ("about three in the morning") and finds herself among "incredible . . . disorder" ([1937] 1961, 78). On arrival, she observes the detritus that the doctor has accumulated: "A pile of medical books, and volumes of a miscellaneous order, reached almost to the ceiling, water-stained and covered with dust. Just above them was a very small barred window, the only ventilation" (78). Barnes further likens this scene, "brimming with abominations," to a vice district in miniature. She compares it to "the rooms in brothels, which give even the most innocent a sensation of having been accomplice" (79). With its multiple references to filth ("dirty linen sheets"), waste ("swill-pail"), squalor, and stench, Nora's journey for sexual knowledge functions as a slumming narrative in the dank depths of the night, one that mirrors Stephen's journey into Parisian haunts (79).

After entering the room, "Nora said, as quickly as she could recover herself: 'Doctor, I have come to ask you to tell me everything you know about the night'" ([1937] 1961, 79). She inquires about "the night" in particular because her lover, Robin, has taken to "directing her steps toward that night life that was a known measure between Nora and the cafés" (59). Following a blissful honeymoon, Robin's withdrawal from the relationship increased, and she began wandering the streets "in a formless meditation" (59). This being the case, for Nora, the night comes to symbolize Robin, and she the night. Hence the two, like the invert and the underworld, are synonymous within her mind.[28]

Like Hall's appeal to Ellis's imprimatur, Nora, too, bows down before the doctor to comprehend the mystery of this (female) homosexuality and the underworlds they inhabit. Though he is irritated that Nora awakens him, Matthew responds at great length to Nora's inquiries. He is more than willing to talk throughout the night and lectures Nora in extended paragraphs on invert life, going so far as to exclaim in glorious detail about "the night of nights—the night you want to know about the most of all" ([1937] 1961, 89). His explanations of the night, however, fail to offer anything knowable about the homosexual condition:

> "I used to think," Nora said, "that people just went to sleep, or if they did not go to sleep that they were themselves, but now—" she lit a cigarette and her hands trembled—"now I see that the night does something to a person's identity, even when asleep."
>
> "Ah!" exclaimed the doctor. "Let a man lay himself down in the Great Bed and his 'identity' is no longer his own, his 'trust' is not with him, and his 'willingness' is turned over and is of another permission. His distress is wild and anonymous. He sleeps in a Town of Darkness, member of a secret brotherhood. He neither knows himself nor his outriders; he berserks a fearful dimension and dismounts, miraculously, in bed!" (81)

While Hall's nightlife—in all of the term's multiple meanings—enables Stephen and other outcast inverts to inhabit a definable sexual community, the Barnesian night that Matthew details does the reverse. In contrast to Hall, Barnes does not find nonnormative subjects asking for acknowledgment. The Great Bed is not a well publicized meeting place such as Alec's, which functions as a safe zone that affirms stigmatized sexual identities and fosters cross-identifications. A trembling Nora instead brackets collective identity, and the doctor confirms her growing suspicions of sexual hermeneutics with an exclamatory "Ah!"

This exchange terrifies Nora because she realizes that, within the Barnesian night that her lover has come to exemplify, agency is irrelevant. Personal "trust" is absent and "willingness" has been "turned over," relinquished to "another permission." Since this state prohibits agency, individuals, asleep or awake, slough off their social or communal impulses and fantastically become "wild and anonymous," foreign to themselves and to others. "He neither knows himself nor his outriders," the doctor tells Nora; and communal or self-discovery becomes a joke, since the obliterating night dissolves the personality, which becomes an untrustworthy other within the unknowable self.

Like the journalist Barnes, the doctor here has nothing significant to tell Nora about the modern Anglo-lesbian type (the individual identity) or about modern lesbianism (the subcultural practice). His reply elides any analogy that might be drawn between the homosexual and the bohemian underworld, which also deflects the reader's focus from the deviant female body by universalizing the night as a ubiquitous state of common man. The night, that is to say, loses its "particular" code as homosexual nightlife and begins to take on the aura of "the greatest generality" ([1937] 1961, 89). Hence the doctor can tell Nora that "we wake from our doings in a deep sweat for that they happened in a house without an address, in a street in no town, citizened with people with no names with which to deny them. Their very lack of identity makes them ourselves.... Sleep demands of us a guilty immunity. There is not one of us who, given an eternal incognito, a thumbprint nowhere set against our souls, would not commit rape, murder and all abominations" (88). Again the Barnesian underworld offers no cultural or geographic specificity. While Stephen's body is filled with inversion and vocalizes the homosexuality that she had transported from the dive bar, the sleeping Barnesian body instead evacuates sexual identity to forge everyone into "an eternal incognito," an incognito removed from the cross-class identifications that support the fiction of an essentialized communal identity. This night is deeply anticommunitarian, "a thumbprint nowhere set against our souls." There are no pseudonymous cafés or dive bars in this corporealized underworld. There are no marginalized others who take center stage in an attempt to voice themselves both within and against a dominant language. Rather, as the doctor diagnoses, the night is terrifying because it is wild, anonymous, and generally unfeeling about (homosexual) identity's proper place within any social field, subcultural or not.

Given this lawlessness, Barnes's underworld would seem to take on the appearance of a vice district as it develops a "sense of danger" that was also found in her initial descriptions of New York City's Chinatown or in Park's immoral regions. Yet, like these ineffable urban enclaves, the commonest spot is not recognizable, and in this most daring design the shops have all been wrongly colored. In sum, Barnes does not ask that perverts be assimilated into the communal order; she instead dismisses sociality in toto. The Town of Darkness, that is, sloughs off identities and champions "the eternal incognito" as those who enter the night world find themselves lost amid an anticommunity: houses that fail to reveal their inhabitants, streets without addresses, and citizens who neglect to participate in any public or counter public sphere. This night world is undetectable and dislocated, everywhere because it is nowhere at all. Unlike the prototypical mystery title, the scenes in *Nightwood*'s dark worlds remain unveiled.

This antiunderworld—an Eliotic unreal city—offers a "guilty immunity" from the emerging prescriptions of modern sexual identity politics and the mandates of a subculture's communal imperatives. For Barnes, social outcasts—perverse or not—can be neither denied nor affirmed because everyone fundamentally "lacks" identity. Hence any attempt to enter a gay or lesbian history or demand sexual recognition is impossible, if only because there is nothing significant to recognize. Within this "anonymous" representational wasteland, persons have no content; they are complete nobodies and eternally incognito. And they are not always subliminal versions of the selves late modern self-identified queers don't wish to envision. Quite the contrary: they are liminal selves already beyond sexual recognition. Like the Jolasian underworld, slumming in this Barnesian night thus offers an escape from a literary social history that constructs sexually classifiable bodies. Rolling around is the language of *Nightwood*, as I now show, does likewise.

Hidden from History

To stylize means to deform reality, to derealize; style involves dehumanization. —José Ortega y Gasset, *The Dehumanization of Art*

If you think that this state is a futile art of escapism that exists only within the mind's nether regions, then recall yet another of Matthew's lectures to Nora. "Take history at night," he informs her, "Have you ever thought of that, now? Was it at night that Sodom became Gomorrah? It was at night, I swear. A city given over to the shades, and that's why it has never been countenanced or understood to this day" ([1937] 1961, 86). Though Matthew alludes to the biblical city of Sodom (and Proust's *Remembrance of Things Past*), he also asks if Nora has "thought of the night now, in other countries, in foreign countries, in Paris?" (81).[29] Telling Nora of the eternal incognitos that he finds in "French nights," Matthew again presents her with a radical revision of a gay and lesbian history that Hall (among others) had inaugurated. Rather than being sensationally exposed, the anonymous nights that he describes are shady and obscured. More important, these nights can be experienced in Paris streets just as they can be encountered in the Great Bed: "'I'm telling you of French nights at the moment,' the doctor went on, 'and why we all go into them'" (82). Neither "countenanced" nor "understood," they offer willing participants a chance to dis-articulate their slumming selves from modern technologies of sexuality, to give themselves "over to shades."

Indeed, the one character that embarks on these urban excursions into fantastic night worlds is also a "Great Enigma"—Robin Vote ([1937] 1961, 83). While Matthew tells Nora that everybody becomes nobody when they sleep, Robin has managed to achieve this incognito state in her waking life: "Her movements were slightly headlong and sideways; slow, clumsy, and yet graceful, the ample gait of the night-watch" (41). And while most of *Nightwood*'s characters are quite garrulous about their selves, the "somnambuliste" Vote talks primarily in monosyllables:

> "I'll get out" (49).
> "Why talk?" (49).
> "I'm Robin Vote.... I don't want to be here" (55).
> "Remember me" (121).
> "Shut up" (75).

Though she does announce her name to her lover Nora, Robin rarely, if ever, speaks of herself or about herself. "She did not explain where she had been: she was unable or unwilling to give an account of herself" (49). Throughout *Nightwood*, readers are given no information about her identity. Their ignorance instead mirrors that of the book's other characters. For Felix, who married Vote and fathered a child with her, "[Robin] was an enigma.... He felt that her attention, somehow in spite of him, had already been taken by something not yet in history" (44). And while the doctor, Nora, and Felix each have lengthy biographies that the reader can comprehend, Robin never explains her actions and has no personal background (or motives) that crack her enigmatic core. "She says... 'Remember me,' Matthew notes, 'Probably because she has difficulty in remembering herself'" (121). In contrast to Nora's case history and her pained epistemological searches, Robin is generally unfeeling toward self-understanding and personal revelation. She has a desperate anonymity and is best described as "the borne somnambule" whose sexual identity never coheres into an articulate person (35).

Her anonymous habitats appear to support this unintelligible state. When the reader first encounters Vote, her surroundings fail to explain her. She sleeps in "one of those middle-class hostelries which can be found in almost any corner of Paris, neither good nor bad, but so typical that it might have been moved every night and not have been out of place" ([1937] 1961, 33–34). Like Paul in white suburban Pittsburgh, like Addams in her abstract Hull-House, and like the inhabitants of the Barnesian Chinatown, Robin, too, inhabits an environment that is curiously nondescript, one that is both easily located—"so typical"—yet also easily displaced—"moved every night." Within this impersonal environment, she lies in a literal manifestation of the doctor's figurative Great Bed: "On a bed, surrounded by a confusion of potted plants, exotic palms and cut flowers, faintly over-sung by the notes of unseen birds, which seemed to have been forgotten—left without the usual silencing cover, which, like cloaks on funeral urns, are cast over their cages at night by good housewives—half flung off the support of the cushions from which, in a moment of threatening consciousness she had turned her head, lay the young woman, heavy and dishevelled" (34). Several mixed metaphors embedded in seven thick subordinate clauses separate "on a bed" from "lay the young woman." Though the "typical" realist paragraph would introduce Robin to the curious reader (as Hall does with Stephen), Barnes's convoluted syntax instead stalls our acquaintance as it refuses to size Robin up. By the time the reader reaches the end of this split independent clause, it is easy to forget who or what topic we encountered. The tortuous paragraph, like Robin's tortuous body, is antirevelatory. In lieu of a knowable character, then, readers butt against several grammatical obstacles that pummel with symbolic plants, birds, songs, cloaks, funerals, cages, housewives, and cushions. It is, the narrator notes, "confusion" at the level of the figurative that distorts our knowledge of the literal subculture.

Like her earlier slumming narratives, this misleading style undermines attempts to grasp who or what Robin is and what significance might attach to her. Or, as Judith Roof suggests, "*Nightwood*'s digressions, ruminations, and texture of language furnish a substitute for the more oedipal narrative gratification of mastery and totalized meaning" (1996, 142). Vote's silence ("Why talk?") and her anonymity obstruct personal and sexual knowledges, while Barnes's manipulation of formalistic introductions does the same. In so doing, Vote deflects any system of categorization (including the sexological) and escapes the burdens of sexual group representation (including that of a developing sexual binary). If readers expect realistic illumination, they instead are confronted with a language of night that abets Vote's "eternally incognito" body since she is, fundamentally, a Jolasian underworld.

Further, just as Barnes, like Van Vechten, manipulates the tropes of primitivism to confound our knowledge of these spectacular homosexual subcultures, she also uses the trope of the primitive body to again undermine what one might know about Robin's deviant activities. "The language used to convey her character," remarks Laura Winkiel, "link[s] her to Barnes's earlier critiques of mass [and sub]culture spectacle" (1997, 8). In the paragraph above, Vote is situated next to lush greenery—"exotic palms and cut flowers"—which suggests a Jolasian link between the walking somnambulist and the underworld. This connection is further enhanced in the following paragraph, where Robin's body merges with the subterranean earth: "The perfume that her body exhaled was of the quality of that earth-flesh, fungi, which smells of captured dampness and yet is so dry, overcast with the odour of oil of amber, which is an inner malady of the sea, making her seem as if she had invaded a sleep incautious and entire. Her flesh was the texture of plant life, and beneath it one sensed a frame, broad, porous and sleep-worn, as if sleep were a decay fishing her beneath the visible surface" ([1937] 1961, 34). Critics frequently cite this passage as a coded exploration of Robin's "hidden" lesbian "libido" (Boone 1998, 244) or as a thick metaphor for female genitalia (Allen 1996, 34). I, however, wish that Robin's primitive nature does not have a stable gendered meaning. Like her earlier slumming narratives, Barnes's description instead suggests that Vote's primitivism is incompatible with any geographic, psychic, or corporeal locale: you cannot pinpoint her on the social field. Just as her hotel room is so typical as to be ubiquitous for the Anglo middle classes, so too is her body dislocated from any regional, national, or communal affiliations. She smells of "earth," "plant," "oil," and "sea," all concrete nouns that also suggest unspecified abstraction. Like the "Town of Darkness" (or like Barnes's Chinatown), they cannot be placed.

Because of this chronic "confusion," Robin also cannot be grasped. She is "waking and yet heavy, like one in sleep," locatable while dislocated, lost yet found, primitive and modern, static and mobile, and ahistorically in history ([1937] 1961, 47). For Felix, she is "an enigma" (44). For Nora, "she was lost" (48). And for the doctor, Robin is "lost somewhere without receiving mail" as she withdraws from any situation that might begin to define her, sexually or otherwise (124). Felix finds that "her clothes were of a period that he could not quite place" (42); and even the narrator describes her as a walking paradox, "newly ancient" (42). Everywhere and nowhere, she is "not yet in history" and outside of any intelligible temporal or geographical schema. Indeed, Robin herself is "strangely aware of some lost land in herself, she took to going out, wandering the countryside; to train travel, to other cities, alone and engrossed" (45).

Unlike Stephen, Vote is not filled with sexual group identity politics. Her underworld excursions do not culminate in a plea for communal recognition. On these night ventures, she visits the back alleys of Paris, "the streets of Marseilles, the waterfront of Tangier, the *basso porto* of Naples" and continually loses her self in the process ([1937] 1961, 157).[30] "Robin can go anywhere, do anything," Nora cries, "because she forgets" that she has or might be considered to be a case history (152). And, as the narrator informs readers, "she began to haunt the terminals, taking trains into different parts of the country, wandering without design, going into many out-of-the-way churches" (167). This indeterminate mobility, I have been arguing, leads Robin to lost international lands both within her evacuated self and without. As she sleeps in the hostelry's Great Bed, she ventures into the psychic Town of Darkness that is the Jolasian night. As she nightly tramps across Europe as well as other unspecified locales, she ventures into towns where she is not countenanced or understood since she has no desire to articulate her sexual self. This transience gives Vote over to shades, as her journeys are pointless ("without design") and incoherent ("I'll never understand her"). She "drank with the men" and went "danc[ing] with the women"; and she, like Nugent's Alex, finds herself dislocated in leisurely acts indifferent to modern Anglo-American constructions of middle-class sexual identity (156). And like Addams's cosmopolitan persona, she sidesteps any trace of romantic friendship or modern lesbian identity as she takes off on international tours. And like Cather's eternal incognito Paul, she tramps into an anticommunity. Yet Robin, unlike Paul, also manages to sustain her illegibility. "Newly ancient," she is not only outside of specified space but also removed from a specified time. Coursing through anachronism, she fits in nowhere.

It could be said that this oxymoron—"newly ancient"—also characterizes the modern sapphists of the Parisian Left Bank, those artists who conjoined the Isle of Lesbos with modernist expatriation to help create a novel historical identity that would trickle down through the decades. The central topics that gather around Robin—motel stays, Parisian cafés, promiscuous wanderings, dark underworlds, primitive flesh, nation-hopping—are also the enabling themes of the transatlantic sapphism that Barnes embraced, then shirked across the pond. Taking the interests of this hesitant collective and blending it with her earlier investments in the sensational slumming narrative, Barnes fashions an antislumming narrative about anticommunitarianism. If *The Well of Loneliness* offers a cult guide to the homosexual underworld, then *Nightwood* offers a cult guide to the Town of Darkness. And if Hall's cultural work could be said to inaugurate a transnational lesbian subculture, then Barnes's text could be said to destroy this project. Though it did not succeed, it does offer readers a blueprint for an illegible queer diaspora, a thumbprint set nowhere against anyone's communitarian soul. In so doing, *Nightwood* offers a foreign sense of displacement that, complemented by a new grammar, forges an elemental and a fabulous world where community does not matter: "[Robin] carried the quality of the 'way back' as animals do" ([1937] 1961, 40).

As this unthinking and "unfeeling" being—"an animal"—Vote moves without motive and without sexual self ([1937] 1961, 135). "The proprietor of an unknown land," she operates with a lack of definition as well as a lack of direction as well as a lack of subcultural purpose. Sidestepping the seemingly inevitable teleology of homosexual subculture, she presents an indeterminate subject position where she is neither subjectified nor sexually positioned. As Matthew notes, she is "utterly unknown, particularly to oneself" and, more important, historically unspecified (138). In so doing, she propels herself out of the salvation history that *The Well of Loneliness* had imagined. While Hall humanizes the homosexual, Barnes deforms this reality. Hence Matthew's desire to go down and to slum like Robin into the primitive underworld, "to be an animal, born at the opening of the eye, going only forward, and, at the end of day, shutting out memory with the dropping of the lid" (135). It is no coincidence that this is where readers find her at the book's close as she engages in an impersonally intimate tête-à-tête with a terrified dog: "And down she went, until her head swung against his; on all fours now, dragging her knees" (169).

The Obscure Life

She covered her secrets and lived a mysterious life, but she made certain all her secrets were written down and preserved or revealed over and over again in conversations with me.
—Hank O'Neal, "Reminiscences"

To ask a question that haunts me through these pages: what about the rest? Not every nonnormative subject is eager get down on all fours, or buy a dilapidated mansion, or sleepwalk though everyday life, or launch into a locomotive, or travel to Tangiers on a lark. Not all would if they could, given other lived experiences such as race, region, religion, and socioeconomic standing that constrain flights from (as well as access to) sexual group identity. But just as Barnes offers a cult guide into the Town of Darkness through Robin Vote's subterranean body, I finally suggest that she also presents another means of slumming beyond sexuality that, potentially, you too can accomplish. This escape reveals itself when a homosexual body appears most legible.

Recall that Matthew's conversations with Nora alert her to the fact that her ex-lover has been subsumed by the night. I had argued earlier that these dialogues fail to offer anything knowable about female inversion. They do, however, have much to *say* about homosexuality. I have in mind an exchange that occurs near *Nightwood*'s close. Matthew has detailed the unknown French nights to Nora. He then switches epistemological gears and expounds on the "love we have for the invert, boy or girl":

> It was they who were spoken of in every romance that we ever read. The girl lost, what is she but the Prince found? The Prince on the white horse that we have always been seeking. And the pretty lad who is a girl, what but the prince-princess in point lace—neither one and half the other, the painting on the fan! We love them for that reason. We were impaled in our childhood on them as they rode through our primers, the sweetest lie of all, now come to be in boy or girl, for in the girl it is the prince, and in the boy it is the girl that makes a prince a prince—where what we never had stands waiting; it was inevitable that we should come on them, for our miscalculated longing has created them. They are our answer to what our grandmothers were told love was, and what it never came to be; they, the living lie of our centuries. ([1937] 1961, 136–37)

At this moment, Matthew appears to offer Nora a sexual etiology. He presents her with a genesis for homosexual inversion, an originating tale that, he imagines, has been ubiquitous in Western culture. Though he had argued that those who live in the underworld are unknowable, here he seems to suggest that the minority group identity has been located in popular narrative forms like the fairy tale all along, undermining his oft-quoted claim that "I have a narrative, but you will be put to it to find it" (97). Looking for the invert "we have always been seeking," one finds him or her "in every romance that we ever read." Within these tales, readers rediscover the inverted beings—"the prince-princesses"—that Hall and others had made so visible. Here Matthew seems not only to parrot sexological literatures but to champion them as well by turning stories of inversion into a discourse that is at once "universalizing"—relevant to all—and "minoritizing"—pertinent only to a segment of the sexual population (Sedgwick 1990, 1).

Such moments may seem to support "Barnes's unabashed frankness (and bawdiness) in representing both male and female homosexuality" (Boone 1998, 468). But, as I have been arguing throughout this chapter, what you see with Barnes is never what you get. A "sinister" Chinatown transfigures into a domesticated middle-class suburb. True-to-life Village artists become indiscernible parodies of Village types. A sleeping woman is lost the moment that she is found in bed. In keeping with these textual subterfuges, we should remember, as Felix notices, that Matthew is "a great liar, but a valuable liar. His fabrications seemed to be the framework of a forgotten but imposing plan" ([1937] 1961, 30). This chapter's introduction noted that, for many scholars, this plan signifies Barnes's investment in a modernist schema that trumpets lesbian erotics. But for others, Matthew "presents Nora with several accounts of inversion that sound like attempts to speak the truth. Yet rather than reveal the truth, as Matthew sets out to do, he only reveals the inadequacy of his own formulae" (Harris 1994, 253). To build on this insight, Matthew's purposeful lies could be read as complementary to Barnes's jolting narrative strategies since they undermine his promise for sexual revelation.[31] After all, his medical books are ruined by water and his surgical instruments are "broken" and "rusty" (78).

At times Matthew—at once "a divine idiot and a wise man"—accomplishes these lies explicitly ([1937] 1961, 31). He admits, "I am my own charlatan" (96). And during his lengthy discussions on the Great Bed and the nature of invert love, he warns Nora that "we look to the East for a wisdom that we shall not use—and to the sleeper for the secret that we shall not find" (88). Though the two converse about Robin's condition, and though he appears to say something substantial about sexual identity and its erasure, the doctor informs Nora that she may never be satisfied with any of his explanations. Beyond a false opposition of *scientia sexualis* and an orientalist *ars erotica*, "there are only confusions" Matthew tells her with brutal dishonesty (22). Like Barnes's slumming, these perplexing explanations may be antirevelatory and somewhat antiorientalist. Much like Robin's peripatetic state, their frequent talks about the night may lead to nowhere productive: "In great defaming sentences," readers are told as Matthew later commands an audience at a café, "his betrayals came up; no one ever knew what was truth and what was not" (158).

Getting lost in this epistemological underworld is *Nightwood*'s great contribution to a deepening suspicion of sexual hermeneutics that I have been tracing throughout this book. By *Nightwood*'s publication in America in 1937, twentieth-century media had published reams of discourse about homosexual communal identity, with the two volumes of Havelock Ellis's *Studies in the Psychology of Sex* alone amounting to more than twenty-nine hundred pages. Barnes's novel is no exception, as it details escapist French nights and deceitful invert love. But just as Nora enlists Matthew to "say something, oh, God, say something!" ([1937] 1961, 146), he does "something" rather unexpected. As he tells her everything he knows about the night, his ramblings (which constitute a good chunk of the book) quiet her inquisitiveness. For a few minutes, she stops crying.

Nora does so not because Matthew tells her the hidden truth of sexual group identity or because the doctor initiates her into the rituals of a homosexual community. And he does not permit her to reach any semblance of epistemological certainty. A self-professed "charlatan," the "mighty" doctor admits that his discourse is a "grain-of-salt" that amounts to little more than great betraying sentences ([1937] 1961, 158). It's not the substance of the conversation, he argues, it's what his quackery does—is doing—to Nora. Revealing everything that he knows about the night and about inversion (which is quite insubstantial), Matthew enables Nora to forget her sexual self. She had asked the doctor to "take my mind off," and his chatty monologues accomplish this task (139). Unlike Robin's incognito treks across the transatlantic, Nora never leaves his apartment on this slumming venture yet she still loses her mind. Enraptured by a discourse that reveals nothing, her will to knowledge is silenced for a moment ("Can't you be quiet now?" Matthew begs of her [124]). She stops asking questions. She forgets her present situation: "While the doctor had been speaking Nora had stopped, as if he had got her attention for the first time" (131).

Which is also to say that their conversation enables Nora to step outside her awareness of her self within an evolving discourse of modern gay and lesbian history. This is the crux of *Nightwood*. In an extended slumming venture that gestures back to Hall's dive bar, Barnes has two queers—one male, the other female—meet in the middle of the intimate night. Yet neither Matthew nor Nora reaches any understanding about the other or about the night worlds that surround them. Making it up as he goes along, Matthew instead presents Nora with a tabula rasa of the night, one that defies sexual discourse even as it conforms to the wittiest guidelines of Anglo-invert banter. Like Robin's journeys or Thurman's talks, the two nightly converse in a "formless meditation" that offers no homosexual awakening ([1937] 1961, 59). Rather than filling Nora with information, he wipes her interior slate clean.

To be honest, these are not completely ego-shattering conversations. Matthew is quick to express his longings and, at one point, wails that "it is my mother without argument I want" ([1937] 1961, 149). Nevertheless, his motives behind the blabber are still egoless: for a few brief hours, the doctor gives himself over to Nora to calm her fears. Though his observations masquerade as a mastery of text and context (and no one can deny that he has a way with words), they are also made in the absence of narcissistic self-interest. "Why not rest?" he tells her after one extended session (124). While she is attentive to the doctor's words, these stylized monologues also talk Nora's head off to the point of exhaustion, and she is placed beside her self. As Matthew replaces her sexual misery with sexual mystery, what begins as an epistemological inquiry into the status of the homosexual/invert ("say something, oh, God, say something!") becomes an evasive tactic for discarding sexual selves.

Could I not say the same for Barnes's extended engagement with the emergent transatlantic discourses of modern homosexuality in the United States, Great Britain, and France? "Though bounded by cultural concepts," notes one critic of the surreal practitioners that Barnes so admired and emulated, "they continually problematized them" (Tythacott 2003, 14). When you recall that the doctor is also a cross-dresser as well as a gynecologist, a psychotherapist, a psychologist, a barfly, a sexologist, a sociologist, an amateur historian, an expert on nightlife, a tour guide, and a raconteur, then these meaningless chats that make up the autobiographical *Nightwood* take on an ever more pertinent note for the present moment. Queers talk and talk and talk and talk but reveal nothing about themselves or those in the nightlife. "The more we learn of a person, the less we know," Matthew tells Nora ([1937] 1961, 111). This delusional gift of gab finds its parallel in *Nightwood*'s "night work" (103). Like Barnes's language of the mysterious night, it is not the revelatory substance of words ("This is real—this is the unknown"), but the act of allusiveness that occupies a slumming Nora as well as the book's slumming readers eager to know more about those in the life. After all, *Nightwood*'s original title was to be both summons and mocking interpellation—*Bow Down*.

You could just as well retitle it *Get Lost*. Though you may not always pattern yourself after an animalized Robin or the other queer slummers I have introduced in these pages, you can take *Nightwood* as a tour guide of sorts into "the obscure life" ([1937] 1961, 122): you can, like Nora, subversively bow down before the intersectional discourses that continue to make up the idea of "you" and "us." I know this is a difficult undertaking. But even though most can't—or won't—stop talking through these discourses, you must nevertheless try, like Matthew, to stop making sense through them.[32] Alongside Barnes's underworlds, the doctor's lie-filled axioms about "the nature" of homosexual identity fail to contribute to a meaningful discourse on modern sexuality or modern sexual communities. Though his rants are quite vocal, his oral histories are not sound. They add up to little more than a "mighty-grain-of-salt" (80). And while they may appear to offer a salvation of sorts for one anxious slummer, they do not represent a redemptive reading of lesbian and gay underworlds in the twentieth-century United States or elsewhere. The "story," like Matthew's investigations into the night, "do[es] not amount to much" (15).

Like the bungled slumming literatures that I have entertained throughout this book, Matthew's discourse runs afoul of any hermeneutics of sexual suspicion. Along the way, it models something historically unexpected and, for some, historically unsatisfying—a talking cure for sexual group identity. To do so, *Nightwood* offers readers a rotten urban exposé—a mystery of the Parisian night—where there is nothing sensational to expose, and nothing spectacular to see, and no historical collective to excavate, and no lesbian and gay group subject to join. By anyone's account, this is a different kind of entertainment than the *Drag*-like queer shows that jumpstarted the novel's antihistorical critique. Rather than perform underworld knowledge about a pathologized subculture, it stages this knowledge as a cultural pathology, as a symptom of what some have celebrated as sexual modernity. But, again, what did you expect?

Epilogue: Secrets of the African-American Bisexual Man; or, Double Lives on the Down Low

How do you identify someone who doesn't want to be identified? How do you define someone who doesn't want to be defined? —Keith Boykin, *Beyond the Down Low*

The word "subculture" is loaded down with mystery. —Dick Hebdige, *Subculture: The Meaning of Style*

Straight Outta Compton

At this late date, instances of queer slumming abound.[1] As nineteenth-century secrets of the city morphed into twentieth-century settlement house autobiographies, realist tramping tales, sensational sapphic novels, and outré Renaissance tour guides, so too have these mysteries taken unexpected cultural turns in the twenty-first-century U.S. imaginary. The corollary to this claim also holds true: by no means did slumming literature's obsession with sexual knowledge—or the desperate modes of queer slumming that countered this obsession—vanish once homosexual group identity crystallized across the American scene. If anything, slumming's mania is still too present, extending well beyond literatures into a host of media—lowbrow television talk shows, highbrow independent art films, and gay lifestyle magazine cartoons, to name but three—that contest and confirm persistent forms of spectacularization (fig. 14—note the guide's cap title, "Nite Life Tour").

It would not be too difficult to trace how the reading of mysteries became the mysteries of readability, how the literatures of modern

FIGURE 14. Cartoon by unknown artist, from the *Advocate*, no. 136 (April 24, 1974), 22. Courtesy of the Kinsey Institute for Research in Sex, Gender, and Reproduction.

slumming continued to seep out into other discursive arenas just as lesbian and gay identities continued, over the decades, to congeal into so-called lesbian and gay communities.[2] These proliferations went hand in hand. One could focus on reference guides to underworld homosexual idiom such as *Dictionary of American Underworld Lingo* (Goldin, O'Leary, and Lipsius 1950) and, later, Bruce Rodgers's cheeky *Gay Talk: A (Sometimes) Outrageous Dictionary of Gay Slang* (1972). One could concentrate on best-selling sexology tracts that argue for and against the classification of subterranean homosexual bodies such as Alfred C. Kinsey's *Sexual Behavior in the Human Male* (1948) or Donald Webster Cory's *The Homosexual in America: A Subjective Approach* ([1951] 1960). One could spotlight the rise of Grove Press and its calculated print-runs of profitable novels about queer urban life such as Hubert Selby's *Last Exit to Brooklyn* (1964) or John Rechy's *City of Night* (1963). One could read glossy leisure magazines such as post-Stonewall the *Advocate*, which deemed itself "America's Homophile Community" and whose distribution sometimes functioned as the print equivalent of "gaping tourists in the bars" (Meeker 2006, 77). One could examine mainstream receptions of visual media such as Keith Haring's queer-of-color subway graffiti (roughly 1980–85), or

Nan Goldin's intimate records of East Village bohemians in *The Ballad of Sexual Dependency* (1981), or Martha Rosler's *The Bowery in Two Inadequate Descriptive Systems* (1974–75). One could review films such as Ellen Hovde and Albert and David Maysles's mystery of urban decadence, *Grey Gardens* (1975), John Waters's *Desperate Living* (1977), William Friedkin's *Cruising* (1980), Emile Ardolino's *Dirty Dancing* (1987), Gus van Sant's *My Own Private Idaho* (1991), Shawn Wayans and Marlon Wayans's *Don't Be a Menace to South Central While Drinking Your Juice in the Hood* (1996), or Fenton Bailey and Randy Barbato's *Inside Deep Throat* (2005). One could concentrate, as Joshua Gamson has done, on the production of queerly classed bodies in early 1990s sensational tabloid talk shows like *The Montel Williams Show*. Last but not least, we could turn critical gazes inward to interrogate queer theories such as Lauren Berlant and Michael Warner's "Sex in Public" (1998) or Samuel R. Delany's *Times Square Red, Times Square Blue* (1999)—texts that situate "underground" bodies like the porn-house masturbator or "underground" activities like erotic vomiting at the epicenter of radical sex and gender theories.[3]

Far from exhaustive, this motley archive suggests the rich potential for further interdisciplinary research into queer slumming, its uses, and its abuses. Some of the above (such as *Cruising*) only affirms insidious divisions between dominant U.S. heterosexual cultures and "perverse" subcultures. Others, like Kinsey's *Sexual Behavior in the Human Male*, record—almost despite their disciplinary intentions—strategies of cultural, communal, and sexual unknowability that mirror the slumming literatures of Addams, Cather, Van Vechten's school, and Barnes. Still other texts, such as *My Own Private Idaho*, do both as they realistically document strains of queer U.S. subculture while they also toy with the demands of realistic documentation. A film like *Idaho* confirms what audiences like to think they know about sub-rosa communities and historicized sexual identities even as it presents new ways of seeing beyond these calcified taxonomic forms. Judging from these three conflicting examples alone, the modern slumming narrative's ideologies are more than malleable, so much so that later producers and critics manipulate its conventions for queer and, without question, not-so-queer ends.

If I have concentrated primarily on the literary tactics of early twentieth-century queer slumming—the novels, the sociological autobiographies, the letters, the short stories, the poems, and the sensational newspaper reports that undermined growing demands for underworld sexual knowledge—it's safe to say that these tactics continue to reverberate throughout U.S. multimedia. As I turn away from a heightened moment of increased visibility in the first third of the twentieth century and turn toward a heightened moment of increased visibility in the first third of the twenty-first, I would like to explore some rhetorical echoes of earlier queer slumming literatures. To be more specific, I would like to explore discourses that inform slumming investigations of the down low (DL).

Though its more astute critics have cast doubt on mainstream representations of the DL as a plausible technology of sexual knowledge production, the phrase itself achieved national recognition in the late 1990s when rhythm and blues singer R. Kelly released his autobiographical hit singles "Down Low (Nobody Has to Know)" in 1996 and "Down Low Double Life" in 1998.[4] Kelly's mention of down low referenced his illicit affairs with women, but the term has taken on same-sex overtones as it is thought to illuminate a subculture—a deviant underworld, if you like—of what columnist, lecturer, and self-appointed DL investigator Keith Boykin has termed a "mysterious group of [African-American and Latino] men" who engage in homosex, yet refuse to self-identify as gay or pledge their fidelity to a visible gay community (2005, 19). Though difficult to denote properly ("no one has ever really defined it"), the acts associated with the down low are thought to traverse—and, more importantly, elide—hetero- and homosexual group identity, a traversal that also gravitates around fears of promiscuous straight or bisexual men who are thought to transmit HIV to their unknowing female sex partners (Boykin 2005, 11).

Given such paranoia, it's not surprising that DL men have become objects of intense sexual and racial curiosity—and even more intense sexual and racial scrutiny—beyond The Billboard Hot 100 as various attempts are made to define the DL. In June 2005, none other than the Centers for Disease Control and Prevention (CDC) issued a surveillance report to disseminate sexual knowledge about the down low. As the CDC informs readers on a website entitled "Questions and Answers: Men on the Down Low" (2006):

> What are the origins of this term *down low* and what does it refer to?
>
> The most generic definition of the term *down low*, or DL, is "to keep something private," whether that refers to information or activity.
>
> The term is often used to describe the behavior of men who have sex with other men as well as women and who do not identify as gay or bisexual. These men may refer to themselves as being "on the down low," "on the DL," or "on

> the low low." The term has most often been associated with African American men. Although the term originated in the African American community, the behaviors associated with the term are not new and not specific to black men who have sex with men.

The website notes that "the phenomenon of men on the down low has gained much attention in recent years." It asks:

> What are the sexual risk factors associated with being on the down low?
>
> Much of the media attention about men on the down low and HIV/AIDS has focused on the concept of a transmission bridge between bisexual men and heterosexual women. Some women have become infected through sexual contact with bisexual men. However, many questions have not yet been answered, including:
>
> - Do bisexually active men account for more cases of HIV infection in women than do men who inject drugs?
> - Are bisexually active men more likely than other groups of men to be HIV infected?
> - What proportion of HIV-infected men who have sex with male and female partners identify with the down low?
> - Do men on the down low engage in fewer or more sexual risk behaviors than men who are not on the down low?

Though the CDC first assumes that down low males define themselves against the production of sexual knowledge ("to keep something private") and against a legible sexual binary, it nevertheless traffics in sexual classifications and sexual exposure by the end of its inquiry. Initially, the CDC's definition diagnoses certain acts—"the behavior of men who have sex with other men as well as women"—that strive to be anticommunitarian. These men, after all, "do not identify as gay or bisexual." Yet following the "generic" representation of these males, the CDC presents "the behavior" as a discernible sexual group identity—that of the AfricanAmerican "bisexual"—when it turns to "sexual risk factors." Thus it moves from acts "not specific" to a particular sexual identity to truth claims such as "much of the media attention about men on the down low and HIV/AIDS has focused on... *bisexual* men and heterosexual women" (emphasis added). In other words, much of the media attention has focused on policing these "men on the down low," on specifying men on the down low as recognizable bisexual males in order to place them in taxonomies predicated on legible sexual and racial group identities. Hence while the division of HIV/AIDS prevention within the CDC desensationalizes down low with a seemingly impersonal list of frequently asked questions, it's clear from its not-so-casual mentions of "phenomenon," "attention," and "unanswered" "questions" that the "low low" is not simply a supplement to the ongoing crisis in HIV/AIDS prevention in the twenty-first-century United States and across the globe. It is also an ongoing crisis in sexual and racial definition; an ongoing crisis in how discourses police male (and unmentioned female) queers of color; an ongoing crisis in the reification of queerness; and, I would argue, an ongoing crisis in classifying and constructing the sexual activities that are thought to take place in what some have characterized as a late-modern sexual underworld—the fantasmatic working-class ghetto.[5]

Not surprisingly then, "America's recent obsession" with turning these down low black and Latino men into recognizable gay or bisexual types has reached such a hysterical crescendo that references to the DL appear to be ubiquitous in popular and more elite cultures (Boykin 2005, 5). Most of these references run alongside mentions of "gay" in glossy magazines such as *Details, Ebony*, and *Vibe*, in op-eds for *Salon.com*, the *Guide*, and the *New York Times Sunday Magazine*, in adult entertainment websites like *GhettoSecrets.com*, *ThugBoi.com*, and *BlackandLow.com*, in television talk shows such as *Oprah*, in cable television dramas like *The Wire*, and in a cottage industry of how-to guides for best identifying men on the DL such as Janice Scott-Blanton's *My Husband Is On the Down Low . . . and I Know about It* (2005).[6] As these multiple media suggest, the "phenomenon" of the down low courses through a slew of cultural productions as social commentators, sensational journalists, anxious bourgeois wives, and other culture industries attempt to define—through what can only be called latter-day slumming investigations—this supposedly vice-ridden sexual underworld.

This hysteria has reached such a feverish pitch that it lends itself to formulaic teasing. Take, for a quick example, one September 2005 *Details* magazine photo spread whose title, "Anthropology," recalls the ethnographic accounts of so-called primitive underworlds that I encountered in writings such as Barnes's "Chinatown's Old Glories Crumbled to Dust" ([1913] 1989b). Though I was unable to obtain permission to reprint this image, I offer here a thick description of its visuals. Taken by Vincent Dilio, the photo spread is on the last page of the magazine. It presents an iconographic image of an unidentified black male attired in stereotypical ghetto or street garb—a cape-like white mink fur coat, dog tags, silver necklaces, baggy jeans, oversized rings, Timberland work boots, well-placed tattoos, and, the print tells us, "conspicuous boxers."[7] Such dress, the spread also informs readers, could just as well connote a fashionable urban gay male identity for those in the cosmopolitan know. The fur coat, captions read, "doubles as bedding on those cold nights with Fat Joe [a well-known rapper]." His "showpiece tattoo" explains to readers that "when you're this hard you don't mind a little prick." The "conspicuous boxers" inform the reader that "only Calvin Klein [a well-known fashion designer] knows where I pack mine." And the "dark denim jeans" are "slung low to make access easier for the Lil Jons [another well-known "East Side" rapper]. The photographed male is shirtless, his open torso drawing attention to his "washboard abs." His fingers are covered in diamond rings; his belt buckle is a jeweled dollar sign; his legs are spread; and he stares at the reader with a blasé demeanor. The title above the male asks in bold lettering: "Gay" black male or straight black "Rapper"? "One comes straight outta Compton," *Details* reports to its middle-class readership below this title, "the other just came out last year."

A quick reading of this scene—a reading that the CDC would likely endorse—might erase the uncertainties that the DL produces for spectators as it thrusts a queer of color male into a rigid system of closet logic. But, as I will demonstrate, other possible interpretations emerge once critics by-pass the epistemologies of such a coming-out scenario. As will become clear, I am less invested in the truth value of DL investigations in glossy magazines, in popular self-help books, or in mainstream television shows. Rather, I am much more interested in how the unknowing latent within this spectacular—and far from verifiable—discourse further demonstrates the applicability of queer slumming as a critical project for the early twenty-first century.

Never Apologize, Never Explain

We can see rhetorical carryovers of queer slumming by examining a 2003 DL exposé by Benoit Denizet-Lewis. Written for the *New York Times Sunday Magazine* and salaciously entitled "Double Lives on the Down Low," Denizet-Lewis's article builds on previous exposés published in newspapers such as the *Atlanta Journal-Constitution* and the *Los Angeles Times* as its self-identified white reporter ("There aren't many white men here either [I'm one of them]") is more than eager to delineate the sex acts and the spectacular sex cultures in which urban African American and Latino men supposedly engage (2003, 30).[8]

To do so, Denizet-Lewis presents his subjects as nothing less than secrets of the late-modern U.S. city. But rather than describe the sordid inhabitants of, say, New York, Denizet-Lewis departs from the traditional settings of the mystery genre and instead tantalizes his audience with spectacles of black and Latino bathhouses in Atlanta and Cleveland. The article begins with a surveillance of Cleveland's thriving Flex, which Denizet-Lewis contrasts (for no good reason) to the "openly gay," "predominantly white" Club Cleveland (2003, 28–30). At the Flex, he informs *Times* readers, "the TV's are tuned to porn, and the dimly lighted hallways buzz with sexual energy. A naked black man reclines on a sling in a room called 'the dungeon play area.' Along a hallway lined with lockers, black men eye each other as they walk by in towels. In small rooms nearby, some men are having sex. Others are napping" (28). After presenting this juicy tidbit of sociological realism for *Times* readers, the article then extends its investigations into DL bodies by shifting from the Flex to Atlanta nightclubs to "the world headquarters of the Web site www.streetthugz.com" to the homesteads of DL men such as "Chi" and "Jigga" (33).

Throughout these excursions, Denizet-Lewis repeats narrative conventions of mainstream slumming that I addressed in writings ranging from Jacob Riis to Stephen Crane to Radclyffe Hall. He guides curious readers through urban sex publics. He translates lingo that might be unfamiliar for *Times* readers: "With no wives or girlfriends around," they are told, "Flex is a safe place for men on the DL to let down their guards. There aren't many white men here either (I'm one of them), and that's often the norm for DL parties and clubs. Some private DL events won't even let whites in the door. Others will let you in if you look 'black enough,' which is code for looking masculine, tough and 'straight'" (2003, 30). He relies on what passes as expert knowledge to make sense of males shrouded in "the secrecy of a mysterious underground lifestyle"—his own journalistic observations of "dungeon"-like sex clubs as well as CDC factoids (Boykin 2005, 123). And he is more than willing to hypersensationalize his sociological observations with sentences like the following: "As I look out onto the dance floor, I can't help doing the math. If the CDC is right that nearly 1 in 3 young black men who have sex with men is H.I.V.-positive, then about 50 of the young men on this dance floor are infected, and most of them don't know it" (Denizet-Lewis 2003, 31).

All this is old slumming in new bottles, yet another repetition of generic conventions that categorize, survey, spectacularize, reify, and detect sexual and racial bodies for *Sunday Magazine* readers. What is somewhat innovative about his accounts, however, is the relentless attempt to normalize male queers of color across class lines by thrusting them into a narrative trajectory of U.S. sexual history and sexual visibility. In the midst of his crafted exposé, Denizet-Lewis sizes up the DL phenomenon and observes with bewilderment: "The resulting permutations confounded just about everyone, black and white, straight and gay. How should guys on the DL be regarded? Whose responsibility are they? Are they gay, straight, or bisexual? If they are gay, why don't they just tough it up, come out and move to a big-city gay neighborhood like so many other gay men and lesbians? If they are straight, what are they doing having sex with guys in parks and bathhouses? If they are bisexual, why not just say that?" (2003, 32). Faced with the specter of urban racial populations that fail to conform to late-modern sexual taxonomies (whose numbers don't add up, so to speak), Denizet-Lewis cannot help but situate them in a discernible straight-gay-bisexual troika that he assumes "everyone" holds in common. He then tries to write these baffling men into an all-too-familiar narrative of U.S. gay underworld history as he interviews George Chauncey, "the noted professor of gay and lesbian history" (32).

To his credit, Chauncey fails to provide satisfactory answers to Denizet-Lewis's questions with his historical excavations. When prompted to explain the DL, the historian states that "a lot of people look at these DL guys and say they must really be gay, no matter what they say about themselves, but who's to know?.... In the early 1900's, many men in immigrant and African-American working-class communities engaged in sex with other men without being stigmatized as queer" (2003, 33). But despite Chauncey's questioning of sexual knowledge about DL men, Denizet-Lewis cannot help but insist that the down low must be a black U.S. gay male collective in the historical making. Thus his slumming accounts cannot help but conceptualize the DL as anything but group identity or community formation: "Many black men," he notifies readers in the opening moves of the exposé, "have settled on a new identity, with its own vocabulary and customs and its own name: Down Low" (30).

Yet even with the supposed historical emergence of this "new identity" across various subcultural scenes, readers soon learn that these novel (or are they anachronistic?) subjects are but a step removed from recognizable gay black men. It makes sense, then, that "Double Lives on the Down Low" ends with the sexual history of Jigga, a "middle-class" African-American DL male who now has "a serious boyfriend who is also on the DL" (2003, 53). At the article's conclusion, Denizet-Lewis situates Jigga's once-perplexing subjectivity into a coming-out narrative that silences any epistemological unease that this queer spectacle might produce: "Jigga is proof that being on the DL isn't necessarily a lifelong identity. He seems considerably more comfortable with his sexuality than he was the first time I met him, and I suspect that soon enough, he may be openly gay in all facets of his life without losing his much-coveted masculinity" (53).

Sunday Magazine audiences might now breathe a sigh of relief. But given that Jigga's "new" (and monogamous) "identity" isn't "necessarily" "life-long," let's be honest: who's to know when it comes to making sense of this DL guy? And who's to say how guys on the DL should best be rhetorically regarded? As Denizet-Lewis's narrative slums in order to identify these queers of color, it becomes evident that his subjects' narratives queer this slumming to argue against communal identifications of any kind. In spite of Denizet-Lewis's claims in "Double Lives," DL "thug" males often do speak, but they don't speak communal identity. When they are pressed into compulsory homosexual group "identity," it's clear that they regard any form of communitarianism with utmost disdain. "Never apologize, never explain," states one DL guy (2003, 33). "There's no way I'm gay," insists another (32). "I'm just freaky," states one (33). And it's a "way to dissociate," explains another male (33).[9] For Denizet-Lewis's mainstream gay slumming, these exclamations prove nothing but the sad, sorry fact that down low rationale is thinly veiled closet logic—"a step back into the dark days before liberation, before gay-bashing was considered a crime, before gay television characters were considered family entertainment" (33). Yet for guys like the "middle-class" Jigga (or Chi or Rakeem or Rick or William or the multitude of men that enter and exit "Double Lives" or myriad other sensational DL exposés) it's a step neither back nor forward in a progressive history of U.S. sexual visibility that is marked by "the dark days before liberation." When these bourgeois men discuss the "street" persona of "being on the DL," it is instead—and I stress a parallel to Wallace Thurman's Ray here—a way for them to step outside sexual narratives that seem so obvious to "everyone," to disregard representations of closet logic, to disassociate rhetorically from the static permutations of present-day U.S. sexual community.

Which is also to say that these queer slummers paradoxically speak sexual disarticulation in "Double Lives" as their sensational self-narrations confuse "an already complicated group identity" (Denizet-Lewis 2003, 31). And despite the exposé's anxious attempts to clarify the DL with comparisons to previous "immigrant and African-American working-class communities," personal sexual histories like Jigga's—let alone collective sexual histories that traverse racial and class divides—aren't easily encapsulated in a spectacle of color. Hence when Denizet-Lewis tries to impose narrative closure on DL men by thrusting them into the before and after of "gay liberation," they soon enough resist revealing any ghetto secrets as their queer life narratives mangle the designs of (homo)sexual visibility, community formation, and the metanarrative of U.S. sexual history. In their refusals, these male bodies relish "a certain freedom... in not having to explain yourself, or your sexuality" by denigrating "modern society's rules of self-identification" (31). To be blunt, their queer slumming brings slumming narratives of sexual surveillance and compulsory homosexuality to a standstill. Or, as Denizet-Lewis notes without a hint of irony before he situates his subjects in an epistemology of the ghetto: "Since they generally don't see themselves as gay, there is nothing to 'come out' to, there is no next step" (31).

Undetectability

Similar strategies appear when one focuses on mainstream television talk shows such as *The Oprah Winfrey Show*, which makes mention of a "recent *New York Times Magazine*" article in a special April 16, 2004, episode titled "A Secret Sex World: Living On the 'Down Low'"(Winfrey 2004, 7). Like Denizet-Lewis, Winfrey frames her talk show as a promise of sexual revelation for her predominantly white and black, predominantly female, and predominantly middle-class audience. And like Denizet-Lewis's accounts of Cleveland's Flex, the host, too, offers her viewers the lure of sensational knowledge about a suspicious sexual community in her show's opening moments: "An all-new OPRAH and it is a shocker," she tells the camera. "One man blows the lid off this sexual underground" (1).[10] *Oprah*, in brief, turns into an armchair slumming tour.

This "one man" is J. L. King, a self-professed middle-class DL guy (and rampant opportunist) who exploited and constructed the down low panic with a series of autobiographical guides such as *On the Down Low: A Journey into the Lives of "Straight" Black Men Who Sleep with Men*

([King and Hunter 2004], originally titled *Secrets: The Official Handbook of the Lifestyles of African-American Men Who Have Sex with Men*) and *Coming Up from the Down Low: The Journey to Acceptance, Healing and Honest Love* (2005). Both best-sellers taxonomize the DL male with chapters titled "The Signs" and "DL Behavior Types" such as "the Mature Brother, the Thug Brother, the Professional Brother, the 'I Have a Wife/Girlfriend Brother,' and the 'I'm Just Curious' Brother" (135). King prides himself on disseminating what counts for sexual knowledge, and he frequently boasts that he was one of the first to alert the CDC to the potential harm that DL men might cause African-American women when he distributed a sensationalized pamphlet entitled "Secrets of the African-American Bisexual Man" in 2001.[11] He situates himself—and is situated by *Oprah*—as a DL expert, as one who will reveal the secrets of these bisexual city subjects for audiences that want to know more about a "shocking" twenty-first-century underworld.

But curiously, when King's spectacular story does unveil metropolitan life during *Oprah*'s slumming venture, it—like Jigga's—only frustrates sexual legibility. When the television host asks King to define the DL properly, he replies with what seems like utmost frankness: "To be on the down low means to keep it hush-hush, to be unreadable, to be able to cover your tracks" (Winfrey 2004, 3). He remains true to these words throughout the episode since he is a train wreck of an informant. Though positioned as the one presumed to know, he fails to reveal anything personal about himself—or those in the life—when asked about his sexual relations. And though positioned as a slumming detective into this mysterious sex world, King shows himself to be "unreadable" when he offers nothing but an elusive identity for *Oprah*'s curious spectators, a strategy that opposes the revealing and timely looks into proto–gay black male subjects that commentators like Boykin or Denizet-Lewis imagine they offer.

Cases in point: *Oprah* tries to solicit true confessions from King that will "blow the lid off" the down low, but King refuses to say anything about his sexual self or his affiliations with any sexual group identity. I reproduce a somewhat incoherent exchange between the interviewer and the interviewee as it was recorded for Winfrey's Harpo Productions, Inc.:

WINFREY: Ok. So tell . . .

MR. KING: But . . .

WINFREY: . . . me this 'cause—tell me this. Do you then not consider yourself gay?

MR. KING: No, I don't.

WINFREY: You don't?

MR. KING: No, I don't consider myself...

WINFREY: Explain that to me, 'cause I can't figure that out. How is...

MR. KING: Why do I—and so why do I have to label myself?

WINFREY: Ok.

MR. KING: Why do I have to put a label on myself to make you comfortable?

WINFREY: Ok. I don't want to be comfortable. I just want to know what it is. Ok. Ok... (Winfrey 2004, 5)

And later in the episode:

WINFREY: Ok. Do you still date men and women?

MR. KING: Date?

WINFREY: O—ok, whatever you call it. Do you still have sex with men?

MR. KING: Am I intimately involved with men and women?

WINFREY: Ok. Yeah.

MR. KING: Yes.

WINFREY: What do you call it?

MR. KING: Yes.

WINFREY: Yes.

MR. KING: Yeah.

WINFREY: Ok. So you wouldn't...

MR. KING: But.... (9–10)

As Winfrey tries to excavate King's personal sexual history, King becomes more and more undetectable. When asked to "tell," he interrupts Winfrey with a repeated series of "buts." He undoes the set parameters of the talk show Q&A by interviewing Winfrey ("Why do I—and so why do I have to label myself?"). He refuses to elaborate on Winfrey's questions by answering in repetitive monosyllables. He feigns ignorance about the proper definitions of activities such as "date." He forces Winfrey to clarify herself to the point of definitional absurdity ("Am I intimately involved with men and women?" "Ok. Yeah."). He answers inquiries with non sequitur ("What do you call it?" "Yes." "Yes." "Yeah." "Ok."). And he ends one interview on the same note of irresolution with which he began. The exchange goes nowhere. It's an inarticulation that functions as sexual disarticulation, a "never apologize, never explain" stance that refuses *Oprah*'s slumming desire for sexual comprehension. And in so doing, King "emerges" at what Judith Butler has elsewhere called "the limits of intelligibility" (2004, 74).

Of course King could—and should—be admonished for many of these pithy remarks, since they disdain effeminacy and self-identified white and black gay men and shunt black women to social irrelevance. "The greatest taboo," he informs Winfrey, "is to be black and homosexual and I refuse to be labeled and classified as this character that folk will look at me as something different. I am a man. I don't want to be labeled" (Winfrey 2004, 5). Though I acknowledge the numerous variables that might enable this nasty comment—the unyielding pressures of normative gender constraints for one, homophobia for two—I nevertheless find King's uneasy claims provocative since his verbal manipulations—the same verbal manipulations present in Van Vechten and Barnes and Nugent—make Winfrey and her audience extremely anxious. It's as if the terrifying possibility of HIV infection ("O—ok") is compounded by the terrifying prospect of becoming infected with King's unknowing. While I have little desire to valorize King here or elsewhere, I highlight his calculated refusals to narrate what, exactly, black male sexuality is. Winfrey promises *Oprah*'s slummers some epistemological certainty about a "secret sex world," but King's exchanges present breakdowns not only in underworld sexual knowledge but also in what mainstream U.S. media like to think they know about "foreign" bodies.

Despite her claims to the contrary, this makes the talk-show host extremely uncomfortable. King prompts unease in Winfrey as he undoes the host's pointed Q&A (and, interestingly, his own earlier sensational CDC findings). What should be a moment of subcultural legibility for middle-class viewers across the racial stratum becomes opaque as King spoils *Oprah*'s promise to reveal "DL behavior types"—his "professional brother" self included. Refusing to narrate any sexual group identity, he situates himself outside mass-mediated surveillances of the dreaded CDC bisexual as his televised autobiography becomes a ruse, a series of blocked sexual revelations and "buts." To his credit and to his dismay, Boykin picked up this strategy: "[King's] identity was much less clear when he appeared on *Oprah*. He was not gay, he was not bisexual, he was not on the down low. He simply refused to be labeled. A few months after that, when *A&U* [*Arts & Understanding*] magazine featured him on a cover story, his story changed again" (2005, 128–29).

To put a different spin on these subterfuges: King remains loyal to the hush-hush ideals of the DL since he betrays nothing about the secret sex world when fixed within the narratives of *Oprah*'s slumming. In his refusal to nominalize, in his indecipherable "verbosity," in his inability to tell Winfrey "what it is," and in his cultivated unreadability, he becomes an illegible sexual subject (Foucault 1990a, 33). Pitching himself outside *Oprah*'s demands, he becomes, to borrow a phrase from a 1939 Winston Churchill radio broadcast, a "mystery inside an enigma" (Boykin 2005, 135). And as he cultivates this mystery by queering Winfrey's slumming, his DL activities extend beyond her audience's desire for sexual recognition. A failed sleuth and a worthless interviewee, he situates himself (and those other down low males for whom he metonymically signifies) outside the revelatory promises of a mystery narrative even as he embeds himself within them. Like Jane Addams, King's Chicago-based performance is a disappearing act.

Which is also to say that King the DL expert becomes—to use an adjective often describing DL males—"unclockable" (Boykin 2005, 127). Propelling himself outside of a discernible U.S. sexual history, he, like some of Denizet-Lewis's subjects, also propels himself outside of a collective sexual history, outside of a locatable time, and outside of a locatable taxonomy. To borrow a term with which DL men are thought to characterize themselves and that cultural critic Jason King mentions in a *Village Voice* essay entitled "Remixing the Closet: The Down-Low Way of Knowledge," King is an "incognito" (2003, 44).[12] To borrow a phrase with which this book began, he's a riddle of the underworld.

Beyond Subcultural Studies: A Manifesto

With these brief excursions into *The Oprah Winfrey Show* and the *New York Times Sunday Magazine* complete, I return to the *Details*'s "Gay or Rapper?" photo spread. I had earlier suggested that readers from the CDC (or viewers from *Oprah*) might want to pin down the tongue-in-cheek DL male by turning him into an easy gay read. On closer examination, any communal identifications that the visual suggests are ruined as closet logic fails to encapsulate this spectacular subject. The moment that any reader of *Details*'s "Anthropology" positions the male as "gay" or "rapper," the stylized image begins to suggest so much more or, potentially, so much less. In homage to Henry Louis Gates, Jr., here's thirteen ways of looking at this black man. The image could be:

A black gay male.
A black straight male.

A black bisexual male.
A freaky black male.
A freaky black rapper.
A black straight rapper.
A black gay ghetto rapper.
A middle-class black gay male slumming as a ghetto rapper.
A middle-class black male slumming as a freaky ghetto rapper.
A middle-class black male slumming as a ghetto rapper who dissociates from a middle-class white gay male identity.
A straight black ghetto male rapper upward slumming as a middle-class gay male.
None of these.
All of these.

Thus when a *Details* reader slums in order to visualize this underworld body in set stereotype, its ethnographic object slips beyond its epistemological grasp. The unnamed male is, perhaps, one who has gone queer slumming by going down low, by sidestepping the "gay or rapper?" question the moment it is invoked. Or, paradoxically, by sidestepping the "gay or rapper?" question by invoking it.

Stated in the terms of queer theory: the nonce taxonomy that is this new subcultural identity prisms into a nonce taxonomic overload. A categorical proliferation that works as a categorical breakdown, it's a reification of queerness that queers itself outside of reification. Stated in the terms of the sensational city mysteries exposé: the narrative permutations of this DL guy may confound just about everyone, much like they do in Denizet-Lewis's slumming reports and in *Oprah*'s slumming shocker of an episode. And just as this image routs the ability to read a singular sexual body, so, too, does it obstruct desire to read a larger subcultural body. As much as it spoils the idea of an exemplary black rapper, *Details*'s "Anthropology" also spoils the idea of a working-class urban black ghetto. Likewise, as much as it spoils the idea of an exemplary gay male, it also spoils the idea of a middle- to upper-middle-class urban gay white male ghetto. The photo spread, in sum, spoils the intersectional idea of a ghetto subculture in toto. Easily read, the communal allegiances that the photo spread might announce are just as easily unreadable, unclockable, unlocalizable, and, for some, uncomfortable.

In lieu of epistemological clarity, the DL forces readers, viewers, and critics to reassess their fascinations with subcultural bodies across racial and class borderlines even as these bodies solicit sexual curiosity. Critics in and of queer studies have become more than adept at surveying underworld discourses of all kinds: it's why we call the work we do an investigation. As excavators of sexuality, we have become more than savvy at investigating the sociocultural conditions under which underworlds rendered themselves legible, regardless of whether or not that legibility occurs in the early 1900's or today, and regardless of whether that legibility occurred willfully. This is what Foucault, years before the academic institutionalization of queer studies in a few American universities, dismissed as "the learned volumes, written and read; . . . all the stories told to oneself and to others, so much curiosity, so many confidences" (1990a, 71). If we heed these words, now may be a time to again envision an alternative for studies of homosexual subcultures. You could start by turning epistemological tools against investigations of your epistemological self.[13]

Rather than continue to unearth an archeology of sexual knowledge in its myriad forms, critics might then begin to dabble in sexual unknowing. Imagine sexual mystifications of the sort that down low males, consciously or not, produce for curious slummers—more truthful lies, more unexplained enigmas, more pictures of vice that don't speak, and more words that don't show. Such projects would attend to uncomfortable instances of inarticulation, and they would offer no insight into sexual group identifications across any decade. They would instead be wary of disciplinary forms high, low, and somewhere in the middle that foster collective sexual hermeneutics. Theoretically conceived, a project that goes queer slumming would frustrate, mislead, misrepresent, misguide, misread, play the fool, fail to illuminate, be unoriginal, offer false testimony, give bad impressions, present bad history, improperly cite, cheat, embrace the derivative, veil itself in mystery, go nowhere fast, keep it hush-hush, be unreadable, cover its tracks. It would go down low to push beyond the novelties of queer epistemologies as it refuses to deliver. It would cultivate disappointment in readerly expectation rather than ferret out subcultural knowledge. It would spoil previous projects of sexual modernity from within. It would strive for ineptitude.

I want to believe that I have accomplished such rotten politics. I have offered you no insight into modern U.S. underworlds as I revisited an established canon of modern U.S. slumming literatures, and I've been a worthless tour guide as I made my way through various late nineteenth- and twentieth-century scenes. I trust that I have not initiated you into any city vice heretofore unknown and that I have exposed little on these tours of urban underworld bodies. Clueless, I had no desire to dig up another version of the closet, whether that closet is an individual's or twentieth-century Western culture's. I only wanted to spoil some well-made stories, to further confound some of these insidious connections that reify homosexual bodies across the late nineteenth, twentieth, and early twenty-first centuries. Nor do I conclude with an explanatory framework that would render shadowy communities more intelligible. I instead focused throughout on formulaic slumming ventures that undercut the formulaic mysteries of modern U.S. lesbian and gay history, on nineteenth-century secrets of the city that spread, kudzu-like, into the open secrets of twenty-first-century U.S. literatures and cultures. Such interpretations demanded—and will continue to demand—attention to close readings that fail explication, archives that crumble when opened, metropolitan lives that remain under wraps, and visuals that don't appear.

Now I know what you're thinking. This seems like a cul-de-sac for any study of the mysteries of sexual modernity in the transcontinental United States or, for that matter, anywhere elsewhere. It is. Pushing beyond scrutiny via scrutiny, it ruins the business of communal visibility whose ethos guides much of the institutional labors and popular cultures of decades past and the decade present. As I have recruited a "stubborn will to nonknowledge" throughout these pages, I ask that scholars forgo their sexual curiosities, as well as their quick studies, as well as their apparent sites, as well as their easy reads (Foucault 1990a, 55). As critics move beyond in-depth investigations of how the other half lives, they might then begin the arduous task of reconsidering the cherished strategy of detective work. This is work that, in the long historical march of sexual group identity, updates the mainstream slumming in which my writers refused to participate. So many more underworlds, I can only guess, remain to be undeciphered, unrecognized, unknown, and undone. I have no clue what these antirevelations might look like. I just wish that they would have nothing to show you.

Notes

Introduction

1. For extended discussions of the controversies surrounding *The Drag*'s production in Bridgeport, Connecticut, Bayonne, New Jersey, and its failure to appear on Broadway, see Chauncey (1994, 312–13); Curtin (1987, 68–90); Hamilton (1997, 63–67), and Schlissel (1997, 10–14).

2. My use of the racial marker "white" for this period is sometimes anachronistic, given that the term itself underwent swift definitional shifts across the nineteenth and twentieth centuries. For more on the social construction of U.S. "white" identities in relation to class, sexuality, and other racialized/ethnic bodies, see, among others, Dyer (1997); Frankenberg (1993); Jacobson (1998); Lott (1993); Rasmussen et al. (2001); Roediger (1991); Somerville (2000); and Stokes (2001).

3. By "promise of sexual legibility," I refer to entrenched ideals of spectacular visibility that have guided many influential productions in U.S.-based as well as transnational-based lesbian, gay and queer studies. Perhaps the best examples of this ideology can be found in the titles of three recent projects: *Becoming Visible: An Illustrated History of Lesbian and Gay Life in Twentieth-Century America* (1998) by Molly McGarry and Fred Wasserman; *All the Rage: The Story of Gay Visibility in America* by Suzanna Danuta Walters (2001); and *Up from Invisibility* by Larry Gross (2002). While Gross tacitly equates lesbian and gay invisibility with slavery by drawing on the title of Booker T. Washington's 1901 *Up from Slavery,* several other texts on lesbian, gay, and queer specularity complicate this cross-ethnic analogy of visibility. The following have been instrumental to my thinking on these matters: Bersani (1995); Conor (2004); Edelman (1994, 3–23); Gamson (1998, 209–25); Green (1997); Hall (1997); Johnson (1993); Phelan (1996, 146–66); Quiroga (2001); Reid-Pharr (2001, 1–18); Ricco (2002); Rothenberg and Valente (1997); and Sedgwick (1990).

4. For further discussions of the mysteries slumming genre and its commitment to social classification, see Chauncey's passing mention of the "heights and depths and light and shadow that many middle-class writers used" (1994, 44); Edwards (2001, 121–26); Erickson (2005, 478–530), where he discusses urban sexual perversion in antebellum U.S. sensational fiction; Gilfoyle (1992, 143–60); Greeson (2001); Koven (2004) on "the city as mystery" (38); Reynolds and Gladman (2002); Sante (1991); Streeby (2002); Tolzmann (1996); Trachtenberg (1982a; 198b, 104–28); Walkowitz (1992) on "the narrative tradition of urban exploration" (5) and "spectacular narratives" of "sensational media stories" (80); and Warner (1984).

5. These are only five of the numerous U.S. mysteries of the city published throughout the nineteenth and twentieth centuries. An extended overview of the genre—one yet to be published—could consider the following: the anonymous *Die Geheimnisse von Philadelphia* (1853) and *The Mysteries and Miseries of San Francisco* (1853); Henry Boernstein [Heinrich Börnstein], *The Mysteries of St. Louis* (1850); George G. Foster, *New York by Gas-Light: With Here and There a Streak of Sunshine* (1850); Emil Klauprecht, *Cincinnati, or, The Mysteries of the West* (1854–55); Phudge Phumble's *Adventures of a Greenhorn in Gotham! or, Rawboned Rambles in New York* (1885); *Rand McNally's Handy Guide to New York* (1891) and *Handy Guide to Chicago and the World's Columbian Exposition* (1893); Baron Ludwig von Reizenstein, *The Mysteries of New Orleans* (1854–55); William T. Stead, *Satan's Invisible World Displayed; or, Despairing Democracy: A Study of Greater New York* (1897); and Robert F. Walsh, *Dr. Parkhurst's Crusade; or, New York after Dark* (1892). See Denning, ([1987] 1998, 85–86) and Erickson (2005, 612–29) for complementary listings of nineteenth-century American mysteries.

6. The archive on sensationalism and sexuality—both inside and outside the United States—is growing. See Chauncey (1994, 39–41); Cvetkovich (1992); Duggan (2000, 2003) on the Alice Mitchell–Freda Ward murder story that would contribute to the crystallization of a transatlantic Anglo-lesbian identity in the first third of the twentieth-century; Goldsby (2006); Kaplan (1999); Koven (2004); Looby (1993); Lutes (2006); Miller (1988); Robertson (2003); Singer (2001); Srebnick (1995); and Streeby on nineteenth-century sensationalism as a "sexualizing [and, she emphasizes, imperial] discourse on the body" (2002, 27).

7. For extended considerations of authorial manipulations of the urban mystery formula and their gendered relation to middle- and lower-class reading publics at a time of national socioeconomic reorganization, see Erickson (2003); Looby (1993); Stewart (1997, 679–83); and Streeby (2002).

8. In this regard, slumming literatures parallel other Western travel literatures describing geographic regions and cultures that fail to conform to standards of national normality and bourgeois productivity. For more on this, see Edwards (2001); Grewal (1996); Kaplan (2002); Lowe (1991); McClintock (1995); Mumford (1997); and Pratt (1992).

9. While my support for this claim will be the writings of Jane Addams and several writers of the Harlem Renaissance, I note that critics such as Keith Gandal, Joseph Entin, and Mary Esteve have undertaken similar readings for ideologically suspect slummers like Stephen Crane and Jacob Riis. See Entin (2001, 327–35); Esteve (2003, 112–17); and Gandal (1997, 39–57).

10. For more on the construction of the turn-of-the-century "underclass" body, see Bramen (2000); and Pittenger (1997).

11. This phrase builds on Paul Ricoeur's consideration of modern "masters of suspicion"—Freud, Nietzsche, and Marx (1970, 33).

12. Historians and cultural critics of U.S. sexual identity have tracked how popular and medical U.S. discourses of sexual inversion regarding "abnormal" women and men metamorphosed into a visible urban homo- and heterosexual binary by the 1920s and thereafter. See Chauncey (1994); Duggan (2000); Katz (1995); Ross (2004); Seitler (2004); Somerville (2000); Stokes (2001); and Trask (2003) for more on this formation. For an important intervention into the metropolitan orientations of this history that questions the ubiquity of the binary in the twentieth-century U.S. South, see Howard (2001).

13. Following Chauncey (1994) and Mumford (1997), historian Chad Heap's exploration of early twentieth-century leisurely slumming in Harlem and Greenwich Village (2000) finds that white middle-class audiences found these sites very good. Chauncey maintains that "the spectacle of the pansy allowed men to confirm their manliness and solidarity with other men by distinguishing themselves from pansies" (328). Heap likewise contends that these ventures "provided a concrete means by which white urban residents could identify themselves as 'respectable' middle-class Americans by differentiating themselves from the free-loving bohemians, blacks and homosexuals whom they objectified in a series of commercialized slumming vogues" (8). Lewis Erenberg offers an earlier version of Chauncey's and Heap's arguments, all of which I find indispensable for those studying the macropolitics of U.S. slumming as well as for those such as myself who concentrate on the microcomplications of its urban literary history. "The Village," Erenberg writes in 1984, "then as now, had the reputation for homosexuality, and conventional whites could *see* lesbians and homosexuals on the streets" (253, emphasis added).

14. While I concentrate on resistances figured within the slumming literature's conventions, I also note that resistances from without were just as frequent. See Denning (1996) for a discussion of "the ghetto pastorals" (228), a tradition that he claims opposes writings such as *How the Other Half Lives* and connects disparate works such as Tille Olsen's *Yonnondio: From the Thirties* (1974); Mike Gold's *Jews without Money* (1930); Henry Roth's *Call It Sleep* (1934); and John Dos Passos's *U.S.A.* trilogy (1930, 1932, 1936).

15. The following list is by no means exhaustive and is meant to suggest the potential for further considerations of modern and modernist U.S. slumming

literatures: Stephen Crane's "Experiments" in "Misery" and "Luxury" (1894) and his never-written "Flowers of Asphalt"; Professor Godfrey St. Peter's infatuation with the working-class Tom Outland in Willa Cather's *The Professor's House* (1925); Mildred's desire to philanthropically slum below deck in Eugene O'Neill's *The Hairy Ape* (1921); Amory Blaine's run-in with the Mann Act in F. Scott Fitzgerald's *This Side of Paradise* (1920); Tom Buchanan's love-hate affair with his working-class mistress in *The Great Gatsby* (1922); Rudolph Fisher's "The Caucasian Storms Harlem" (1927); Edna St. Vincent Millay's observations of Village gentrification in *A Few Figs from Thistles* (1920); Henry James's *The American Scene* (1907); the bohemian gambling dens and the slummers at The Club in James Weldon Johnson's *The Autobiography of an Ex-Colored Man* (1912); Nella Larsen's critique of slumming in *Passing* (1929); Ralph Werther's *The Female-Impersonators* (1922); Floyd Dell's urban tramping in *Intellectual Vagabondage* (1913); Gertrude Stein and Alice Toklas's police tour in *Everybody's Autobiography* (1937); unreal cities in T. S. Eliot's *The Waste Land* (1922) and "The Love Song of J. Alfred Prufrock" (1915); Claude McKay's notorious best-seller *Home to Harlem* (1928); the shadowlands of Blair Niles's *Strange Brother* (1931); James Agee and Walker Evans's displaced urban sexual anxieties in the rural Alabama setting of *Let Us Now Praise Famous Men* (1939); West's *The Pleasure Man: A Comedy Drama* (1928), her companion piece to *The Drag*; Wallace Thurman's early Harlem tour guides (1927); Herbert Asbury's *The Gangs of New York: An Informal History of the Underworld* (1928) and one of its follow-ups, *The French Quarter: An Informal History of the New Orleans Underworld* (1936); Tom Kromer's tramping in *Waiting for Nothing* (1935); Margaret Bourke-White and Erskine Caldwell's *You Have Seen Their Faces* (1937); Robert McAlmon's bitter accounts of Weimar Berlin's expatriate Anglo-American slummers in stories such as "Miss Knight" and "Distinguished Air" in *Distinguished Air* (*Grim Fairy Tales*) (115 copies first appearing in 1925 by McAlmon's Contact Edition Press, then a limited run in 1927 by Carl Van Doren's *Americana Esoterica*, and later reprinted by the University of New Mexico Press in 1992); (William) Clyde Fitch's drama *The City* (1909); Nathanael West's ventures into surreal homosexual brothels in *A Cool Million* (1934); plus the countless glossaries, dictionaries of slang and underworld language, and cheap paperback tour guides into major U.S. cities published from the turn-of-the-century onward.

16. Of course, many lesbians and gays of any color and any historical period are—and were—not immune to undertaking sexual identifications of their own when they went slumming to search for underworld belonging. For more on the suspect erotics of such "sexual colonialism" and "the desire for a [sexual] relationship across class lines," see Weeks (1997, 273); and see also Chauncey (1994, 44).

17. Though I focus primarily on U.S. writers, I note that several contemporary modern western European writers undertook similar projects. In Bersani's analysis (1995, 127) of Michel's "radical slumming" in Gide's *The Immoralist*, he offers

a line that contains one of the germs of this present book: "Gide was certainly not immune to colonizing impulses (as he himself recognized), and yet those very impulses were perhaps the precondition for a potentially revolutionary eroticism. By abandoning himself to the appearances of sexual colonialism Gide was able to free himself from the European version of relationships that supported the colonialism" (1995, 122).

18. This strategy of minor literature has been a guiding creed in queer theories, literary-focused or not. A brief genealogy must include Berlant and Freeman on the productions of "queer counterspectacle" (1997, 170); Butler on the rearticulations of sexological discourses concerning trans subjects, discourses which the philosopher suggests enable recalcitrant bodies to go on "refusing the interrogations that besiege [them], reversing their terms, and learning the ways in which [they] might escape" (2004, 73); Cobb (2006) on queer redeployments of religious rhetoric in twentieth-century and early twenty-first century U.S. public spheres; Duggan on the way in which insidious sensational narratives such as the turn-of-the-century "lesbian murder plot" "were available to be read, reworked, or reinvented in quite unpredictable ways for a variety of social purposes" (2000, 155); Freeman (2002) on queer reimaginings that engage with the normative marriage plot in U.S. literatures and cultures; Fuss (1995) on the reformatting of psychoanalytic concepts of identification; Muñoz on the "smoky, mysterious, and ultimately contestory" forms of what he, following Fuss, theorizes as "disidentification," the "partial disavowal of that cultural form that works to restructure it from within" (1999, 34, 28); and Juana María Rodríguez's writings on queer Latin identities (2003).

19. Framed in this manner, this book engages with ongoing debates over a key concept in queer studies—communitarianism—that informs many of the field's productions. See, for starters, Berlant and Warner (1998); Bersani (1995); Bersani and Dutoit (1998); Joseph (2002); Muñoz (1999, 32–34); Nealon (2001); and Ricco (2002).

20. See Scott (2001) for a theoretical consideration of the role that "history" plays in the construction of discernible sexual and gender group identity bases. For an engagement that links historical being with the emergence of lesbian and gay communities in twentieth-century U.S. literary public spheres, see Nealon (2001). And for a discussion of the role of historical undoing and unmaking that has influenced my thinking on how queer slummers refuse to illuminate or assimilate to the narrative norms of lesbian and gay history, see Gallagher (2002).

Chapter One

1. See Chauncey (1994, 99–127); Faderman (1991, 62–92); and Weeks (1997, 272–76) for more on these subcultures. For more on the interconnections between

the working-class passing woman, middle-class romantic friendships between Anglo women, and their link to modern gay and lesbian group identity, see Duggan (2000). To this far from exhaustive list, I add Heap (2000); Koven (2004); Ross (2004); Trask (2003); and White (1993).

2. While some may question my use of the term "philanthropic slumming" to describe these ventures, I note that several historians, sociologists, and other social commentators during the first third of the twentieth century—as well as later critics—have been quick to employ the phrase. Three examples illuminate this point. First, in his 1933 review of urban bohemian living in Chicago and New York, Albert Parry finds that the late nineteenth century and early twentieth century was "an era of early settlement houses" where "the spirit was missionary." "Young men and women," he claims, "became seriously and socially minded and went slumming amid the newly arrived East European immigrants" (63). Likewise, University of Chicago sociology student Nels Anderson states that "the word 'slum'" originated "with the wave of humanitarianism that swept the country in the eighties and nineties" and that it has "come into disrepute" "with the decline of slumming as a philanthropic pastime" (1998b, 95). And in its most recent historical formula, Kevin J. Mumford's analysis of slumming literatures maintains, "social reformers, intellectuals, sociologists, bohemians, white urban sophisticates—all can be understood as modern-day slummers" (1997, 135).

3. Here I distinguish between slumming for pleasure or entertainment—or leisurely slumming—and a more altruistic-oriented slumming, or philanthropic slumming. The former, which I will discuss in my third and fourth chapters, dominated white-led urban tourism during the cabaret-crazy Jazz Age. The latter was much more prevalent during the 1890s, though resorts and clubs in New York's Bowery, as Chauncey notes, were frequented by middle-class white men looking for "a chance to cultivate and explore sexual fantasies" (1994, 36). For more on philanthropic slumming as cross-class and cross-racial contact, see Cocks (2001, 174–203). For more on leisurely slumming as cross-racial contact, see Erenberg (1984, 252–59).

4. For extended analyses of Progressivism and questions of assimilation, immigration, and U.S. imperialism, see Davis (1967); Deegan (1988); Duis (1998); Feffer (1993); Horowitz (1976); Jackson (2000); Jacobson (2000); Meyerowitz (1988); and Rosen (1982).

5. For more on the link between racial bodies and homosexual identifications at the turn of the century, see Hatheway (2003). Also, see Somerville (2000, 15–38), who explores the connection between the body of the tragic mulatto and the body of the invert across late nineteenth- and early twentieth-century film, literature, legal discourse, and sexology.

6. Though I do take Faderman's claim at face value, I also emphasize that other historians and cultural critics have pointed out the difficulty of properly identifying romantic female friendships as proto-lesbian. On the pleasures and difficulties

of tracking same-sex Anglo friendship across the centuries, see Vicinus, who notes that a historical figure sometimes "remains tantalizingly beyond full historical reconstruction" (2004, 24). For more general accounts of same-sex white female relations such as smashing and crushing, see Inness (1995). And for an insightful account of nineteenth-century same-sex passion that ruptures the traditional teleology between romantic friendship and lesbianism, see Diggs (1995).

7. This relation, however, does not fall under the category of what Judith Halberstam, following Eve Kosofsky Sedgwick, terms "nonce taxonomies" or "classifications of desire, physicality, and subjectivity that attempt to intervene in the hegemonic processes of naming and defining" (1998, 8). To my mind, Addams does not enhance taxonomic productions of sexual identity for those who may be typed as white, middle-class lesbians. As I will later argue, she instead flattens the Progressive Era project of taxonomic identification in her cultivation of unnamed cultural—and personal—abstractions in *Hull-House*.

8. Duggan's analysis of the highly sensationalized Alice Mitchell murder case supports this point, as Mitchell was constructed as a "sapphic slasher" after her trial for murdering her intimate female friend Freda Ward (2000, 2003). See, also, Chauncey (1994, 121–22); Coyle and Van Dyke (1997); and Terry (1999, 97–100) for more on these sensational sex panics.

9. Over four decades, the settlement house fostered more than forty clubs, many catering exclusively to women. A small sample would include the Arnold Toynbee Club (1892), the Chicago Question Club (1892), the Hull-House Girls' Club (1895), the Hull-House Kitchen, Hall, Coffee House, Dining Hall and Restaurant (1891–1916), the Hull-House Woman's Club (1892–1935), the Old Settlers Party (1905), the Jane Club (1893–98, 1917), the Mary Crane Nursery and League (1908–35) and the Practical Housekeeping Center (1909).

10. I note that this attempt to construe romantic friendships and spinsters as perverse lesbians has become a standard historiographic move in U.S.-based lesbian and gay studies as well. One instance of this would be Trisha Franzen's *Spinsters and Lesbians: Independent Womanhood in the United States* (1996).

11. For another extended discussion of how queer domesticity—particularly San Francisco's Chinatown opium dens—"produced alternative environments and relations of intimacy and social ethics . . . perceived to be a formidable threat to the norms of respectable domesticity," see Shah (2001, 104). For a reading that links queer domesticity to the reproduction and instantiation of hetero norms outside the U.S. nation-state, see Fiol-Matta (2002).

12. I borrow the phrase "domestic cosmopolitanism" from Joseph Valente's study of sexuality and race in relation to Irish national identity. Through his focus on Bram Stoker's *Dracula*, Valente finds that the author moves from "the pathos of metrocolonial immixture to an ethos of domestic cosmopolitanism" (2002, 41). *Twenty Years at Hull-House*, I believe, does more of the same.

13. A notable exception is Shannon Jackson (2000), who provides exemplary

readings of Hull-House's cultivation of cosmopolitan theatrical performances. See 48–60 and 223–36.

14. For a sustained theoretical thinking through of the "politics of nonrecognition," see Dean (1998, 154–57).

15. This impetus to universalism is, perhaps, one of the lasting legacies of modern cosmopolitan writing (though the project was undermined by the simultaneous popularization of cultural pluralism). See, for example, Michael North's analysis (1999) of Lawrence, Houdini, Chaplin, and Wittgenstein, as well as Michaels (1995, 13–23).

16. As historian Cocks suggests, "slumming, like other forms of tourism, offered a new way of forging social and spatial relationships" (2001, 203).

17. Though I focus here on sensational yellow journalism, we could also find instances of this realistic technique in highbrow transatlantic literatures such as Henry James's *The Princess Casamassima* (1886). See Seltzer (1982) and McGurl (2001, 79–83) for readings of James's relation to underworld surveillance.

18. In *Types from City Streets*, Hutchins Hapgood provides a similar typologization of "low" urban scenes that mirrors the taxonomies Riis introduces. Published the same year as *Hull-House*, Hapgood divides New York city life into "The Real Bowery," "The Tammany Man," "The Bohemian," and detailed accounts of "Life's Little Misfits" (1910, 3–4).

19. Though Addams recognized the absurdity of racial categorization in *Hull-House*, she was also in close contact with antilynching campaigns led by Ida B. Wells and Progressive race activists such as Mary Church Terrell. In a January 1901 article entitled "Respect for Law," Addams whole-heartedly supported the antilynching campaigns, though she did not question the veracity of Southern white claims against so-called Negro rapists. Five months later, Wells provided a firm corrective to Addams's false characterization in her reply, "Lynching and the Excuse for It." The two went on to fight segregation in Chicago's public schools and to organize for the National Association for the Advancement of Colored People (Aptheker 1977, 6–7). For more on their intense interaction, see Addams's and Wells's conversations in *Lynching and Rape* ([1901] 1977).

20. Addams herself acknowledges her debt to this developing field when she explains, "Certainly the difficulties of our committee [on social science] were not minimized by the fact that the then new science of sociology had not yet defined its own field. The University of Chicago [under Dewey's leadership], opened only the year before the World's Fair, was the first great institution of learning to institute a department of sociology" ([1910] 1990, 108). For more on the connections between U.S. sociology and the settlement movement, see Davis (1967); Deegan (1988); Feffer (1993); and Jackson (2000).

21. Alongside the genres of the slumming narrative and the sociological treatise, both key productions of the Progressive Era, emerged the immigrant autobiography, a genre on which Addams draws. One of the most famous, *The Life*

Stories of Undistinguished Americans, as Told by Themselves (1906), presents twenty-seven accounts of everyday early twentieth-century life. Each story functions as a personalized impersonal narrative, much like Addams's autobiography. In fact, the anonymous tales are structured according to types: "The Life Story of a Farmer's Wife," "The Life Story of a Japanese Servant," "The Life Story of a Lithuanian," "The Life Story of a Greek Peddler," to name but four.

22. Seltzer terms this process "the mass in person," the "intimation of a vast community within" an individual subject (1998, 146). And Warner sees the public sphere as a failed, utopian promise of personal "self-abstraction," an impersonal, indifferent "we" excluding personal differences (1992, 379). As I have already suggested, Addams typifies this process by becoming a typical person—the "MOTHER of races," the generic internationalist, the mass body who connects disparate classes, ethnicities, and races into a universalized one. This conflation—or, better, confusion—of inside and outside becomes most apparent in the first three chapters of her autobiography, whereby Addams mimics the press's public image of her self to such an extent that her authentic self becomes nonexistent.

23. See Thornton (1997) for a rich theoretical analysis of this minority strategy. While cultural theorists have charted a similar move in urban subcultures such as punk, rave kids, and hardcore, I note that Addams's strategy of transcending social distinctions rests on an initial binary of middle class/working poor that she herself immediately dismisses in her autobiography's first chapters.

24. While Addams does queer her personal life and intimate identifications with women, she nevertheless publicly spoke against sexual practices such as prostitution. For more on this, see her *The Spirit of Youth and the City Streets* (1909) and *A New Conscience and an Ancient Evil* (1912).

25. I am thinking in particular of historian Seth Koven's claim: "Elite women's willingness to 'go dirty'... made it possible for them to flout bourgeois class and gender expectations even as they acted as missionaries bringing bourgeois values and culture to the working poor. It also created a space in which they could explore their own same-sex and opposite-sex feelings and identities" (2004, 198). While I agree with these claims for many philanthropic slummers, I nevertheless see Addams's life project as not as one of sexual exploration but of homosexual identitarian disruption.

Chapter Two

1. In *Making American Boys*, Kenneth B. Kidd (2004) provides a historical overview of "boyology" that links the scientific discipline to contemporary Continental psychoanalysis and turn-of-the-century realist writings such as that by William Dean Howells. I note that Cather's white boys could easily fall into such as schema as well.

2. For a definitive genealogy of the term "perversion" and its integral relationship to burgeoning transatlantic psychological and psychoanalytic discourses, see Davidson (1987).

3. Kevin White (1993) is one of the first revisionist historians to pinpoint intersections between adolescence, homosexuality, and early twentieth-century American literatures (see, esp., 36–56).

4. This seemingly innocuous charge is more severe than twenty-first-century readers would imagine. For more on the politics of social control, spectatorship, and the disciplining of the late nineteenth-century body, see Kasson (1990) and Levine (1988).

5. Though I am indebted to many of his insights, for the moment I depart from Claude J. Summers's contextual reading of "Paul's Case." Summers's central thesis is that "the thing not named [in the story] is Paul's homosexuality, a presence made palpable not by direct statement but by numerous hints and a distinct emotional aura and verbal mood" (1990, 108). For a similar account of Catherian sexuality, see Anders (1999).

6. The forms of mobility I am describing are primarily Anglo-American and male. This is not to imply, however, that questions of mobility and travel were peripheral to the formation of urban, suburban, or regional female and racial/ethnic identities. Far from it, particularly when one takes into consideration the Great Migrations made by African-American men and women over the first half of the twentieth century as well as various sensational exposés of black and white working-class passing women. Nor do I want to suggest that female transience was foreign to the Catherian aesthetic, as critics such as Joseph Urgo (1995) have ably shown. After all, Cather herself was a mobile artist, and her international transience reflects in her writings. In her later novel *Lucy Gayheart* (1935), the titular protagonist seeks an "invisible, inviolable world" where she, like Paul, escapes through art ([1935] 1985, 104); and the novel closes with Harry Gordon pondering the concrete image of Lucy's "three light footprints, running away" (231). See Bowlby (1995); Buck-Morss (1991); Chisholm (2005); Nord (1991); Parsons (2001); and Wilson (1995) for further accounts of female mobility in the city. And for a reading of regional transience that has influenced my thinking on anticommunal relationality, see Galehouse (2000).

7. Again I find José Esteban Muñoz's theorizations of "disidentification" useful. Muñoz defines "disidentification" as a tactic used by minority queers to distance themselves from social norms in order to construct novel counter publics (1999, 4–11). I extend Muñoz's findings to chart how certain perverse individuals attempt to overcome the demands of any discernible community, collective, or subculture.

8. Bersani's call for "an anticommunal mode of connectedness" finds its echo in Michael Warner's claim that "queer politics opposes society itself" (1993, xxvii). But I note that the two theorists differ radically with regards to the aims of these

politics. For Warner, queer politics opposes society to imagine a queerer world that coheres around gender and sexual nonconformity. For Bersani, the queer world is more atomistic, even as individuals sexually merge together only, as he notes, to break with each other: "Sexuality is socially dysfunctional in that it brings people together only to plunge them into a self-shattering and solipsistic *jouissance*" (1987, 222). Like Bersani, Cather is deeply suspicious of traditional modes of political resistance on any queer's behalf. Art, in her aesthetic, is an escape from the social, not an intervention that indelibly alters it. Hence my later claim that Cather forges a company of transient queers rather than a prescient queer nation.

9. Though Paul is never explicitly referred to as a tramp boy, Cather does use this term to describe the wandering adolescent in *The Professor's House*. Inquiring about the vagabond Tom Outland, Mrs. St. Peter states, "'Well, this is something new in students, Godfrey. We ask a poor perspiring tramp boy to lunch, to save his pennies, and he departs leaving princely gifts'" ([1925] 1990, 121).

10. Though I concentrate specifically on urban and suburban explorations made by the deviant male body, Urgo (1995) and Reynolds (1996) both provide readings of mobility and migration in a variety of Cather's writings that historicize her works within global currents of late nineteenth- and early twentieth-century immigration, empire, and race within the city and without.

11. This is not the stereotypically free-loving, socialist bohemian of Greenwich Village that would come to dominate fantasies of metropolitan life, though the Village's sexual make-ups did inform Cather's later works. Cather often resided in the Village from 1906 until her death in 1947. Like other Village writers such as Henry James before her, she became a notable part of the neighborhood landscape, a writer who indirectly commented on novel identify formations of the sexed city in her more modernist writings of the 1920s and 1930s. Or, as Merrill Maguire Skaggs has suggested, "All of New York—its high arts and sidewalk low life, and all the sights a habitual walker in the city glimpsed in between—enriched her mind and imagination" (2000, 14). So much so, we find, that "the bohemian ferment of Greenwich Village in which she lived . . . challenged and provoked her," according to Skaggs. Given that she wrote "Paul's Case" in Pittsburgh, however, Cather's unique bohemian ideal was somewhat removed from these Village overtones. It was instead based on Continental decadent movements such as the French symbolists and the British aesthetes, her previous interactions with mobile immigrant settlers from eastern Europe, and her encounters with bohemian realists through her editorship at *McClure's*.

12. Here I follow Slote again, who suggests that "Willa Cather had by 1896 gravitated to a fundamentally primitivistic position—historical, cultural, human" (1967, 33). Yet I also reconsider her claim that Cather rejected discourses of bohemian primitivism that were circulating in early-century popular literatures. In my mind, Cather tweaks this model to her own ends in "Paul's Case," and vestiges of this ideal continue in some of her most critically lauded texts. One has

only to recall Jim's infatuation with Ántonia and his journey back into the "primitive" heartland in *My Ántonia*, or Godfrey St. Peter's obsession with Tom Outland and the temporally frozen Cliff City in *The Professor's House* to see how Cather extended the bohemian infatuation with supposedly exotic locales into an overarching aesthetic.

13. Though I combine these writers under the rubric of realist trampers, distinctions between their representation of themselves as tramps and their depictions of working-class tramp cultures differ drastically. See Entin (2001) for more on their various manipulations of tramp realism. And see Denning ([1987] 1998, 149–66) for more on the relation between tramp literature, working-class culture, and popular fiction.

14. On British acts of "incognito slumming," sensational slumming, and their relation to sexual identity during the Victorian Era, see Koven (2004, 82, 25–74).

15. Crane, of course, complements this "Experiment in Misery" with the antirealist sexual experiment that would become *Maggie: A Girl of the Streets* (1893). I also note that he may have worked on a counterpart to *Maggie* after witnessing "a boy with purple-painted eyes on Broadway one night in 1894, but Hamlin Garland found the manuscript—tentatively called "Flowers of Asphalt"—so shocking that Crane abandoned the work" (Austen 1977, 20). Given the twists, ironies, and disruptions of Crane's realism, one can only imagine his take on this fairy's body.

16. To get a quick sense of how influential these tramping tales were for Cather, we have only to recall that she met Crane when she worked as a journalist for the *Nebraska State Journal*; that she published a few of his stories when she worked as an editor at *McClure's* (Lewis 1953, 63); that she too dabbled in literary muckraking outside of her damning account of Wilde; and that when she wrote for a magazine entitled the *Library*, she embarked on her own tramping excursions into Pittsburgh under a variety of male pseudonyms. The most famous of these incognitos was "Henry Nicklemann," whom, M. Catherine Downs maintains, continues a tradition of sensational slumming that can first be found in "the early muckraker Jacob Riis [and] author and journalist Stephen Crane" (1999, 77). For a detailed account of such muckraking that includes *McClure's*, see Tichi (2004, 63–104).

17. As a figure of supreme social disruption, the tramp inspired numerous attempts at classification and control. In the late 1880s and 1890s, several states, such as Illinois and Connecticut, passed vagrancy laws that condemned the tramp's wandering as illegal and perverse. See Cresswell (2001) for more on juridical moves to suppress the tramp body and Nissen for how male tramps engage in relations that "are hard to define, be it in nineteenth-century or twentieth-century terms" (2005, 58).

18. For an alternate representation of tramping life in America, see Flynt ([1899] 1972, 1942).

19. Matei Calinescu (1987, 171–78) provides a strong reading of "the decadent euphoria," one thankfully devoid of Nordau's hysterical tone.

20. This is even more striking given the critical concern with Cather's names. See Butler (1993a).

21. The connection between perversity and tramping that I have been tracing should be even more apposite given the telling phrase, "double life." As Chauncey points out, though the closet was not a commonly used metaphor to describe homosexual life in urban U.S. environments, queers nevertheless referred to themselves as living a double life. "Many gay men," he writes, "described negotiating their presence in an often hostile world as living a double life, or wearing a mask and taking it off" (1994, 6). Though Cather acknowledges Verlaine's double life, she explodes this implicit closet logic when she revises decadent aesthetic wandering through Paul's upper-class slumming.

22. Here I build on Marilee Lindemann's *Willa Cather: Queering America* (1999), whose central thesis maintains that Cather dedicated her artistic life to plugging perversity into American ideals of progress, individualism, and nation building. In my mind, Cather was adamantly opposed to not only nationalism but also the burdens of affiliating one's self with any institution, including the body politic. For an account similar to Lindemann, see Abraham (1996).

23. For more regimes of masculinity and normalization at the turn-of-the-century, see Chauncey (1994); Chudacoff (1999); Gustav-Wrathall (1998); Kasson (2001); Ross (2004); Rotundo (1993, 227–46); Townsend (1996); and White (1993).

24. See Jackson (1985); Jurca (2001); and Marchand (1985) for more on the suburbanization of white middle-class U.S. populations in the early twentieth century and beyond.

25. Cather is not alone in hammering this point home. For other analyses of turn-of-the-century work and play, see Brown (1996) and Gleason (1999, esp. 211–58).

26. Another way to frame this argument is to see how Paul, like the readers of dime novel fictions, relishes this literature as an escapist fiction that "is largely the continual story of capture by and escape from the narrative paradigms of middle-class culture" (Denning [1987] 1998, 61).

27. Paul's theatrical project of losing himself gestures to what Foucault sees as one of the primary goals of queer cultures past and present—impersonal self-fashioning. As outlined in vols. 2 and 3 of *History of Sexuality* (1990b, 1988), this ideal, based heavily on Grecian and Roman practices of *acsesis*, permits the subject to form an impersonal relationship with his self and society. Critics such as historian David Halperin have extended this project to contemporary U.S. subcultural practices such as gay male bodybuilding and sex acts such as fisting. While I agree with Halperin and Foucault that these practices might sometimes lead to "the affirmation of non-identity" (Halperin 1995, 36), they are nevertheless predicated on the idea of building on a self while Cather advances the dissolution of the self. Overwhelmed by the spectacle on the stage, Paul discards his neurotic

identity as well as his spectacular (im)personal self. He sloughs off his presumably perverse sexuality by losing his body and becoming a transparently opaque set of sightseeing eyes.

28. Though I have been unable to trace the intertextual reference to Cather's description of "subterranean halls" and "fabulously rich Jews," I hypothesize that she refers to Eugène Sue's internationalist *The Wandering Jew* (1845). In a December 1897 edition of the *Home Monthly*, Cather reviews Sue's anti-Semitic slumming narrative, links it to her own adolescent reading, and remarks that "the story has all the youth of yesterday and will charm generations yet to be" ([1897] 1970a, 368).

29. The critics I have in mind are Edward Said (1993), Joseph Allen Boone (1995), and several contributors to the special edition of *GLQ: A Journal of Lesbian and Gay Studies* titled "Queer Tourism: Geographies of Globalization" (Puar 2002). Though they operate in disparate disciplines, all agree that Western queer sightseeing in foreign locales does a supreme disservice to native residents. In brief, these sightseers appropriate. I wholly agree with these critiques, yet I also point out that Paul's subterranean fantasy, while orientalist in form, is ambiguous in its content. Paul inhabits the scene but he does not inhabit—or overtake—a subaltern Jewish subjectivity. He instead sits alongside side these others rather than displacing them, a process that may not attenuate what Boone sees as the primary trope of the homoerotic orientalist narrative, namely, "phallocentric collusions and resistant excitations" (1995, 104). I highlight this point not to salvage Cather or her character from charges of racism and ethnocentrism (the evidence is there for the taking) but to open a space that considers the complexities of her chronic stereotyping and how her stereotyping sometimes—not always—courses into unexpected critical spaces. For more on her harsh relation to Jewish identity in her later novels, see Michaels (1995, 46–48 and 50–52).

30. See Herring (2002, 422–23) for more on how urban fantasies can depersonalize the wandering artist. And for a psychoanalytic theorization that mirrors my own cultural readings, see Dean's thinking on Freud and Lacan in *Beyond Sexuality*, which argues that "fantasy *impersonalizes* the subject, decomposing his or her ego in the *mise-en-scène* of desire. Thus it is owing to the subject's mercurial positioning in a sequence of mutating terms that fantasy permits identifications across a number of socially regulated boundaries—between active and passive, masculine and feminine, gay and straight, black and white, perhaps even the boundary between the living and the dead. In so doing, fantasy undermines the distinctions such categories are intended to uphold, thereby disqualifying these social categories from providing the grounds for anything but *imaginary* identities" (2000, 261–62).

31. On question of queer cross-identification and popular media forms such as the cinema, see DeAngelis (2001).

32. Now-classic formulations of highbrow and lowbrow lifestyles can be found in Bourdieu (1984); Levine (1988); and Lynes (1985).

33. See Love's (2001) instructive essay on *The Well of Loneliness* for more on how a spoiled identity—a term she borrows from Erving Goffman and Eve Kosofsky Sedgwick—can shed light on early twentieth-century sexual identity as well as more pride-filled cultural moments of the twenty-first. For a deconstructive rethinking of shame and pride that has also informed my reading here, see Ricco (2002, 15–18).

34. While Paul's death may play into traditional homophobic narratives of homosexual suicide, we should also read this self-annihilation as a form of social critique. For more on queer suicide as a link between "self/social destruction and self/social reconstruction," see Robertson (2003, 191).

Chapter Three

1. Ann Douglas documents the literary public spheres that Van Vechten traversed and helped forge in *Terrible Honesty* (1995). See, esp., 287–89.

2. Robert F. Worth provides a reading of *Nigger Heaven*'s reception. He concludes by claiming that "the controversy *Nigger Heaven* aroused was instructive. Never again would white writers roar uptown with such feckless glee, and never would blacks admit them again so freely" (1995, 472). Yet historians such as Chauncey and Heap have shown that interracial interactions continued throughout the late 1920s and well into the 1930s in Harlem nightclubs and cabarets. Building on their findings, I argue that *Nigger Heaven* did not close the book on white and black contact. It opened a novel form of relationality for a few New Negro artists independent of the communal ideals of race pride.

3. Torgovnick (1990); Somerville (2000); and Lemke (1998) provide analyses of the modern white infatuation with primitive bodies and locales. See, esp., Torgovnick (1997, 3–41). Also, see Terry (1999) for a detailed discussion of sensational "interbreeding" between U.S racial bodies in the first decades of the twentieth century—what sexologists and paranoid commentators held to be "the frightening specter of white and black 'perverts' congregating in bizarre sexual rituals involving cross-dressing and clandestine orgies" (94).

4. While Brown's folk poems frequently present sensational moments of sexual abuse, infidelity, abandonment, and promiscuity, these salacious acts nevertheless fall under violations of developing African-American hetero-norms. Likewise, while critics have explored the underlining (homo)sexual tensions in Larsen's slumming narrative *Passing*, the novel's critical reception remains embedded within a tradition of psychological realism from which it often does not deviate. See McDowell (1993) and Butler (1993b) for more on Larsen's sexual—and racial—transgressions.

5. Following Bernard, I note that the intimate, life-long relationship between Hughes and Van Vechten was "complicated by race, power, and money" but was

nevertheless based on mutual "fondness, respect, and compassion" (2001, xxvi, xxvii). See Bernard (2001, xiii–xxvii) for a detailed analysis of their connection.

6. Edwards (2001); Gloster (1948); Heap (2000); Herrmann (2000, 123, 127); Kellner (1987); Mumford (1997); and Ross (2004) each provide critiques of this project as an intrusive form of white patronage and white exploitation that shored up distinctions between black and white bodies.

7. For carryovers and critiques of this ideal, see Mercer (1994).

8. See Akam (1991); Carby (1992); Dewey ([1927] 1954); Reid-Pharr (2001, 54–55); and Royce (1950) for more on this imperative for a legibly redemptive—and legibly gendered—community. Carby, in particular, concentrates on the sanctions against improper admixture for the black female body in Harlem. Also, see Hutchinson (1995) for an exhaustive reading of how Locke's obsessive concern with "communal identity" (82) and "true community" (82)—alongside his equally obsessive focus on pluralism—informs his thinking on the New Negro.

9. This rich interracial interaction has been "rediscovered" by scholars of the Harlem Renaissance. For the definitive account of how black and white literary public spheres operated in tandem in the 1920s, see Hutchinson (1995). And for a comprehensive account of late nineteenth- and twentieth-century African-American literature that explores how some writings complicate the compulsory demand solely to produce art for, by, and about black writers, see Jarrett (2006).

10. While definitional battles over what exactly constituted "the Negro race" and "group thinking" flourished during the Harlem Renaissance and beyond, and while I understand group thinking to be an ongoing process, I am most concerned here with the developing compulsion to identify as a collective body that can be treated as an object of critical scrutiny in the first place, rather than call attention to arguments over how, precisely, that body should be nominalized. For accounts of racial minoritization, group policing, and the questions of communal naming, see Cohen (1999) and Harper (1996).

11. The idea that Negro—or any racial—culture could be a form of personal property is discussed in detail in Michaels's *Our America* (1995), which argues that movements such as a Lockean-influenced Harlem Renaissance constituted themselves through the rubric of communal-based cultural pluralism. See 110–35.

12. See Berlant and Warner (1998) and Muñoz (1999) for more on this ideal.

13. For an early critical exploration of the "mysterious" urban "other" and Park's concept of moral region, see Trachtenberg (1982a, 140–41). For more on the links between DuBois, the Park school, and early twentieth-century African-American sociology as a particular form of slumming, see Mumford (1997, 138–39). For more on the connections between Park, Locke, "belonging and community," see Edwards (2001, 159–60). For a queer-of-color critique of Park that focuses on white-led sociological endeavors, see Ferguson (2004, 56–58, 76). For links between Park's 1920s sociology and later subcultural theory, see Hebdige

([1979] 2002, 75). And for considerations of sociological U.S. discourses as they dovetail with high Anglo-American literary productions, see Trask (2003).

14. For more on the modern—and modernist—project of racial intelligibility and the oppressive dynamics of visuality, see Wallace (2002) and Wiegman (1995, 21–42).

15. Though I (and almost all of its critics) concentrate primarily on a white tourist response to *Nigger Heaven*, I note that professional, middle-class black readers also constituted some of the novel's armchair slummers and also contributed to the slumming literature's best-seller status.

16. While McCoy's analysis of the Van Vechten scene has been influential on my thinking, I defer from her closing remarks that Van Vechten's inscrutably spectacular strategies culminate in a desire "to be" a black body (2003, par. 42). In my mind, the author instead thwarts any process of cross-identification at the precise moment that he advances a queer interracialism. This is not to disregard McCoy's central claim that Van Vechten's corpus—both the novels and his photographs—are inherently indeterminate: it certainly is. In fact, we might apply McCoy's observations to Van Vechten's friend Langston Hughes, who adopts a similar strategy in his earlier poetry collections, most notably *The Weary Blues* (1926b) and *Fine Clothes to the Jew* (1927). Often read as a proponent of folksy négritude (and essays such as "The Negro Artist and the Racial Mountain" [1926a] support this claim), Hughes also, at times, strategically cultivated an unknowing relationship to race and sexuality that makes his identity incognito. For more on this tactic, see Jarraway (1996).

17. This strategy, I note, disrupts the dominant paradigm for Anglo modernism's use of minoritarian language that North discusses in *The Dialect of Modernism* (1994, 59–99). Unlike North's Pound, Eliot, Stein, and Picasso, Van Vechten does not always deploy primitivism in order to buttress his privileged white racial identity—or that of another.

18. One could also apply this complex, contradictory form of spectatorship to Van Vechten's interracial photography. As James Smalls remarks, "Van Vechten's 'fetish and fantasy' photographs emphasize ambivalent interracial relations of looking and desiring that often destabilize any subject/object dichotomy in terms of seeing and being seen" (1998, 94).

19. For more on the interconnections between racial group formation, homosexual group formation, and illegibility, see Somerville (2000).

20. For more on the links between primitivism and "the idea of merging," see Torgovnick (1997, 14–17).

21. Simmel elaborates further on the impersonal nature of the party scene in "On the Significance of Numbers in Social Life" (1950a). See also Simmel's "The Social Gathering" ('Party')" where he argues that, at social venues such as "the modern ball," "relations are impersonal and as it were anonymous, because of the magnitude of the group and the associated formalism of behavior" (1950b, 114).

22. This form of contact could be characterized as "a relation of simultaneity and togetherness, in which singular encounters rather than unity or obligation become the condition of community" (Kawash 1997, 169). For a similar analysis of cosmopolitan queer friendship, see O'Hara (1991).

23. Here Ray seems prescient, not only in his call for racial cosmopolitanism but also in his insistence that identity politics may have already reached its useful limits in the year 1932. For another discussion that longs for identitarianism's eventual obsolescence, see Paul Gilroy's *Against Race: Imagining Political Culture beyond the Color Line* (2000). In a closing line that Thurman and Ray would both have appreciated, Gilroy invites his readers to "bring even more powerful visions of planetary humanity from the future into the present and to reconnect them with democratic and cosmopolitan traditions that have been all but expunged from today's black political imaginary" (356).

24. Though they may appear to be strange bedfellows, Thurman's desires here mirror those of Larsen's in *Quicksand*, where Helga Crane searches for a viable "consciousness" "apart from racial or cultural identity" (Esteve 2003, 171).

25. Other critics who read this friendship as a closeted cover for homosexual desire, homosexual subculture, and/or an interracial gay romance include Blackmore (1997); Kellner (1987); Knadler (2002); and Mumford (1997).

26. I'm thinking about Michael Lynch's essay on phrenology, friendship, and homosexuality in trans-Atlantic literature and culture (1985). Lynch argues that nonnormative individuals such as Whitman used the discourse of adhesive friendship—a discourse the poet borrowed from phrenology—to fashion a modern homosexual identity. My reading of queer Harlem reverses this teleology. While both Thurman and Van Vechten, like many writers of the New Negro Renaissance, were beholden to Whitman, they both engaged in discourses of friendship and interracial slumming to distance themselves from discourses of reified homosexual group identity and community. For an argument similar to my own that promotes deviant identity, see Jarraway (2002).

27. By "once middle class," I refer to Nugent's own blue-vein childhood in Washington, D.C. Given the autobiographical quality of the story, it is difficult not to see Alex as a stand in for Nugent's own adolescent ambiguity.

28. These disruptions could also be considered a form of queer misbehavior given the proper protocols that guided the first wave of the Harlem Renaissance. See Cobb (2000) for more on Nugent's insolent textuality.

29. In his introduction to Nugent's writings and drawings, Wirth notes that Nugent would have been directly influenced by Van Vechten's decadent novels: "Nugent began squarely in what might be characterized as the tradition of perfumed decadence . . . [that] flowered in the United States in the 1920s in the novels of Carl Van Vechten" (2002, 41).

30. For more on the sexual cultures of working-class Italian-American males in the first third of the twentieth century, see Chauncey (1994, 72–76).

31. Similar critical moves that both confirm and queer Nugent's homosexual identity can be found in Schwarz's *Gay Voices of the Harlem Renaissance* (2003) and Silberman (2004). While Schwarz notes Nugent's voice was "gay," the critic also states that, throughout the artist's oeuvre, "Nugent widens his challenge and transgression of sexual norms, transcending the issue of sexual orientation per se" (133).

32. For more on the politics of queer ephemera and the archive, see Cvetkovich (2003); Halberstam (2005, 169–74); Muñoz (1996); Quiroga (2001); Román (2005, 137–78); and Seitler (2004).

Chapter Four

1. For more on the interconnections between Barnes and high (male) modernism, see Lamos (1998); Lyon (2005); McGurl (2001); and Reizbaum (1998).

2. For a detailed analysis of the social construction of the freak and the cultural evolution of the freak show, see Adams (2001) and Bogdan (1988). For Barnes's interest in the carnivalesque, see Marcus (1991) and Stevenson (1991).

3. I have in mind Barnes's interest in the spectacular force-fed body of the militant suffragette; the New York Zoological Society's Dinah the gorilla; the elevator man who spent "twenty-four years in a cage" ([1913] 1989e, 94); hypermuscular prize-fighters; and her own surrealist investment in what James Clifford calls "an aesthetic that values fragments, curious collections, unexpected juxtapositions—that works to provoke the manifestation of extraordinary realities drawn from the domains of the erotic, the exotic, and the unconscious" (1988, 118).

4. McAlmon's Berlin expatriate stories in *Miss Knight and Others* (1992) provide a disdainful counterpart to these urban scenarios that Barnes comments on in her journal articles and later fiction writings.

5. For a similar argument, see Kennedy's reading of *Nightwood* as an exilic text that poses "the condition of uncertainty as the distinguishing sign of modernist experience" (1993, 223).

6. A notable exception is Nancy J. Levine, who finds that Barnes's "career as a journalist was the seedbed of her greatest novel, *Nightwood*" (1991, 27).

7. See Chauncey (1994, 228–44, esp. 234 on sensational Village exposés); Dorman (1993, 19–20); Edwards (1999, 138–39); Heap (2000); Stansell (2000); Ware (1935); and Wilson (2000) for detailed accounts of bohemianism's relationship to sensationalism and sexualized slumming.

8. For broad overviews of bohemianism on American soil, see Barnet (2004); Chisholm (2005); Churchill (1959); Cowley (1934); Haskell (1987, 54–57); McGurl on "critique[s] of middle-class conventionality and moral probity" (2001, 15); Watson (1995); and Wetzsteon (2002).

9. I'm thinking about another bohemian depiction of white male perversion as a metonymic display of hands—Sherwood Anderson's tragically "grotesque"

Wing Biddlebaum. As the opening tale in Anderson's widely influential *Winesburg, Ohio*, "Hands" attempts to reveal why Biddlebaum's flighty digits "made more grotesque an already grotesque and elusive individuality" (1960, 29). To do so, it shows how a small-town gendered body is forced into a homosexual identity. *Nightwood*'s queer slumming narrative, I argue, does the reverse of Anderson's small-town imagist scenes of homosexual surveillance. For more on how "hands" in modern U.S. literature and culture often came to signify "complex representations that at once crudely stereotype homosexuals," see Corn (1999, 199).

10. It might be apropos to hypothesize that Barnes culled some of these strategies from her observations of Villager interaction with slummers. As Parry notes, there was such dizzying intermixture between the two groups that it was sometimes difficult to tell who was watching and who was being watched (1933, 312).

11. Justin Edwards, whom I extend here, is also quick to note that Barnes is eager "to satisfy middle-class curiosity and reinstate structures of [racial/ethnic] difference" (2001, 136) and to suggest that Barnes will "disclose [Chinatown's] mysteries for her readers" (135) even as she traffics in "uses of primitivism" (141) when she "combat[s] the mysteries and otherness" of this population (131). Likewise, in his introduction to Barnes's *Collected Stories*, Phillip Herring diplomatically addresses this matter: "Like some writers of her time, Barnes was often indelicate about race" (1996, 10). More to the point: Barnes's repeated use of the racial slur "nigger" to refer to African-Americans in her short stories supports his claim, as does a quick glance at the Duchess's anecdote about "Nikka the nigger" in *Nightwood*. Like countless Anglo-modernist writers, Barnes undeniably had racist tendencies. Her unfortunate language use, I add to these critiques, is sometimes countered by a surprising attentiveness to how racialized bodies can overwrite racist discourses on their skin. Nikka, for instance, though marked as "the nigger who used to fight the bear in the *Cirque de Paris*," tattoos his body with brilliant markings "in no way befitting the great and noble British Empire that he was brought up with a start" ([1937] 1961, 16). And when Matthew asks Nikka about this textual "barbarity" that marks his entire body, he replies, "he loved beauty and would have it about him" (17). That Barnes's racism eddies into discourses of aestheticism and anti-imperalism in one extended paragraph only begins to illuminate the intricacies of her complex thoughts on racially marked bodies. For further critiques of her racism, see Hackett (2004); Hovey (1996); and more from Edwards (2001). And for a more general overview of the Continental orientalisms that Barnes may have fostered and manipulated, see Lowe (1991).

12. See Bramen (2000, 187–92); Foote (2001, 142–53); Lee (2001); Lowe (1996); Takaki (1989) for extended discussions of turn-of-the-century sensational realism such as that of Riis and its anxious representation (and desperate surveillance) of urban Asian immigrant populations. For more on the relationship between "perverse" Chinese bachelor cultures and Anglo-American sexual policing, see Eng (2001).

13. Though the archive is currently slim, fears over the Chinese mafia circulated throughout the mass Anglo-American press (and particularly in San Francisco) around the time Barnes composed some of her slumming literatures.

14. As I have noted throughout, traits of surveillance and spectacularization are just two of the technologies of empire writing, external, internal, or both. For more on the discursive forms of colonial journalisms, see Spurr (1993).

15. This inversion of intent refers back to Riis's characterization of Chinatown, where he tells his curious audience that "Chinatown as a spectacle is disappointing. Next door neighborhood to the Bend, it has little of its outdoor stir and life, none of its gayly-colored rags or picturesque filth and poverty" ([1890] 1996, 120). While Riis begins with disappointment, the Barnesian Chinatown procures the same emotional response after skewering the reader's sensationally realistic expectations. For more on Riis's "discourse of regionalism," see Foote (2001, 144).

16. Such textual crossovers—and such a broad historical leap that I track here—makes more sense given that a portion of the Village populace migrated overseas following what could be called a gentrification of the Village. According to Parry's colorful account, "by the middle 1920s, the loss of Greenwich Village to the impudent Babbitts was another excuse to go to Montparnasse" (1933, 331).

17. While Barnes, to my knowledge, is the only novelist to mock Hall in high-modernist style, there were many parodies written as jibes at *The Well of Loneliness*: Beresford Egan's *Sink of Solitude* (1928); Henry von Rhau's *Hell of Loneliness* (1929); Percy Reginald Stephensen's *Well of Sleevelessness: A Tale for the Least of These Little Ones* (1929); and Robert Leicester's *Hell of Comeliness* (1933). For an extended reading of these largely homophobic and misogynistic texts, see Behling (2001, 133–41), from whom I take this list.

18. It also proved to be a formative text for many readers in the United States. For more on the novel's successful publication and its sensational New York trial for obscenity, see Taylor (2001).

19. For a comprehensive overview of sexological discourse, see the edited collection *Sexology in Culture* (Bland and Doan 1998). For readings of Hall's traffic in sexology, "perverse desire," "female masculinity," and "the mannish woman," see, respectively, de Lauretis (1994), Halberstam (1998), and Newton (1990). On Hall's use of race as a metaphor for inversion, see Walton (2001). For her suspect use of orientalism as a permissible outlet for female Anglo-invert desire, see Chinn (2001). For her connection to late nineteenth-century U.S. sexology and sensationalism, see Duggan (2000, 188–91). And for her relationship to twenty-first-century identifications and recuperations of disavowed affect, see Love (2001).

20. Another intertextual and intercultural dialogue is the loose friendship forged between Miss Knight/Charlie Knight and the "lumberjack-looking lesbian" in McAlmon's "Miss Knight" (1992, 10). Like Hall, McAlmon presents his readers with a disdainful view of international queer life in continental Europe. But unlike

The Well of Loneliness, McAlmon's slumming portrayal of this invert connection seethes with disgust at the idea of homosexual subculture as its mocking narrator adopts a hetero-spectatorial point of view.

21. My reading of *The Well of Loneliness* extends Love's (2001) overarching historiographic intent. I want to emphasize how Hall, in her specific cultural context, infuses a call for a minoritizing sexual history into an underworld narrative that queers of any present may now reconsider. For other useful considerations of queer historiography and prolepsis (irrespective, in some cases, of sexual object choices or sexual and gender identifications), see Bersani and Dutoit (1998); Copjec (1994); Dean (2000); Freeman (2000); Goldberg and Menon (2005); Halberstam (2005); Halperin (2002); Lane (1999); Nealon (2001); Rohy (2006); Shah (1998); and Umphrey (2003).

22. While later historians of Western sexuality and cultural and literary critics have rejected Hall's history as politically suspicious, their methodologies sometimes parallel Stephen's in their presentations of political acknowledgment and historical legibility. *Boots of Leather, Slippers of Gold* finds that "the struggle for public recognition and acceptance" has always been a desirable facet of working-class lesbian U.S. communal life (Kennedy and Davis 1994, 29). Historian Leila J. Rupp, too, defines her "short history of same-sex love in America" as *A Desired Past* (1999). And more theoretical analyses of queer history often replace the recovery of lost minority identities with "the production of a counterdiscursive *deviant subjectivity*" (Terry 1991, 55). For an important reading of these historical frameworks, see Scott (1993, 2001).

23. In "Great Cities," Julie Abraham (2001) takes Hall's dialogue with sexology and sociological realism a step further to suggest a hypothetical link between *The Well of Loneliness* and the Chicago school of sociology when she draws parallels between Hall's sexual liberation and the Chicago school's analyses of urban homosexual community.

24. Christopher Lane accounts for "highly sophisticated" fiction's attraction to antimimetic writing in an essay on the ideological pratfalls of New Historicism in particular and historicism in general (2003, 465–66). Also, for another astute reading of the literary's relation to antirepresentation, see Jackson ([1981] 1993).

25. There is an array of scholarship on high modernism's ambivalent relationship to history as various artists, singularly and collectively, attempted to undermine a Victorian infatuation with historical progress. See Frank (1963); Hamilton (1996, esp. 110–32); Lane (2003); Levenson (1984); Longenbach (1987); Hayden White (1973, 1978, 1987); and Williams (2002). For broader considerations of "history" and literary studies that have influenced my thinking here, see Elias (2001); Hutcheon (1988); and Michaels (1996).

26. Following Kannenstine (1977), Boone (1998), too, notes this connection in his endnotes on 470.

27. Given Barnes's allegiance to Jungian psychology's racial unconscious as well as the popularization of Freudian theories during the twenties, it makes sense that *Nightwood*'s grammar is also indebted to *Interpretation of Dreams*. I hesitate, however, to see modernist variations of Freudian unconscious as the royal road to *Nightwood*'s meaning. All too frequently, the indeterminacy of dream work (and *Nightwood*) is erased through revelatory interpretation. Barnes, in contrast, defers the gratification that meaning something may offer to a body that finds itself to be a nonnormative subject.

28. For an extended reading of Nora's traumatic relationship to Robin, see Allen, whose argument "depends on micro-reading only the narratives within each text that engage affective exchanges between women as lovers" and who opens up an anti-identitarian (and anticommunitarian) reading of *Nightwood* (1996, 17).

29. Barnes appears to echo and revise the international frame that closes part 1 of Marcel Proust's *Cities of the Plain*. Discussing the bathetic nature of invert communities, the narrator notes that "they would repair to Sodom only on days of supreme necessity, when their own town was empty, at those seasons when hunger drives the wolf from the woods. In other words, everything would go on very much as it does to-day in London, Berlin, Rome, Petrograd or Paris" (1981, 656).

30. Again another parallel to McAlmon emerges. "Miss Knight" closes with the exclamation that its invert protagonist, having disappeared from Berlin's gay and lesbian society, will "turn up" to "appear in Paris or London or Madrid or Singapore. She's just that international" (1992, 20). See Lorusso (1992) for more on Barnes's revisions of McAlmon's slumming narratives.

31. Here I have been influenced by Lamos's reading of the Proustian lie, one that offers "semiotic proliferation and semantic vacancy" (1998, 204) and "culturally contingent confusion with specific historical determinants" (227). *Nightwood* is rife with allusions to *Remembrance of Things Past*, and Lamos notes in her conclusion how Barnes extends Proustian strategies of homosexual misunderstanding and lying that holds no secrets (229). I suspect that Barnes may have been influenced by one translation—"The Mysteries of Albertine"—that was reproduced in English in 1927 by Scottish writer Charles Kenneth Scott Moncrieff. Also, for a reading of *Remembrance of Things Past* that ties with my attention to Barnes's sexual mystery, see Jonathan Freedman, who argues that "both Jewishness and perversion return over and over as topics of mystery and interrogation" in Proust (2001, 527).

32. In my reading of such silence, I recall Leo Bersani's and Ulysse Dutoit's call for "life-sustaining and even self-expansive modes of losing your head" at the close of *Caravaggio's Secrets* (1998, 99). These moments could also be considered "the insertion of nonhistorical modes of being in time" (64). *Nightwood*'s reading experience offers a concrete way to achieve this theoretical dream, if you are game for losing your mind and your head.

Epilogue

1. To track in detail further evolutions of slumming literatures in mid-twentieth-century and late twentieth-century U.S. public spheres is beyond this book's scope, but scholars would need to consider the following: first, the rise of a heteronormative proletariat realism and its heightened attention to proper or improper representations of the working class as well as its refiguration of bourgeois Anglo-modernisms as perverse and effete; second, what Chauncey has termed "the exclusion of [overt] homosexuality from the public sphere" during the onset of the Great Depression following "the spectacle of the pansy" (1994, 331); third, how the city mystery genre was remixed into what cultural critic Michael Denning terms the ghetto pastoral—"the flip side of the slumming stories that ran from Stephen Crane to Dos Passos"—throughout the 1930s and the early 1940s (1996, 230); and fourth, how subsequent strains of the city mystery genre such as pulpy crime fiction and film noir translated reader curiosity about homosexual subcultures into curiosity about the city's criminal "shadowlands." That said, I do not wish to imply that fascinations with sexual subcultures and nonnormative bodies—or the slumming that enabled these fascinations—have ever vanished in U.S. cultural milieus, literary or otherwise. Historian Joanne Meyerowitz has shown this to be true in her investigation of numerous sensational trans narratives (and their accompanying specter of homosexual knowledge) produced during Cold War America (2002, 2). And as Justin Edwards notes in his closing remarks on U.S. erotic travel literatures, "although the Depression of the 1930s and World War II shifted the focus of American travel literature away from erotic imagery, the Beat writers of the 1950s returned to the erotics of travel with a vengeance" (2001, 172).

2. For more on the crystallization of post–World War II lesbian and gay urban communities in the United States, see D'Emilio (1983).

3. Though it might seem odd to imagine contemporary queer studies as advancing the earlier ideals of queer slumming, one could turn to the closing scenes of Berlant and Warner's "Sex in Public" to witness how matters of sexual spectacularization and fascination with underworld knowledge inform their thinking on urban U.S. public sex cultures of the late 1990s. As both note in a critical discussion of the growing interest of a "young straight couple" in risqué sex toys,

> in order not to feel like perverts, they had to make *us* into a kind of sex public. Later, the question of aversion and perversion came up again. This time we were in a bar that on most nights is a garden-variety leather bar, but that, on Wednesday nights, hosts a sex performance event called 'Pork.' . . . That night, word was circulating that the performance was to be erotic vomiting. This sounded like an appetite spoiler, and the thought of leaving early occurred to us but was overcome by a simple curiosity: what would the

foreplay be like? Let's stay until it gets messy. Then we can leave. (1998, 564)

4. While the phrase's popularity skyrocketed after R. Kelly's late 1990s hits, it is important to remember that previous incarnations of down low can also be found in song lyrics by TLC and Naughty by Nature. For more on these earlier mentions, see Boykin (2005, 40–60).

5. See Osofsky (1966) for a history of what some have (knowingly at times, dismissively at others) called the African-American ghetto in the twentieth century. And for analyses that both explore and critique the production of scientific and popular knowledge about urban ghetto cultures, see Hannerz ([1969] 2004); Perry (2004); Rose (1994, 10–12); and, esp., O'Connor (2001).

6. This list goes on and on: you could include hip hop artists such as Deadlee and Homothug as well as a growing catalog of writings—both fictional and nonfictional—like Asante Kahari's *Homo Thug* (2004); Kevin Ames's *Down Low Secrets: A Story about Black Men Who Have Sex with Other Men* (2005); Christopher David's *I'm on My Way* (2005); Nubia's *20 Warning Signs of Down Low Brothers* (2005); D. L. Smith's *Down Low, Double Life* (2004); Adam Phillips's "Down Low Blues" in a 2004 *Salon* article; and Matthew Phillip's "Homothugs: Hip-Hop's Secret Homo Underside" in his 2005 *The Guide: Gay Travel, Entertainment, Politics and Sex* exposé.

7. Though the photographer agreed to the image's reproduction in this book, the model refused to have his image republished because "he is uncomfortable with his image being used" (Hassett 2006, n.p.).

8. The article builds on what Boykin sees as a "2001 down low craze" that appeared in numerous international, national, and regional presses such as the February 11, 2001, *New York Times*; the March 15, 2001, *USA Today*; the April 22, 2001, *Chicago Sun-Times*; and the June 4, 2001, *San Francisco Chronicle*. For a detailed chronology of these writings, see Boykin's exhaustive listing of them (2005, 101–5). For a critical exploration of the bisexual black male that haunts many of these articles, see Cohen (1999). And for further explorations of contemporary responses and shifts in black (homo)sexual U.S. media cultures, see Collins (2004) and Neal (2005).

9. These forms of dissociation, I note, are not solely particular to the black and Latino DL. For a contemporary account of queer slumming undertaken by a middle-class white urban male, see English (2002).

10. My readings of *Oprah* and the complexities of talk show sexual recognition have been influenced by Gamson's analyses of tabloid TV, which finds that sensational shows sometimes offer resistant possibilities as they negotiate "the tight rope of visibility" (1998, 208).

11. See King's detailed account of this brochure (King and Hunter 2004, 8–11).

12. As Jason King argues, DL men "call themselves incognitos, playas, real nikkas, thug bottoms, and pretty thugs" (2003, 44). I have found King's readings of DL men suggestive and instrumental for my own thinking, since he, too, implicitly sees some of these men as queer slummers—"thugs"—who define themselves against "bourgie" gay black males (46). I'd stress, however, that DL males may not necessarily want to associate with ideals or codes that inform mainstream, middle-class (white) gay U.S. community of any sort, and they may not necessarily want to see their activities framed under the disciplinary rubric of "sexual knowledge" or revealed as city mysteries, even though King contends at the close of his article that "their demand for self-determination extends a core value in gay liberation. Will the movement acknowledge the rap at the door?" (46). In my reading, the DL cultivates an anticommunal disconnect to the core values in (white) U.S.-based lesbian and gay liberation—visibility and recognition—that undermines these entrenched ideals and is indifferent to their acknowledgment or revelation. I thank Keguro Macharia for helping me think through the differences just outlined.

13. Methodological investigations of queer subcultures ground some of the most innovative research in the field since its inception in the early 1980s—and continue to do so. A cursory list would include Chauncey on "the gay male world" of Manhattan (1994); Faderman on lesbian subcultures (1991); Halberstam on transgender and dyke subcultures in the United States (2005, 152–87); Koestenbaum on gay male opera subcultures (1993); Nealon on the "secret public of [male] physique culture" (2001, 99–139); Rubin (1993); Warner on late twentieth-century urban queer New York City sex publics (1999).

Works Cited

Manuscript and Archival Collections

Addams, Jane, Memorial Collection. Hull-House Archives. University Library, University of Illinois at Chicago.

———, Papers. Peace Collection. Swarthmore College.

Thurman, Wallace, Papers. James Weldon Johnson Memorial Collection. The Beinecke Rare Book and Manuscript Library. Yale University.

Van Vechten, Carl, Papers. Carl Van Vechten Collection. The Beinecke Rare Book and Manuscript Library. Yale University.

Primary and Secondary Sources

Abraham, Julie. 1996. *Are Girls Necessary? Lesbian Writing and Modern Histories*. New York: Routledge.

———. 2001. "Great Cities: Radclyffe Hall at the Chicago School." In *Palatable Poison: Critical Perspectives on* The Well of Loneliness, edited by Laura Doan and Jay Prosser, 336–54. New York: Columbia University Press.

Adams, Rachel. 2001. *Sideshow U.S.A.: Freaks and the American Cultural Imagination*. Chicago: University of Chicago Press.

Addams, Jane. [1912] 1972. *A New Conscience and an Ancient Evil*. New York: Arno.

———. [1909] 1972. *The Spirit of Youth and the City Streets*. Urbana and Chicago: University of Illinois Press.

———. [n.d.] 1985. "The 'mine' and 'thine' of wedded folk." In *The Jane Addams Papers*, ed. Mary Lynn McCree Bryan, microfilm reel 113.45.1585. Ann Arbor, MI: University Microfilms International.

———. [1910] 1990. *Twenty Years at Hull-House with Autobiographical Notes*. Urbana and Chicago: University of Illinois Press.

Addams, Jane, and Ida B. Wells. [1901] 1977. *Rape and Lynching: An Exchange of Views*. New York: American Institute for Marxist Studies.

Akam, Everett H. 1991. "Community and Cultural Crisis: The 'Transfiguring Imagination' of Alain Locke." *American Literary History* 3 (2): 255–76.

Allen, Carolyn. 1996. *Following Djuna: Women Lovers and the Erotics of Loss*. Bloomington: Indiana University Press.

Alonso, Harriet Hyman. 2004. "Jane Addams: Thinking and Acting Locally and Globally." *Journal of Women's History* 16 (1): 148–64.

Anders, John P. 1999. *Willa Cather's Sexual Aesthetics and the Male Homosexual Literary Tradition*. Lincoln: University of Nebraska Press.

Anderson, Amanda. 1998. "Cosmopolitanism, Universalism, and the Divided Legacies of Modernity." In *Cosmopolitics: Thinking and Feeling beyond the Nation*, ed. Pheng Cheah and Bruce Robbins, 265–89. Minneapolis: University of Minnesota Press.

———. 2001. *The Powers of Distance: Cosmopolitanism and the Cultivation of Detachment*. Princeton, NJ: Princeton University Press.

Anderson, Nels. 1998a. "The Juvenile and the Tramp." In *On Hobos and Homelessness*, ed. Raffaele Rauty, 99–119. Chicago: University of Chicago Press.

———. 1998b. "The Slum: A Project for Study" (1928). In *On Hobos and Homelessness*, ed. Raffaele Rauty, 95–98. Chicago: University of Chicago Press.

Anderson, Sherwood. [1919] 1960. *Winesburg, Ohio*. New York: Viking.

Aptheker, Bettina. 1977. Introduction to *Rape and Lynching: An Exchange of Views*, by Jane Addams and Ida B. Wells, 1–21. New York: American Institute for Marxist Studies.

Austen, Roger. 1977. *Playing the Game: The Homosexual Novel in America*. Indianapolis: Bobbs-Merrill.

Barnes, Djuna. [1937] 1961. *Nightwood*. New York: New Directions.

———. [1916] 1989a. "Becoming Intimate with the Bohemians." In *New York*. Edited by Alyce Barry, 233–45. Los Angeles: Sun & Moon.

———. [1913] 1989b. "Chinatown's Old Glories Crumbled to Dust." In *New York*. Edited by Alyce Barry, 123–30. Los Angeles: Sun & Moon.

———. [1916] 1989c. "Greenwich Village as It Is." In *New York*. Edited by Alyce Barry, 223–32. Los Angeles: Sun & Moon.

———. [1916] 1989d. "How the Villagers Amuse Themselves." In *New York*. Edited by Alyce Barry, 246–52. Los Angeles: Sun & Moon.

———. [1913] 1989e. "Veterans in Harness." In *New York*. Edited by Alyce Barry. Los Angeles: Sun & Moon. 77–118.

———. [1928] 1992. *Ladies Almanack: Showing Their Signs and Their Tides; Their Moons and Their Changes; the Seasons as It Is with Them; Their Eclipses and Equinoxes; as Well as a Full Record of Diurnal and Nocturnal Distempers / Written & Illustrated by a Lady of Fashion*. Normal, IL: Dalkey Archive.

Barnet, Andrea. 2004. *All-Night Party: The Women of Bohemian Greenwich Village and Harlem, 1913–1930*. Chapel Hill, NC: Algonquin Books.

Bartley, Sarah Elizabeth. [1910] 1985. "Spinsters." *Woman's National Daily* November 24. Reprinted in *The Jane Addams Papers*, ed. Mary Lynn McCree Bryan, microfilm reel 113.58.95. Ann Arbor, MI: University Microfilms International.

Baudelaire, Charles. [1863] 1997. From "The Painter of Modern Life." Translated by Jonathan Mayne. In *From Modernism to Postmodernism: An Anthology*, ed. Lawrence E. Cahoone, 136–44. Malden, MA: Blackwell.

Behling, Laura L. 2001. *The Masculine Woman in America, 1890–1935*. Urbana: University of Illinois.

Benstock, Shari. 1986. *Women of the Left Bank: Paris, 1900–1940*. Austin: University of Texas Press.

———. 1990. "Expatriate Sapphic Modernism: Entering Literary History." In *Lesbian Texts and Contexts: Radical Revisions*, ed. Karla Jay and Joanne Glasgow, 183–203. New York: New York University Press.

Berlant, Lauren. 1997. "Live Sex Acts (Parental Advisory: Explicit Material)." In *The Queen of America Goes to Washington City: Essays on Sex and Citizenship*, 55–81. Durham, NC: Duke University Press.

Berlant, Lauren, and Elizabeth Freeman. 1997. "Queer Nationality." In *The Queen of America Goes to Washington City: Essays on Sex and Citizenship*, 145–73. Durham, NC: Duke University Press.

Berlant, Lauren, and Michael Warner. 1998. "Sex in Public." *Critical Inquiry* 24 (2): 547–66.

Berlin, Irving. [1937] 1991. "Slumming on Park Avenue." In *Novelty Songs*. Milwaukee: H. Leonard; New York: I. Berlin Music. [From the score for the movie *On the Avenue*, directed by Roy Del Ruth.]

Berman, Jessica. 2001. *Modernist Fiction, Cosmopolitanism, and the Politics of Community*. Cambridge: Cambridge University Press.

Bernard, Emily. 1997. "What He Did for the Race: Carl Van Vechten and the Harlem Renaissance." *Soundings* 80 (4): 531–42.

———, ed. 2001. *Remember Me to Harlem: The Letters of Langston Hughes and Carl Van Vechten, 1925–1964*. New York: Knopf.

Bersani, Leo. 1987. "Is the Rectum a Grave?" *October* 43:197–222.

———. 1995. *Homos*. Cambridge, MA: Harvard University Press.

———. 2002. "Sociability and Cruising." *Umbr(a): A Journal of the Unconscious* 2:9–24.

Bersani, Leo, and Ulysse Dutoit. 1998. *Caravaggio's Secrets*. Cambridge, MA: MIT Press.

Blackmer, Corrine E. 1996. "Selling Taboo Subjects: The Literary Commerce of Gertrude Stein and Carl Van Vechten." In *Marketing Modernisms: Self-Promotion, Canonization, Rereading*, ed. Kevin J. H. Dettmar and Stephen Watt, 221–52. Ann Arbor: University of Michigan Press.

Blackmore, David. 1997. "'Something . . . Too Preposterous and Complex to Be Recognized or Considered': Same-Sex Desire and Race in *Infants of the Spring*." *Soundings* 80 (4): 520–29.

Bland, Lucy, and Laura Doan, eds. 1998. *Sexology in Culture: Labeling Bodies and Desires*. Chicago: University of Chicago Press.

Bogdan, Robert. 1988. *Freak Show: Presenting Human Oddities for Amusement and Profit*. Chicago: University of Chicago Press.

Boone, Joseph A. 1995. "Vacation Cruises; or, The Homoerotics of Orientalism."

Publications of the Modern Language Association of America 110 (1): 89–107.
———. 1998. *Libidinal Currents: Sexuality and the Shaping of Modernism.* Chicago: University of Chicago Press.
Bourdieu, Pierre. 1984. *Distinction: A Social Critique of the Judgement of Taste.* Translated by Richard Nice. Cambridge, MA: Harvard University Press.
Bourne, Randolph. [1920] 1969. *History of a Literary Radical and Other Essays.* Edited by Van Wyck Brooks. New York: Biblo & Tannen.
Bowlby, Rachel. 1985. *Just Looking: Consumer Culture in Dreiser, Gissing, and Zola.* New York: Methuen.
Boykin, Keith. 2005. *Beyond the Down Low: Sex, Lies, and Denial in Black America.* New York: Carroll & Graf.
Brace, Charles Loring. [1872] 1967. *The Dangerous Classes of New York; and Twenty Years Work among Them.* Montclair, NJ: Patterson Smith.
Bramen, Carrie Tirado. 2000. *The Uses of Variety: Modern Americanism and the Quest for National Distinctiveness.* Cambridge, MA: Harvard University Press.
Broe, Mary Lynn. 1991. Introduction to *Silence and Power: A Reevaluation of Djuna Barnes*, ed. Mary Lynn Broe, 3–23. Carbondale and Edwardsville: Southern Illinois University Press.
Brown, Bill. 1996. *The Material Unconscious: American Amusement, Stephen Crane, and the Economies of Play.* Cambridge, MA: Harvard University Press.
Brown, Sterling. 1932. *Southern Road: Poems.* New York: Harcourt, Brace, & Co.
———. 1974. “Sterling Brown: A Living Legend.” Interview by Genevieve E. Kaete. *New Directions: The Howard University Magazine* 1:9.
———. [1937] 1978. *The Negro in American Fiction.* New York: Atheneum.
Buck-Morss, Susan. 1991. *The Dialectics of Seeing: Walter Benjamin and the Arcades Project.* Cambridge, MA: MIT Press.
Buel, James W. 1883. *Metropolitan Life Unveiled; or, The Mysteries and Miseries of America’s Great Cities, Embracing New York, Washington City, San Francisco, Salt Lake City, and New Orleans.* San Francisco: A. L. Bancroft.
Buntline, Ned. 1848. *The Mysteries and Miseries of New York: A Tale of Real Life.* London: Milner & Co.
Burroughs, William S. [1985] 1991. Letter to Mary Lynn Broe. January 14. In *Silence and Power: A Reevaluation of Djuna Barnes*, ed. Mary Lynn Broe, 206. Carbondale and Edwardsville: Southern Illinois University Press.
Butler, Judith. 1993a. “‘Dangerous Crossing’: Willa Cather’s Masculine Names.” *Bodies That Matter: On the Discursive Limits of “Sex,”* 143–66. New York: Routledge.
———. 1993b. “Passing, Queering: Nella Larsen’s Psychoanalytic Challenge.” *Bodies That Matter: On the Discursive Limits of “Sex,”* 167–85. New York: Routledge.
———. 2004. *Undoing Gender.* New York, London: Routledge.
Calinescu, Matei. 1987. *Five Faces of Modernity: Modernism, Avant-Garde, Decadence, Kitsch, Postmodernism.* Durham, NC: Duke University Press.

Carby, Hazel V. 1992. "Policing the Black Woman's Body in an Urban Context." *Critical Inquiry* 18 (4): 738–55.

Carson, Mina Julia. 1990. *Settlement Folk: Social Thought and the American Settlement Movement, 1885–1930*. Chicago: University of Chicago Press.

Castle, Terry. 1993. *The Apparitional Lesbian: Female Homosexuality and Modern Culture*. New York: Columbia University Press.

Cather, Willa. 1894. "More or Less Personal." Unsigned review of *The Green Carnation* by Robert Smythe Hitchens. *Nebraska State Journal*, November 4, 12.

———. 1918. *My Ántonia*. Boston and New York: Houghton Mifflin.

———. 1922. *One of Ours*. New York: Knopf.

———. [1905] 1928a. "The Sculptor's Funeral." In *Youth and the Bright Medusa*. New York: Knopf.

———. [1920] 1928b. "Coming, Aphrodite!" In *Youth and the Bright Medusa*. New York: Knopf.

———. 1966. "Verlaine." In *The Kingdom of Art: Willa Cather's First Principles and Critical Statements, 1893–1896*, ed. Bernice Slote, 393–97. Lincoln: University of Nebraska Press.

———. [1897] 1970a. "The Wandering Jew." *Home Monthly* December 19, n.p. Reprinted in *The World and the Parish: Willa Cather's Articles and Reviews, 1893–1902*, 2 vols., ed. William M. Curtin, 1:367–68. Lincoln: University of Nebraska Press.

———. [1935] 1985. *Lucy Gayheart*. London: Virago.

———. [1925] 1990. *The Professor's House*. New York: Vintage Classics.

———. [1905] 1991. "Paul's Case." In *The Story and Its Writer: An Introduction to Short Fiction*, ed. Ann Charters, 221–36. Boston: St. Martin's Press, Bedford.

———. 1992a. "Escapism" (1936). In *Willa Cather: Stories, Poems, and Other Writings*. Edited by Sharon O'Brien, 968–73. New York: Library of America.

———. 1992b. "Miss Jewett." In *Willa Cather: Stories, Poems, and Other Writings*. Edited by Sharon O'Brien, 849–58. New York: Library of America.

———. 1992c. "The Novel Démeublé." In *Willa Cather: Stories, Poems, and Other Writings*. Edited by Sharon O'Brien, 834–37. New York: Library of America.

Centers for Disease Control. 2006. "Men on the Down Low." October 19. Department of Health and Human Services, Centers for Disease Control and Prevention. http://cdc.gov/hiv/topics/aa/resources/qa/downlow.htm.

Chauncey, George. 1994. *Gay New York: Gender, Urban Culture, and the Making of the Gay Male World, 1890–1940*. New York: Basic Books.

Chinn, Sarah. 2001. "'Something Primitive and Age-Old as Nature Herself': Lesbian Sexuality and the Permission of the Exotic." In *Palatable Poison: Critical Perspectives on* The Well of Loneliness, ed. Laura Doan and Jay Prosser, 300–315. New York: Columbia University Press.

Chisholm, Dianne. 2005. *Queer Constellations: Subcultural Space in the Wake of the City*. Minneapolis: University of Minnesota Press.

Chudacoff, Howard P. 1999. *The Age of the Bachelor: Creating an American Subculture*. Princeton, NJ: Princeton University Press.

Churchill, Allen. 1959. *The Improper Bohemians: A Re-Creation of Greenwich Village in Its Heyday*. New York: Dutton.

Clifford, James. 1988. "On Ethnographic Surrealism." In *The Predicament of Culture: Twentieth-Century Ethnography, Literature, and Art*, 117–51. Cambridge, MA: Harvard University Press.

Cobb, Michael L. 2000. "Insolent Racing, Rough Narrative: The Harlem Renaissance's Impolite Queers." *Callaloo* 23 (1): 328–51.

———. 2006. *God Hates Fags: The Rhetorics of Religious Violence*. New York: New York University Press.

Cocks, Catherine. 2001. *Doing the Town: The Rise of Urban Tourism in the United States, 1850–1915*. Berkeley: University of California Press.

Cohen, Cathy J. 1999. *The Boundaries of Blackness: AIDS and the Breakdown of Black Politics*. Chicago: University of Chicago Press.

Coleman, Leon. 1998. *Carl Van Vechten and the Harlem Renaissance: A Critical Assessment*. New York: Garland.

Collins, Patricia Hill. 2004. *Black Sexual Politics: African Americans, Gender, and the New Racism*. New York: Routledge.

Commager, Henry Steele. [1910] 1961. Foreword to *Twenty Years at Hull-House with Autobiographical Notes*, by Jane Addams, vii–xvi. New York: New American Library.

Conor, Liz. 2004. *The Spectacular Modern Woman: Feminine Visibility in the 1920s*. Bloomington: Indiana University Press.

Copjec, Joan. 1994. *Read My Desire: Lacan against the Historicists*. Cambridge, MA: MIT Press.

Corn, Wanda M. 1999. *The Great American Thing: Modern Art and National Identity, 1915–1935*. Berkeley: University of California Press.

Cory, Daniel Webster. [1951] 1960. *The Homosexual in America: A Subjective Approach*. New York: Castle Books.

Cowley, Malcolm. 1934. *Exile's Return: A Literary Odyssey of the 1920s*. New York: Viking.

Coyle, Katy, and Nadiene Van Dyke. 1997. "Sex, Smashing, and Storyville in Turn-of-the-Century New Orleans: Reexamining the Continuum of Lesbian Sexuality." In *Carryin' On in the Lesbian and Gay South*, ed. John Howard, 54–103. New York: New York University Press.

Crane, Stephen. [1894] 1966a. "An Experiment in Misery." *New York Press*, April 22. Reprinted in *The New York City Sketches of Stephen Crane, and Related Pieces*. Edited by R. W. Stallman and E. R. Hagemann, 33–43. New York: New York University Press.

———. [1894] 1966b. "An Experiment in Luxury." *New York Press*, April 29. Reprinted in *The New York City Sketches of Stephen Crane, and Related Pieces*. Edited by R. W. Stallman and E. R. Hagemann, 43–51. New York: New York University Press.

Cresswell, Tim. 2001. *The Tramp in America*. London: Reaktion.

Curtin, Kaier. 1987. *We Can Always Call Them Bulgarians: The Emergence of Lesbians and Gay Men on the American Stage*. Boston: Alyson.

Cvetkovich, Ann. 1992. *Mixed Feelings: Feminism, Mass Culture, and Victorian Sensationalism*. New Brunswick, NJ: Rutgers University Press.

———. 2003. *An Archive of Feelings: Trauma, Sexuality, and Lesbian Public Cultures*. Durham, NC: Duke University Press.

Davidson, Arnold I. 1987. "How to Do a History of Psychoanalysis: A Reading of Freud's *Three Essays on the Theory of Sexuality*." *Critical Inquiry* 13 (2): 252–77.

Davis, Allen F. 1967. *Spearheads for Reform: The Social Settlements and the Progressive Movement*, New York: Oxford University Press.

———. 1973. *American Heroine: The Life and Legend of Jane Addams*. New York: Oxford University Press.

Dean, Tim. 1998. "What's the Point of Psychoanalytic Criticism?" *Oxford Literary Review* 20 (1–2): 143–62.

———. 2000. *Beyond Sexuality*. Chicago: University of Chicago Press.

DeAngelis, Michael. 2001. *Gay Fandom and Crossover Stardom: James Dean, Mel Gibson, and Keanu Reeves*. Durham, NC: Duke University Press.

DeCordova, Richard. 1990. *Picture Personalities: The Emergence of the Star System in America*. Urbana: University of Illinois Press.

Deegan, Mary Jo. 1988. *Jane Addams and the Men of the Chicago School, 1892–1918*. New Brunswick, NJ: Transaction.

Delany, Samuel R. 1999. *Times Square Red, Times Square Blue*. New York: New York University Press.

De Lauretis, Teresa. 1994. *The Practice of Love: Lesbian Sexuality and Perverse Desire*. Bloomington: Indiana University Press.

Deleuze, Gilles, and Félix Guattari. 1986. "What Is a Minor Literature?" (1975). In *Kafka: Toward a Minor Literature*, 16–27. Translated by Dana Polan. Minneapolis: University of Minnesota Press.

Dell, Floyd. 1926. *Intellectual Vagabondage*. New York: George H. Doran Co.

D'Emilio, John. 1983. *Sexual Politics, Sexual Communities: The Making of a Homosexual Minority in the United States, 1940–1970*. Chicago: University of Chicago Press.

———. 1993. "Capitalism and Gay Identity." In *The Lesbian and Gay Studies Reader*, ed. Henry Abelove, Michèle Aina Barale, and David M. Halperin, 467–76. New York: Routledge.

Denizet-Lewis, Benoit. 2003. "Double Lives on the Down Low." *New York Times Sunday Magazine*, August 3, 28–33, 48, 52–53.

Denning, Michael. 1996. *The Cultural Front: The Laboring of American Culture in the Twentieth Century*. London and New York: Verso.

———. [1987] 1998. *Mechanic Accents: Dime Novels and Working-Class Culture in America*. New York: Verso.

Dewey, John. [1927] 1954. *The Public and Its Problems*. Athens, OH: Swallow.

Diggs, Marylynne. 1995. "Romantic Friends or a 'Different Race of Creatures'? The Representation of Lesbian Pathology in Nineteenth-Century America." *Feminist Studies* 21 (2): 317–40.

Doan, Laura. 2001. *Fashioning Sapphism: The Origins of a Modern English Lesbian Culture*. New York: Columbia University Press.

Donzel, Catherine, Alexis Gregory, and Marc Walter. 1989. *Grand American Hotels*. New York: Vendome.

Dorman, Robert L. 1993. *Revolt of the Provinces: The Regionalist Movement in America, 1920–1945*. Chapel Hill: University of North Carolina Press.

Doughty, Frances M. 1991. "Gilt on Cardboard: Djuna Barnes as Illustrator of Her Life and Work." In *Silence and Power: A Reevaluation of Djuna Barnes*, ed. Mary Lynn Broe, 137–54. Carbondale and Edwardsville: Southern Illinois University Press.

Douglas, Ann. 1995. *Terrible Honesty: Mongrel Manhattan in the 1920s*. New York: Farrar, Straus, & Giroux.

Downs, M. Catherine. 1999. *Becoming Modern: Willa Cather's Journalism*. Selinsgrove, PA: Susquehanna University Press.

DuBois, W. E. B. 1926. "The Negro in Art: How Shall He Be Portrayed? A Symposium." *Crisis* 31 (March): 219.

———. [1926] 1994a. "Criteria of Negro Art." In *The Portable Harlem Renaissance Reader*, ed. David Levering Lewis, 100–105. New York: Penguin.

———. [1926] 1994b. Review of *Nigger Heaven* by Carl Van Vechten. In *The Portable Harlem Renaissance Reader*, ed. David Levering Lewis, 106–8. New York: Penguin.

Duggan, Lisa. 2000. *Sapphic Slashers: Sex, Violence, and American Modernity*. Durham, NC: Duke University Press.

———. 2003. "The Trials of Alice Mitchell: Sensationalism, Sexology, and the Lesbian Subject in Turn-of-the-Century America." In *Queer Studies: An Interdisciplinary Reader*, ed. Robert J. Corber and Stephen Valocchi, 73–87. Malden, MA, and Oxford: Blackwell.

Duis, Perry R. 1998. *Challenging Chicago: Coping with Everyday Life, 1837–1920*. Urbana: University of Illinois University Press.

Dyer, Richard. 1997. *White*. New York: Routledge.

Edelman, Lee. 1994. *Homographesis: Essays in Gay Literary and Cultural Theory*. New York: Routledge.

Edwards, Justin. 1999. "Carl Van Vechten's Sexual Tourism in Jazz Age Harlem." In *American Modernism across the Arts*, ed. Jay Bochner and Justin D. Edwards, 167–84. New York: Peter Lang.

———. 2001. *Exotic Journeys: Exploring the Erotics of U.S. Travel Literature, 1840–1930*. Hanover, NH: University of New England.

Elias, Amy J. 2001. *Sublime Desire: History and Post-1960s Fiction*. Baltimore: Johns Hopkins University Press.

Eliot, T. S. 1961. Introduction to *Nightwood*, by Djuna Barnes, xi–xvi. New York: New Directions.

Ellis, Havelock. [1928] 1990. Commentary to *The Well of Loneliness*, by Radclyffe Hall, n.p. New York: Anchor Books.

Ellis, Havelock, and John Addington Symonds. [1897] 1915. *Sexual Inversion*. Vol. 2 of *Studies in the Psychology of Sex*. 3d ed. Philadelphia: F. A. Davis.

Elshtain, Jean Bethke. 2002. *Jane Addams and the Dream of American Democracy: A Life*. New York: Basic Books.

Eng, David. 2001. *Racial Castration: Managing Masculinity in Asian America.* Durham, NC: Duke University Press.
English, Camper. 2002. "The Joys of Slumming." *Instinct* 5 (1): 40–42.
Entin, Joseph. 2001. "'Unhuman Humanity': Bodies of the Urban Poor and the Collapse of Realist Legibility." *Novel* 34 (3): 313–37.
Erenberg, Lewis A. 1984. *Steppin' Out: New York Nightlife and the Transformation of American Culture, 1890–1930.* Chicago: University of Chicago Press.
Erickson, Paul. 2003. "New Books, New Men: City-Mysteries Fiction, Authorship, and the Literary Market." *Early American Studies* 1 (1): 273–312.
———. 2005. "Welcome to Sodom: The Cultural Work of City-Mysteries Fiction in Antebellum America." Ph.D. diss. University of Texas at Austin.
Esteve, Mary. 2003. *The Aesthetics and Politics of the Crowd in American Literature.* Cambridge: Cambridge University Press.
Evening Transcript. [n.d.] 1985. "In Desert of Individualism," n.p. Reprinted in *The Jane Addams Papers*, ed. Mary Lynn McCree Bryan, microfilm reel 113.58.656. Ann Arbor, MI: University Microfilms International.
Faderman, Lillian. 1991. *Odd Girls and Twilight Lovers: A History of Lesbian Life in Twentieth-Century America.* New York: Penguin.
Fauset, Jessie. 1924. *There Is Confusion.* New York: Boni & Liveright.
Feffer, Andrew. 1993. *The Chicago Pragmatists and American Progressivism.* Ithaca, NY: Cornell University Press.
Ferguson, Roderick A. 2004. *Aberrations in Black: Toward a Queer of Color Critique.* Minneapolis: University of Minnesota Press.
Fiol-Matta, Licia. 2002. *A Queer Mother for the Nation: The State and Gabriela Mistral.* Minneapolis: University of Minnesota Press.
Fisher, Rudolph. 1932. "Harlem Manor." *New York Herald Tribune Books*, February 21, 16.
Flynt, Josiah. 1942. "Homosexuality among Tramps." In *Studies in the Psychology of Sex*, 2 vols., by Havelock Ellis, 1:359–67. New York: Random House.
———. [1899] 1972. *Tramping with Tramps: Studies and Sketches of Vagabond Life.* Montclair, NJ: Patterson Smith.
Foote, Stephanie. 2001. *Regional Fictions: Identity and Culture in Nineteenth-Century American Literature.* Madison: University of Wisconsin Press.
Foucault, Michel. 1988. *The History of Sexuality.* Vol. 3, *The Care of the Self.* Translated by Robert Hurley. New York: Vintage.
———. 1990a. *The History of Sexuality.* Vol. 1, *An Introduction.* Translated by Robert Hurley. New York: Vintage.
———. 1990b. *The History of Sexuality.* Vol. 2, *The Use of Pleasure.* Translated by Robert Hurley. New York: Vintage.
———. 1994. "Friendship as a Way of Life." In *Ethics: Subjectivity and Truth*, vol. 1, ed. Paul Rabinow, 135–40. Translated by Robert Hurley et al. New York: New Press.
Frank, Joseph. 1963. *The Widening Gyre: Crisis and Mastery in Modern Literature.* New Brunswick, NJ: Rutgers University Press.
Frankenberg, Ruth. 1993. *White Women, Race Matters: The Social Construction of Whiteness.* Minneapolis: University of Minnesota Press.

Franzen, Trisha. 1996. *Spinsters and Lesbians: Independent Womanhood in the United States*. New York: New York University Press.

Freedman, Estelle B. 1998. "'The Burning of Letters Continues': Elusive Identities and the Historical Construction of Sexuality." *Journal of Women's History* 9 (4): 181–200.

Freedman, Jonathan. 2001. "Coming Out of the Jewish Closet with Marcel Proust." *GLQ: A Journal of Lesbian and Gay Studies* 7 (4): 521–51.

Freeman, Elizabeth. 2000. "Packing History, Count(er)ing Generations." *New Literary History* 31 (4): 727–44.

———. 2002. *The Wedding Complex: Forms of Belonging in Modern American Culture*. Durham, NC: Duke University Press.

Fuss, Diana. *Identification Papers*. New York: Routledge, 1995.

Galehouse, Maggie. 2000. "Their Own Private Idaho: Transience in Marilynne Robinson's *Housekeeping*." *Contemporary Literature* 41 (1): 117–37.

Gallagher, Catherine. 2002. "Undoing." In *Time and the Literary*, ed. Karen Newman, Jay Clayton, and Marianne Hirsch, 11–29. New York: Routledge.

Gamson, Joshua. 1998. *Freaks Talk Back: Tabloid Talk Shows and Sexual Nonconformity*. Chicago: University of Chicago Press.

Gandal, Keith. 1997. *The Virtues of the Vicious: Jacob Riis, Stephen Crane, and the Spectacle of the Slum*. New York: Oxford University Press.

Garber, Eric. 1989. "A Spectacle in Color: The Lesbian and Gay Subculture of Jazz Age Harlem." In *Hidden from History: Reclaiming the Gay and Lesbian Past*, ed. Martin Duberman, Martha Vicinus, and George Chauncey, Jr., 318–31. New York: Meridian.

Gerstenberger, Donna. 1989. "The Radical Narrative of Djuna Barnes's *Nightwood*." In *Breaking the Sequence: Women's Experimental Fiction*, ed. Ellen G. Friedman and Miriam Fuchs, 129–39. Princeton, NJ: Princeton University Press.

Gilfoyle, Timothy J. 1992. *City of Eros: New York City, Prostitution, and the Commercialization of Sex, 1790–1920*. New York: Norton.

Gilroy, Paul. 2000. *Against Race: Imaging Political Culture beyond the Color Line*. Cambridge, MA: Belknap Press.

Gleason, William A. 1999. *The Leisure Ethic: Work and Play in American Literature, 1840–1940*. Stanford, CA: Stanford University Press.

Gloster, Hugh M. 1948. *Negro Voices in American Fiction*. Chapel Hill: University of North Carolina Press.

Goldberg, Jonathan. 2001. *Willa Cather and Others*. Durham, NC: Duke University Press.

Goldberg, Jonathan, and Madhavi Menon. 2005. "Queering History." *Publications of the Modern Language Association of America* 120 (5): 1608–17.

Goldin, Hyman E., Frank O'Leary, and Morris Lipsius, eds. 1950. *Dictionary of American Underworld Lingo*. New York: Twain.

Goldsby, Jacqueline. 2006. *A Spectacular Secret: Lynching in American Life and Literature*. Chicago: University of Chicago Press.

Green, Barbara. 1997. *Spectacular Confessions: Autobiography, Performative Activism, and the Sites of Suffrage, 1905–1938*. New York: St. Martin's Press.

Greeson, Jennifer Rae. 2001. "The 'Mysteries and Miseries' of North Carolina: New York City, Urban Gothic Fiction, and *Incidents in the Life of a Slave Girl*." *American Literature* 73 (2): 277–309.

Grewal, Inderpal. 1996. *Home and Harem: Nation, Gender, Empire, and the Cultures of Travel*. Durham, NC: Duke University Press.

Gross, Larry. 2001. *Up from Invisibility: Lesbians, Gay Men, and the Media in America*. New York: Columbia University Press.

Gustav-Wrathall, John Donald. 1998. *Take the Young Stranger by the Hand: Same-Sex Relations and the YMCA*. Chicago: University of Chicago Press.

Hackett, Robin. 2004. *Sapphic Primitivism: Productions of Race, Class, and Sexuality in Key Works of Modern Fiction*. New Brunswick, N.J.: Rutgers University Press.

Halberstam, Judith. 1998. *Female Masculinity*. Durham, NC: Duke University Press.

———. 2005. *In a Queer Time and Place: Transgender Bodies, Subcultural Lives*. New York: New York University Press.

Hall, G. Stanley. 1904. *Adolescence*. 2 vols. New York: Appleton & Co.

Hall, Radclyffe. [1928] 1990. *The Well of Loneliness*. New York: Anchor Books.

Hall, Stuart. 1997. "The Spectacle of the 'Other.'" In *Representation: Cultural Representations and the Signifying Process*, ed. Stuart Hall, 12–74. London: Sage.

Halperin, David M. 1995. *Saint Foucault: Towards a Gay Hagiography*. New York: Oxford University Press.

———. 2002. *How to Do the History of Homosexuality*. Chicago: University of Chicago Press.

Hamilton, Marybeth. 1997. *"When I'm Bad, I'm Better": Mae West, Sex, and American Entertainment*. Berkeley: University of California Press.

Hamilton, Paul. 1996. *Historicism*. New York: Routledge.

Hannerz, Ulf. [1969] 2004. *Soulside: Inquiries into Ghetto Culture and Community*. Chicago: University of Chicago Press.

Hapgood, Hutchins. 1910. *Types from City Streets*. New York: Funk & Wagnalls Co.

Harper, Phillip Brian. 1996. *Are We Not Men? Masculine Anxiety and the Problem of African-American Identity*. Oxford: Oxford University Press.

Harris, Andrea L. 1994. "The Third Sex: Figures of Inversion in Djuna Barnes's *Nightwood*." *Genders* 20: 233–59.

Harris, Bertha. 1973. "The More Profound Nationality of Their Lesbianism: Lesbian Society in Paris in the 1920s." In *Amazon Expedition: A Lesbian Feminist Anthology*, ed. Phyllis Birkby. et al., 77–88. New York: Times Change Press.

Haskell, Barbara. 1987. *Charles Demuth*. New York: Harry M. Abrams, Inc.

Hassett, Gillian. 2006. "Re: permission to reprint image of Kalon Jackson." E-mail to author, August 14.

Hatheway, Jay. 2003. *The Gilded Age Construction of Modern American Homophobia*. New York: Palgrave Macmillan.

Hayner, Norman S. 1936. *Hotel Life*. Chapel Hill: University of North Carolina Press.

Heap, Chad Cottrell. 2000. "'Slumming': Sexuality, Race, and Urban Commercial Leisure, 1900–1940." Ph.D. diss. University of Chicago.

Hebdige, Dick. [1979] 2002. *Subculture: The Meaning of Style*. London: Routledge.

Hemingway, Ernest. 1964. *A Moveable Feast*. New York: Simon & Schuster.

Herring, Phillip. 1995. *Djuna: The Life and Work of Djuna Barnes*. New York: Penguin.

———. 1996. Introduction to *Collected Stories* by Djuna Barnes, 7–24. Los Angeles: Sun & Moon.

Herring, Terrell Scott. 2002. "Frank O'Hara's Open Closet." *Publications of the Modern Language Association of America* 117 (3): 414–27.

Herrmann, Anne. 2000. *Queering the Moderns: Poses/Portraits/Performances*. New York: Palgrave.

Holt, Hamilton, ed. [1906] 2000. *The Life Stories of Undistinguished Americans, as Told by Themselves*. New York and London: Routledge.

Horowitz, Helen Lefkowitz. 1976. *Culture & the City: Cultural Philanthropy in Chicago from the 1880's to 1917*. Lexington: University of Kentucky.

Hovey, Jaime. 1996. "Sapphic Primitivism in Gertrude Stein's *Q.E.D.*" *Modern Fiction Studies* 42 (3): 547–68.

Howard, John. 2001. *Men Like That: A Southern Queer History*. Chicago: University of Chicago Press.

Howells, William Dean. 1896. "An East-Side Ramble." In *Impressions and Experiences*. New York: Harper & Brothers.

Hughes, Langston. 1926a. "The Negro Artist and the Racial Mountain." *Nation* 122 (June 23): 693–94.

———. 1926b. *The Weary Blues*. New York: Knopf.

———. 1927. *Fine Clothes to the Jew*. New York: Knopf.

———. [1940] 1986. *The Big Sea*. New York: Pluto.

———. 1995. "Café: 3 A.M." (1951). *The Collected Poems of Langston Hughes*. Edited by Arnold Rampersad and David Roessel. New York: Vintage.

Hurt, James. 1990. Introduction to *Twenty Years at Hull-House with Autobiographical Notes*, by Jane Addams, ix–xix. Urbana and Chicago: University of Illinois Press.

Hutcheon, Linda. 1988. *A Poetics of Postmodernism: History, Theory, Fiction*. London: Routledge.

Hutchinson, George. 1995. *The Harlem Renaissance in Black and White*. Cambridge: Belknap Press.

Inness, Sherrie A. 1995. *Intimate Communities: Representation and Social Transformation in Women's College Fiction, 1895–1910*. Bowling Green, KY: Bowling Green State University Popular Press.

Jackson, Kenneth T. 1985. *Crabgrass Frontier: The Suburbanization of the United States*. Oxford: Oxford University Press.

Jackson, Rosemary. [1981] 1993. *Fantasy: The Literature of Subversion*. London, New York: Methuen.

Jackson, Shannon. 2000. *Lines of Activity: Performance, Historiography, Hull-House Domesticity*. Ann Arbor: University of Michigan Press.

Jacobs, George W. 1928. "New Yorker Flays McKay's Book, 'Home to Harlem.'" *Pittsburgh Courier* April 7.

Jacobson, Matthew Frye. 1998. *Whiteness of a Different Color: European Immigrants and the Alchemy of Race*. Cambridge, MA: Harvard University Press.

———. 2000. *Barbarian Virtues: The United States Encounters Foreign Peoples at Home and Abroad, 1876–1917*. New York: Hill & Wang.

Jarraway, David R. 1996. "Montage of an Otherness Deferred: Dreaming Subjectivity in Langston Hughes." *American Literature* 68 (4): 819–47.

———. 2002. "Tales of the City: Marginality, Community, and the Problem of (Gay) Identity in Wallace Thurman's 'Harlem' Fiction." *College English* 65 (1): 36–52.

Jarrett, Gene Andrew, ed. 2006. *African American Literature beyond Race: An Alternative Reader*. New York: New York University Press.

Jeffreys, Sheila. 1985. *The Spinster and Her Enemies: Feminism and Sexuality, 1880–1930*. London: Pandora.

Johnson, Barbara. 1993. "Lesbian Spectacles: Reading *Sula*, *Passing*, *Thelma and Louise*, and *The Accused*." In *Media Spectacles*, ed. Marjorie Garber, Jann Matlock, and Rebecca L. Walkowitz, 160–66. New York: Routledge.

Johnson, James Weldon. [1912] 1966. *The Autobiography of an Ex-Colored Man*. New York: Knopf.

Jolas, Eugene. 1932. *The Language of Night*. The Hague: Servire Press.

Joseph, Miranda. 2002. *Against the Romance of Community*. Minneapolis: University of Minnesota Press.

Jurca, Catherine. 2001. *White Diaspora: The Suburb and the Twentieth-Century American Novel*. Princeton, NJ: Princeton University Press.

Kannenstine, Louis F. 1977. *The Art of Djuna Barnes: Duality and Damnation*. New York: New York University Press.

Kaplan, Amy. 2002. *The Anarchy of Empire in the Making of U.S. Culture*. Cambridge, MA: Harvard University Press.

Kaplan, Morris. 1999. "Who's Afraid of John Saul? Urban Culture and the Politics of Desire in Late Victorian London." *GLQ: A Journal of Lesbian and Gay Studies* 5 (3): 267–314.

Kasson, John F. 1990. *Rudeness and Civility: Manners in Nineteenth-Century Urban America*. New York: Hill & Wang.

———. 2001. *Houdini, Tarzan, and the Perfect Man: The White Male Body and the Challenge of Modernity in America*. New York: Hill & Wang.

Katz, Jonathan Ned. 1995. *The Invention of Heterosexuality*. New York: Dutton.

Kawash, Samira. 1997. *Dislocating the Color Line: Identity, Hybridity and Singularity in African-American Literature*. Stanford, CA: Stanford University Press.

Kellner, Bruce. 1987. "'Refined Racism': White Patronage and the Harlem Renaissance." In *The Harlem Renaissance Re-examined*, ed. Victor A. Kramer, 93–106. New York: AMS Press.

———, ed. 2000. *Letters of Charles Demuth, American Artist, 1883–1935*. Philadelphia: Temple University Press.

Kennedy, Elizabeth Lapovsky, and Madeline Davis. 1994. *Boots of Leather, Slippers of Gold: A History of a Lesbian Community*. New York: Penguin.

Kennedy, J. Gerald. 1993. *Imagining Paris: Exile, Writing, and American Identity*. New Haven, CT: Yale University Press.

Kidd, Kenneth B. 2004. *Making American Boys: Boyology and the Feral Tale*. Minneapolis: University of Minnesota Press.

King, J. L., and Karen Hunter. 2004. *On the Down Low: A Journey into the Lives of "Straight" Black Men Who Sleep with Men*. New York: Broadway Books.

King, Jason. 2003. "Remixing the Closet: The Down-Low Way of Knowledge." *Village Voice*, June 25–July 1, 38, 44, 46.

Kinsey, Alfred C. 1948. *Sexual Behavior in the Human Male*. Philadelphia: W. B. Saunders Co.

Knadler, Stephen. 2002. "Sweetback Style: Wallace Thurman and a Queer Harlem Renaissance." *Modern Fiction Studies* 48 (4): 899–936.

Koestenbaum, Wayne. 1993. *The Queen's Throat: Opera, Homosexuality, and the Mystery of Desire*. New York: Vintage.

Koven, Seth. 2004. *Slumming: Sexual and Social Politics in Victorian London*. Princeton, NJ: Princeton University Press.

Krafft-Ebing, Richard von. [1893] 1998. *Psychopathia Sexualis, with Especial Reference to Contrary Sexual Instinct: A Medico-Legal Study*. Translated by Franklin S. Klaf. New York: Arcade.

Lamos, Colleen. 1998. *Deviant Modernism: Sexual and Textual Errancy in T. S. Eliot, James Joyce, and Marcel Proust.* Cambridge: Cambridge University Press.

Lane, Christopher. 1999. *The Burdens of Intimacy: Psychoanalysis and Victorian Masculinity*. Chicago: University of Chicago Press.

———. 2003. "The Poverty of Context: Historicism and Nonmimetic Fiction." *Publications of the Modern Language Association* 118 (3): 450–69.

Laplanche, Jean, and Jean-Bertrand Pontalis. 1986. "Fantasy and the Origins of Sexuality." In *Formations of Fantasy*, ed. Victor Burgin, James Donald, and Cora Kaplan, 5–34. London: Methuen.

Lee, Anthony E. 2001. *Picturing Chinatown: Art and Orientalism in San Francisco*. Berkeley: University of California Press.

Lemke, Sieglinde. 1998. *Primitivist Modernism: Black Culture and the Origins of Transatlantic Modernism*. Oxford: Oxford University Press.

Levenson, Michael H. 1984. *A Genealogy of Modernism: A Study of English Literary Doctrine*. Cambridge: Cambridge University Press.

Levine, Lawrence W. 1988. *Highbrow/Lowbrow: The Emergence of Cultural Hierarchy in America*. Cambridge, MA: Harvard University Press.

Levine, Nancy J. 1991. "'Bringing Milkshakes to Bulldogs': The Early Journalism of Djuna Barnes." In *Silence and Power: A Reevaluation of Djuna Barnes*, ed. Mary Lynn Broe, 27–34. Carbondale and Edwardsville: Southern Illinois University Press.

Lewis, David Levering. [1979] 1997. *When Harlem Was in Vogue.* New York: Penguin.

Lewis, Edith. 1953. *Willa Cather Living: A Personal Record*. New York: Knopf.

Lindemann, Marilee. 1999. *Willa Cather: Queering America*. New York: Columbia University Press.

Linn, James Weber. [1937] 2000. *Jane Addams: A Biography*. Urbana, and Chicago: University of Illinois Press.

Lissak, Rivka Shpak. 1989. *Pluralism and Progressives: Hull-House and the New Immigrants, 1890–1919*. Chicago: University of Chicago Press.

Locke, Alain. 1925. "Enter the New Negro." *Survey Graphic* 6 (March): 631–34.

———. 1928. "Art or Propaganda?" *Harlem* 1 (November): 12.

———. 1937. "Spiritual Truancy." *New Challenge* 2 (Fall): 81–85.

London, Jack. [1903] 1982. *The People of the Abyss*. In *Jack London: Novels and Social Writings*, 1–184. Edited by Donald Pizer. New York: Literary Classics of the United States.

Longenbach, James. 1987. *Modernist Poetics of History: Pound, Eliot, and the Sense of the Past*. Princeton, NJ: Princeton University Press.

Looby, Christopher. 1993. "George Thompson's 'Romance of the Real': Transgression and Taboo in American Sensation Fiction." *American Literature* 65 (4): 651–72.

Lorusso, Edward N. S. 1992. Introduction to *Miss Knight and Others*, by Robert McAlmon, xv–xxvi. Albuquerque: University of New Mexico Press.

Lott, Eric. 1993. *Love and Theft: Blackface Minstrelsy and the American Working Class*. New York: Oxford University Press.

Love, Heather K. 2001. "'Spoiled Identity': Stephen Gordon's Loneliness and the Difficulties of Queer History." *GLQ: A Journal of Lesbian and Gay Studies* 7 (4): 487–519.

Lowe, Lisa. 1991. *Critical Terrains: French and British Orientalisms*. Ithaca, NY: Cornell University Press.

———. 1996. *Immigrant Acts: On Asian American Cultural Politics*. Durham, NC: Duke University Press.

Lutes, Jean Marie. 2006. *Front-Page Girls: Women Journalists in American Culture and Fiction, 1880–1930*. Ithaca, NY: Cornell University Press.

Lynch, Michael. 1985. "'Here Is Adhesiveness': From Friendship to Homosexuality." *Victorian Studies* 29 (1): 67–96.

Lynes, Russell. 1985. *The Lively Audience: A Social History of the Visual and Performing Arts in America, 1890–1950*. New York: Harper & Row.

Lyon, Janet. 2005. "Gender and Sexuality." In *The Cambridge Companion to American Modernism*, ed. Walter Kalaidjian, 221–41. Cambridge: Cambridge University Press.

Marchand, Roland. 1985. *Advertising the American Dream: Making Way for Modernity, 1920–1940*. Berkeley: University of California Press.

Marcus, Jane. 1991. "Laughing at Leviticus: *Nightwood* as Woman's Circus Epic." In *Silence and Power: A Reevaluation of Djuna Barnes*, ed. Mary Lynn Broe, 221–50. Carbondale and Edwardsville: Southern Illinois University Press.

Martin, Edward Winslow. 1868. *The Secrets of the Great City: A Work Descriptive of the Virtues and the Vices, the Mysteries, Miseries and Crimes of New York City*. Philadelphia: Jones, Brothers & Co.

McAlmon, Robert. 1992. "Miss Knight." In *Miss Knight and Others*. Edited by Edward N. S. Lorusso, 3–20. Albuquerque: University of New Mexico Press.

McCabe, James Dabney, Jr. 1872. *Lights and Shadows of New York Life; or, The Sights and Sensations of the Great City, a Work Descriptive of the City of New York in All Its Various Phases; with Full and Graphic Accounts of Its Splendors and Wretchedness; Its High and Low Life; Its Marble Palaces and Dark Dens; Its Attractions and Dangers; Its Rings and Frauds; Its Leading Men and Politicians; Its Adventurers; Its Charities; Its Mysteries; and Its Crimes*. Philadelphia and Chicago: National Publishing Co.

McClintock, Anne. 1995. *Imperial Leather: Race, Gender, and Sexuality in the Colonial Contest*. New York: Routledge.

McCoy, Beth. 1998. "Inspectin' and Collecting: The Scene of Carl Van Vechten." *Genders* 28, 43 pars. http://www.genders.org/g28/g28inspectin.txt (accessed March 15, 2003).

McDowell, Deborah. 1993. "'It's Not Safe. Not Safe at All': Sexuality in Nella Larsen's *Passing*." In *The Lesbian and Gay Studies Reader*, ed. Henry Abelove, Michèle Aina Barale, and David M. Halperin, 616–25. New York and London: Routledge.

McGarry, Molly, and Fred Wasserman. 1998. *Becoming Visible: An Illustrated History of Lesbian and Gay Life in Twentieth-Century America*. New York: Penguin Studio.

McGurl, Mark. 2001. *The Novel Art: Elevations of American Fiction after Henry James*. Princeton, NJ: Princeton University Press.

Meeker, Martin. 2006. *Contacts Desired: Gay and Lesbian Communications and Community, 1940s–1970s*. Chicago: University of Chicago Press.

Meese, Elizabeth A. 1992. *(Sem)erotics: Theorizing Lesbian : Writing*. New York: New York University Press.

Meier, Nellie Simmons. [1909] 1985. "Characteristics Read in the Palm of the Hand." *Indianapolis News*, November 16. Reprinted in *The Jane Addams Papers*, ed. Mary Lynn McCree Bryan, microfilm reel 113.57.702. Ann Arbor, MI: University Microfilms International.

Mencken, H. L. 1926. "Response to 'The Negro in Art: How Shall He Be Portrayed? A Symposium.'" *Crisis* 31 (March): 219–20.

Mercer, Kobena. 1994. "Black Art and the Burden of Representation." In *Welcome to the Jungle: New Positions in Black Cultural Studies*, 233–58. New York and London: Routledge.

Meyerowitz, Joanne. 1988. *Women Adrift: Independent Wage Earners in Chicago, 1880–1930*. Chicago: University of Chicago Press.

———. 2002. *How Sex Changed: A History of Transsexuality in the United States*. Cambridge, MA: Harvard University Press.

Michaels, Walter Benn. 1995. *Our America: Modernism, Nativism, Pluralism*. Durham, NC: Duke University Press.

———. 1996. "'You who never was there': Slavery and the New Historicism, Deconstruction and the Holocaust." *Narrative* 4 (1): 1–16.

Miller, D. A. 1988. *The Novel and the Police*. Berkeley: University of California Press.

———. 1992. *Bringing out Roland Barthes*. Berkeley: University of California Press.

Morris, Lloyd. 1951. *Incredible New York: High and Low Life of the Last Hundred Years, 1850–1950*. New York: Random House.

Mumford, Kevin J. 1997. *Interzones: Black/White Sex Districts in Chicago and New York in the Early Twentieth Century*. New York: Columbia University Press.

Muñoz, José Esteban. 1996. "Ephemera as Evidence: Introductory Notes to Queer Acts." *Women and Performance* 8 (2): 5–16.

———. 1999. *Disidentifications: Queers of Color and the Performance of Politics*. Minneapolis: University of Minnesota Press.

Murphy, Kevin P. 2000. "Socrates in the Slums: Homoerotics, Gender, and Settlement House Reform." In *A Shared Experience: Men, Women, and the History of Gender*, ed. Laura McCall and Donald Yacovone, 273–96. New York: New York University Press.

Neal, Mark Anthony. 2005. *New Black Man*. New York: Routledge.

Nealon, Christopher. 2001. *Foundlings: Lesbian and Gay Historical Emotion before Stonewall*. Durham, NC: Duke University Press.

Newton, Esther. 1990. "The Mythic Mannish Lesbian: Radclyffe Hall and the New Woman." In *Hidden from History: Reclaiming the Gay and Lesbian Past*, ed. Martin Duberman, Martha Vicinus, and George Chauncey, Jr., 281–93. New York: Meredian.

New York Times Book Review. 1932. "Harlem's Bohemia." February 28, 22.

New York World. [1905] 1985. "Race Suicide Laid to Women's Clubs." December 4. Reprinted in *The Jane Addams Papers*, ed. Mary Lynn McCree Bryan, microfilm reel 113.56.74. Ann Arbor, MI: University Microfilms International.

———. [1916] 1985. "Defends Bachelor Maids, Rebuked by Helen Gould." July 26. Reprinted in *The Jane Addams Papers*, ed. Mary Lynn McCree Bryan, microfilm reel 113.58.1172. Ann Arbor, MI: University Microfilms International.

Nissen, Axel. 2005. "A Tramp at Home: *Huckleberry Finn*, Romantic Friendship, and the Homeless Man." *Nineteenth-Century Literature* 60 (1): 57–86.

Nord, Deborah Epstein. 1991. "The Urban Peripatetic: Spectator, Streetwalker, Woman Writer." *Nineteenth-Century Literature* 46 (3): 351–75.

Nordau, Max. 1895. *Degeneration*. New York: Appleton & Co.

North, Michael. 1994. *The Dialect of Modernism: Race, Language, and Twentieth-Century Literature*. New York and Oxford: Oxford University Press.

———. 1999. *Reading 1922: A Return to the Scene of the Modern*. New York, Oxford: Oxford University Press.

Nugent, Richard Bruce. 2002a. "Geisha Man" (selections). In *Gay Rebel of the Harlem Renaissance: Selections from the Work of Richard Bruce Nugent*. Edited by Thomas H. Wirth, 90–111. Durham, NC: Duke University Press.

———. 2002b. "On Carl Van Vechten." In *Gay Rebel of the Harlem Renaissance: Selections from the Work of Richard Bruce Nugent*. Edited by Thomas H. Wirth, 226–30. Durham, NC: Duke University Press.

———. 2002c. "Smoke, Lilies, and Jade." In *Gay Rebel of the Harlem Renaissance: Selections from the Work of Richard Bruce Nugent*. Edited by Thomas H. Wirth, 75–86. Durham, NC: Duke University Press.

———. 2002d. "You See, I Am a Homosexual." Interview by Thomas H. Wirth. In *Gay Rebel of the Harlem Renaissance: Selections from the Work of Richard Bruce Nugent*. Edited by Thomas H. Wirth, 268–72. Durham, NC: Duke University Press.

O'Brien, Sharon. 1987. *Willa Cather: The Emerging Voice*. New York, Oxford: Oxford University Press.

O'Connor, Alice. 2001. *Poverty Knowledge: Social Science, Social Policy, and the Poor in Twentieth-Century U.S. History*. Princeton, NJ: Princeton University Press.

O'Hara, Daniel T. 1991. "Michel Foucault and the Fate of Friendship." *Boundary 2* 18 (1): 83–103.

O'Neal, Hank. 1991. "Reminiscences." In *Silence and Power: A Reevaluation of Djuna Barnes*, ed. Mary Lynn Broe, 348–61. Carbondale and Edwardsville: Southern Illinois University Press.

Ortega y Gasset, José. 1948. *The Dehumanization of Art*. Translated by Willard R. Trask. Princeton, NJ: Princeton University Press.

Osofsky, Gilbert. 1966. *Harlem: The Making of a Ghetto: Negro New York, 1890–1930*. New York: Harper & Row.

Park, Robert E. [1915] 1997. From *The City: Suggestions for the Investigation of Human Behaviour*. In *The Subcultures Reader*, ed. Ken Gelder and Sarah Thornton, 16–27. New York: Routledge.

Parry, Albert. 1933. *Garrets and Pretenders: A History of Bohemianism in America*. New York: Covici Friede.

Parsons, Deborah L. 2000. *Streetwalking the Metropolis: Women, the City, and Modernity*. Oxford: Oxford University Press.

Perry, Imani. 2004. *Prophets of the Hood: Politics and Poetics in Hip Hop*. Durham, NC: Duke University Press.

Pfeiffer, Kathleen. 2000. Introduction to *Nigger Heaven*, by Carl Van Vechten, ix–xxxix. Urbana: University of Illinois Press.

Phelan, Peggy. 1996. *Unmarked: The Politics of Performance*. New York: Routledge.

Pittenger, Mark. 1997. "A World of Difference: Constructing the 'Underclass' in Progressive America." *American Quarterly* 49 (1): 26–62.

Poirier, Richard. 1987. *The Renewal of Literature: Emersonian Reflections*. New York: Random House.

Pratt, Mary Louise. 1992. *Imperial Eyes: Travel Writing and Transculuration*. New York: Routledge.

Proust, Marcel. 1981. *Cities of the Plain*. Vol. 2 of *Remembrance of Things Past*. Translated by C. K. Scott Moncrieff and Terence Kilmartin. New York: Random House.

Puar, Jasbir Kaur. 2002. "Queer Tourism: Geographies of Globalization." Special issue, *GLQ: A Journal of Lesbian and Gay Studies*, vol. 8, nos. 1–2.

Quiroga, José. 2001. *Tropics of Desire: Interventions from Queer Latino America*. New York: New York University Press.

Rasmussen, Birgit Brander, Irene J. Nexica, Eric Klinenberg, and Matt Wray. 2001. *The Making and Unmaking of Whiteness*. Durham, NC: Duke University Press.

Rechy, John. 1963. *City of Night*. New York: Grove Press.

Record Herald. [1909] 1985. "Genius of Hull House Is 'First Citizen of Chicago.'" December 2. Reprinted in *The Jane Addams Papers*, ed. Mary Lynn McCree Bryan, microfilm reel 113.57.735. Ann Arbor, MI: University Microfilms International.

Reid-Pharr, Robert F. 2001. *Black Gay Man: Essays*. New York: New York University Press.

Reimonenq, Alden. 1993. "Countee Cullen's Uranian 'Soul Windows.'" *Journal of Homosexuality* 26 (2–3): 143–65.

Reizbaum, Marilyn. 1988. "A 'Modernism of Marginality': The Link between James Joyce and Djuna Barnes." In *New Alliances in Joyce Studies: "'When It's Aped to Foul a Delfian,'"* edited by Bonnie Kime Scott, 179–89. Newark: University of Delaware Press.

Residents of Hull-House, a Social Settlement at 335 South Halsted Street, Chicago, Ill. 1895. *Hull-House Maps and Papers: A Presentation of Nationalities and Wages in a Congested District of Chicago, Together with Comments and Essays on Problems Growing Out of the Social Conditions*. New York: Thomas Y. Crowell & Co.

Reynolds, David, and Kimberley R. Gladman. 2002. Introduction to *"Venus in Boston" and Other Tales of Nineteenth-Century City Life*, by George Thompson, ix–liv. Amherst: University of Massachusetts Press.

Reynolds, Guy. 1996. *Willa Cather in Context: Progress, Race, Empire*. New York: St. Martin's.

Rich, Adrienne. 1993. "Compulsory Heterosexuality and Lesbian Existence." In *The Lesbian and Gay Studies Reader*, ed. Henry Abelove, Michèle Aina Barale, and David M. Halperin, 227–54. New York: Routledge.

Rich, B. Ruby. 2002. "The Gay Escape." *Advocate*, July 23, 43.

Ricco, John Paul. 2002. *The Logic of the Lure*. Chicago: University of Chicago Press.

Ricoeur, Paul. 1970. *Freud and Philosophy: An Essay on Interpretation*. New Haven, CT: Yale University Press.

Riis, Jacob. [1890] 1996. *How the Other Half Lives: Studies among the Tenements of New York*. New York: St. Martin's.

Robertson, Jennifer. 2003. "Dying to Tell: Sexuality and Suicide in Imperial Japan." In *Queer Studies: An Interdisciplinary Reader*, ed. Robert J. Corber and Stephen Valocchi, 187–205. Malden, MA, and Oxford: Blackwell.

Rodgers, Bruce. 1972. *Gay Talk: A (Sometimes) Outrageous Dictionary of Gay Slang*. New York: Paragon.

Rodríguez, Juana María. 2003. *Queer Latinidad: Identity Practices, Discursive Spaces*. New York: New York University Press.

Roediger, David R. 1991. *The Wages of Whiteness: Race and the Making of the American Working Class*. New York: Verso.

Rohy, Valerie. 2006. "Ahistorical." *GLQ: A Journal of Lesbian and Gay Studies* 12 (1): 61–83.

Román, David. 2005. *Performance in America: Contemporary U.S. Culture and the Performing Arts*. Durham, NC: Duke University Press.

Roof, Judith. 1996. *Come as You Are: Sexuality and Narrative*. New York: Columbia University Press.

Rose, Tricia. 1994. *Black Noise: Rap Music and Black Culture in Contemporary America*. Hanover, NH: Wesleyan University Press.

Rosen, Ruth. 1982. *The Lost Sisterhood: Prostitution in America, 1900–1918*. Baltimore: Johns Hopkins University Press.

Ross, Marlon. 2004. *Manning the Race: Reforming Black Men in the Jim Crow Era*. New York: New York University Press.

Rothenberg, Molly Anne, and Joseph Valente. 1997. "Performative Chic." *College Literature* 24 (1): 295–305.

Rotundo, E. Anthony. 1993. *American Manhood: Transformations in Masculinity from the Revolution to the Modern Era*. New York: BasicBooks.

Royce, Josiah. 1950. *The Social Philosophy of Josiah Royce*. Edited by Stuart Jerry Brown. Syracuse: Syracuse University Press.

Rubin, Gayle. 1993. "Thinking Sex." In *The Lesbian and Gay Studies Reader*, ed. Henry Abelove, Michèle Aina Barale, and David M. Halperin, 3–44. New York: Routledge.

Rupp, Leila J. 1999. *A Desired Past: A Short History of Same-Sex Love in America*. Chicago: University of Chicago Press.

Said, Edward W. 1993. *Culture and Imperialism*. New York: Knopf.

Sante, Luc. 1991. *Low Life: Lures and Snares of Old New York*. New York: Farrar, Straus, Giroux.

Schlissel, Lillian. 1997. Introduction to *The Drag: A Homosexual Comedy in Three Acts* (1927). In *Three Plays by Mae West*: Sex, The Drag, The Pleasure Man, by Mae West. Edited by Lillian Schlissel, 1–29. New York: Routledge.

Schoonmaker, Edwin Davies. [1912] 1985. "MOTHER of Races." *Kansas City News Gazette*. May 2. Reprinted in *The Jane Addams Papers*, ed. Mary Lynn McCree Bryan, microfilm reel 113.58.568. Ann Arbor, MI: University Microfilms International.

Schuyler, George S. 1926. "Views and Reviews." *Pittsburgh Courier*, November 6, 14.

———. 1950. "The Van Vechten Revolution." *Phylon* 11(4): 362–68.

Schwarz, A. B. Christa. 2003. *Gay Voices of the Harlem Renaissance*. Bloomington: Indiana University Press.

Scott, Joan W. 1993. "The Evidence of Experience." In *The Lesbian and Gay Studies Reader*, ed. Henry Abelove, Michèle Aina Barale, and David M. Halperin, 397–415. New York: Routledge.

———. 2001. "Fantasy Echo: History and the Construction of Identity." *Critical Inquiry* 27 (2): 284–304.

Scott-Blanton, Janice. 2005. *My Husband Is on the Down Low . . . and I Know about It*. Kearney, NE: Morris Publishing.

Scruggs, Charles. 1987. "Crab Antics and Jacob's Ladder: Aaron Douglas's Two Views of *Nigger Heaven*." In *The Harlem Renaissance Re-examined*, ed. Victor A. Kramer, 149–84. New York: AMS Press.

Sedgwick, Eve Kosofsky. 1990. *Epistemology of the Closet*. Berkeley: University of California Press.

———. 1993a. "Queer and Now." In *Tendencies*, 1–20. Durham, NC: Duke University Press.

———. 1993b. "Willa Cather and Others." In *Tendencies*, 167–76. Durham, NC: Duke University Press.

Seitler, Dana. 2004. "Queer Physiognomies, or, How Many Ways Can We Do the History of Sexuality?" *Criticism* 46 (1): 71–102.

Selby, Hubert, Jr. 1964. *Last Exit to Brooklyn*. New York: Grove Press.

Seltzer, Mark. 1982. "*The Princess Casamassima*: Realism and the Fantasy of Surveillance." In *American Realism: New Essays*, ed. Eric J. Sundquist, 95–118. Baltimore and London: Johns Hopkins University Press.

———. 1996. *Bodies and Machines*. New York: Routledge.

———. 1998. *Serial Killers: Death and Life in America's Wound Culture*. New York: Routledge.

Shah, Nayan. 1998. "Sexuality, Identity, and the Uses of History." In *Q & A: Queer in Asian America*, ed. David L. Eng and Alice Y. Hom, 141–56. Philadelphia: Temple University Press.

———. 2001. *Contagious Divides: Epidemics and Race in San Francisco's Chinatown*. Berkeley: University of California Press.

Silberman, Seth Clark. 2004. "Reading Black Queer Vernacular in the 'Streetgeist and Folklore' of Harlem's Renaissance." In *Public Space, Private Lives: Race, Gender, Class, and Citizenship in New York, 1890–1929*, ed. William Boelhower and Anna Scacchi, 129–52. Amsterdam: VU University Press.

Simmel, Georg. 1950a. "On the Significance of Numbers for Social Life." In *The Sociology of Georg Simmel*, 87–104. Translated by Kurt H. Wolff. New York: Free Press.

———. 1950b. "The Social Gathering ('Party')." In *The Sociology of Georg Simmel*, 111–14. Translated by Kurt H. Wolff. New York: Free Press.

———. 1971. "Sociability." In *On Individuality and Social Forms*, ed. Donald N. Levine, 127–40. Chicago: University of Chicago Press.

Singer, Ben. 2001. *Melodrama and Modernity: Early Sensational Cinema and Its Contexts*. New York: Columbia University Press.

Singh, Amritjit. 1992. Foreword to *Infants of the Spring*, by Wallace Thurman, vii–xxix. Boston: Northeastern University Press.

Singh, Amritjit, and Daniel M. Scott III. 2003. Introduction to "Essays on Harlem" by Wallace Thurman. In *The Collected Writings of Wallace Thurman: A Harlem Renaissance Reader*, edited by Amrijit Singh and Daniel M. Scott III, 29–31. New Brunswick, NJ: Rutgers University Press.

Skaggs, Merrill Maguire. 2000. Introduction to *Willa Cather's New York: New Essays on Cather in the City*, ed. Merrill Maguire Skaggs, 13–16. London: Fairleigh Dickinson.

Slote, Bernice. 1967. Introduction to *The Kingdom of Art: Willa Cather's First Principles and Critical Statements, 1893–1896*. Edited by Bernice Slote, 1–88. Lincoln: University of Nebraska Press.

Smalls, James. 1998. "Public Face, Private Thoughts: Fetish, Interracialism, and the Homoerotic in Carl Van Vechten's Photographs." In *The Passionate Camera: Photography and Bodies of Desire*, ed. Deborah Bright, 78–102. London and New York: Routledge.

Smith, Charles Michael. 1986. "Bruce Nugent: Bohemian of the Harlem Renaissance." In *In the Life: A Black Gay Anthology*, ed. Joseph Beam, 209–21. Boston: Alyson.

Smith-Rosenberg, Carroll. 1990. "Discourses of Sexuality and Subjectivity: The New Woman, 1870–1936." In *Hidden from History: Reclaiming the Gay and Lesbian Past*, ed. Martin Duberman, Martha Vicinus, and George Chauncey, Jr., 264–80. New York: Meredian.

Somerville, Siobhan B., 2000. *Queering the Color Line: Race and the Invention of Homosexuality in American Culture*. Durham, NC: Duke University Press.

Spokane Spokesman. [n.d.] 1985. "Pastor's Criticism of Old Maids Properly Resented." Reprinted in *The Jane Addams Papers*, ed. Mary Lynn McCree Bryan, microfilm reel 113.58.1134. Ann Arbor, MI: University Microfilms International.

Spurr, David. 1993. *The Rhetoric of Empire: Colonial Discourse in Journalism, Travel Writing, and Imperial Administration*. Durham, NC: Duke University Press.

Srebnick, Amy Gilman. 1995. *The Mysterious Death of Mary Rogers: Sex and Culture in Nineteenth-Century New York*. New York: Oxford University Press.

Stallybrass, Peter. 1990. "Marx and Heterogeneity: Thinking the Lumpenproletariat." *Representations* 31:69–95.

Stansell, Christine. 2000. *American Moderns: Bohemian New York and the Creation of a New Century*. New York: Metropolitan Books.

Stevenson, Sheryl. 1991. "Writing the Grotesque Body: Djuna Barnes' Carnival Parody." In *Silence and Power: A Reevaluation of Djuna Barnes*, ed. Mary Lynn Broe, 81–91. Carbondale and Edwardsville: Southern Illinois University Press.

Stewart, David M. 1997. "Cultural Work, City Crime, Reading, Pleasure." *American Literary History* 9 (4): 676–701.

Stokes, Mason. 2001. *The Color of Sex: Whiteness, Heterosexuality, and the Fictions of White Supremacy*. Durham, NC: Duke University Press.

Streeby, Shelley. 2002. *American Sensations: Class, Empire, and the Production of Popular Culture*. Berkeley: University of California Press.

Summers, Claude J. 1990. "'A Losing Game in the End': Aestheticism and Homosexuality in Cather's 'Paul's Case.'" *Modern Fiction Studies* 36 (1): 103–19.

Takaki, Ronald T. 1989. *Strangers from a Different Shore: A History of Asian Americans*. Boston: Little, Brown.

Talmage, Thomas DeWitt. 1878. *The Night Sides of City Life*. Chicago: J. Fairbanks & Co.

Taylor, Leslie A. 2001. "'I Made up My Mind to Get It': The American Trial of *The Well of Loneliness*, New York City, 1928–1929." *Journal of the History of Sexuality* 10 (2): 250–86.

Taylor, Louis. 1932. Review of *Infants of the Spring*, by Wallace Thurman. *Opportunity*, March 10, 89.

Terry, Jennifer. 1991. "Theorizing Deviant Historiography." *Differences* 3 (2): 55–74.

———. 1999. *An American Obsession: Science, Medicine, and Homosexuality in Modern Society*. Chicago: University of Chicago Press.

Thompson, George. [1849] 2002. *City Crimes; or Life in New York and Boston, a Volume for Everybody—Being a Mirror of Fashion, a Picture of Poverty, and a Startling Revelation of the Secret Crimes of Great Cities;* Reprinted in *"Venus in Boston" and Other Tales of Nineteenth-Century City Life*. Edited by David S. Reynolds and Kimberley R. Gladman, 107–310. Amherst: University of Massachusetts Press.

Thornton, Sarah. 1997. "The Social Logic of Subcultural Capital." In *The Subcultures Reader*, ed. Ken Gelder and Sarah Thornton, 200–209. London: Routledge.

Thurman, Wallace. 1928. Letter to Harold Jackman, May 17. James Weldon Johnson Memorial Collection. The Beinecke Rare Book and Manuscript Library, Yale University, New Haven, Connecticut.

———. [1932] 1992. *Infants of the Spring*. Boston: Northeastern University Press.

———. 2003a. "Autobiographical Statement." James Weldon Johnson Memorial Collection. The Beinecke Rare Book and Manuscript Library, Yale University, New Haven, Connecticut. Reprinted in *The Collected Writings of Wallace Thurman: A Harlem Renaissance Reader*. Edited by Amritjit Singh and Daniel M. Scott III, 91–92. New Brunswick, NJ: Rutgers University Press.

———. [1926] 2003b. "'Fire Burns': A Department of Comment." *Fire!!* November. Reprinted in *The Collected Writings of Wallace Thurman: A Harlem Renaissance Reader*. Edited by Amritjit Singh and Daniel M. Scott III, 193–95. New Brunswick, NJ: Rutgers University Press.

———. [1927] 2003c. "Harlem: A Vivid Word Picture of the World's Greatest Negro City." *American Monthly*, May. Reprinted in *The Collected Writings of Wallace Thurman: A Harlem Renaissance Reader*. Edited by Amritjit Singh and Daniel M. Scott III, 32–34. New Brunswick, NJ: Rutgers University Press.

———. [1929] 2003d. Letter to William Jourdan Rapp, May 7. Reprinted in *The Collected Writings of Wallace Thurman: A Harlem Renaissance Reader*. Edited by Amritjit Singh and Daniel M. Scott III, 137–39. New Brunswick, NJ: Rutgers University Press.

———. [1927] 2003e. "Negro Life in New York's Harlem: A Lively Picture of a Popular and Interesting Section." *Haldeman-Julius Quarterly*, Fall. Reprinted in *The Collected Writings of Wallace Thurman: A Harlem Renaissance Reader*. Edited by Amritjit Singh and Daniel M. Scott III, 39–62. New Brunswick, NJ: Rutgers University Press.

———. [1926] 2003f. "A Stranger at the Gates: A Review of *Nigger Heaven*, by Carl Van Vechten." *Messenger*, September. Reprinted in *The Collected Writings of Wallace Thurman: A Harlem Renaissance Reader.* Edited by Amritjit Singh and Daniel M. Scott III, 191–93. New Brunswick, NJ: Rutgers University Press.

Thurman, Wallace, and William Jourdan Rapp. [1929] 2003. "Few Know Real Harlem, the City of Surprises: Quarter Million Negroes Form a Moving, Colorful Pageant of Life." *New York World*, March 3. Reprinted in *The Collected Writings of Wallace Thurman: A Harlem Renaissance Reader*. Edited by Amritjit Singh and Daniel M. Scott III, 66–67. New Brunswick, NJ: Rutgers University Press.

Tichi, Cecelia. 2004. *Exposés and Excess: Muckraking in America, 1900/2000.* Philadelphia: University of Pennsylvania Press.

Tolzmann, Don Heinrich. 1996. "Introduction: The Great Cincinnati German Novel." In *Cincinnati, or, The Mysteries of the West: Emil Klauprecht's German-American Novel.* Edited by Don Heinrich Tolzmann, xi–xxv. Translated by Steven Rowan. New York: Peter Lang.

Torgovnick, Marianna. 1990. *Gone Primitive: Savage Intellects, Modern Lives.* Chicago: University of Chicago Press.

———. 1997. *Primitive Passions: Men, Women, and the Quest for Ecstasy*. New York: Knopf.

Townsend, Kim. 1996. *Manhood at Harvard: William James and Others*. New York: Norton.

Trachtenberg, Alan. 1982a. "Experiments in Another Country: Stephen Crane's City Sketches." In *American Realism: New Essays*, ed. Eric J. Sundquist, 138–54. Baltimore: Johns Hopkins University Press.

———. 1982b. *The Incorporation of America: Society in the Gilded Age*. New York: Hill & Wang.

Trask, Michael. 2003. *Cruising Modernism: Class and Sexuality in American Literature and Social Thought.* Ithaca, NY: Cornell University Press.

Tythacott, Louise. 2003. *Surrealism and the Exotic*. London and New York: Routledge.

Umphrey, Martha M. 2003. "The Trouble with Harry Thaw." In *Queer Studies: An Interdisciplinary Reader*, ed. Robert J. Corber and Stephen Valocchi, 21–30. Malden, MA, and Oxford: Blackwell.

Urgo, Joseph R. 1995. *Willa Cather and the Myth of American Migration*. Urbana, IL: University of Illinois.

———. 2002. "The Iconic Willa Cather." *Modernism/Modernity* 9 (2): 327–33.

Valente, Joseph. 2002. *Dracula's Crypt: Bram Stoker, Irishness, and the Question of Blood*. Urbana: University of Illinois Press.

Van Notten, Eleonore. 1994. *Wallace Thurman's Harlem Renaissance*. Atlanta, GA: Rodopi.

Van Vechten, Carl. 1923. *Peter Whiffle: His Life and Works*. New York: Knopf.

———. 1925a. *Firecrackers*. New York: Knopf.

———. 1925b. Letter to Langston Hughes, May 1925. James Weldon Johnson Memorial Collection. The Beinecke Rare Book and Manuscript Library, Yale University, New Haven, Connecticut.

———. 1926. Response to "The Negro in Art: How Shall He Be Portrayed? A Symposium." *Crisis* 31 (March): 219.

———. [1927] 1966. Introduction to *The Autobiography of an Ex-Colored Man*, by James Weldon Johnson. New York: Knopf.

———. [1930] 1977. *Parties: Scenes from Contemporary New York Life*. New York: Bard.

———. [1926] 2000. *Nigger Heaven*. Urbana: University of Illinois Press.

Vicinus, Martha. 2004. *Intimate Friends: Women Who Loved Women, 1778–1928*. Chicago: University of Chicago Press.

Walker, Lisa. 2001. *Looking Like What You Are: Sexual Style, Race, and Lesbian Identity*. New York: New York University Press.

Walkowitz, Judith A. 1992. *City of Dreadful Delight: Narratives of Sexual Danger in Late-Victorian London*. Chicago: University of Chicago Press.

Wallace, Maurice O. 2002. *Constructing the Black Masculine: Identity and Ideality in African American Men's Literature and Culture, 1775–1995*. Durham, NC: Duke University Press.

Walters, Suzanna Danuta. 2001. *All the Rage: The Story of Gay Visibility in America*. Chicago: University of Chicago Press.

Walton, Jean. 2001. "'I Want to Cross Over into Camp Ground': Race and Inversion in *The Well of Loneliness*." In *Palatable Poison: Critical Perspectives on* The Well of Loneliness, ed. Laura Doan and Jay Prosser, 277–99. New York: Columbia University Press.

Ware, Caroline F. 1935. *Greenwich Village, 1920–1930: A Comment on American Civilization in the Post-War Years*. New York: Harper & Ware.

Warner, Michael. 1992. "The Mass Public and the Mass Subject." In *Habermas and the Public Sphere*, ed. Craig Calhoun, 377–401. Cambridge, MA: MIT Press.

———. 1993. Introduction to *Fear of a Queer Planet: Queer Politics and Social Theory*, ed. Michael Warner, vii–xxxi. Minneapolis: University of Minnesota Press.

———. 1999. *The Trouble with Normal: Sex, Politics, and the Ethics of Queer Life*. New York: Free Press.

———. 2002. *Publics and Counterpublics*. New York: Zone Books.

Warner, Sam Bass, Jr. 1984. "Slums and Skyscrapes: Urban Images, Symbols, and Ideology." In *Cities of the Mind: Images and Themes of the City in the Social Sciences*, ed. Lloyd Rodwin and Robert M. Hollister, 181–95. New York and London: Plenum.

Washington, Booker T. 1901. *Up from Slavery: An Autobiography*. New York: Doubleday Page & Co.

Watson, Steven. 1995. *The Harlem Renaissance: Hub of African-American Culture, 1920–30*. New York: Pantheon.

Weber, Max. [1904–5] 2001. *The Protestant Ethic and the Spirit of Capitalism*.

Translated by Stephen Kalburg. Chicago: Fitzroy Dearborn.

Weeks, Jeffrey. 1997. "Inverts, Perverts, and Mary-Annes." In *The Subcultures Reader*, ed. Ken Gelder and Sarah Thornton, 268–80. London: Routledge.

Weinberg, Jonathan. 1994. "'Boy Crazy': Carl Van Vechten's Queer Collection." *Yale Journal of Criticism* 7 (2): 25–49.

Welter, Barbara. 1966. "The Cult of True Womanhood: 1820–1860." *American Quarterly* 18 (2): 151–74.

Werther, Ralph. [1918] 1975. *Autobiography of an Androgyne*. New York: Arno.

———. [1922] 1975. *The Female-Impersonators*. New York: Arno.

West, Mae. [1927] 1997. *The Drag: A Homosexual Comedy in Three Acts*. In *Three Plays by Mae West:* Sex, The Drag, The Pleasure Man. Edited by Lillian Schlissel, 95–140. New York: Routledge.

Wetzsteon, Ross. 2002. *Republic of Dreams: Greenwich Village: The American Bohemia, 1910–1960*. New York: Simon & Schuster.

White, Hayden. 1973. *Metahistory: The Historical Imagination in Nineteenth-Century Europe*. Baltimore: Johns Hopkins University Press.

———. 1978. "The Historical Text as Literary Artifact." In *Tropics of Discourse: Essays in Cultural Criticism*, 81–100. Baltimore: Johns Hopkins University Press.

———. 1987. "The Value of Narrativity in the Representation of Reality." In *The Content of the Form: Narrative Discourse and Historical Representation*, 1–25. Baltimore: Johns Hopkins University Press.

White, Kevin. 1993. *The First Sexual Revolution: The Emergence of Male Heterosexuality in Modern America*. New York: New York University Press.

Wiegman, Robyn. 1995. *American Anatomies: Theorizing Race and Gender*. Durham, NC: Duke University Press.

Wilde, Oscar. [1891] 1962. Preface to *The Picture of Dorian Gray*. New York: New American Library.

Williams, Louise Blakeney. 2002. *Modernism and the Ideology of History: Literature, Politics, and the Past*. Cambridge: Cambridge University Press.

Wilson, Elizabeth. 1995. "The Invisible Flâneur." In *Postmodern Cities and Spaces*, ed. Sophie Watson and Katherine Gibson, 57–79. Oxford: Blackwell.

———. 2000. *Bohemians: The Glamorous Outcasts*. New Brunswick, NJ: Rutgers University Press.

Winfrey, Oprah. 2004. "A Secret Sex World: Living on the 'Down Low.'" Transcript of April 16, 2004, episode of *Oprah: The Oprah Winfrey Show*. Livingston, NJ: Burrelle's Information Services.

Winkiel, Laura. 1997. "Circuses and Spectacles: Public Culture in *Nightwood*." *Journal of Modern Literature* 21 (1): 7–28.

Wirth, Thomas H. 2002. Introduction to *Gay Rebel of the Harlem Renaissance: Selections from the Work of Richard Bruce Nugent*. Edited by Thomas H. Wirth, 1–61. Durham, NC: Duke University Press.

Worth, Robert F. 1995. "*Nigger Heaven* and the Harlem Renaissance." *African American Review* 29 (3): 461–73.

Wyckoff, Walter. 1897. *The Workers: An Experiment in Reality*. New York: Scribner's.

Ziff, Larzer. 1966. *The American 1890s: Life and Times of a Lost Generation*. Lincoln: University of Nebraska Press.

Zorbaugh, Harvey Warren. 1929. *The Gold Coast and the Slum: A Sociological Study of Chicago's Near North Side*. Chicago: University of Chicago Press.

Index

Note: Page numbers in *italics* indicate illustrations.